*To my family,
and to nurses
and their clients*

PREFACE

It is a pleasure to present the sixth edition of *Mental Health and Mental Illness*. This text is written to provide you with a current understanding of the important role of nurses and their compassionate care for clients and their families who are experiencing the pain of mental disorders.

The changes in mental health care in the United States during the past decade have markedly altered the way in which nurses plan and deliver care to clients with mental disorders. The financial constraints imposed by rapidly escalating health care costs, the care needs of changing populations, and the increasing number of sites where care is delivered are some of the more noticeable changes. Overall, governmental and insurance industry cost-containment measures are ensuring that the focus of treatment is on delivering therapeutic care in much shorter periods of time.

The urgency of this "time-effective" requirement has led to a refinement of the role of nursing in mental health care delivery. The roles that nurses perform in mental health settings contribute significantly to restabilizing clients who are learning to cope with their life circumstances in new ways.

In fact, some would say that the primary reason for hospital admission is to provide an environment of nursing care in which an individual's health status can be stabilized, and to provide health care teaching so that effective self-care is possible when discharge occurs.

The sixth edition continues to expand on the knowledge of stress adaption theory. All chapters have been revised to integrate the concepts of effecting coping with the theoretical base of mental health and mental illness. In addition, the role of ineffective coping has been emphasized to assist the student in understanding the continuum of maladaptive behaviors that may be encountered in mental illness.

◆ TEXT ORGANIZATION

The text uses the Diagnostic and Statistical Manual of Mental Disorders (DSM), the most widely used classification of mental disorders, as an organizing framework for discussing mental disorders. The DSM is published every 5 to 7 years by the American Psychiatric Association (APA). Committees of psychiatrists, psychologists, nurses, and social workers meet in every region of the United States to discuss revisions to the previous list of categories of mental disorders.

The text is organized into seven units and 31 chapters. The first five units present an overview of psychiatric mental health nursing today: Unit 1 presents the Current and Evolving Patterns of Mental Health Care; Unit 2 addresses the Concepts of Psychiatric Mental Health Nursing; Unit 3 reviews the Basic Concepts of Mental Health; Unit 4 compares Mental Health and Mental Disorder; and Unit 5 focuses on Nursing the Client With a Mental Disorder.

Unit 6 covers eight Categories of Mental Disorders: Disorders Usually First Diagnosed During Infancy, Childhood, or Adolescence; Cognitive Impairment Disorder; Substance-Related Disorders; Schizophrenia and Other Psychotic Disorders; Mood Disorders; Anxiety and Somatoform Disorders; Dissociative Disorders; and Personality Disorders.

And last, Unit 7 describes Intervention and Treatment of Mental Disorders and includes chapters on Crisis Intervention, Milieu Therapy and Behavior Modification, Group Therapy, and Psychopharmacology and Electroshock Treatment of Mental Disorders.

◆ TEXT FEATURES

- **Pedagogy to enhance learning** includes behavioral objectives for each chapter, end-of-chapter review questions, end-of-unit case study–based questions for class discussion, glossary.

- **Developing critical thinking skills through class discussion:** Case studies, located at the end of each unit, provide the basis for class discussion exercises, prompting students to examine their own responses to the circumstances described. In addition, this material provides the opportunity to increase individual understanding of the personal vulnerability, sensibility, and individual value systems that are an important foundation of mental health nursing and that have a significant influence on the quality of mental health nursing care.

- **Unique unit:** Nursing the Client with a Mental Disorder includes chapters on the use of nursing diagnosis and nursing care planning in the mental health setting. The chapter on nursing care planning provides nursing care guidelines for clients with the altered mental states most commonly seen in inpatient settings, such as psychosis, depression, mania, anxiety, confusional state, and violence. Each chapter uses a case study format that consists of a clinical history followed by nursing diagnosis care planning recommendations.

All content in this edition has been reviewed and updated to reflect the important developments in mental health care in all types of settings.

■ **Content:** Content has been added or strengthened in many areas including eating disorders, substance-related disorders, geri-psychiatric content (particularly Alzheimer's, schizoaffective disorders, patient and family teaching), codependency, posttraumatic stress disorder, and updated psychopharmacology content.

■ **New chapter:** Chapter 3, Home Care Setting: Client and Family Issues, addresses the increased challenge inherent in providing competent psychiatric nursing care in settings outside of the hospital.

■ **New chapter:** Chapter 8, Delivering Mental Health Care in a Continuum of Settings, covers the multiple site in which mental health care is provided, including the home care setting, community outpatient treatment options, partial hospitalization programs, and inpatient acute care.

Two new features introduced in this edition include:

■ **Chapter summaries** that provide a focus for studying chapter content;

■ **End-of-chapter NCLEX–style review questions** enable students to self-test on what they've learned from studying the chapter content.

As Mental Health and Mental Illness enters its next stage of development, I want to thank those faculty members who generously gave of their time and expertise to evaluate and provide feedback about this edition. It is particularly important for them to have shared their views on the changing needs of mental health nursing faculty and students. This strong revision was born of their ability to respond to our inquiries about how and where to strengthen this text and by their thoughtful, well-analyzed, and organized comments about the content. As in previous editions, these comments formed the foundation of planning for this, the sixth edition. I am indebted to you all and thank the many faculty and students who have used this text to prepare to practice in today's nursing care environment.

Patricia D. Barry, PhD, APRN, CS
Hartford, Connecticut
April 1997

ACKNOWLEDGMENTS

I want to thank the nursing faculty who select this text for their students. I hope that it will meet your needs and their as we all work to provide compassionate nursing care to individuals whose quality of life is deeply affected by mental illness.

I want to say thank you also to Lippincott editor Margaret Belcher Zuccarini. Her vision of the overall goals of this revision as they relate to the identified needs of faculty was unwavering. I have strong appreciation for her keen intellect, as well as her understanding of the scope of nursing education in today's mental health environment. I also want to thank her capable assistant, Emily Cotlier, who cheerfully provided me with information during all stages of the writing.

Beth Richards provided excellent assitance in the preparation of this edition in myriad ways. It has been a pleasure to work with her. Her skills and organizational abilities always kept our work on track. I am deeply indebted to her editorial assistance and overview of the project. Judy Logan provided valuable library assistance in the research of information and references used in the new and revised chapters in this edition. She also contributed significantly to the updating of chapter bibliographies.

Nancy Jeresak, a clinical nurse specialist at the Institute of Living in Hartford, Connecticut, provided expert clinical consultation for the case material described in Chapter 13, Nursing Care Planning with Specific Types of Disordered Mental States. It is important to note that each mental state description includes a composite of hypothetical clinical information. In no case is the clinical material descriptive of an actual client in the Institute of Living.

CONTENTS

Unit 3 ◆ BASIC CONCEPTS OF MENTAL HEALTH, **91**

Unit 4 ◆ MENTAL HEALTH AND MENTAL DISORDER, **133**

Unit 6 ◆ CATEGORIES OF MENTAL DISORDERS, 231

Unit 7

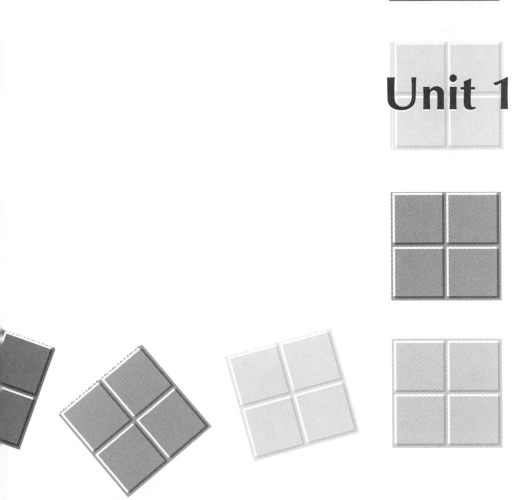

Unit 1

PATTERNS OF MENTAL HEALTH CARE

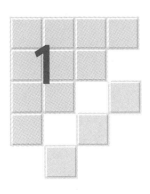

Current and Evolving Patterns of Mental Health Care

Behavioral Objectives

After reading this chapter the student will be able to:

■ Name the three major forces that have caused changes in mental health care since the 1940s.

■ Explain how each of the above forces is continuing to cause changes in mental health care services.

■ Explain the shift from inpatient to community-based mental health services that began in the late 1950s.

■ Describe the current economic factors that have affected the availability of mental health care services.

■ List three of the major plans designed to decrease mental health care costs.

The treatment of mental disorders has gone through many stages of development during the past 100 years. The guiding principle throughout has been to move the mentally disordered person from his or her normal family, social, and community surroundings to a sheltered environment. During the past 20 years, the **sheltered environment** has shifted from one that was primarily custodial to one that is dynamically oriented toward community-based rehabilitation of the person with a mental disorder. This philosophical change in treatment is evident from the preadmission through the active treatment and postdischarge phases of mental health care.

◆ CHANGES IN INPATIENT MENTAL HEALTH TREATMENT

There are many forces that have shaped these changes. The most significant forces have been the following:

- The development of medications that significantly decrease the major symptoms of psychiatric disorders, psychosis, and depression. These medications, when properly used, can allow those who formerly required long-term institutionalization to return to outpatient community care.

- Economic forces that do not support long-term psychiatric care. Funding emphasis has shifted from chronic inpatient care to community models of outpatient care.

- The advent of a variety of mental health disciplines that train individuals to work with different aspects of a mental health client's psychological and social functioning in both inpatient and community care settings. With their combined skills, these individuals comprise a treatment team that utilizes a comprehensive mental health care approach.

A discussion of the medications used to treat various symptoms of mental disorders can be found in Unit 7, Interventions and Treatment of Mental Disorders (Chapter 31, Psychopharmacology and Electroshock Treatment of Mental Disorders). The economic forces that are shaping the changing patterns of mental health care in the United States will be addressed in this chapter. The mental health treatment team and its approaches to therapeutic care will be presented in Chapter 4, Inpatient Hospitalization: The Mental Health Treatment Team and the Therapeutic Milieu.

◆ HISTORY OF THE SHIFT FROM INPATIENT TO COMMUNITY-BASED MENTAL HEALTH SERVICES

The original change in philosophy from inpatient to outpatient care of seriously mentally disordered individuals began in the late 1950s and early 1960s. This change was the result of a number of factors:

- Research on psychiatric disorders was increasingly demonstrating that environmental and social factors contributed strongly to the development of mental illness.

- An increase in the incidence of mental illness in the community can be inferred by the incidence of mental disorders in inductees into the Armed Services. During the preinduction process of U.S. citizens in World War II, 1,875,000 men were found to be emotionally unfit for service and 850,000 (40% of *all* discharges) were released from active service because of mental illness.

- The introduction of phenothiazines (the major tranquilizers) in the mid-1950s followed in the last decade by "second" and "third" generations of effective antipsychotic medications reduced the incidence of active psychotic episodes in people with schizophrenia and other types of psychotic mental disorders. The use of these psychotropic medications has been the primary contributing factor to reduction in the cost of mental health care in the United States.

- Studies in state mental institutions revealed that clients were living under poor conditions.

As a result of these findings, many government agencies were eager to develop community-based programs in which formerly state-supported mental health clients could receive care as outpatients in their home communities.

The premise of community psychiatry is that custodial, institution-based care should be reserved only for acutely ill individuals; thus, many people formerly treated in long-term residential care centers should be returned to their home environments. Community psychiatry also focuses on prevention, using community-based programs.

These findings and related recommendations are at the heart of the concept of deinstitutionalization. **Deinstitutionalization** is the act of transferring formerly institutionalized individuals to sheltered community environments or to homes in the community.

T

◆ THE EMERGING IMPORTANCE OF ECONOMIC FACTORS IN DECISION MAKING ABOUT MENTAL HEALTH TREATMENT

During the 1980s, the cost of health care in the United States increased at a greater rate than any other cost of living factor in our national economy. These costs have been addressed in both the public and private sectors. The result has been strategic planning to reduce costs. Mental health care costs have been targeted in the following areas:

- Deinstitutionalization of seriously mentally disordered individuals in public-funded mental health care.
- Community versus inpatient mental health care for individuals with acute mental health disturbances.
- Changes in payment mechanisms by private insurers for both inpatient and outpatient care.
- The use of diagnostic related groups by federal and state funding agencies to create guidelines for lengths of hospital stay. **Diagnostic related groups (DRGs)** are the categories of mental disorders listed with the guidelines for normal days expected for inpatient hospitalization.
- Quality assurance programs mandated by public and private agencies to ensure the quality of health care to all people, regardless of whether their care is paid by the individual, public funding, or insurance.

These factors have brought about many changes in current mental health treatment and will continue to be important forces in the future. The reasons are described below.

Deinstitutionalization. Rather than serving as centers for chronic care, federal and state-funded, long-term psychiatric care institutions have adapted to treat people in crisis or with serious mental disorders requiring acute (7 days or less) and midterm (usually 14–21 days) treatment. The effects of deinstitutionalization on mental health care will be discussed in Chapter 2, Community-Based Treatment Settings for Mental Disorders. Alternative, community-based mental health treatment programs are intended to provide ongoing treatment for the chronically mentally ill individual.

Changes in payment mechanisms used by private insurers for mental health care. Because mental health care costs have escalated faster than general physical health care costs, stringent limits have been set for both inpatient and outpatient mental health treatment. The limit on inpatient care costs has resulted in a more aggressive treatment process during acute "crisis" admissions, usually 7 days or less in duration.

Longer-term admissions are becoming increasingly rare because of the stringent criteria used to justify inpatient hospitalization.

The emphasis on short lengths of inpatient admissions is being driven by a policy known as "capping." Capping is the practice of allowing a limited dollar amount for lifetime psychiatric care. For example, an insurance company may set a limit of $50,000 on the amount that it will reimburse to a person during his or her lifetime for any type of psychiatric care, whether in the hospital or in the community. A person with a chronic psychiatric disorder such as schizophrenia can exhaust the "lifetime" psychiatric benefit before the age of 30.

Biological psychiatry. **Biological psychiatry** is the use of biological means to treat mental disorders. Because the majority of mental disorders show laboratory findings of changes in the normal patterns of neurophysiology, there is a strong emphasis on the use of psychopharmacology to produce rapid results in treating acute mental states. Increasingly, health maintenance organizations that are overseeing managed mental health services disallow ongoing psychotherapy services and urge the primary use of medication to manage mental health symptoms.

Use of DRGS by federal and state funding agencies. In another effort to reduce unnecessary hospital costs, DRGs are being used to establish guidelines for appropriate lengths of stay. Using these guidelines, hospitals are permitted to charge for a specific number of days of treatment. The approved number of days can be extended only when there are unusual complications that meet previously defined criteria. Payments for Medicaid and Medicare admissions cut off after the DRG deadline is reached. Accordingly, short-term aggressive treatment that discharges clients as soon as they are reasonably able to leave the hospital is rewarded. On the other hand, if hospitals lag in discharging a significant number of their clients, they can quickly encounter major financial difficulties.

Quality assurance programs mandated by public and private agencies. **Quality assurance programs** are designed to monitor the quality of health care delivered in hospitals and communities. The services of all health care providers, including nurses, are reviewed, whether in inpatient or outpatient settings and public or privately funded health care. Using quality assurance guidelines, the following aspects of health care are evaluated:

- Assessment
- Accuracy of diagnosis
- Rationale for diagnostic testing
- Effectiveness of care planning
- Evaluation of outcomes

The quality assurance programs in hospitals actively review the care planning of nurses in the psychiatric setting. Good quality inpatient and outpatient mental health care is strongly dependent on the effective use of the nursing process by psychiatric nurses. The nursing process will be described in Unit 2, Concepts of Psychiatric-Mental Health Nursing.

CHAPTER 1 SUMMARY

■ Three significant forces have shaped the treatment of mental disorders:
  — Development of medications that decrease major symptoms of mental disorders
  — Shifts in economic focus
  — Development of a range of mental health disciplines to treat clients

■ Beginning in the late 1950s and early 1960s, many seriously mentally disordered people were transferred from inpatient settings to outpatient or community-based care. This shift is known as deinstitutionalization.

■ Community mental health treatment uses social and environmental measures to prevent mental illness and to treat and care for those who develop mental disorders.

■ To reduce the rising cost of mental health care, fewer clients are treated in inpatient settings, spending limits are set on lifetime care, and length and quality of client care are closely monitored.

■ Quality assurance programs actively review the care plans of all mental health providers, including those of psychiatric nurses.

CHAPTER 1 QUESTIONS

1. The major forces that have changed mental health care since the 1940s are
   a. an increased emphasis on institution-based care and greater funding for psychiatric hospitals.
   b. significant government support of inpatient and outpatient mental health care.
   c. more clinical psychologists available for consultations.
   d. development of medications, shift in funding emphasis from in-

patient to outpatient, and increased variety of people trained to care for mental health clients.

2. Capping means
   a. setting a limited dollar amount for lifetime psychiatric care.
   b. allowing a mental health client to limit his or her own treatment schedule.
   c. adding 10% of mental health care costs to the approved hospital budget.
   d. wearing a specific hat to designate one's role on the treatment team.

3. Quality assurance programs evaluate the quality of health care in accuracy of diagnosis, rationale for diagnostic testing, effectiveness of care planning, *and*
   a. availability of board-certified psychiatrists.
   b. community cooperation and support.
   c. assessment and evaluation of outcomes.
   d. number of clients treated per month.

4. The purpose of diagnostic related groups (DRGs) is
   a. to group similar mental health caregivers for greater efficiency.
   b. to make organized lists of client diagnoses.
   c. to create a monopoly of services.
   d. to create guidelines for length of hospital stay.

BIBLIOGRAPHY

Barry, P.D. (1996). *Psychosocial nursing: Care of physically ill patients and their families* (3rd ed.). Philadelphia: Lippincott-Raven.

Burgess, A.W. (1995). *Advanced practice in psychiatric mental health nursing.* Norwalk, CT: Appleton & Lange.

Johnson, B. (1996). *Psychiatric mental health nursing* (4th ed.). Philadelphia: Lippincott-Raven.

Lego, S. (1996). *Psychiatric nursing: A comprehensive reference* (2nd ed.). Philadelphia: Lippincott-Raven.

McFarland, G.K., Wasli, E.L., & Gerety, E.K. (1996). *Nursing diagnosis and process in psychiatric mental health nursing* (3rd ed.). Philadelphia: Lippincott-Raven.

Mental health and psychiatric nursing (2nd ed.). (1996). Lippincott's Review Series. Philadelphia: Lippincott-Raven.

Shives, L.R. (Ed.). (1994). *Basic concepts of psychiatric mental health nursing* (3rd ed.). Philadelphia: J.B. Lippincott.

Wilson, H.S., & Kneisl, C.R. (1996). *Psychiatric nursing* (5th ed.). Redwood City, CA: Addison-Wesley.

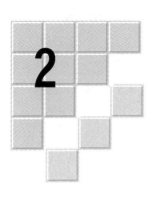

2

Community-Based Treatment Settings for Mental Disorders

Behavioral Objectives

After reading this chapter the student will be able to:

■ Name three different groups of individuals who are outpatient mental health care consumers.

■ List the different types of payment mechanisms that are used for community mental health services.

■ Describe the five basic mental health services of a community mental health center.

■ Explain two benefits of partial hospitalization programs.

■ Name the three most common problems of the homeless mentally ill.

■ Describe the differences between the services offered by community mental health centers and the assertive community treatment model of mental health care.

In order to decrease all health care costs, pressure is being actively exerted to treat people with mental disorders in their communities. There are three major populations of individuals who may be community-based or outpatient mental health care consumers:

1. *The physically disabled or elderly infirm who require home services for mental health care.* These individuals use a variety of payment options that affect the quality and duration of their care at home: Medicare or Medicaid, private health insurance, health maintenance organizations, self-pay, or indigent with no available funds. The clinical options open to these individuals include contracting for mental health services from visiting nurse associations, other public or private mental health caregiver groups, or private practitioners.

2. *Individuals with nondisabling mental disorders who are able to continue working and fulfilling their normal social roles.* The ability of such individuals to continue their normal roles is supported by the use of psychotropic medications. **Psychotropic medications** alter the neurochemistry of the brain so that brain chemistry approaches more normal levels. Disabling mental symptoms are reduced to more comfortable levels. Pharmacotherapy is augmented by outpatient individual or outpatient group therapy.

Funding options for outpatient therapy and medications include partial funding by private health insurance, limited numbers of therapy sessions funded by health maintenance organizations, very restricted numbers of sessions funded by Medicaid and Medicare, or self-payment by those who have adequate resources. The individual who lacks financial or insurance resources will most often function at a borderline disabled level. This type of disabled mental functioning usually increases the risks not only to the individual, but also to his or her family members.

3. *Individuals who are psychiatrically disabled.* Because of the decreasing public and private support for mental health services, there is a growing percentage of people with chronic, disabling mental disorders. This segment of the population is particularly affected by the current crisis in health care costs. The Community Mental Health Act legislated by the U.S. Congress in the 1960s was originally designed to provide a range of mental health care options to all people. Inadequate funding and lack of comprehensive policy planning left woeful gaps in care, particularly when accompanied by the national trend of deinstitutionalization. Currently, the most commonly used treatment option open to the chronically mentally ill client is the community mental health center.

◆ COMMUNITY MENTAL HEALTH CENTERS (CMHCs)

The Community Mental Health Act states that a community mental health center should be accessible to the community it serves and that it should provide five basic services:

1. Inpatient treatment
2. Outpatient treatment
3. Partial hospitalization (day or night programs)
4. Emergency services on a 24-hour-a-day basis
5. Consultation and education services to community agencies, groups, and individuals

Several other services, although not mandatory, are desirable in order to assist in the functioning, implementation, and continuity of these five basic services:

6. Diagnostic services
7. Rehabilitation
8. Precare and aftercare
9. Training programs for professionals and nonprofessionals
10. Research and evaluation

When a center has all 10 of these services and they are fully operational, the center is known as a **comprehensive community mental health center.**

The Community Mental Health Act specifies that such a center must serve a specific area with a population between 75,000 and 200,000. This geographic area is known as a **catchment area.** In a densely populated urban area, such a maximum population may be found in fewer than 100 square blocks; in some remote rural areas, the minimum population may be scattered over hundreds of square miles. Thus, the community mental health center is not always in close proximity to area residents wanting or needing services. Ideally, though, travel time to the center should not exceed 1 hour.

Of the delivery modalities within the community mental health system, two have enjoyed outstanding growth and appear to have permanently changed the face of psychiatric practice. They are crisis intervention and partial hospitalization or day-treatment programs. Almost all private and public mental hospitals have both partial hospitalization and crisis intervention services. Community-based home crisis intervention programs will be described in the next chapter, as will community-based home care.

Partial hospitalization and day or evening treatment programs. These programs are designed to meet the needs of two types of clients:

1. Those who were recently discharged from acute care institutions but require an overview by mental health professionals to continue their rehabilitation

2. Mentally ill individuals who are currently living at home or are homeless and who require stabilization in order to avoid inpatient hospitalization

Partial hospitalization programs are designed to meet the needs of their clients. They provide a structured environment that can avert inpatient hospitalization. These programs are designed to accommodate the schedules of clients who are employed; these individuals usually attend partial evening programs.

In an evening program, clients have an opportunity to discuss their coping concerns about work and family and find support from staff members and fellow attendees. Other clients who require supportive care during the daytime, when their family members may be out of the home at work or school, attend partial daytime programs.

Assessment in a partial day or evening program. The assessment of a newly admitted individual to a partial mental health program is comprehensive. It includes a review of the following factors:

- Physical health
- Psychosocial functioning
- Emotions
- Behavior
- Recreation
- Vocation
- Legal circumstances
- Nutrition

As each of these factors is assessed and addressed in the partial program, it is possible to plan interventions that support the individual in his or her normal social environment. Interventions that are based on daily reports of the individual's coping challenges can provide strong support for a successful return to his or her precrisis level of functioning.

◆ THE HOMELESS AND MENTAL ILLNESS

The political decision to deinstitutionalize people with chronic mental illness began with the active use of phenothiazine medications in the 1960s. These medications dramatically reduced the psychosis-induced instability of many individuals with serious mental disorders. Legislators at both the state and federal levels looked at the high cost of long-term psychiatric hospitalization. Social scientists assured them that community-based care would be in the best interests of all concerned: the mentally ill and the general tax-paying public.

It was believed that chronically mentally ill people who were institutionalized developed a social breakdown syndrome. This syndrome included the following characteristics: lack of initiative, submission to authority, withdrawal, and excessive dependence on the institution.

Although deinstitutionalization was humane in its original philosophy, the actual implementation of the concept has been seriously undermined by the lack of good community alternatives. It has been widely recognized that the largest group of users of public community mental health services are the poor. At this time, a large proportion of the individuals using community mental health treatment services are the "homeless" poor.

Of the homeless, nearly half are chronically mentally ill. The chronically mentally ill may frequently experience the dual diagnosis of functional mental illness, such as schizophrenia, and addiction disorders. A **dual diagnosis** is the presence of two major types of mental disorder in one individual.

Chronic mentally ill individuals are often alienated from their families and are socially isolated. They avoid contact with social structures, such as community mental health treatment centers. Because of these factors they often discontinue their medications, become psychotic and disorganized, and begin to live on the street. Their lives are seriously endangered by their disordered mental states.

As noted above, community-based crisis intervention and partial hospitalization programs are the most important deterrents to inpatient hospitalization. These two types of outpatient care are currently being offered by two intervention models: community mental health centers, described earlier, and assertive community treatment.

◆ ASSERTIVE COMMUNITY TREATMENT (ACT)

During the 1980s, community mental health professionals recognized that the use of assertive, active outreach to the homeless mentally ill and others who avoided coming to community mental health centers was an important intervention model. Table 2–1 compares the differences in approach of these two major intervention models.

Early research on the cost-effectiveness of these two programs indicates that clients who are participating in ACT programs have fewer hospitalizations on an annual basis than those using CMHCs. The cost of the ACT program is higher on a per-client basis than that of the

TABLE 2–1. Comparison of Characteristics of Assertive Community Treatment (ACT) and Community Mental Health Center (CMHC) Programs

Characteristic	ACT	CMHC
Treatment base	Predominantly in the community	In the community, but predominantly in the clinic
Staffing	Clinical staff-to-client ratio of around 1 : 10	Clinical staff-to-client ratio of around 1 : 30–50
Frequency of contact	Daily in most cases	Usually once every 1 or 2 weeks
Frequency of contact with family or support structure	Average of once a week	Occasional
Medication	Responsibility of staff; can be administered by staff daily if needed	Responsibility of client or family
Physical health	Monitored by program staff	Therapist and case manager encourage a healthy lifestyle
After-hours service	Monitored by program staff; team on call	Provided by therapist or case manager during day hours, emergency room or mobile team otherwise
Occupational rehabilitation	Actual job placement or volunteer job	Psychosocial programs
Housing arrangement	Responsibility of staff	Varies, but usually responsibility of client and family
Continuity of care	Team follows case through hospitalization; maintains legal, health system, and other contacts	Responsibility of therapist and case manager
Staff structure	Team structure: integration of clinical and case management roles	Individual staff model: therapist and case manager are different individuals

From *Hospital and Community Psychiatry*, 41(6), p. 643, 1990. Copyright 1990, the American Psychiatric Association. Reprinted by permission.

CMHC. The higher cost is offset by the higher psychiatric hospitalization patterns of CMHC clients or, more important, the higher psychiatric hospitalization patterns of the mentally ill who do not customarily use the CMHC services.

In contrast to the CMHC model, which requires that clients seek out services at the mental health center, the direct searching out of mentally ill people in the community ensures that a larger percentage of potential clients are reached. Additionally, the ACT model uses a case manager. The **case manager** is the member of the mental health team who oversees all aspects of support, including direct mental health services, housing, physical care, and so on. The case manager is also the clinician providing direct care.

A case manager's ideal case load is around 10 to 12 clients, and allows for more active support of the client during precrisis periods. Government financial support for community mental health services for the indigent continues to be cut, however; accordingly, the numbers of clients managed by many community mental health case managers is increasing to a level that can cause a breakdown in the delivery system of such care.

An important component of the ACT care model is ongoing training in activities of daily living, such as communication, problem-solving, and coping skills. Other important aspects of the case manager approach are medication overview and support regarding adequate housing and physical care. More detailed research on the ACT model and its cost effectiveness can support its use and increased availability to the chronically mentally ill, who are the primary users of community psychiatry services.

◆ GENERAL HOSPITAL EMERGENCY ROOM TREATMENT OF PSYCHIATRIC EMERGENCIES AMONG THE HOMELESS

When community programs are unsuccessful in averting psychiatric hospital admission, the triage of psychiatric clients in the emergency rooms of general hospitals is instituted. **Triage** is the term used to describe the way that the care of people with mental or physical health problems is prioritized. Those who are most acutely ill with a prognosis of surviving their current illness are prioritized at the highest level. Health care resources are apportioned according to the priority of care assigned to a specific health problem.

In the current health care environment, there are large numbers of homeless or unemployed people with no health insurance. Particularly during the past decade, the use of the general hospital emergency room as the initial care setting has markedly increased. Many homeless individuals suffer from chronic mental disorders such as schizophrenia, substance abuse, or cognitive mental disorders. Sometimes they are diagnosed with all three disorders concurrently. Adding to their psychiatric distress is their noncompliance in taking the medications that could stabilize their mental conditions.

Changes in the law have allowed law enforcement agencies to involuntarily admit seriously mentally disturbed, antisocial, or dangerous individuals to general hospital emergency rooms for crisis assessment and intervention services. Inner city hospitals have shown an increase of nearly 100% in the number of admissions of mentally ill people to their emergency rooms during the past decade.

Because of deinstitutionalization, transfer of these individuals to mental institutions has been severely restricted by sharp decreases in mental hospital bed capacities. Accordingly, emergency rooms may have to hold these individuals in cramped, inadequate quarters for several days before discharging them to the street or to a mental institution. The use of a triage evaluation system prioritizes rapid transfer to the general hospital inpatient unit or mental institution. Those individuals who are not stabilized within 4 hours by psychotropic medication or who pose a high risk of danger to themselves, staff members, or other emergency room clients will most likely be transferred.

CHAPTER 2 SUMMARY

- Three major populations may be treated in community-based or outpatient settings:
  - Physically disabled or elderly individuals needing mental health care
  - Individuals with nondisabling mental disorders
  - Individuals who are psychiatrically disabled

- Community mental health centers should be accessible to the community and provide inpatient and outpatient services, day or night programs (partial hospitalization), 24-hour emergency services, and consultation/education services.

- Nearly half the homeless population is chronically mentally disordered, and the homeless poor are a large proportion of those using community mental health services.

- Assertive community treatment (ACT) focuses on direct outreach to and supervision of clients. ACT also provides ongoing training for clients in communication, coping, and other activities of daily living.

CHAPTER 2 QUESTIONS

1. The largest user group for public community mental health services is
   a. people with schizophrenia.
   b. people with substance-related mental disorders.
   c. poor people.
   d. people recently released from psychiatric hospitals.

2. Of the following, which is *not* one of the five basic services offered by a community health center?
   a. Inpatient and outpatient treatment
   b. Partial hospitalization
   c. Emergency service
   d. Research

3. Two community mental health delivery modalities are important deterrents to inpatient hospitalizations. They are
   a. intervention and partial hospitalization/day-treatment programs.
   b. medication assessment and adjustment.
   c. housing assistance and social services.
   d. medication adjustment and family therapy.

4. A catchment area is
   a. the 10-square-mile area directly adjacent to a psychiatric hospital.
   b. an area zoned for a community mental health center (CMHC).
   c. a geographic area with population between 75,000 and 200,000.
   d. an urban area where people with mental disorders tend to meet.

BIBLIOGRAPHY

Bunn, H. (1995). Preparing nurses for the challenge of the new focus on community mental health nursing. *Journal of Continuing Education in Nursing, 26*(2), 55–59.
Byrne, C., Brown, B., Voorberg, N., & Schofield, R. (1994). Wellness education for individuals with chronic mental illness living in the community. *Issues in Mental Health Nursing, 15*(3), 239–252.
Community psychiatry: A reappraisal. (1983). New York: Mental Health Materials Center.
George, M. (1995). Mental health: Who's caring in the community? *Nursing Standard, 9*(38), 21.
Heifner, C. (1996). Designing a partial hospitalization program. In S. Lego (Ed.). *Psychiatric nursing: A comprehensive reference.* Philadelphia: Lippincott-Raven.
Kaplan, H.I., & Sadock, B.J. (1995). *Comprehensive textbook of psychiatry/VI* (6th ed.). Baltimore: Williams & Wilkins.
Kwakwa, J. (1995). Alternatives to hospital-based mental health care. *Nursing Times, 91*(23), 38–39.
Lego, S. (1996). *Psychiatric nursing: A comprehensive reference* (2nd ed.). Philadelphia: Lippincott-Raven.
Lewis, J.A., & Lewis, M.D. (1997). *Community counseling* (2nd ed.). Pacific Grove, CA: Brooks-Cole.
Shives, L.R. (Ed.). (1994). *Basic concepts of psychiatric-mental health nursing* (3rd ed.). Philadelphia: J.B. Lippincott.

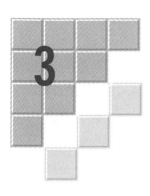

Home Care Setting: Client and Family Issues

B e h a v i o r a l   O b j e c t i v e s

After reading this chapter the student will be able to:

■ Identify the core value of mental health home care.

■ List the six holistic health care priorities.

■ Describe the importance of nursing assessment in the home care environment.

■ List the six reasons why mental health home care is preferable.

■ Define intense brief intervention and describe how it is different from traditional home care.

Home care nursing has seen a nearly three-fold increase in size and scope during the last decade. All specialties in nursing, except for intensive and emergency care, have shifted to the home care arena. As described in earlier chapters, this shift is a response to the rapidly changing insurance programs of managed medical care. These programs, which, increasingly, are dictating the health services that are available to the general public, have mandated a decrease in the cost of all health care. It is interesting to note that the practice arena of nursing has returned to its roots—the home.

◆ THE NEW OPTION OF HOME CARE FOR TREATMENT OF MENTAL DISORDERS

HOME CARE VERSUS HOSPITALIZATION OF THE MENTALLY DISORDERED CLIENT

Traditionally, psychiatric-mental health nursing in the general hospital setting has focused directly on the client. Hospital-based care shifts the client from his or her normal social environment into the unnatural location and experience of the hospital for assessment, treatment, and stabilization.

Table 3–1 compares and contrasts the different perspectives of the

◆ TABLE 3–1. Comparison of Medical and Psychosocial Rehabilitation Models

Medical	Psychosocial Rehabilitation
Illness, disease, symptoms	Wellness, health, symptoms deemphasized
Person's disability	Person's ability
Institutional settings	Normalizing settings
Unnatural environments	Natural environments
Intrapsychic functioning	Functional behavior
Expert to patient	Adult to adult
Minimize stress	Take risks
Medicate until symptoms are controlled	Minimum amount of medication, symptoms okay
Practitioner makes decisions, prescribes treatment	Member and case manager identify strengths and develop a plan for change
Dependence and caretaker approach	Self-help, interdependence, support symptoms approach
Low expectancy	High expectancy

Thompson, J., & Strand, K. (1994). Psychiatric nursing in a psychosocial setting. *Journal of Psychosocial Nursing, 32*(2), p. 27. Used with permission.

medical model, which is practiced in the majority of hospital settings, with the psychosocial rehabilitation model that can be used in home care nursing. In contrast to the medical model of care, the psychosocial model contains components of openness that can support the unique needs and strengths of a client and the family in their normal surroundings.

Inpatient admission to the hospital setting is essential in many circumstances. These circumstances include times when the mental symptoms cause the following:

- The life of the client or others to be at risk
- The inability of the client and/or family to medicate with appropriately ordered psychotropic medications
- Exhaustion, dysfunction, or any other circumstance that prevents the family or social network from providing a secure environment for the client
- A need for community mental health services with no adequate services available to meet the individual's needs

In this text, **family** is an inclusive term that means a person's immediate and extended family members who are blood relatives. In addition, the term *family* will be used to designate individuals who are not relatives but who reside in the same home and provide significant support for the client. A **social network** comprises all those people whom an individual views as important sources of support. A **social system** is a comprehensive term that includes an individual's social network as well as the general social environment in which he or she lives.

The following section describes the care philosophy and approaches that can contribute to positive outcomes for the client, family or social system, and health care providers.

◆ THE PHILOSOPHY OF HOME CARE NURSING

The core value that underlies the philosophy of home care nursing is the ideal of returning the individual to a precrisis level of functioning within his or her normal social environment. This ideal also includes recognition of the potential for psychosocial adaptation and growth to the highest innate ability of the client and family.

The philosophy of home care nursing is based on the following six **holistic health care priorities,** listed in order of their importance:

1. Life sustenance
2. Security
3. Family/social system integrity and balance
4. Integrity of the individual (physical, mental, and spiritual)

5. Discovery of inner strengths and resources to support growth and change

6. Contribution to the betterment of self and others

Assessment of the status of each of these goals can provide the structure for prioritizing decision making at each stage of the nursing process.

These goals are formulated to provide a framework for humane and responsible care of individuals who have mental or physical conditions. They can be generalized to psychosocial nursing care. This home care nursing framework is intended to guide the nurse in maintaining, restoring, or supporting the development of an environment in which the client's holistic sense of well-being can potentially occur. Implicit in these goals is the collaborative planning process with nurse, client, and family.

The use of this model in the home care setting recognizes the important role of the family in providing the environment in which rehabilitation and restoration of health and balance can occur. The significance of the assessment phase of the nursing process in the home care environment is emphasized. The nurse's astuteness is essential in recognizing the capabilities and resources within the family to provide the first three of the requirements listed during an acute phase of mental disorder in a family member.

Also implicit in this model of care planning is the recognition that the client's ability to regain his or her precrisis level of functioning will depend partly on the family's capacity to provide a stable environment. The assessment of the home environment's capacity to support the provision of adequate care includes the nurse's awareness of the capabilities and current needs of the primary caregiver to provide and maintain the precrisis home environment.

IDENTIFYING COMMUNITY SUPPORT SERVICES DURING THE ASSESSMENT PHASE

During this initial phase of assessment, the nurse reviews current and potential gaps in family or caregiver resources that can decrease effective client rehabilitation or exhaust the family's caregiving resources. Recognition of these gaps in resources motivates the nurse to plan collaboratively with the client and primary caregiver for community services to support the home care environment during the time of increased demand on the family.

IDENTIFYING SOURCES OF SUPPORT WITHIN THE FAMILY OR SOCIAL NETWORK

The nurse can also talk with the client and primary caregiver about calling on the extended family or social network for additional support during times of greater need. It is important to note that, during the initial phase of mental crisis, the primary caregiver is often unable to ascertain his or her personal reserves and the availability of additional family or social supports who can be available to provide respite care.

Respite care is possible when extended family or community resources can be called on to provide care for the ill individual in the home to allow rest and recovery for the primary caregiver. Early discussion of the importance of respite care will be more likely to ensure the ongoing health of the caregiver and to enhance his or her ability to provide an optimal environment for the client's rehabilitation.

◆ Basic Principles of Mental Health Rehabilitation

In 1986, the California Nurses' Association presented an outline of the belief system that can be used as a foundation for mental health and psychosocial rehabilitation. The five basic principles of this belief system are as follows:

1. Each individual has an inherent capacity for change.
2. Ideologies and practices that define the person in terms of mental illness dehumanize the individual.
3. Individual freedom of choice and conscious self-direction are central to change.
4. Interpersonal relationships are essential for bringing about change.
5. Behavior cannot adequately be understood apart from the context in which it occurs.

The principles of psychosocial rehabilitation outlined in Box 3–1 review the overall values that can contribute to the restoration of the individual to his or her highest potential. The use of these principles in planning and implementing the mental health nursing care plan can enhance the holistic health and integrity of the home care client and family.

◆ Criteria for Assessment of Safe Mental Health Home Care

When adequate community mental health services are present and the home environment is relatively stable, with a capable caregiver in attendance, home care is preferable for the following reasons:

- Nursing staff are able to assess the status of the client in his or her normal social surroundings and plan the individual and home support in a more realistic setting.

BOX 3-1. PRINCIPLES OF PSYCHOSOCIAL REHABILITATION

- All people have an underused capacity that should be developed.
- All people can be equipped with skills (eg, social, vocational, educational, interpersonal).
- People have the right to and responsibility for self-determination.
- Services should be provided in as normalized an environment as possible.
- Assessment of needs and care should be differential (ie, based on the unique needs, abilities, deficiencies, and environment of each client).
- Maximum commitment is required from staff members.
- Care is provided in an intimate environment without professional authoritative shields and barriers.
- Early intervention is preferable.
- Environmental agencies and forces are recruited to assist in the provision of service.
- Attempts are made to modify the environment in terms of attitudes, rights, services, and behavior (social change).
- All clients are welcome for as long as they want to be served (with the exception of specific, short-term, high-demand programs).
- Work and vocational rehabilitation are central to the rehabilitation process.
- Emphasis is on a social rather than a medical model of care.
- Emphasis is on the client's strengths rather than on pathologies.
- Emphasis is on the here and now rather than on problems from the past.

Cnaan, R.A., Blankertz, L., & Saunders, M. (1992). Perceptions of consumers, practitioners, and experts regarding psychosocial rehabilitation principles. *Psychosocial Rehabilitation Journal, 16*(1), 93–119. Adapted with permission.

- The capacity of the client to perform normal activities of daily living can be observed and specific planning can be more reliably recommended.
- Restoration of the normal role in the home of the mentally disordered individual can be more rapidly resumed.
- The client and family are spared the social stigma of psychiatric hospitalization.
- The client and family are saved the financial burden of hospitalization.
- The home health nurse is able to serve as a role model for effective communication with the client and with others in the home setting.

Two stages of mental health care are most frequently treated in the home:

1. The acute initial phase of the mental health crisis, when hospitalization can be averted.

2. The stabilization phase of the mental health crisis, when discharge from a traditional inpatient setting to an adequately supported home environment may occur.

◆ HOME CARE SERVICES FOR THE PERSON IN A MENTAL HEALTH CRISIS

Forward-thinking community mental health programs have instituted a new segment of community mental health nursing: home-based mental health crisis intervention. The operating mode and the intention of this intervention model are to provide emergency mental assessment and nursing care for individuals using the following general criteria for the assessment of clients at risk:

• The person lives in a predetermined geographic location.

• The person meets specific age criteria (eg, aged 16 to 65).

• The person who is referred may either have a prior psychiatric history or be having his or her initial mental health crisis.

• There is a stable home environment with adequate community or home support available for the individual to be treated in the home.

The key to success in early intervention community crisis treatment is the presence of a team or teams of mental health nurses who are trained and prepared to intervene in the home when a mental health crisis threatens the well-being of a client or that of others. This type of model uses a rapid assessment team of nurses that respond to a primary caregiver or medical specialist's call for emergency mental health assessment.

These nurses are authorized to arrange direct hospital admission or referral to an acute care mental health home treatment team. In a study reported in 1994, 25% of the individuals referred to the service were admitted directly to the hospital, rather than being treated at home.

ACUTE CARE MENTAL HEALTH HOME TREATMENT TEAM

The purpose of the acute care mental health home treatment team is to provide intensive support in the community to those in mental health crisis. An essential part of this referral is a planning meeting between the nurses who perform the initial rapid mental and home assessment and nurses on the acute care team who will direct the home care process and provide care.

It is important to note that this form of acute mental health home treatment differs from traditional mental health home care (described in the next section). The character of this early mental health intervention can be described as **intense brief intervention.** When inclusion criteria are met, mental health providers, clients, and their families describe the acute home treatment model as preferable to hospitalization.

An essential aspect of readiness to provide this type of community care is the immediate availability of a psychiatrist for consultation about treatment setting and other critical issues that can determine successful intervention outcomes. Research about client outcomes and cost effectiveness of this type of early intervention acute mental health care will continue to determine refinements of this approach.

TRADITIONAL MENTAL HEALTH COMMUNITY AND HOME CARE

The functions of the mental health home care nurse are to provide mental health assessment and nursing care planning and intervention when changes in mental state occur in the following individuals:

- Older adults

- Those with neuropsychiatric changes associated with AIDS

- Those being treated at home for physical health problems who develop ineffective coping

- Those with chronic mental disorders

- Family members of seriously mentally disturbed children

- Another function of the mental health home care nurse is to provide psychosocial support to the primary caregiver and others involved in the care of these clients. The mental health home care nurse may also be called on to consult with the home care nurse generalist in the physical care setting to obtain clinical recommendations for clients or their family members who are coping ineffectively with the strain of physical illness.

◆ COLLABORATIVE CARE WITH OTHER HEALTH CARE DISCIPLINES

The nurse who is providing psychiatric home care will be developing collaborative care plans with caregivers from other disciplines.

Communication in home care can be more challenging than in general hospital settings where the client's chart is in a central location and accessible at all times by all care disciplines.

The multidisciplinary home care team can include an occupational therapist, social worker, home care generalist (in the event there is a concurrent physical condition), physical therapist, speech therapist, and home health aide.

AVOIDANCE OF CONFLICT WITH OTHER CAREGIVERS

Because of the variety of care disciplines in the home care setting, it can be helpful to be aware of the potential for creating conflict when making statements to the client or his or her family. The following scenario illustrates a common example.

While the nurse is with the client, a family member states that the social worker disagreed with a statement the nurse had made the day before. The nurse becomes angry and expresses her anger to the family member. The nurse then returns to her office and tells her clinical supervisor who makes a call to the social worker's manager to report the incident.

In this scenario, the dynamic of **triangulation** occurs. A **triangle** is a social dynamic that begins with a conflict between two people. Instead of addressing the problem directly, however, one of the two people describes the conflict to a third person. The third person may then become embroiled in a conflict that he or she never witnessed. The third person may even go on to describe the alleged incident to yet another individual who may also become enmeshed.

Indeed, the initial event described above by the family member may have been misunderstood by the family member. To reduce the possibility of this type of miscommunication, it is wise not to discuss an alleged statement with anyone other than the individual to whom it has been attributed. Another recommendation is not to discuss it with the family member; the nurse can discuss it later with a clinical supervisor for recommendations about the best course of action to pursue.

CHAPTER 3 SUMMARY

- The philosophy of home care nursing has the core value of returning the individual to his or her precrisis level of functioning and recognizes the client's and family's potential for psychosocial growth and adaptation.

- Home care nursing recognizes six holistic health care priorities: life sustenance, security, family/social system integrity and balance, in-

tegrity, discovery of inner resources to support growth, and contribution to the betterment of self and others.

■ Assessment of the home environment includes the client's needs as
well as the ability of those in the home environment to provide adequate support, including community support, family or social network, and respite care.

■ Home care is preferable because the nursing staff can assess the status of clients in their normal social surroundings, plan individual and
home support in a more realistic setting, restore mentally disordered
individuals to their normal role in the home, and spare the client and
family the stigma and expense of psychiatric hospitalization.

■ The key to success in early intervention community crisis treatment
is the presence of a team or teams of mental health nurses who are
trained to intervene when a client experiences a mental health crisis.

■ Nurses must often work closely with other disciplines involved in a
client's health care. Developing collaborative care plans and avoiding conflict and poor communication practices such as triangulation are essential.

CHAPTER 3 QUESTIONS

1. The philosophy of home care nursing has the core value of
   a. teaching the family to live with a client's maladaptive behavior.
   b. returning the client to his or her precrisis level of functioning.
   c. closing all inpatient facilities.
   d. accepting that most mental health clients don't really improve.

2. Which of the following is a holistic health care priority?
   a. Security
   b. Life sustenance
   c. Family/social system integrity and balance
   d. All of the above

3. Home care is preferable because
   a. home care can substitute for community care.
   b. nursing staff are able to assess the client's status in his or her nor-
      mal social surroundings.
   c. home care costs more.
   d. the client does not have to participate in activities of daily living.

4. Successful collaborative care plans include
   a. communication with other care disciplines such as social work or
      occupational therapy.

b. using the dynamic of triangling to resolve conflict.
c. discussing disagreements with everyone to make sure they are fully informed.
d. all of the above.

BIBLIOGRAPHY

California Nurses' Association. (1986). *The psychiatric-mental health position statement.* San Francisco: California Nurses' Association.

Cnaan, L., & Blankertz, M. (1992). Perceptions of consumers, practitioners, and experts regarding psychosocial rehabilitation principles. *Psychosocial Rehabilitation Journal, 16*(1), 93–119.

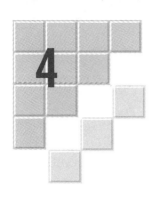

Inpatient Hospitalization: The Mental Health Treatment Team and the Therapeutic Milieu

Behavioral Objectives

After reading this chapter the student will be able to:

- Name the conditions that precede admission to an inpatient mental health treatment setting.

- Explain two benefits to the use of critical paths.

- Describe six members of the inpatient mental health treatment team and the clinical roles they fill.

- List three characteristics that contribute to effective mental health team communication.

- Describe the meaning of the concept **therapeutic milieu**.

- List the characteristics of a therapeutic environment.

- Describe the objectives of a therapeutic treatment team.

Inpatient hospitalization of clients with mental disorders becomes necessary when one or more of the following conditions is present:

1. There is a change in mental status that increases the risk of harm to self or others so that safety must be provided. Admission can be voluntary or court ordered.

2. The normal social environment of the individual is not able to continue the emotional, physical, or financial support of the vulnerable, mentally disabled person.

3. There is a self-perception that the emotionally vulnerable individual is unable to cope effectively. The mental status of the individual must then meet the admission criteria of an inpatient psychiatric unit.

Because of legislation supporting outpatient mental health care, plus increasingly stringent mental health care reimbursement mechanisms, the average number of inpatient hospitalization days continues to decrease. Clients once regularly treated on an inpatient basis now often receive outpatient treatment or a combination of inpatient intervention and outpatient follow-up. (See also Chapter 2, Community-Based Treatment Settings for Mental Disorders).

Thus, when inpatient care is indicated, it must be planned in an aggressive manner designed to restore a person's effective coping ability as soon as possible. Such an objective requires rapid preadmission assessment; this includes selection of the appropriate inpatient setting to meet the particular needs of the person with a mental disorder. For example, a person with a substance-related disorder can sometimes be effectively treated in a partial hospitalization drug program. Certain characteristics of the client's history may indicate that he or she would be better suited to inpatient hospitalization in a local drug treatment center, whereas another person would be recommended to a residential drug treatment program in a different location.

◆ PRELIMINARY CARE PLANNING IN THE INPATIENT TREATMENT SETTING

Care planning for a newly admitted person with a mental disorder ideally begins before he or she is admitted. Consultation between the clinical director, usually a physician, and the head nurse or unit manager can assist in assigning an incoming client to a particular location on the unit that will provide a proper level of safety. In addition, the newly admitted person is often preassigned by the clinical director to a particular treatment team. The clinical leader of the team is called the **team**

leader. He or she will usually begin to consider treatment options before the newly admitted person arrives on the unit.

◆ CRITICAL PATHS

Quality assurance mechanisms have tracked the most effective client care outcomes and cost-effective approaches in mental health settings. As data were assembled, patterns emerged indicating that certain types of care, when paired with specific diagnoses, produced better outcomes than others. These data were used to identify the most effective care for individuals with specific types of diagnoses. A critical path is the use of a specific care protocol for individuals with specific diagnoses. These diagnoses include the following:

Major depression

Cognitive mental disorder

Schizophrenia

Chemical dependency

Bipolar disorder

The advantage of using critical paths is that interventions can be predictably sequenced and planned; discharge planning within a specific number of days can occur more reliably. In addition, all members of the mental health team are working with a very specific treatment protocol. Integration of the goals of all members of the multidisciplinary team is more assured.

The primary goal of inpatient hospitalization is to stabilize the client in a short period of time, so that a more rapid return to his or her normal environment can occur. The information in Table 4–1 demon-

◆ TABLE 4–1. Critical Paths Reduce Lengths of Stay

Following are examples of reductions in length of stay (LOS) that have resulted from critical pathways implemented in The Center For Mental Health at EHS Good Samaritan Hospital in Downers Grove, IL.

Critical Path	1992 Avg. LOS	1993 Avg. LOS
Major depression/adult	11.06 days	8.9 days
Schizophrenia	17.2 days	14.6 days
Major depression/adolescent	14.8 days	11.0 days

Homan, C. (1994). Critical path™ network: Five hospitals succeed with critical paths for psychiatric inpatients. *Hospital Case Management, 2*(9), p. 138. Used with permission.

strates the changes in length of stay (LOS) of clients with major mental disorders in a midwestern general hospital.

◆THE MENTAL HEALTH TREATMENT TEAM

The ability to provide rapid and aggressive assessment and treatment in the inpatient setting requires a cohesive team of clinicians with comprehensive skills in assessing and treating mental disorders in a secure and supportive environment. These team members are named below with a brief description of their roles.

The **clinical director** is usually a psychiatrist. The care of inpatients is his or her ultimate responsibility. In addition to the clinical director, there usually are other inpatient staff psychiatrists who assist in the care of clients by providing overall direction in assessment and care planning, provision of safety, and prescription of appropriate medications to ensure a therapeutic treatment outcome.

The **head nurse** or **unit manager**, usually a registered nurse, manages the physical environment and resources of the unit. He or she also supervises other registered nurses and nursing personnel on the unit.

The **registered nurse** in the psychiatric setting uses the nursing process to plan and implement the care of his or her assigned clients. The philosophy and scope of practice of psychiatric nursing will be presented in Chapter 7, Building A Person-Centered Therapeutic Relationship. The nursing process will be presented in Chapter 16, Nursing Process in the Mental Health Setting. The role of the registered nurse on the mental health team is to assess collaboratively the client's current problems and personal resources and develop a nursing care plan that provides for the client's safety and hygiene needs, as well as the safety and hygiene needs of other inpatients and the mental health team. The safety of all individuals on the unit, whether clients or staff members, is a major priority in nursing care. In inpatient settings, the nurse may also coordinate the therapeutic milieu (discussed later in this chapter). The administration of medications is a nursing function on most psychiatric units. Some units, however, have **medication technicians**, supervised by hospital pharmacists, who prepare and deliver medications to clients.

Other aspects of the nurse's role will depend on a client's specific symptoms, the level of expertise of the nurse, and the particular norms of the unit regarding the functions of nurses. Other nursing personnel who work under the direction of the registered nurse include the licensed practical nurse, the psychiatric aide, and the orderly.

The role of the **licensed practical nurse** is to assist in the implementation of the nursing care plan, including assessing, implementing, and evaluating the client's current status. These observations are reported to the registered nurse, who uses the new data to evaluate the current nursing plan and modify nursing interventions to achieve the desired outcomes. Licensed practical nurses may also be asked to prepare and deliver medication on psychiatric units.

The **psychiatric aide** is a member of the therapeutic team who receives his or her training in programs developed by the psychiatric institution. Usually this job category is found in large psychiatric institutions. Typically, general hospital psychiatric units do not have the in-service training capability to develop such a position. The psychiatric aide in most instances develops good assessment and intervention skills and is a valuable asset to the nursing team.

The **orderly** may be a permanently assigned member of the psychiatric team, depending on the size and resources of the psychiatric unit. This individual's presence is most important during critical incidents on the unit, when numbers of physically strong personnel are needed as a deterrent to loss of control in a client or group of clients.

Another member of the mental health team is the **clinical psychologist**. He or she is trained to administer psychological tests that can identify the specific causes of a person's mental dysfunction. Such information can be used to design strategic, symptom-related intervention. In addition, the targeting of the cause of symptoms can usually assist physicians in selecting appropriate medications for reducing these symptoms.

Another important member of the mental health treatment team is the **psychiatric social worker**. He or she brings knowledge of community resources that can assist in the recovery of the person with mental illness. A psychiatric social worker is knowledgeable about the effect of family on the development, course, and treatment of mental disorders. He or she meets with family members during periods of hospitalization to obtain information about the client's family history and the context of the client's current need for hospitalization.

Expressive therapists are trained to use a special medium, such as art, music, drama, or other creative modalities, to allow expression of the emotional conflict that has caused the client's need for hospitalization. The client may be able to express the underlying conflict using one of these modalities, even though he or she may not have an intellectual understanding of the cause of his or her conflict. By using the insights gained through expressive work, therapists can assist clients in reaching a deeper understanding of why they became ill and how they can address the resulting problems.

The **occupational therapist** is another important contributor to the treatment team. He or she designs activities in conjunction with clients that provide structured outlets for emotional or physical tensions.

These activities also test the client's abilities to solve problems, set goals, maintain concentration, and perform purposeful tasks. The inability to participate in one or more of these functions can provide information to the team about the client's current clinical status and rate of improvement.

◆ COMMUNICATION WITHIN THE TREATMENT TEAM

The goals of inpatient treatment are as follows:

- To identify rapidly the symptoms that caused the need for hospitalization

- To develop a treatment plan that will modify the symptoms

- To identify the effective coping behaviors that are necessary to meet discharge requirements.

Skilled mental health clinicians work as a team to assess and intervene in the comprehensive range of ineffective client behaviors that indicate mental disorder. The inherent factor that contributes to cohesive teamwork is mutual trust. Mutual trust can occur in an environment where there is general respect for the unique role and skills of each clinical discipline.

Team communication is the essence of effective care planning. Each discipline includes skills that can be used to evaluate specific aspects of behavior and functioning: mental status, social skills, cognitive status, vocational capacities, and so on. When the observations and identified client care goals of each discipline are discussed, the result can be a comprehensive plan designed to meet the unique and specific needs of each client.

An important consideration in team communication is that the unit management and members of the team recognize the value of **ongoing evaluation** of the team communication process. For example, does the team take time to discuss and evaluate its own communication patterns? Does it recognize conflict? Does it provide a mechanism to work through the conflict? Does it take time away from the unit for a "day away" or "retreat" to evaluate its current status, ongoing goals, and deterrents to achieving those goals? Most teams find that prioritizing such questions allows for a higher level of professional performance and job satisfaction for each member of the team. Effective communication within the team supports the concept of the therapeutic milieu.

◆ THE THERAPEUTIC MILIEU

The term **milieu** is derived from the French words *ma*, meaning "my," and *lieu*, meaning "place." The phrase "my place" signifies a trusted environment where one can be real and authentic and be respected for these qualities. The concept of the therapeutic milieu is based on the premise that an individual's current, "here and now" behavior is a reflection of his or her current reality and normal social interactions. This reflection offers insights about why the individual is having difficulty in his or her internal reality or social interactions with others. The treatment team can be most effective by assessing these "here and now" behaviors and designing interventions to modify them so that therapeutic client insights and outcomes can be realized.

Several characteristics of a therapeutic milieu have been identified by Jack (1989). They are as follows:

- Every interaction is an opportunity for therapeutic intervention.
- Clients must assume responsibility for their own behavior.
- Problem solving is achieved by discussion, negotiation, and consensus, rather than by a few authority figures.
- Community meetings exist to discuss information and interactions that apply to all staff and clients.
- Peer pressure is a useful and powerful tool.
- Inappropriate behaviors are dealt with as they occur.
- Communication is open and direct between the staff and the clients.
- Clients are encouraged to participate actively in their own treatment and in decision making on the unit.
- The unit remains in close contact with the community, and there is frequent communication with family and significant members of the client's social network.
- Usually the unit's door is open, and the clients have access to areas beyond the unit (p. 70).

◆ THERAPEUTIC TEAM TREATMENT

By using these "here and now" therapeutic milieu concepts, the treatment team is able to develop a comprehensive list of the mental status symptoms, social interactive style, and behaviors that caused the client to be hospitalized. Therapeutic team treatment includes the following objectives:

1. Developing a team treatment plan to modify specific ineffective coping and social behaviors.

2. Naming the objectives or goals of inpatient treatment for each of these ineffective behaviors.

3. Describing the intervention plan for each member of the mental health treatment team with the client.

4. Listing the mental status and coping criteria necessary for discharge.

5. Describing the outpatient discharge recommendations of the team.

The most therapeutic inpatient hospitalizations are ensured when team planning occurs as described earlier. Well-synchronized team planning is the result of good clinical leadership and professional participation by each member of the team. Such planning and therapeutic outcomes can contribute significantly to the ongoing job satisfaction of each team member.

C H A P T E R   4   S U M M A R Y

- Inpatient hospitalization of a person with a mental disorder is necessary when:
  - A change in mental status increases risk of harm to self and others
  - The individual's normal environment cannot support him or her
  - The individual's self-perception is that he or she cannot cope effectively

- Therapeutic team treatment includes five objectives:
  - Develop a team treatment plan to modify ineffective behaviors and coping devices.
  - Name objectives or goals in the treatment for these behaviors.
  - Describe the plan and the role of each team member to the client.
  - List the mental status and coping criteria necessary for discharge.
  - Describe the team's recommendations for outpatient discharge.

- Communication and mutual trust are essential for effective functioning of a mental health treatment team.

- The concept of the therapeutic milieu focuses on addressing current client behavior, assessing how it reflects the client's inadequate coping or relational skills, and determining interventions to modify the ineffective behaviors.

CHAPTER 4 QUESTIONS

1. The treatment team member who generally assesses client problems, develops a care plan for inpatient client safety and hygiene needs, and administers medication is the
   a. clinical psychologist.
   b. psychiatric social worker.
   c. registered nurse.
   d. orderly.

2. Care planning for a newly admitted person with a mental disorder ideally begins
   a. before the person is admitted.
   b. during the first 24 hours after admission.
   c. after an assessment is complete and medication is administered.
   d. none of the above.

3. Milieu ("my place") therapy includes which of the following concepts?
   a. The mentally disordered person is best treated at home.
   b. "Here and now" behavior reflects the client's current reality.
   c. Odd or disruptive client behavior should be ignored.
   d. Peer pressure has little impact on the treatment of mentally disordered individuals.

4. The factors that contribute *most* to cohesive teamwork on the treatment team are
   a. shared philosophies on therapeutic milieu and behavior.
   b. adequate certification and experience of all team members.
   c. abilities to avoid conflict and set treatment timetables.
   d. mutual trust and communication.

BIBLIOGRAPHY

Butterworth, T. (1994). Working in partnership: A collaborative approach to care. The review of mental health nursing. *Journal of Psychiatric and Mental Health Nursing, 1*(1), 41–44.

Homan, C. (1994) Critical path network. Five hospitals succeed with critical paths for psychiatric inpatients. *Hospital Case Management, 2*(9), 135–138.

Jack, L.W. (1989). Use of milieu as a problem-solving strategy in addiction treatment. *Nursing Clinics of North America, 24*, 69–80.

Kaplan, H.I., & Sadock, B.J. (1995). *Comprehensive textbook of psychiatry/VI* (6th ed.). Baltimore: Williams & Wilkins.

Kaplan, H.I., & Sadock, B.J. (1994). *Synopsis of psychiatry: Behavioral sciences, clinical psychology* (7th ed.). Baltimore: Williams & Wilkins.

Lego, S. (1996). *Psychiatric nursing: A comprehensive reference* (2nd ed.). Philadelphia: Lippincott-Raven.

Mental health and psychiatric nursing (2nd ed.). (1996). Lippincott's Review Series. Philadelphia: Lippincott-Raven.

Mohr, W.K. (1995). A critical reappraisal of a social form in psychiatric care settings: The multidisciplinary team meeting as a paradigm case. *Archives of Psychiatric Nursing, 9*(2), 85–91.

Murray, R.B., & Baier, M. (1993). Use of therapeutic milieu in a community setting. *Journal of Psychosocial Nursing and Mental Health Services, 31*(10), 11–16.

Shives, L.R. (Ed.). (1994). *Basic concepts of psychiatric-mental health nursing* (3rd ed.). Philadelphia: J.B. Lippincott.

Stuart, G.W., & Sundeen, S.J. (Eds.). (1994). *Principles and practice of psychiatric nursing* (5th ed.). St. Louis: Mosby Year Book.

Walker, M. (1994). Principles of therapeutic milieu: An overview. *Perspectives in Psychiatric Care, 30*(3), 5–8.

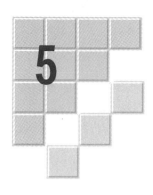

5

Legal and Ethical Issues in Mental Health Nursing

Behavioral Objectives

After reading this chapter the student will be able to:

■ Summarize the ethical codes for nurses.

■ Define **socialization, values,** and **ethics.**

■ Name six standards of nursing practice and the rationale for each.

■ Describe the following rights of mentally ill people who are hospitalized:

Right to treatment

Confidentiality

Habeas corpus

Right to refuse treatment

■ Explain the following legal terms:

Competency

Dangerousness as it pertains to the mentally ill person

Involuntary commitment

◆ THE CODE OF NURSING

The role of nurses is to safeguard the well-being of people entrusted to their care. The Code of Nursing, revised by the American Nurses Association in 1985*, describes the ways in which a nurse should carry out this role:

1. The nurse provides services with respect for human dignity and the uniqueness of the client unrestricted by considerations of social or economic status, personal attributes, or the nature of health problems.

2. The nurse safeguards the client's right to privacy by judiciously protecting information of a confidential nature.

3. The nurse acts to safeguard the client and the public when health care and safety are affected by the incompetent, unethical, or illegal practice of any person.

4. The nurse assumes responsibility and accountability for individual nursing judgments and actions.

5. The nurse maintains competence in nursing.

6. The nurse exercises informed judgment and uses individual competence and qualifications as criteria in seeking consultation, accepting responsibilities, and delegating nursing activities to others.

7. The nurse participates in activities that contribute to the ongoing development of the profession's body of knowledge.

8. The nurse participates in the profession's efforts to implement and improve standards of nursing.

9. The nurse participates in the profession's efforts to establish and maintain conditions of employment conducive to high-quality nursing care.

10. The nurse participates in the profession's efforts to protect the public from misinformation and misrepresentation and to maintain the integrity of nursing.

11. The nurse collaborates with members of the health professions and other citizens in promoting community and national efforts to meet the health needs of the public.

The code is based on the assumption that a nurse has a well-formulated sense of ethics and legal responsibilities. The field of mental health nursing involves working with people who have varying levels of mental competence or judgment. Accordingly, it becomes essential

---

*As the sixth edition of *Mental Health and Mental Illness* goes to press, the Code of Nursing is being updated. Anticipated publication date is 1997.

that mental health nurses be aware of ethics within their scope of practice. **Ethics** is defined as the knowledge of the principles of good and evil. When the ethics of a particular field or discipline are discussed, it is expected that the individual within that field possesses a basic set of ethical values about his or her conduct individually and in interpersonal relationships. Professional ethics are then built on the foundation of personal ethics.

The Social Policy Statement issued by the American Nurses' Association has become the basis of the nursing practice acts in many states. This statement defines nursing as "the diagnosis and treatment of the human response to illness." This broad definition of nursing practice encompasses a very wide range of nursing care functions. It implies that the nurse is aware of the moral obligations of his or her care of clients.

Personal ethics are formed as a person is socialized. **Socialization** is a developmental process during which the young child gains acceptance from his or her parents and other authority figures by conforming to their rules. These rules are the "do's and don'ts" that are gradually internalized to form the child's value system. A **value** is a basic internal guideline that causes an emotional response in a person.

These values or personal guides develop and evolve throughout one's lifetime. They form the basis, either consciously or unconsciously, of a person's decisions and actions. Values, which are at the core of a person's selfhood, do not change easily or quickly. Ideally they are dynamic and are subject to modification and change as a person matures and acquires more wisdom and knowledge about himself or herself and others. When this does not happen, the outcome is an inflexible personality. This type of inflexibility is the result of insecurity and the need to avoid anxiety.

◆ THE CODE FOR LICENSED PRACTICAL/VOCATIONAL NURSES

The Code for Licensed Practical/Vocational Nurses* provides a motivation for establishing, maintaining, and elevating professional standards. Each LP/VN, upon entering the profession, inherits the responsibility of adhering to the standards of ethical practice and conduct as set forth in the following code:

1. Know the scope of maximum use of the LP/VN as specified by the nursing practice act of the state in which one is licensed and function within this scope.

*The Code and the Nursing Practice Standards are adapted from Nursing Practice Standards for the Licensed Practical/Vocational Nurse, a brochure published by the National Federation of Licensed Practical Nurses, Inc.

2. Safeguard the confidential information acquired from any source about the client.

3. Provide health care to all clients regardless of race, creed, cultural background, disease, or lifestyle.

4. Refuse to give endorsement to the sale and promotion of commercial products or services.

5. Uphold the highest standards in personal appearance, language, dress, and demeanor.

6. Stay informed about issues affecting the practice of nursing and delivery of health care and, where appropriate, participate in government and policy decisions.

7. Accept the responsibility for safe nursing by keeping oneself mentally and physically fit and educationally prepared to practice.

8. Accept responsibility for membership in the National Federation for Licensed Practical Nurses (NLFPN) and participate in its efforts to maintain the established standards of nursing practice and employment policies which lead to quality client care.

◆ NURSING PRACTICE STANDARDS FOR THE LICENSED PRACTICAL NURSE

The Nursing Practice Standards for the Licensed Practical/Vocational Nurse were developed and adopted by the National Federation of Licensed Practical Nurses. These standards provide a basic model to measure and evaluate the quality of health service and nursing service and care given by LPNs and VNs. These practice standards are applicable in any practice setting.

Education

1. Complete a formal education program in practical nursing approved by the appropriate nursing authority in a state.

2. Successfully pass the National Council Licensure Examination for Practical Nurses.

3. Participate in initial orientation within the employing institution.

Legal/Ethical Status

1. Hold a current license to practice nursing as an LP/VN in accordance with the law of the state where employed.

2. Know the scope of nursing practice authorized by the nursing practice act in the state where employed.
3. Have a personal commitment to fulfill the legal responsibilities inherent in good nursing practice.
4. Take responsible actions in situations in which there is unprofessional conduct by a peer or other health care provider.
5. Recognize and have a commitment to meet the ethical and moral obligations of the practice of nursing.
6. Do not accept or perform professional responsibilities outside of one's areas of competence.

Practice

1. Accept assigned responsibilities as an accountable member of the health care team.
2. Function within the limits of educational preparation and experience as related to the assigned duties.
3. Function with other members of the health care team in promoting and maintaining health, preventing disease and disability, caring for and rehabilitating individuals who are experiencing an altered health state, and contributing to the ultimate quality of life until death.
4. Know and use the nursing process in:
   a. Planning (assessment of health status, analysis of information gained from the assessment, and identification of health goals)
   b. Implementing (put the nursing care plan into practice to achieve the stated goals)
   c. Evaluating (measure progress toward the stated goals of the nursing care plan)
5. Participate in peer review and other evaluation processes.
6. Participate in the development of policies concerning the health and nursing needs of society and in the roles and functions of the LP/VN.

Continuing Education

1. Be responsible for maintaining the highest possible level of professional competence at all times.
2. Periodically reassess career goals and select continuing education activities to help achieve these goals.
3. Take advantage of continuing education opportunities that will lead to personal growth and professional development.

4. Seek and participate in continuing education activities that are approved for credit by appropriate organizations, such as the NFLPN.

Specialized Nursing Practice

1. Have at least 1 year's experience in nursing at the staff level.

2. Present personal qualifications that indicate potential abilities for practice in the chosen specialized nursing area.

3. Present evidence of completion of a program or course approved by an appropriate agency to provide the knowledge and skills necessary to effective nursing services in the specialized field.

4. Meet all of the standards of practice as set forth in this document.

◆ STANDARDS OF PSYCHIATRIC-MENTAL HEALTH CLINICAL NURSING PRACTICE

In these authoritative statements, the nursing profession describes the responsibilities for which nurses are accountable in the field of psychiatric and mental health nursing. In 1994, the American Nurses' Association developed the following psychiatric-mental health nursing practice standards to reflect the values and priorities of the profession. They also provide direction for professional nursing practice and a framework for evaluating the practice. These standards apply to the care that is provided to all clients. The standards and the rationale for each are listed below.

Standard 1: Assessment

The psychiatric-mental health nurse collects client health data.

Rationale: The assessment interview (which requires linguistically and culturally effective communication skills, interviewing, behavioral observation, database record review, and comprehensive assessment of the client and relevant systems) enables the psychiatric-mental health nurse to make sound clinical judgments and plan appropriate interventions with the client.

Standard 2: Diagnosis

The psychiatric-mental health nurse analyzes the assessment data in determining diagnoses.

Rationale: The basis for providing psychiatric-mental health nursing care is the recognition and identification of patterns of response to actual or potential psychiatric illnesses and mental health problems.

Standard 3: Outcome Identification

The psychiatric-mental health nurse identifies expected outcomes individualized to the client.

Rationale: Within the context of providing nursing care, the ultimate goal is to influence health outcomes and improve the client's health status.

Standard 4: Planning

The psychiatric-mental health nurse develops a plan of care that prescribes interventions to attain expected outcomes.

Rationale: A plan of care is used to guide therapeutic intervention systematically and achieve the expected client outcomes.

Standard 5: Implementation

The psychiatric-mental health nurse implements the interventions identified in the plan of care.

Rationale: In implementing the plan of care, psychiatric-mental health nurses use a wide range of interventions designed to prevent mental and physical illness and promote, maintain, and restore mental and physical health. Psychiatric-mental health nurses select interventions according to their level of practice. At the basic level, the nurse may select or participate in counseling, milieu therapy, self-care activities, physician-ordered psychobiological interventions, health teaching, case management, health promotion and health maintenance, and a variety of other approaches to meet the mental health needs of clients. In addition, at an advanced level, the certified specialist may provide consultation, engage in psychotherapy, and prescribe pharmacological agents where permitted by state statutes or regulations.

Standard 6: Evaluation

The psychiatric-mental health nurse evaluates the client's progress in attaining expected outcomes.

Rationale: Nursing care is a dynamic process involving change in the client's health status over time, giving rise to the need for new data, different diagnoses, and modifications in the plan of care. Therefore, evaluation is a continuous process of appraising the effect of nursing interventions and the treatment regimen on the client's health status and expected health outcomes.

◆ THE ETHICS OF NURSING

Because the primary function of mental health nursing is relating with people, it is important to review the way in which nursing "care" occurs. Richards has examined the concepts of "caring for" versus "caring about." When a person *cares for* another, the implication is that the other is like a child and is incapable of self-care; he or she is dependent and cannot make any contributions to his or her own well-being. *Caring about*, on the other hand, demonstrates respect for the other as a full human being. Although a client may be temporarily incapacitated (to a greater or lesser degree), the nurse should continually relate to him or her in a manner that promotes self-acceptance, ability to care for self, and ultimate restoration of health.

It can be helpful to review one's own philosophy of client care to determine which approach to use in practice. Consistent use of the caring-for approach described above does not contribute to the ultimate well-being or potential autonomy of clients.

The Code of Nursing Practice noted earlier describes the ethical relationship that ideally exists between a nurse and a mental health client. These ethical codes, although clearly stated, can sometimes create internal conflicts in the nurse. Because nursing practice deals with all aspects of human existence, it cannot consist of circumstances that fit within perfect guidelines. In actual practice, it is possible to be caught between a personal belief and a professional ethic or a law that causes strong disagreement and consternation. If this occurs and the dilemma seems unresolvable, it can be helpful to seek the counsel of someone in the profession who is knowledgeable about the issues involved.

◆ LEGAL ASPECTS OF MENTAL HEALTH NURSING

Physically or mentally ill individuals are in a dependent position when hospitalized. Accordingly, the legal systems in various states have instituted laws designed to safeguard their well-being. Laws regarding mentally ill people differ from state to state, so it is important that nurses obtain specific information about the statutes affecting their delivery of care during orientation programs in their respective institutions or agencies.

Laws are developed by a society as an outcome of personal and professional values and ethics. A single instance of violation of another's well-being does not usually result in a law designed to forbid its recurrence. Instead, repetition of similar types of violations causes people to respond with indignation and call for a law to control and punish its continued occurrence.

RIGHT TO TREATMENT

All people who are hospitalized for mental illness have the right to treatment. As the result of lawsuits brought to court during the 1960s and 1970s, mental health professionals are increasingly aware of their legal responsibilities to clients. A court decision of the mid-1960s (*Rouse v Cameron*) (373 F. 2d 451 [D.C. Cir. 1966]) declared that a mentally ill person has the following rights to treatment:

- A treatment plan that is continuously reviewed by a qualified mental health professional and modified, if necessary
- A mental examination and review of a client's care plan every 90 days by a qualified mental health professional other than the professional responsible for supervising and implementing the plan
- A statement of client problems and needs
- A statement of the least restrictive treatment conditions necessary
- Intermediate and long-range goals and a timetable for implementing them
- A statement of rationale for the plan
- A description of proposed staff involvement
- Criteria for release to a less restrictive environment and discharge
- Notation of therapeutic tasks to be performed by the client

CONFIDENTIALITY

The client in the mental health setting has many rights to safeguard his or her well-being. These include the right to confidentiality. **Confidentiality** requires that the nurse's knowledge of all aspects of the client's condition belong, in essence, to the client. The nurse cannot reveal this information publicly without the client's informed consent. Obviously, the nurse's documentation of information revealed in the nurse–client relationship falls within this guideline.

In the nurse–client relationship, the client may share sensitive or potentially damaging information with the nurse. It is important that the nurse be aware of the specific guidelines regarding documentation or verbal reporting of this information developed by the institution in which he or she is working. A wise rule is that, if in doubt, do not chart such material until the situation is discussed with a supervisor.

It is also important to remember that a client's chart can be used at any time in a legal proceeding. The client's chart should contain accurate documentation using guidelines established by the institution in which the nurse is working. Upon changing institutions, it is important for the nurse to determine what information is recorded in what manner in the new setting. Guidelines can vary among different institutions. If it should be necessary to change any charted material, the following recommendations should be closely followed:

1. The record should never be erased.
2. A line should be drawn through the erroneous material in the chart and the corrected version substituted.
3. The correction should be dated and initialed.
4. A chart should never be altered after material has been subpoenaed in a lawsuit. This may be considered tampering with evidence and could result in a serious penalty.

Another important aspect of confidentiality or privacy is the disclosure of information by a client who requests that the nurse not share it with anyone else. It is unwise for the nurse to agree to such a request. Because the nurse is a member of a treatment team, such information should be shared verbally with the director of the team, whose clinical judgment forms the basis of the decisions about whether and how this information should be shared with the team. Inexperienced students or nurses sometimes may want to maintain this requested confidentiality, but it can sometimes have tragic consequences if the information would have averted danger to the client or others. In addition, a request for confidentiality is often an attempt by the client, conscious or otherwise, to split the members of the health care team.

INFORMED CONSENT AND COMPETENCY

Consent is a person's agreement to an act that will affect his or her body or to disclosure of information about himself or herself. There are four general types of consent. **Informed consent** is the agreement by a competent person who has been given the information necessary to weigh the advantages and disadvantages of the treatment that is being proposed to him or her. **Implied consent** is the consent a person gives when allowing himself or herself to undergo routine laboratory work or x-rays, or to take medications administered by a caregiver. **Presumed consent** comes into play when an unconscious person is given life-saving treatment in a life-threatening situation. **Vicarious consent** is given by parents, guardians, or conservators when a person is incapable of deciding for himself or herself.

In addition to decisions regarding treatment, another type of informed consent (particularly important to a person with past or present mental illness) refers to the release of information about a client's outpatient treatment or hospitalization. Such consent is usually sought so that health care insurance firms, future employers, or the legal system can obtain information about the client. Because such information can be potentially damaging to a client, he or she has the right to know exactly what information will be given and why it is needed. The person explaining the informed consent procedure should be knowledgeable and serve as a client advocate.

Competency is a person's mental status that renders him or her capable of sound decision making and management of his or her own life circumstances. The concept of competency is subject to different legal definitions, depending on circumstances and the particular state in which a person lives.

The decision to obtain a court decision on mental competency is usually made when family members or caregivers have serious concerns about a person's judgment and ability to handle his or her own affairs. If sufficient data are presented to the judge, he or she can order that a guardian, conservator, or committee be appointed to make and implement decisions that will safeguard all aspects of the client's well-being.

The case described below is one that can cloud an interpretation of competency.

> Mary is a 52-year-old, single schoolteacher who was diagnosed with acute leukemia 3 years ago. Since that time she has undergone two rounds of chemotherapy, which caused excessive nausea, fatigue, and alopecia (baldness). Although her mental status has not deteriorated, she was physically weakened. Following the second round of chemotherapy she had to resign her teaching position, which was a major focus in her life. Because of other medications she is receiving, her bones have become brittle. She has broken her collarbone, femur, and humerus in falls in her home. She is excessively frail and lives in near isolation.

It is possible that a physician could attempt to treat this client with a third round of chemotherapy. The client could refuse, choosing instead to allow the natural evolution of death.

What is your reaction to this example?

Do you believe the client has the right to refuse treatment?

In some medical-surgical care settings, the rule of maintaining life, no matter what the cost to the mental health or quality of life of the client and his or her family, may appear to be the only factor considered in making treatment decisions. In such hospitals, when a terminally ill, but mentally competent, client refuses to undergo prolonged or painful treatment, the physicians may try to obtain a legal ruling of mental incompetence in order to give the client such treatment.

Values in our society are shifting to include consideration of quality of life in the decision about radical treatment. As a result, the medical and legal systems are more often responding with sensitive and thoughtful decisions that support the needs of clients and their families.

It is important to know that the client has a right to review his or her own chart. It is recommended and required in many institutions that such a request by a client be forwarded to his or her physician. It is wise for the physician to be present when the client is reading the chart in order to answer any questions and clarify any misunderstandings.

INVOLUNTARY COMMITMENT

Most people who are mentally ill recognize their need for treatment and are relieved when they are hospitalized. Others, whose sense of reality and judgment are markedly altered, do not submit to hospitalization. When lack of treatment poses a danger to the client or others, it is often necessary to obtain a court order for commitment. The state is empowered by law to fulfill its obligation to protect its citizens.

Each state has adopted different definitions of the mental state that constitutes **dangerousness.** Generally, it is a serious mental condition that has existed during the previous 30 days. The person must be examined by a psychiatrist when commitment is believed necessary. If suicide, homicide, serious bodily harm to self or others, or neglect that can lead to harm of self or others is believed by the examining psychiatrist to be a potential outcome, emergency commitment can be carried out immediately. The case must be reviewed by a judge with strong supporting evidence submitted for a continued court-ordered hospitalization.

HABEAS CORPUS

If a person is being held in a hospital against his or her will, he or she may apply for a writ of habeas corpus. A writ of **habeas corpus** has the purpose of requiring an immediate court hearing to determine a person's sanity. If the person is declared sane, then he or she must be released from the institution immediately.

RIGHT TO REFUSE TREATMENT

Most of the rights of clients have been established because of legal precedents that were determined when former mental clients went to court to sue former caregivers for denial of their rights when they were hospitalized. Two of the most common treatments that have potentially negative side effects are electroshock treatment (EST) and all psychotropic medications. Phenothiazine medications have been specifically identified in lawsuits because of the permanent side effect called tardive dyskinesia, described in Chapter 31, Psychopharmacology and Electroshock Treatment of Mental Disorders. Mentally ill hospitalized clients, whether voluntarily or involuntarily admitted, have the right to information about these treatments and the right to refuse them.

In conclusion, the knowledge regarding ethics and legal issues in mental health nursing is expanding rapidly. As the issue of client rights became more urgent, nurses began to review their own ethical responsibilities to clients. One of the major reasons for the increase in knowledge of legal issues was consumer awareness that their needs were not being adequately met by the mental health care system. Lawsuits that mandated change in particular states often had effects beyond the boundaries of those states. Other states, in viewing the outcomes of these lawsuits, began to review and revise some of their own questionable practices.

CHAPTER 5 SUMMARY

- The Code of Nursing describes how nurses should carry out their role of safeguarding the well-being of people in their care.

- The Code of Nursing assumes that nurses have a strong sense of ethics (knowledge of the principles of good and evil) and understand the legal responsibilities involved in client care.

- Mentally disordered clients have a right to
  — Treatment
  — Confidentiality
  — A determination of competency (habeas corpus)
  — Refuse treatment

- In cases where a mentally disordered client is dangerous to self or others, the client can be committed involuntarily. The definition of "dangerous" may vary from state to state.

CHAPTER 5 QUESTIONS

1. It is necessary for a nurse to be aware of the ethics of treating mentally disordered clients because
   a. each care plan contains an "ethics" section that must be completed.
   b. otherwise clients cannot become socialized.
   c. the Code of Nursing requires it.
   d. mental health nursing involves working with people who have varying degrees of mental competence or judgment.

2. Vicarious consent is given
   a. by the client at least 6 months before hospitalization occurs.
   b. when the client is competent but not able to decide for himself or herself.

   c. by parents, guardians, or conservators when the client cannot decide for himself or herself.
   d. only in cases of outpatient treatment.

3. If a person held in a hospital applies for a writ of habeas corpus, what must happen?
   a. The person is immediately released from the hospital.
   b. The person must undergo blood tests to check for substance abuse.
   c. The person must sign a document declaring that he or she is mentally disordered.
   d. The person immediately receives a court hearing to determine his or her sanity.

4. Which of the following statements about competency is true?
   a. It is the mental status that allows sound decision making and management.
   b. It is subject to different legal definitions in different states.
   c. It can include clients refusing painful or prolonged medical treatment.
   d. All of the above

BIBLIOGRAPHY

American Nurses Association Code of nurses with interpretive statements. (1985). Washington, D.C: American Nurses Association.

Bandman, E.L., & Bandman, B. (1995). *Nursing ethics across the life span* (3rd ed.). Norwalk, CT: Appleton & Lange.

Caverly, S. (1994). Legal and ethical issues related to psychopharmacology. *ANA Publication PMH-13 10 M*, 34–37.

Coletta, S. (1978). Values clarification in nursing: Why? *American Journal of Nursing, 78*, 2057.

Fisher, A. (1995). The ethical problems encountered in psychiatric nursing practice with dangerous mentally ill persons. *Scholarly Inquiry in Nursing Practice, 9*(2), 193–208.

Lego, S. (1996). *Psychiatric nursing: A comprehensive reference* (2nd ed.). Philadelphia: Lippincott-Raven.

Mental health and psychiatric nursing (2nd ed.). (1996). Lippincott's Review Series. Philadelphia: Lippincott-Raven.

Nursing practice standards for the licensed practical/vocational nurse. (1996). Garner, NC: National Federation of Licensed Practical Nurses.

Nursing social policy statement. (1995). Kansas City, MO: American Nurses Association.

Offer, P.A. (1994). Nurse and patient rights: Can both be protected? *Journal of Psychosocial Nursing and Mental Health Services, 32*(12), 48.

Richards, F. (1975). Do you care for, or care about? *AORN Journal, 22*, 792–798.

Spensley, J. (1995). Ethics: The last execution. *Nursing Standard, 9*(17), 50–51.

DEVELOPING CRITICAL THINKING SKILLS THROUGH CLASS DISCUSSION

UNIT ONE Case Study
Patterns of Mental Health Care

Alice is a 26-year-old woman who was diagnosed with schizophrenia, a chronic mental illness, when she was 16 years old. She lives with her widowed mother, Ann Price, who has chronic emphysema. Because of her chronic illness Mrs. Price is unable to work. She and her daughter live on the meager income from their Social Security payments.

As her own physical condition has deteriorated, Mrs. Price has lacked the energy and motivation to be involved in the care of her daughter's mental illness. Alice has been noncompliant in taking her antipsychotic medication since her original diagnosis. She has been hospitalized seven times in the past 10 years as her psychoses have become severe.

She is being treated by the outpatient department of psychiatry at her local hospital, approximately 4 miles from her apartment. Because of her poor motivation and lack of interest in treatment, she has been assigned to a chronic schizophrenic medication group led by a clinical nurse specialist in psychiatry. She does not attend the group nor does she take her medication on a regular basis.

DISCUSSION QUESTIONS

1. As you hear the story of Alice, what are you major concerns?

2. What types of intervention from community resources could assist Alice to become more responsible for her own care while she is living with her mother?

3. What can happen to Alice if her mother becomes too ill to maintain her apartment?

4. Can Alice live alone? Why?

5. What are the significant risks to Alice's safety if she is no longer able to live with her mother?

6. If you were Alice's cousin, what would you do to investigate possible housing options for her? Health care options?

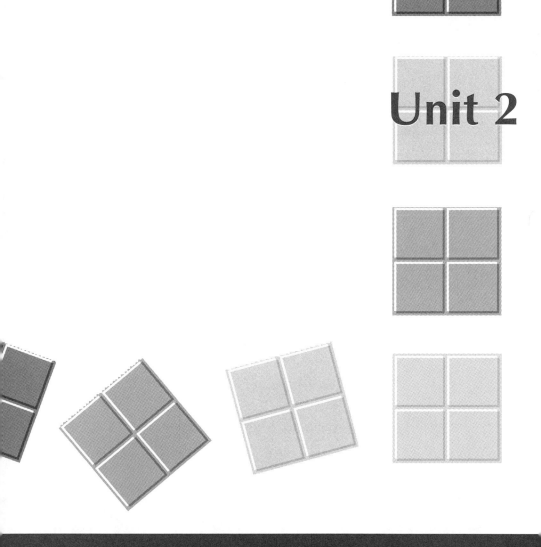

Unit 2

CONCEPTS OF PSYCHIATRIC-MENTAL HEALTH NURSING

6

Establishing the Therapeutic Nursing Environment

After reading this chapter the student will be able to:

■ Define empathic care and list four characteristics of empathic caring.

■ Explain the concept of acceptance and describe why it is an important part of the therapeutic relationship.

■ Describe why explanations are important to the person with mental illness.

■ Define **trust**.

■ Explain the difference between empathy and sympathy and give an example of each.

■ Describe why limit setting is important in the treatment of the mentally ill person.

■ Define **reality** and explain why the ego may alter a person's awareness of reality.

◆ CARING

There are many qualities that support therapeutic nursing practice. Regardless of the pattern of behavior that may characterize a client's illness, certain general principles apply to the care of all who show behavior disorders. Everyone has certain basic and psychosocial needs that must be met, no matter how different the surface behavior may be. **Caring** is a distinguishing characteristic of nursing practice. This characteristic of nursing practice and of nurses themselves has been studied by Dr. Patricia Benner. Benner says that nurses have the potential to provide skilled, empathic, and effective care. She describes the heart of caring as the ability to be empathic. **Empathy** is placing oneself within the experience of another without losing one's own sense of identity. Other abilities that expand one's empathy are "being there" and understanding the meaning of illness to the client; touching; listening; communicating verbally and nonverbally so that the client feels that he or she is understood; and demonstrating technical competence.

◆ ACCEPTANCE

The client needs to be accepted exactly as he or she is, as a person of worth and dignity. An emotionally ill person cannot be expected to meet normal standards of behavior, nor should he or she be rewarded or punished as his or her behavior approaches or recedes from such standards.*

Each of us has certain standards of conduct that we strive to maintain. When others fail to meet our standards, we tend to pass judgment upon them and to punish them in one way or another for their transgressions. This is acceptable behavior for normal individuals, but an emotionally ill person needs a *very low-pressure social environment* in order to learn to live again with others.

Acceptance does not mean that we sanction or approve of a client's behavior, but neither do we judge or punish him or her for it. Do not call attention to defects, or show disapproval by word, action, attitude, or expression. You must show interest in a client as a human being—as an individual possessed of dignity and worth.

Acceptance often starts out as one-sided. Frequently, the client wants no part of you or other staff members, nor of your help. He or she may be fearful of any closeness and be suspicious of your intentions. If

---

*When a behavior modification program (see Chapter 29, Milieu Therapy and Behavior Modification) is in operation, however, this tenet no longer holds. The behavior modification contract will describe the acceptable and unacceptable behavior on which staff interventions will be based.

previous interpersonal experiences have convinced the client that he or she is not acceptable to others, it may be difficult to change this self-concept. However, you must convey to the client that he or she is a worthwhile person, and that even though some behavior may be unacceptable, he or she—as a person—is acceptable. If you set limits on behavior in order to help the client behave more appropriately, but demonstrate warmth and support while doing so, he or she will slowly begin to feel accepted and viewed as a worthwhile person.

The mentally ill person may need to test the sincerity of the therapeutic relationship over and over again before fears and doubts are all swept away. Acceptance is a way of expressing belief in the fundamental worth of another person. We all have a need for acceptance; the mentally ill have a very great need for it.

◆ EXPLANATIONS

Routines and procedures should always be explained at the client's level of understanding. Most of us like to be informed about what to expect in any given situation. Mentally ill clients are no exception. Always explain what is being done and why it is being done in such a way that full allowance is made for the client's symptom-imposed limitations. A client with a limited attention span needs a brief, clear, pointed explanation; an apprehensive client needs a firm explanation that assumes he or she will accept the procedure; and an indecisive client needs us to make decisions for him or her and to outline procedures to minimize the necessity of deciding. The purpose behind an explanation is to reduce anxiety whenever possible by preparing the client for what is to come.

◆ EXPRESSION OF FEELINGS

The client needs to be able to ventilate feelings without fear of retaliation. Encouraging the client to express feelings helps lower his or her frustration level and assists you in assessing real feelings and the motivation for behavior. Talk and *actively listen* to the client. Conversation should center on the client—on his or her needs, wants, and interests—not on those of the listener. Allow the client to express emotions such as anxiety, fear, hostility, hatred, and anger.

A client's ability to express a negative emotion can be a very healthy sign, for strong emotions, bottled up, are potentially explosive and dangerous. Strange as it may seem, we can frequently be more help to a psychiatric client if we are the objects of his or her hostility rather than if the client likes us. Our quiet acceptance of hostility permits him or her to discharge emotion without retaliation. One of the real dangers of hatred and hostility to the person who feels these emotions is the fear of retribution they carry. Therefore, the client needs an atmosphere in which his or her behavior is calmly accepted.

◆ MUTUAL TRUST

Like the need for acceptance, the need for mutual trust is vital to a therapeutic relationship. If we find our world a friendly and trustworthy place in which to live, we will bring this ability to trust to our work. If a series of experiences have convinced the client that he or she cannot trust others, we must start at the beginning to establish a basis for trust, building slowly and carefully. Honesty, integrity, and consistency are all building blocks in laying such a foundation.

Explain in clear, simple language what you intend to do with and for your clients and let nothing interfere with carrying out your contract or pact. If you promise to visit a client daily, arrive at the appointed time, stay the length of time promised, and leave when the time is up. Should something unavoidably cause a delay or prevent a visit, notify the client. This is the way to build trust.

If you tell a client that he or she may discuss problems, it is important to sit quietly and listen openly. Chapter 7, Building a Person-Centered Therapeutic Relationship, discusses counseling techniques that are helpful in this process. If the client's behavior becomes unacceptable, it is important to set reasonable limits so he or she can express emotions constructively, not destructively.

◆ UNDERSTANDING

When we as staff members increase our own self-understanding, we are better able to understand client behavior. We each need to analyze our own feelings and motivations and usually need some help in developing skills in interpersonal relationships. Group discussions on emotions and their effects are very valuable in deepening self-awareness. We can become comfortable in our relationships with clients only when we feel secure about our ability to respond appropriately to client behavior.

When we are able to understand a client's behavior and find the underlying motivation, then and only then can we organize these findings into a truly therapeutic care plan designed to meet his or her needs. We must then constantly evaluate the client's behavior to see if those needs are being effectively met. This is called the **dynamic approach.** A **therapeutic relationship** uses professional knowledge and skill in a manner that is constructive to the well-being of the client. Place yourself in the client's position to understand whatever he or she is experiencing. At the same time, make efforts to establish and improve communication, especially in the field of active listening.

◆ EMPATHY AND SYMPATHY

As discussed at the beginning of the chapter, one of the important qualities in a helping relationship is **empathy**. Empathy is the ability to hear what another person is saying and be able to borrow the other person's feelings temporarily but still maintain one's own. When with a client, it is important to maintain one's own objectivity in order to assess accurately the client's mental functioning. **Sympathy** occurs if objectivity is lost by the caregiver who adopts the same feelings as the client.

The following scenario illustrates the difference between empathy and sympathy. You are in a boat with someone who falls overboard. Choosing to throw him a line and pull him to safety is comparable to an empathic therapeutic intervention. Jumping into the water with him, even if you don't know how to swim, is comparable to sympathy.

◆ CONSISTENCY

Consistency is a measure that contributes much to client security. All mentally ill clients are insecure and uncertain. Not knowing what to expect produces anxiety. Consistency in all areas of experience is valuable to the psychiatric client, for it builds into his or her environment something to depend on. A consistent hospital routine with firm limit setting is tremendously important to the client. It reduces the number of decisions that must be made daily, and he or she learns what to expect from the environment. The attitude of the entire hospital staff toward the client, likewise, must be consistent; this consistency in attitude should extend from person to person and from shift to shift. Continuous exposure to an atmosphere of quiet understanding causes the client's anxiety to lessen, and he or she becomes increasingly aware of the acceptance of the staff.

◆ SETTING LIMITS

We have been stressing the acceptance of client behavior and the value of a permissive, therapeutic atmosphere. However, permissiveness must have a limit. The client cannot be allowed to do exactly as he or she pleases. The actual limitations on a client's behavior should be determined by the entire team to whom he or she is assigned, and those limitations should be consistently enforced by everyone who comes in contact with him or her.

If, through suspiciousness, a client refuses food and threatens starvation, do not permit it; if a client tries to take his or her life or the life of another on the ward, prevent it; if a client is overactive, do not allow him or her to become exhausted. We accept the fact that the client has a right to feel the way he or she feels, but limitations must be drawn and behavior kept within these limits. If these limits are enforced in a consistent, quiet, matter-of-fact way, they contribute to the client's security.

Avoid physical and verbal force if possible. Force always traumatizes. None of us likes being forced to comply with the wishes of others. However, in spite of every precaution, occasions may arise in which the use of force cannot be avoided. When it must be used, adequate help should be secured and the action carried out quickly and efficiently. When employing force, never show annoyance or anger toward the client. Self-control in this situation is very important.

◆ REALITY

The ego, in an attempt to protect itself from intrapsychic or environmental awareness that is potentially anxiety-provoking, may use defense mechanisms that alter a person's perception of what is really happening. **Reality** is a person's accurate perception of what is really happening intrapsychically or environmentally.

The ability to differentiate between reality and unreality is often seriously affected in a mentally ill person. What he or she observes and hears may be very distorted. If a client is hallucinating, what the client hears and sees may cause him or her to respond to his or her own unconscious motivation. Because of this faulty perception, the client may interpret and respond to the behavior of others in a very inappropriate way. If you can gain the trust and acceptance of such a client, you will be in a position to help validate his or her concepts of reality and to bring him or her back gently and slowly into the real world. While making the assessment, always try to establish the approximate degree of the client's distortion and ability or inability to respond to reality.

◆ REASSURANCE

All of us need reassurance occasionally; the psychiatric client needs it constantly. Make every effort to see a situation as the client sees it. Reassurance is effective only if it does not contradict a false concept that the client holds (ie, a concept or defense mechanism to protect his or her ego). The best way to reassure a client, in addition to well-placed verbal assurance, is by giving attention to matters that are important to him or her and by doing things for and with the client without asking anything in return, such as showing appreciation for an improvement in his or her behavior.

We do not change a client's behavior by reasoning with him or her. Simply telling a client why he or she ought to do something is not an effective way of getting cooperation, especially when he or she has emotional difficulties. The client has developed a pattern of behavior that functions as a defense against anxiety-producing stress, and the client uses what reason he or she is capable of using to bolster defensive patterns of thinking. If a false belief is based on strong emotional needs, the more we challenge it, the more the client will defend it. Work at helping to develop the client's emotional security. With an improvement in this area, the client will slowly tend to develop some insight into his or her behavior and the forces behind it. However, insight can be a threat as well as a help to the emotionally disturbed client. Thus, behavior should only be interpreted when the client is ready for it, secure enough to tolerate it, and able to apply it to alter his or her behavior. This help is best left in the hands of the psychiatrist.

Do not try to meet your own emotional needs through your clients. Be trained and prepared to understand their needs and to meet them, with no thought of return for yourself other than to see your clients recover. Whenever we find ourselves evaluating a client's behavior in terms of right or wrong, or criticizing a client or defending or justifying ourselves, we are in danger of letting our own emotional needs take precedence over those of the client.

CHAPTER 6 SUMMARY

- Mentally disordered individuals need the following:
- *Acceptance*—acknowledges the client's basic worth and dignity
- *Explanations*—explain routines and procedures, at the client's level of understanding
- *Expression of feelings*—allows the client to vent feelings without fear of retaliation
- *Mutual trust*—consists of honesty, integrity, and consistency in dealings with client
- *Consistency*—reduces client's anxiety about not knowing what to expect
- *Reassurance*—helps client feel secure and develop insight about his or her behavior

- Nurses must understand client behavior and its underlying motives to organize a therapeutic care plan most effectively.

- Empathy means that the nurse temporarily borrows client feelings to gain insight but maintains his or her own feelings and boundaries.

- Sympathy means adopting the same feelings as the client, which is not effective for assessing a client's status or needs.

- Even though a permissive atmosphere is valuable for clients, nurses must set limits on client behavior that is harmful to the clients or staff.

CHAPTER 6 QUESTIONS

1. The best definition of *empathy* is
   a. the ability to feel exactly what a client feels.
   b. the ability to transcend interpersonal boundaries.
   c. the ability to feel a client's feelings without losing personal boundaries.
   d. the ability to ignore improper client behavior and focus on the underlying problem.

2. Explanations to mentally disordered clients are important because
   a. clients insist on being fully informed of their care plan.
   b. appropriate explanations greatly reduce client anxiety.
   c. nurses enjoy explaining treatment plans to clients.
   d. explanations are required by law.

3. Which of the following is *not* true?
   a. An emotionally ill person needs a very low-pressure social environment.
   b. Physical and verbal force toward clients should be avoided if possible.
   c. Accepting client behavior means setting no limits that confine the client.
   d. Clients need to express emotions such as anxiety, fear, hostility, and anger.

4. Which of the following is true?
   a. Reality is a person's accurate perception of what is happening.
   b. A mentally disordered client often cannot distinguish between reality and unreality.
   c. Nurses who gain a client's trust can help the client move back into the real world.
   d. All of the above

BIBLIOGRAPHY

Barrett-Lennard, G.T. (1993). The phases and focus of empathy. *British Journal of Medical Psychology, 66*(pt. 1), 3–14.

Barry, P.D. (1996). *Psychosocial nursing: Care of physically ill patients and their families* (3rd ed.). Philadelphia: Lippincott-Raven.

Benner, P.E., Tanner, C., & Chesla, C. (1995). *Expertise in nursing practice: Caring, clinical, judgment, and ethics.* New York: Springer.

Clarke, S. (1995). Let the caring show. *Imprint, 42*(3), 67.

Denman, J.Z. (1995). Caring in the nursing profession is being forgotten. *Journal of Nursing Care Quality, 9*(4), 86–87.

Doyle, B. (1995). Maintaining cultural awareness when caring for patients. *Oncology Nursing Forum, 22*(8), 1289.

Eriksson, K. (1994). Theories of caring as health. In D. Gaut & A. Boykin (Eds.). *Caring as healing: Renewal through hope.* New York: National League for Nursing.

Friedman, M.M. (1997). *Family nursing: Theory and practice* (4th ed.). Norwalk, CT: Appleton & Lange.

Harrison, E. (1995). Nurse caring and the new health paradigm. *Journal of Nursing Care Quality, 9*(4), 14–23.

Heifner, C. (1993). Positive connectedness in the psychiatric nurse-patient relationship. *Archives of Psychiatric Nursing, 7*(1), 11–15.

Kaplan, H.I., & Sadock, B.J. (1995). *Comprehensive textbook of psychiatry/VI* (6th ed.). Baltimore: Williams & Wilkins.

Kaplan, H.I., & Sadock, B.J. (1994). *Synopsis of psychiatry: Behavioral sciences, clinical psychiatry* (7th ed.). Baltimore: Williams & Wilkins.

Kozier, B. (1995). *Fundamentals of nursing* (5th ed.). Redwood City, CA: Addison-Wesley.

Lego, S. (1996). *Psychiatric nursing: A comprehensive reference* (2nd ed.). Philadelphia: Lippincott-Raven.

Mental health and psychiatric nursing (2nd ed.). (1996). Lippincott's Review Series. Philadelphia: Lippincott-Raven.

Phillips, S.S., & Benner, P.E. (Eds.). (1994). *The crisis of care: Affirming and restoring caring practices in the helping professions.* Washington, DC: Georgetown University Press.

Shives, L.R. (Ed.). (1994). *Basic concepts of psychiatric mental health nursing* (3rd ed.). Philadelphia: J.B. Lippincott.

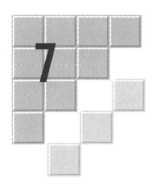

Building a Person-Centered Therapeutic Relationship

Behavioral Objectives

After reading this chapter the student will be able to:

■ Explain the concepts of nursing and the four themes of nursing practice.

■ Define the terms **psychopathology**, **psychosocial adaptation**, and **psychosocial maladaptation**.

■ Describe the nurse's role in treating a mentally ill individual.

■ Name the important personal qualities in a therapeutic relationship.

■ Describe the two main types of communication.

■ Discuss the differences between open-ended and close-ended questioning.

■ Explain the importance of contracting and terminating of the counseling relationship.

The essence of nursing practice is to provide care to a person who is experiencing physical or mental distress. The goal of nursing is to restore the person to his or her highest potential for quality of life.

◆ CONCEPTS OF NURSING PRACTICE

Nursing is an art and a science that combines and integrates the theories and practices of many different fields: social sciences, such as psychology and sociology; basic sciences, such as anatomy, physiology, microbiology, and biochemistry; and medical science, the diagnosing and treating of illness. Nursing is a biopsychosocial science—that is, in assessing and planning care for the human responses to illness, it draws on knowledge of human biology, psychology, and the human social systems of family, friends, and community as the foundations of its practice. This approach to assessment is called a **holistic** model of care.

Many nursing scientists have developed theoretical models about the concepts of nursing practice. As a whole, nursing models generally address four critical aspects or themes of nursing. These themes are as follows:

1. Person
2. Nursing
3. Environment
4. Health

Person is viewed by the nurse as a human being composed of biological, psychological, and social functions or domains. These functions or domains are blended in a complex system that results in a unique individual.

Nursing is a role that includes the following dimensions of person-centered care: comfort, including physical and emotional care and the monitoring and maintenance of safety and hygiene.

Environment includes all the internal and external forces that affect the well-being of the person. These forces include biological, psychological, and social dynamics, as well as the external physical surroundings.

Health is a state of physical and mental functioning. It can exist in a continuum that ranges from wellness to death.

The concept of what constitutes health can be affected by a person's value judgments. What is subjectively viewed as "good" or "bad" health by one person may be viewed differently by another. The perception of what constitutes good health by health care professionals may depend on the professional discipline of the caregiver, for example, nursing, medicine, psychology, or social work.

◆ THE ROLE OF NURSING IN ADDRESSING PSYCHOSOCIAL NEEDS

According to the prior definition of nursing practice, the nurse assesses the whole person using knowledge of normal and pathologic physical, psychological, and social functioning. In psychiatric-mental health nursing the whole-person focus continues, so that all aspects of a client's functioning are being assessed. The primary cause of admission to a mental health setting, however, is some form of mental disorder or psychopathology that has caused a temporary incapacity in the client's ability to function in his or her normal social environment. **Psychopathology** is defined as disease of the mind. The medical approach to caregiving is based on a model of curing pathology or disease, whether physical or mental. Using this approach, there is usually a specific focus on curing the identified disease.

Nursing, on the other hand, views the disease process as the cause of distress to the whole person. The distress resulting from disease affects the person's overall sense of well-being—physical, mental, and social. Nursing care involves assessing each of these functional domains. Care planning intervenes directly with the disease process using physicians' orders when necessary, as well as the guiding principles of nursing practice described above. In addition, the nurse assesses, plans, and implements care and continually evaluates the outcomes of care as measured by client responses in the physical, mental, and social domains. This assessment process uses the same holistic principles whether the person has a mental or physical disorder.

In the mental health setting the primary focus is on the cause of the admission. The client has a mental disorder that has changed his or her mental functioning. When mental functioning is disordered, it results in behavioral changes that affect social relationships. The major goals of nursing care planning and intervention are to work collaboratively with other mental health disciplines to set a cohesive set of therapeutic goals that support the client's recovery and return to psychosocial adaptation.

◆ BIOPSYCHOSOCIAL RESPONSES TO STRESS

Psychosocial adaptation is the ability of the human being to perceive reality and respond to it in a way that supports his or her own emotional and physical well-being and that of others in the social environment. When some aspect of mental functioning is disordered, it can result in misperceptions of reality and misjudgments that alter effective decision making. When effective decision making is altered, healthy coping processes deteriorate.

Psychosocial maladaptation is the result of ineffective coping. When maladaptation occurs, it is the symptom of disordered perception or cognitive processes. The result of maladaptation is tension and distress in those who share the client's social environment.

Hospital admission occurs when the client or members of his or her social environment determine that the level of distress requires professional intervention that is not available in the home, outpatient, or community mental health care system. It is important to note that the clinical role of nursing, that of assessing the whole-person response to illness, is a unique caregiving perspective. In contrast, other disciplines focus on specific aspects of functioning in their treatment models.

The nurse has the most intimate ongoing contact with the client. Accordingly, he or she can observe the subtle clinical changes that indicate improvement or deterioration in the client's condition. These changes can be the first indicators that the treatment plan is working or needs modification. The role of nursing is to implement the nursing care plan, and also to be the first observer of clinical changes for the treatment team. Reporting clinical observations can alert the treatment team about the effectiveness of the team assessment and treatment plan. The nursing role is a critical factor in the successful treatment of mental disorders.

The previous chapter presented many general concepts that form the basis of beginning a therapeutic relationship. This section covers the various counseling techniques that promote a therapeutic relationship.

◆IMPORTANT PERSONAL QUALITIES IN A THERAPEUTIC RELATIONSHIP

In order to establish a helping relationship with a client, be aware of the personal qualities of a caregiver that help the client to establish trust. They are described by Carl Rogers as the following:

1. **Unconditional positive regard**. Accept the client without negative judgment of his or her basic worth.

2. **Empathic understanding of the client's internal frame of reference**. Be aware of and have the capacity to empathize with the client's situation and the various dynamics that are contributing to it. Another word for the circumstances that led up to the client's current difficulty is **context.**

3. **Authenticity**. Allow yourself to be known to others (also called **transparency** or **genuineness**).

◆ COMMUNICATION PATTERNS IN THE COUNSELING RELATIONSHIP

Chapter 6, Establishing the Therapeutic Nursing Environment, discusses general concepts of communication with individuals who are mentally ill. The following section discusses specific counseling approaches that can ease conversations with a client and contribute toward a therapeutic outcome.

NONVERBAL COMMUNICATION IN THE COUNSELING SETTING

The essence of a helping relationship is the communication or message that is relayed from the helper to the client *and* from the client to the helper. There are two types of messages: verbal and nonverbal. In the field of psychiatry, the way that we communicate nonverbally is very important. Psychiatric clients are particularly sensitive to the many nonverbal messages they receive from caregivers. They know whether they are liked, respected, distrusted, or considered a nuisance. We give off messages, usually without being aware of them. Clients give the same messages to us.

The means with which we tell clients how we are feeling about them are our eyes, posture, and gestures. The ability to maintain consistent eye contact is a strong indicator of relationship potential. When a person frequently looks away or keeps his or her eyes in a downcast position, we know that he or she is not comfortable. Posture is another indication of what a person's true feelings are about a given situation. A person who is standing or sitting erect is usually interested in what he or she is doing or who he or she is with. Conversely, one who is slouched and half turned away is saying "I really don't want to be here." Finally, gestures that we unconsciously make can be important nonverbal signs. For example, a quick movement by a caregiver in the presence of a markedly paranoid client can trigger a defensive reaction. A depressed client would meet the same movement with hardly a glance.

VERBAL COMMUNICATION IN THE COUNSELING SETTING

When we are talking with a client we are essentially inviting him or her to join in verbal communication. The words we speak may prompt him or her to engage in a discussion or to "shut down" and not respond. The various methods of leading the client into discussion are as follows:

Indirect statements

Direct statements

Focusing

Questioning

Advice-giving

Summarizing

An **indirect leading statement** is intentionally general and non-specific, such as "Tell me about when you were growing up." A **direct leading statement** is more specific: "You said your mother died when you were 6 years old." **Focusing** is a helpful technique when you have explored a broad range of subjects and have a general idea about the client's circumstances. When you focus, you pay particular attention to a topic that seems especially sensitive for him or her. For example, you might ask, "Do you remember how you felt when your mother died?"

Questioning, particularly when open-ended questions are used, is a helpful way to encourage the client's insights into his or her difficulties. An **open-ended question** invites the client to give as much information as he or she wants. For example, you could ask, "You told me earlier you went to live with your aunt when your mother died. How was it for you to live with her?" In contrast, a **close-ended question** is one that frequently requires a one-word answer that ultimately closes off further discussion. You might say, "John, are you sad today?" If John answers "no" it shuts off further therapeutic discussion. Instead say, "John, how are you feeling today?" His answer to this will make it easier to explore how he is feeling.

Advice-giving is a counseling technique that *rarely* should be used in the counseling or psychiatric setting. Advice is actually "the easy way out" that can encourage the client's dependence and delay his or her rehabilitation. When a client asks for advice, gently turn the question back to him or her. The response, "John, what would you like to do?" for example, allows him to explore his options out loud with a caring, but impartial, person. Often, clients learn to form their own conclusions and trust their own judgments when this process is implemented.

If the client is in crisis or experiencing severe anxiety, turning the question back to him or her is not helpful. Before responding to such a client, check with the client's primary nurse, who knows the client well and may be able to recommend alternate approaches.

Summarizing is a skilled form of verbal communication that occurs at the end of a session in which the nurse and the client have explored a number of issues. The nurse briefly describes the affective and intellectual experiences that occurred during their time together. The use of summarizing leaves the client with the feeling that he or she accomplished something during the interview.

◆ OTHER ASPECTS OF THE THERAPEUTIC RELATIONSHIP

CONTRACT

Whenever we tell someone that we will do something, we are entering into a contract. In a therapeutic relationship, a **contract** is an agreement, direct or indirect, with another person. A **direct contract** is one that involves setting formal appointment times with a client or entering a primary nurse–client type of commitment. An **indirect contract** is less formal. Here you can commit to see a client at some time during a working shift. But remember, clients will come to depend on you. It promotes their trust in you and their sense of security, both important aspects of returning to good mental health. For example, if you will be off the next day, or working a different shift, let your clients know when they can expect to see you next. Keep clients informed of your schedule; this indicates your respect for them and your regard for their needs and feelings.

TERMINATION OF RELATIONSHIP

The therapeutic relationship is a very close, delicate, and intimate relationship between two people. During the course of interaction, if the client fully accepts the nurse or health care professional and cooperates toward an improved mental health goal, he or she tends to become quite dependent on and emotionally attached to the nurse. It is not easy to terminate an emotional dependency. It is usually quite traumatic for the client, and it may also be hard for us as staff members. If we give deeply of our professional skills, we will terminate those relationships with genuine regret and loss.

It is not easy to determine, at the start of a therapeutic relationship, just how long it may take to help a client gain enough insight to be able to manage his or her feelings and behavior in an acceptable way. Ideally, you can indicate, both at the initiation of the relationship and at intervals during it, that hopefully the day will arrive when the client will no longer need specific help, when he or she will reach a plateau of emotional stability that will enable him or her to handle problems without your intervention.

The client is often fearful of his or her inability to make decisions and to act responsibly. He or she may fear the approaching time of return to family and job, and be concerned about not being well enough yet to carry on work and family responsibilities. He or she may be fearful about acceptance by family and friends or may wonder whom to call on for help. The client may feel quite threatened by the withdrawal of your help—you have earned his or her trust and helped him or her face personal needs and adjust behavior to an acceptable level.

In anticipation of these fears, discuss them long before the relationship is terminated. Find ways to handle the client's fears. Slowly include other members of the treatment team to prepare the client for discharge or for further therapy in or out of the hospital, as his or her needs may indicate. As you slowly withdraw from the relationship, include other clients on the ward in an enlarging circle to help promote the client's ability to socialize with others.

To make termination easier, assure the client that you would like to hear from him or her to know how he or she is. Encourage the client to come back to visit you in the hospital from time to time. The invitation to maintain contact is rarely abused by clients. Instead, such assurances, during the period before discharge when the client's anxiety about independence is high, will enhance his or her sense of security. In addition, during the immediate postdischarge period, the knowledge that he or she can call you often provides security without his or her ever actually placing a telephone call.

CHAPTER 7 SUMMARY

- Nursing practice provides care to a person who is experiencing physical or mental distress. The primary goal of nursing is to restore the person to his or her highest potential for quality of life.

- Nursing combines and integrates theories and practices of a number of fields, including the social sciences, basic sciences, and medical science.

- The four critical themes that nursing models address are person, nursing, environment, and health.

- Nursing perceives mental disorders as causing distress to the whole person and nursing care involves intervening directly with the disease or disorder process.

- Psychosocial adaptation is a person's ability to perceive reality and respond to it in a way that supports emotional and physical well-being. Psychosocial maladaptation is the result of ineffective coping.

- Caregiver qualities that help a client establish trust are
  — Unconditional positive regard
  — Empathic understanding of the client's internal frame of reference
  — Genuineness or authenticity

- Effective verbal communication techniques include indirect and direct leading statements, focusing, open-ended questioning, and summarizing.

- Nonverbal communication includes posture, gesture, and eye contact.

- In a therapeutic relationship, a contract is an agreement with another person. A caregiver's contract with a client may be direct (formal) or indirect (informal).

- Termination of the therapeutic relationship can be difficult for both clients and caregivers. It is important to discuss client fears about the end of the relationship well before termination.

CHAPTER 7 QUESTIONS

1. The *primary* goal of nursing is to
   a. release the client from the hospital setting as soon as possible.
   b. provide care of the person's physical well-being without interfering with his or her family or other problems.
   c. restore the person to his or her highest potential for quality of life.
   d. record any psychosocial maladaptation behaviors for evaluation by a psychologist.

2. The nurse's role in the mental health care setting is to
   a. observe the changes in client behavior that show improvement or deterioration in the client's condition.
   b. implement the nursing care plan.
   c. report clinical observations to the treatment team.
   d. all of the above.

3. Which of the following is true?
   a. Open-ended questions require a one-word response.
   b. Close-ended questions are very useful in establishing a therapeutic relationship.
   c. Open-ended questions can help encourage a client's insights.
   d. Close-ended questions help clients express and explore their feelings.

4. Contracting between a caregiver and client is important because
   a. it helps the client better manage his or her time.
   b. it promotes the client's sense of trust and security.
   c. the caregiver must control time spent with clients.
   d. it keeps clients from depending on caregivers.

BIBLIOGRAPHY

Barry, P.D. (1996). *Psychosocial nursing: Care of physically ill patients and their families* (3rd ed.). Philadelphia: Lippincott-Raven.

Brooke Army Medical Center. (1973). *Interpersonal skills.* (Videocassette). Fort Sam Houston, TX: Academy of Health Sciences.

Denman, J.Z (1995). Caring in the nursing profession is being forgotten. *Journal of Nursing Care Quality, 9*(4), 86–87.

Harrison, E. (1995). Nurse caring and the new health care paradigm. *Journal of Nursing Care Quality, 9*(4), 14–23.

Kaplan, H.I., & Sadock, B.J. (1995). *Comprehensive textbook of psychiatry/VI* (6th ed.). Baltimore: Williams & Wilkins.

Lewis, J.A., & Lewis, M.D. (1997). *Community counseling* (2nd ed.). Pacific Grove, CA: Brooks-Cole.

Litwack, L., Litwack, J., & Ballou, M. (1980). *Health counseling.* New York: Appleton-Century-Crofts.

Phillips, S.S., & Benner, P.E. (Eds.). (1994). *The crisis of care: Affirming and restoring caring practices in the helping professions.* Washington, DC: Georgetown University Press.

Wilson, H.S., & Kneisl, C.R. (1996). *Psychiatric nursing* (5th ed.). Redwood City, CA: Addison-Wesley.

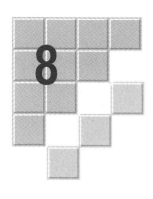

8

Delivering Mental Health Care in a Continuum of Settings

B e h a v i o r a l   O b j e c t i v e s

After reading this chapter the student will be able to:

■ Name the determining factors that contribute to a continuum of care.

■ List the five most important factors that determine decisions made about care.

■ Discuss the role of the nurse in various settings such as outpatient, home care, partial hospitalization, and residential programs.

■ Name the eight goals of community residential care programs.

The delivery of health care is changing rapidly, being driven by health insurance and government reform of the payment systems for health care. Nurses are often important buffers and interpreters of those changes. When an individual becomes ill, there is a profound effect on that person and his or her loved ones. The role of the nurse includes assisting them to understand the cause and nature of the illness and the means of restoring health. These important nursing values can be expressed regardless of the site where care is administered.

The guiding principle of nursing care will continue to be the nursing process. The openness and flexibility of the nursing process allows it to be used in all settings. As a response to the variety of needs affecting health care decision making today, many treatment settings have been developed to provide adequate care levels to clients and their families.

◆ DETERMINING FACTORS THAT CONTRIBUTE TO A CONTINUUM OF CARE

The time frame of the health care decision-making process is often influenced by the overriding expectation of providing the most cost-effective care in a succession of settings ranging from acute inpatient care to community-based partial hospitalization and, finally, to home care. This succession of care settings is known as a **continuum of care**. When a client requires medical care, the primary medical caregiver will examine the options available.

Large urban centers usually have a greater variety of home care, community, partial hospitalization, and inpatient hospitalization sites available. In these urban centers and their surrounding suburbs, the concept of a continuum of care is more likely to be put into practice. In medium-sized and rural communities, the availability of a continuum of services ranging from home to inpatient care options will depend primarily on the vision of the leaders of the community health institutions and agencies. Have those leaders recognized the rapidly changing trends and planned accordingly?

Another important factor that contributes to the availability of a range of services is government funding to assist community health care planners. Government funds include those from federal, state, and local community resources. Often the federal government will provide grants for innovative health care programs whose effectiveness has been documented by research. Federal grants usually require that state and local communities also provide funds from their own treasuries as evidence of their involvement with and commitment to the successful implementation of a new program.

◆Selecting the Appropriate Care Site

The concept of **triage** was discussed in Chapter 2. An important consideration in triage is the selection by a knowledgeable health care provider of the setting that can most effectively provide care. The triage decision also includes assessment of the state of the client, his or her family or home environment, the availability of community resources, and the financial resources for different levels of care.

The most important considerations that guide decision making are:

1. The state of the client
2. The site where care can be most effectively provided in order to promote stabilization and well-being

These factors can be determined by considering the following:

- Is the client's life at risk from a mental or physical disorder?

  - Is there a life-threatening physical disorder that must be stabilized?

  - Is there a mental disorder that poses a threat to the life of the client or another?

- Are there services necessary to stabilize the client that can be provided only in an inpatient setting?

- Is there an unstable home environment that is inadequate in providing safe care to the client?

- Are there no supportive community services available that can provide the care required to stabilize the client?

- If the client has insurance, will the insurance company approve financial reimbursement for one site rather than another?

Whenever the answer to one of these questions is yes, the choices then become focused around that factor in identifying the appropriate environment, out of those options available in the individual's community, that can provide the safest and most cost-effective care. Ideally, the following services will be available:

1. Outpatient clinic or private treatment options
2. Home care
   a. Crisis assessment and intervention
   b. Family therapy consultation
3. Partial hospitalization programs
4. Residential programs
5. Inpatient settings (described in Chapter 4, Inpatient Hospitalization)

These options will be discussed, with an overview of the role of the nurse in each of these settings.

A significant outcome of health care policy making in the past decade is that clients are rapidly moved from one treatment setting and focus to another. These rapid changes occurring during a time of emotional crisis can be further unsettling to a client and family.

As individuals move from one treatment setting to another, their care providers often change as well. The effectiveness of communication between care sites is an important aspect of the "seamlessness" of a continuum of care. Nurses often provide the bridge of understanding about the specific needs of a patient from one setting to another.

◆ THE ROLE OF THE NURSE IN DIFFERENT SETTINGS

OUTPATIENT CLINIC OR PRIVATE TREATMENT OPTIONS

Many individuals who are coping ineffectively with life's challenges are able to obtain community treatment in clinic or private clinical therapy settings. Generally, nurses are not used in an adjunctive role in the private treatment setting. Nurses are often adjunctive care providers in outpatient clinic settings to give medications and monitor the clinical environment.

HOME CARE

It is understandable that the least disruptive care site for the client is his or her home. The home care setting offers the client the opportunity to test new ways of coping in his or her natural environment. This is the environment that offers the highest degree of control to the client. The nurse is the case manager or team leader in the home, responsible for the coordination of care. The client's primary need is to have a plan with structure that will augment and strengthen his or her normal coping methods. If the home care admission was coordinated by a crisis assessment home care team, the teams's recommendations and orders will direct the initial nursing care and structure of the home care setting.

Another important client need is to have support from immediate family or others who live in the home. The nurse is in a good position to observe the quality and nature of these relationships; in addition, the nurse can help the client in interpreting and responding to others in an adaptive manner. The nurse is also in an important position to interpret the behavior and needs of the client to his or her family or those in the home environment.

The steps of the nursing process are in a more fluid and changing state in the home because events that can affect the client are more likely to occur than when he or she is in a protected hospital environment. When events in the home appear to have a direct impact on the stability of the client, family therapy can be considered in order to provide a more supportive and adaptive home environment.

The client participates in all aspects of assessment, planning, implementation, and evaluation. The discussions between nurse, client, and home caregiver can become the model for communication in the family. Review by the nurse of the daily activities and events that are most challenging or threatening for the client can assist in supporting decision making and effective coping. Adaptive coping can be supported with the following types of questions:

- What is the most difficult crisis you have faced in the past?
- What did you do that helped you to cope with it?
- What are some of the effective choices that help you to cope?
- What are some of the negative choices that undermine your coping?

The home care nurse communicates and coordinates care with other members of the home care team. The nurse will communicate with and provide direction to the home health aide, an important member of the team. The communication supports the nursing care plan addressing specific behaviors or problems. Other team members can include occupational, physical, and speech therapists and social workers. If any dimension of the multidisciplinary team requires modification, the nurse assumes the role of client advocate in identifying and communicating the client's needs.

PARTIAL HOSPITALIZATION PROGRAMS

When the client requires more structure and personal or medication monitoring than may be available in the home or community, partial hospitalization programs are an important alternative. There are two types of clinical populations who are well-served in these settings: chronic mentally disordered individuals and those requiring brief crisis stabilization.

Partial hospitalization programs can be scheduled during the following periods: daytime, Monday through Friday; evenings, Monday through Friday; weekends; or overnight. The purpose of a partial program is to provide an alternative that supports the person in his or her normal home, work, or community environment and provides additional structure, without which inpatient admission might be required. The nurse's role in this setting is adjunctive; the primary functions are

◆ TABLE 8–1. Types and Characteristics of Housing in Aftercare of the Mentally Ill

Type of Housing	Purpose	Staffing on Site	Provisions	Average Length of Stay	Number of Residents	Counseling Available	Responsibilities of Residents
Transitional halfway house	Transition from the hospital to the community	Available 24 hours a day	Room, board, and help with activities of daily living	6–8 months	10–20, varies with available space and staff	Yes	Cooking and cleaning the house
Long-term group home	Transition from the hospital to the community; sometimes residency	Available 24 hours a day	Room, board, and help with activities of daily living	Years to a lifetime	10–20, varies with available space and staff	Yes, as residents are often dependent and symptomatic	Cooking and cleaning the house
Single-room occupancy hotels	Residency	Dependent on availability of an outreach program	Room	Years to a lifetime	Up to hundreds	If a PMH CNS is available for outreach	Independent living
Cooperative apartments	Residency	None	Room	Years to a lifetime	2–4 clients per apartment	If a PMH CNS is available	Independent living
Foster care	Residency	None, but family is often supervised by case manager	Room and board	Years to a lifetime	Usually one	No	As required by foster family
Nursing home	To provide physical care as well as shelter	Nursing staff and sometimes PMH CNS or geriatric CNS	Room and board, custodial care by nursing staff	Dependent on physical care needed	Varies	If a PMH CNS is available	None
Crisis center	To prevent admission to a psychiatric unit, if client has begun to deteriorate	Available 24 hours a day. At least one staff member is a nurse.	Close observation, support, medication, counseling	1–2 weeks	Varies	Yes	Participation in program

In Husseini, M.B. (1996). Designing residential aftercare and outreach programs. In S. Lego (Ed.) *Psychiatric nursing: A comprehensive refrence.* Philadelphia: Lippincott-Raven, p. 400, as adapted from Budson, R.D. (1983). Residential care for the chronically mentally ill. In I. Barofsky & R.D. Budson (eds.), *The chronic psychiatric patient in the community: Principles of treatment* (pp. 281–308). New York: SP Medical & Scientific Books.

medication administration and monitoring of safety and activities of daily living.

RESIDENTIAL PROGRAMS

There are two primary types of mental health residential care:

1. Crisis stabilization
2. Community residential care for the chronically mentally ill

The goal of the crisis stabilization residential option is to remove a mentally disordered adult who is in crisis from an unsafe or unstable environment. This brief-treatment residential option also avoids admission to a hospital facility. During the voluntary crisis residential admission, the individual is linked with community resources that will be available to him or her after discharge.

These centers are usually staffed by individuals with graduate degrees in mental health services, such as clinical nurse specialists, social workers, or counselors. Additional staff members may have undergraduate degrees in counseling.

Community residential care programs for the chronically mentally ill offer a long-term (usually 6 to 9 months) option to those with chronic mental disorders. These programs provide a stable, structured environment for people who are homeless or without stable support systems. Community residential care programs are designed to achieve the following goals:

- Decrease social isolation
- Improve social skills
- Develop relationships within the residential program
- Support activities of daily living (eg, good hygiene and nutrition)
- Allow for overview of medication compliance
- Promote independent living
- Obtain and maintain employment
- Decrease crises and need for hospitalization

Table 8–1 shows the variety of options developed in communities to provide residential aftercare for chronically mentally disordered clients.

CHAPTER 8 SUMMARY

- The guiding principle of nursing care is the nursing process, no matter where the care occurs.

■ A variety of factors contributes to the availability of care in a community, including community size and local and federal resources.

■ The client's current state and where care can most effectively be provided to promote stabilization and well-being are crucial to the decision on the caregiving setting. Factors to consider are as follows:
— Is the client or the community at risk from the client's illness?
— Can the needed services only be provided in an inpatient setting?
— Can the home environment provide a safe setting for client care?
— Are supportive community services available?
— If the client has insurance, does the coverage favor one site over another?

■ Options along the care continuum include outpatient or private treatment, home care, partial hospitalization, residential programs, and inpatient settings.

■ In the home care setting, the nurse is often responsible for coordination of care, including support of the client's family; being a role model for communication; and assisting the client in learning decision making and effective coping.

■ The goals of a community residential care program include decreasing social isolation, improving social skills, and supporting activities of daily living, medicine compliance, and other living skills such as employment.

CHAPTER 8 QUESTIONS

1. Which of the following is a factor in determining where care can be most effectively provided?
   a. Stability or lack of stability of the home environment
   b. Whether the client has a life-threatening physical or mental disorder
   c. Presence of supportive community services
   d. All of the above

2. The concept of a continuum of care is most likely to be operational in
   a. rural communities where people know each other.
   b. large urban centers that have a variety of care options available.
   c. the hospital setting.
   d. programs that do not accept government funding.

3. In which of the following settings are nurses generally *not* used?
   a. Private clinical therapy
   b. Home care

c. Community-based programs

d. Partial hospitalization programs

4. Community residential care programs for the chronically mental ill

a. are short-term (no more than 3 months).

b. provide housing but no other structured support.

c. support goals such as decreasing clients' social isolation, improving social skills, and supporting activities of daily living.

d. increase the need for hospitalization.

BIBLIOGRAPHY

Husseini, M.B. (1996). Designing residential aftercare and outreach programs. In S. Lego (Ed.). *Psychiatric nursing: A comprehensive reference*. (2nd ed.). Philadelphia: Lippincott-Raven.

Lewendowski, W. (1996). Designing a crisis center. In S. Lego (Ed.). *Psychiatric nursing: A comprehensive reference*. (2nd ed.). Philadelphia: Lippincott-Raven.

DEVELOPING CRITICAL THINKING SKILLS
THROUGH CLASS DISCUSSION

UNIT TWO Case Study

Concepts of Psychiatric-Mental Health Nursing

Gloria is 28 years old. She and her husband, Tom, have a 1-month-old infant. Almost as soon as Gloria arrived home from the hospital she began to have difficulty coping with her baby. She became acutely suicidally depressed and had frequent waves of anxiety about taking care of her baby. She was referred by her obstetrician to a psychiatrist, who admitted her to the hospital inpatient psychiatric unit.

D I S C U S S I O N   Q U E S T I O N S

1. What are your personal reactions as you hear about Gloria and her circumstances?

2. Would you describe your reactions as sympathetic or empathic? Why? What are the differences between sympathy and empathy?

3. What difference does it make to the nurse whether he or she is responding to a client's distress with sympathy or empathy? And what difference can it make to the client?

4. If you wanted to ask Gloria why she was admitted to the hospital so that you could determine her own understanding and insight about why her doctor decided to admit her, how would you phrase the question?

5. What are the nonverbal cues that you can give to Gloria to indicate your caring for her well-being?

6. How can you tell whether Gloria trusts you?

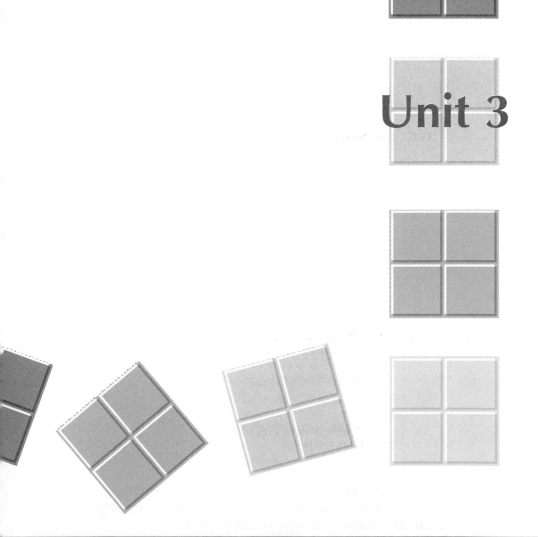

Unit 3

BASIC CONCEPTS OF MENTAL HEALTH

Human Development and Needs

Behavioral Objectives

After reading this chapter the student will be able to:

■ Identify the physical and mental characteristics that constitute a person's heredity.

■ Name three forces that influence the development of personality.

■ Explain the process of identification and how it influences personality development.

■ Describe the four steps involved in learning.

■ Explain the role of reinforcement in the learning process.

■ List the five childhood experiences that are very important to development.

■ Explain the human hierarchy of needs identified by Maslow.

■ Discuss the differences in moral development and decision making between males and females identified by Gilligan.

■ Describe the concept of ego ideal.

◆ HEREDITY

When a sperm and an ovum unite to form a new life, each germ cell contributes 23 chromosomes on which a vast number of genes or genetic factors are arranged. These genes determine the type of body build the child will have, his or her skin and hair texture, eye color, general intellectual capacity and abilities, talents, and many other physical and mental characteristics. In short, they constitute the child's heredity. Heredity can also be described as genetic endowment.

Part of an infant's heredity includes the makeup of his or her neurologic system. **Neurotransmitters** are the biochemical substances that send messages from the central nervous system to the body tissues. These substances include adrenaline (epinephrine), noradrenaline (norepinephrine), and serotonin, to name a few of the many that are present in the body. Theorists believe these neurotransmitters strongly influence the human drives for sleep, nourishment, and sexual gratification. Neurotransmitters also affect the intensity of drives, as well as emotions and stress tolerance.

After 9 months of sheltered prenatal life, when every need of the growing fetus is supplied by the mother's body, the baby emerges from the uterus into a world that immediately begins to make demands on him or her and will continue to do so throughout his or her life. However, if the child has developed normally, he or she is well designed to live in and adapt to this world.

Babies come into the world with basic temperaments or personality dispositions. For example, some infants are more placid than others. In addition, the temperaments of the baby's parents can be similar to or quite unlike that of their newborn. Depending on the compatibility of the baby's inborn disposition and those of his or her parents, the environment may hold varying degrees of conflict for the developing child.

Certain inborn personality characteristics have been identified by Terry Brazelton, a pediatrician who researches the development of newborns. These personality characteristics include 26 behaviors and 20 reflexes that can be observed and rated. The most easily observable of these appear in the following list.

Alertness
General physical tone
Cuddliness
Motor maturity
Tremulousness
Activity

Irritability

Startle reflex during examination

Lability of skin color

Lability of states

Self-quieting activity

Hand-to-mouth facility

Smiles

Response to light

Response to rattle

Response to bell

Response to pinprick

Orientation to various auditory and visual stimuli

Defensive movements

Consolability with intervention

Peak of excitement

Buildup of excitement

Pull to sit

◆ ENVIRONMENT

The child's environment is a limited world—one reflected by his or her parents and their home—and it causes him or her to react to a multitude of new situations and to other human beings. The child's personality forms as the result of interaction between environment and heredity.

One important effect of environmental influences is the child's acquisition of values. **Values** are deeply held beliefs the child acquires during the formative years as the result of exposure to people who are important to him or her. In the desire to be accepted and to avoid disapproval, the child gradually takes on their values and beliefs. Conversely, the child will also develop a value system based on exposure to individuals who displease him or her, forming values unlike theirs in order to be different from them. Values are the basis of much of adult behavior and decision making.

◆ DEVELOPMENTAL STAGES

Just as bodies go through successive stages of physical development until they reach adulthood, so, too, personalities normally undergo developmental stages until they reach maturity. Harmful influences may interfere with the normal physical growth and functioning of a tissue, an organ, or the entire body. Similarly, disturbing early experiences and unsatisfied emotional needs may lead to an arrest or **fixation** of the normal growth pattern of the personality and can result in personality distortions and immaturities.

Psychologists consider a wholesome mother–child relationship to be essential for the normal growth and personality development of the child. The child must feel wanted, loved, and enjoyed by his or her parents, and especially by his or her mother or the mother-figure.

If the child feels loved and cared for, a desirable sense of security will follow. If, on the other hand, the child experiences rejection, harshness, and frustration, his or her personality will often be characterized by anxiety, insecurity, and depression. He or she may develop hostile and aggressive tendencies. The emotional experiences of early years leave permanent imprints on the personality, although they may no longer be a part of the individual's consciousness.

One of the most important processes in influencing personality development is called **identification.** Through this process, the child, because of his or her love for and wish to be like the parent, particularly the parent of the same sex, molds himself or herself after that parent and adopts the parent's characteristics and attitudes. This is not a conscious imitation; it is automatic. If the parent is emotionally mature and well adjusted, this process of identification can greatly contribute to the development of similar characteristics in the child's personality.

As the personality continues to grow, it is influenced and molded by many factors. Some of the child's experiences will stimulate personality growth; others will block or distort its development. If the child experiences difficulties with the issues of security, love, aggression, and dependence, he or she may develop emotional problems. As the child begins to strive for independence, he or she will find it difficult to meet the new responsibilities that independence entails. Growth brings new problems and contradictory urges. Such challenges may sometimes result in emotional turmoil and sometimes in healthy, adaptive behavior.

Emotional development often progresses on an uneven course; but, if early identifications have been healthy and if most conflicts have been successfully resolved, eventually a mature, adult personality should emerge. A person with a mature personality has achieved a harmonious adjustment to his or her environment and can meet life's inevitable stresses realistically and effectively.

In order to understand deviant personality, it is important to understand how a normal personality develops. For our purposes, **personality** does not mean personal charm and distinction; rather, it is the total of all individual tendencies—including strengths and weaknesses, attributes, aspirations, and drives—that determines a person's adjustments to his or her material and social environment. Personality has been referred to as the internal psychophysiologic organization of an individual as he or she interacts with the external organization of the environment.

Personality is always in a state of flux. It is always in the process of becoming something else, yet ordinarily it retains an identifiable continuity from situation to situation, from year to year, and from birth to death.

Although definitions of personality vary greatly, most theorists agree on the following six points:

1. Personality is a relatively enduring organization of patterns of behavior characteristic of the individual.

2. Personality results from the complex interactions of heredity and environment. (Theorists do not agree whether biological forces or psychosocial factors are more important.)

3. Dynamic forces, including psychobiological drives produced by neurotransmitters, cause behavior.

4. Some of these dynamic forces are unknown to the individual; that is, unconscious causes of behavior do exist.

5. Childhood is an important time for forming and organizing relatively enduring patterns of behavioral characteristics of an individual.

6. Behavior, both in its outward and inward manifestations, is a function or expression of personality.

◆ PERSONALITY DEVELOPMENT AND LEARNING

Few subjects have been as fully studied as the field of animal and human learning. Yet much remains to be understood about how learning occurs. Psychologists studying the process of learning have organized it into four steps:

1. First a person must want something (the drive, the **need**, or the motivation).

2. The person must then notice something that will satisfy his or her need (the **stimulus**, or the cue).

3. The person must then act on the stimulation (the **response**).

4. He or she must then get something (the reward, the **reinforcement**, or the need reduction).

These four steps of learning are, of course, much oversimplified. Learning is a process; each step can be infinitely elaborated. For example: A newborn baby becomes hungry, and needs impel him or her to restless activity. Mother offers food, the baby sucks, and the hunger pangs subside. The baby becomes comfortable and drowsy. Here are all the ingredients of a learning situation—a need (hunger), a stimulus (the feel of a nipple in the baby's mouth), a response (sucking), and reinforcement (relief from hunger). Accordingly, learning takes place.

At birth, a baby will actively seek the nipple, turning his or her head from side to side and making sucking responses if his or her cheek is stroked when he or she is hungry. The baby then learns that food (nipple plus sucking) brings relief. After a few weeks, the learning extends to include other elements of this sequence. Now the baby may stop crying from hunger when he or she is picked up. New cues have been tied in or associated with the food-brings-comfort pattern. Soon baby will smile when mother bends over him or her, even when he or she is not hungry, which indicates that the original food-brings-comfort learning has been elaborated into "mother is something good." The baby may learn to associate the feel of his or her mother's body with nursing, and he or she will wiggle with anticipation.

Reinforcement is the process by which behavior is learned. A reinforcer is anything that causes behavior to be repeated. The greater the reinforcement, the stronger the learning. The reinforcement may have to come in succeeding episodes, or, if strong enough, a single reinforcement may result in fixing the pattern of learning. For instance, toilet training or learning to eat with fingers and later with a spoon becomes effective only after repeated efforts followed by the reinforcement. For example, reinforcement of eating behavior can be the pleasant feeling of satiety, a smile from mother, or the feeling of accomplishment from feeding oneself.

On the other hand, a single experience that is very painful or surprising, such as a burnt finger or tumbling down several stairs, will usually result in a clearly remembered learning experience. The baby will avoid the hot object and refuse, even when coaxed, to try the stairs again until his or her coordination is much better.

When the pattern of learning no longer serves the need, reinforcement ceases to operate. When this happens, the learning process progressively decreases and finally ceases altogether. This is called **extinction,** or in ordinary language, forgetting. Although lack of reinforcement is just one cause of forgetting, it is the chief one. Many things that are important to a child lose importance as the child matures, and lack of reinforcement causes a progressive decrease in the sharpness of the mental image, until memory finally ceases.

However, something well learned once is never fully forgotten. We store it in our subconscious mind, and it can be brought back to immediate awareness. Sometimes remembrance is immediate; sometimes we must concentrate quite a bit before a dim memory emerges clearly to view. Learning of many activities, such as playing the piano, typing, or tying an intricate knot, improves with reinforcement but will fade away or become extinct if the activity is not used. However, relearning a once-acquired skill is usually accomplished with a little practice.

◆ DEVELOPMENT OF NEEDS

The newborn shows a generalized response to all stimuli. Emotions develop as the baby reacts to his or her environment. For the infant, life is first of all a biological fact. The infant responds physiologically to the unpleasantness of hunger and cold and to the need to move his or her muscles. It soon becomes necessary for the infant to react to a multitude of new situations and to other human beings.

One ability the infant possesses is highly significant—the inexplicable power to communicate emotional feeling tones (the power of **empathy**). The baby is able to sense and respond to feelings of approval and disapproval from the mother or mother-figure. Feelings of approval increase the newborn's sense of well-being, and the opposite feelings cause discomfort. This happens long before the baby is capable of understanding the meaning of either feeling.

Although all experiences are planted forever in the mind, at this time the infant only vaguely associates them with the mother-figure. Satisfactions are achieved with the first magic tool, crying, and comfort and discomfort are known but not understood. The baby's responses to comfort and discomfort begin to form a patterned behavior.

Experiences in childhood that are particularly important in future development are as follows:

- Availability of a consistent, concerned caregiver
- The feeding situation in early infancy (including weaning)
- Toilet and cleanliness training
- Early training about sexuality
- Training for control of anger and aggression

Adjusting to these situations can be quite upsetting to the child, and it takes patience and understanding on the part of the parents to help him or her accept social rules and regulations. If the parents approve of the child as a person, even when they may disapprove of his or her actions, the child will usually accept their rules and values as his or her own and build them into a growing personality.

◆ HIERARCHY OF HUMAN NEEDS

Abraham Maslow, a psychologist, was one of the founders of the field of humanistic psychology. He believed that humans have levels of needs that must be met before each can develop into a psychologically mature person. Maslow called these the hierarchy of human needs:

1. Physiologic needs
2. Safety needs
3. Love and belonging needs
4. Esteem needs
5. Self-actualization needs

According to Maslow, it is impossible to progress from one stage of psychological development to the next higher stage until the needs at the lower level are met. For example, until a person has obtained the basic physiologic needs of the first level, it is impossible for him or her to move to the level of feeling safe and secure. Accordingly, until a person has a safe and secure environment, he or she will be unable to continue the process of feeling loved and accepted in that social environment.

PHYSIOLOGIC NEEDS

The growing child has many needs; some are physiologic and some are psychosocial. The physiologic needs are often called **basic** or **primary** needs because they are basic to physical survival. Six basic requirements are oxygen, food, water, sleep, protection from temperature extremes (clothing and shelter), and excretion. Extreme deprivation of any one will result in a person's death.

To these six should be added a seventh—sexual activity—not because deprivation of this activity would result in death, but because, without it, the human race would become extinct. If these physiologic or biologic needs were humans' only concern, they would live on a very primitive level indeed. Brute force would determine survival.

SAFETY NEEDS

In order to develop in a psychologically healthy way, it is important that a person feel **safe and secure from harm**. This requires a predictable social and physical environment. Without feelings of safety, humans of any age, from infants to elderly adults, live with a chronic sense of fear that inhibits personal growth and fulfillment.

It is important to note that, in a psychiatric inpatient setting, the client's need for feeling safe and secure is crucial. These safety requirements and the nursing care measures needed to provide them are discussed in the chapters covering specific mental disorders and appear later in this book. Clients whose needs for safety in the inpatient setting are not met will not be able to progress to higher levels in the hierarchy.

LOVE AND BELONGING NEEDS

Probably the deepest psychosocial need most of us have is the need for **love** or **emotional security**. Love is a complex feeling of trust, warmth, and understanding—of closeness, intimacy, and emotional give-and-take. From infancy, humans need to feel accepted. All babies need a sense of emotional security; they need to be "mothered" regularly— held against the mother's body, stroked, caressed, cuddled, spoken and sung to, and rocked. So deep is this need that some psychologists place it with the seven basic needs. Humans do not outgrow the need to love and be loved. They merely shift where they look for the need to be filled—from the parental figure to peers (those of one's own age).

ESTEEM NEEDS

A person must feel accepted and loved by others in order to love and accept himself or herself. The young child's sense of self-worth or self-esteem forms the basis of his or her supply of self-esteem in adulthood. Self-esteem is a feeling of **self-acceptance** and **positive self-image**. Esteem needs have two main parts: a sense of competence about oneself and the need for recognition and a good reputation. If these needs are not fully met, a person lacks the feelings of confidence and competence necessary to move to the next and highest level of human needs.

Within the esteem level of human needs is the need for **status** and **recognition**. Status is a person's particular place in society; this place is allotted to him or her by virtue of age, sex, abilities, vocation or profession, his or her parents' status, and his or her socioeconomic standing. Recognition is the approval or acceptance given the individual by society as he or she performs in keeping with the role society has accorded. The esteem of others nourishes and supports an individual's self-esteem.

Although in the United States we have a so-called classless society—that is, one without aristocratic titles—we do have criteria, such as success and money, that substitute for aristocracy and help to determine status. The pressure to succeed, to achieve, and to excel begins very early in our lives. Power and possessions are two very important symbols of success. The need for status and recognition is probably related directly to our need to belong—the need for approval and acceptance—first within the family, and then within the group.

SELF-ACTUALIZATION NEEDS

Finally, there is the need to achieve—the need to accomplish and do. Maslow believed that the need to self-actualize or fully **develop one's**

potential is a constant driving force in all people, regardless of age. When adults feel vague discontent with their lives, it is often because they have not fully developed their potentials. This usually occurs because a person is limiting his or her own capacity to further develop, either personally, educationally, or in the working environment. It also can happen when a person's attempts at full personal development are thwarted by another person, financial circumstances, or other environmental factors. Full actualization requires that these self-created or other-created obstacles be overcome.

If the child's struggle to crawl, stand, walk, talk, and master the environment is rewarded by the approval of the significant figures in his or her life, the child will learn the satisfaction of accomplishment and will build a healthy concept of himself or herself as a "doer of deeds," a success. If the child fails to earn the approval of those around him or her, if small achievements are ignored, or worse yet, criticized severely, the child will build a picture of himself or herself as "one who fails." The child whose pride is diminished may lose the ambition or drive to develop his or her potential in adulthood. The child's rights and limits should be clearly defined and respected by the family. Accordingly, the child will grow to respect his or her own rights, as well as the rights of others.

Self-development in the child is vital. The child must gradually acquire a concept of *who* he or she is, *what* he or she is, and *what he or she can do*. By the time the child is 4 or 5 years old, he or she tends to have an exaggerated self-concept, and feels able to do anything. The lessons slowly learned from the environment, however, level off this concept to a more realistic one. Some self-idealization continues in most adults. They have a strong tendency to see themselves much closer to perfection than they really are. This is the **ego ideal** Freud spoke of in relation to his concept of personality development. It is a strong motivation for continued growth.

◆ DIFFERING NEEDS OF MEN AND WOMEN

Carol Gilligan, a psychologist interested in the differences in the social development of males and females, has found that the sexes have somewhat different values underlying their relationship potential, as well as their moral development. She has found in her research that the basic need of women is to maintain relationships. They promote communication as a means of keeping relationships intact. Women tend to feel strong responsibility in relationships. Men, on the other hand, tend to shy away from relationships and instead seek achievement as their basic need. The need for achievement, according to Gilligan, is a strong factor in male decision making and ethical considerations.

CHAPTER 9 SUMMARY

- A child's heredity, also known as genetic endowment, includes genetic traits such as eye and skin color, general intellectual capacity, talents, and the makeup of his or her neurologic system.

- Just as a child's body goes through successive stages of physical development, the child's personality undergoes developmental stages. Disturbing early experiences or unsatisfied emotional needs may lead to an arrest of normal development.

- Most theorists agree that:
  - Personality results from complex interactions between heredity and environment
  - Dynamic forces cause behavior
  - Some of these dynamic forces are unconscious or unknown to the individual
  - Childhood is an important time for forming these enduring behavior patterns
  - Behavior is a function or expression of personality

- Learning consists of four steps: need, stimulus, response, reinforcement. Extinction or forgetting occurs when reinforcement ceases.

- Certain experiences are crucial in a child's development:
  - Availability of a consistent, concerned caregiver
  - Feeding situation (including weaning) in early infancy
  - Toilet and cleanliness training
  - Early sex training
  - Training for control of anger and aggression

- According to Abraham Maslow's theory, a hierarchy of needs must be met for people to develop psychological maturity. These needs, from lowest to highest, are physiologic, safety, love and belonging, esteem, and self-actualization.

- Carol Gilligan's research shows that a basic need for women is to maintain relationships, whereas a basic need for men is achievement.

CHAPTER 9 QUESTIONS

1. Which of the following is true?
   a. Babies seldom display any reflex behavior at birth.
   b. Babies are born with basic temperaments or personalities.

c. Heredity is less important than environment in personality development.
d. All of the above

2. Identification is important in personality development because
   a. children can identify their parents' outdated ideas and attitudes and avoid them.
   b. it indicates a child's intelligence.
   c. healthy identifications can help people develop mature adult personalities.
   d. it means the child's personality is never in a state of flux.

3. Which of these childhood experiences is *not* particularly important in future psychosocial development?
   a. Feeding
   b. Training about cleanliness, sex, and aggression control
   c. Exposure to bright light
   d. Availability of a consistent, concerned caregiver

4. According to Carol Gilligan, which of the following is true?
   a. Men and women have the same values underlying their moral development.
   b. Men tend to maintain relationships rather than seek achievement.
   c. Women tend to strive for achievement rather than maintain relationships.
   d. The need for achievement is a strong factor in male decision making and ethical considerations.

BIBLIOGRAPHY

Brazelton, T. (1991). What we can learn from the status of the newborn. *NIDA Research Monograph, 114,* 93–105.
Gilligan, C. (1982). *In a different voice.* Cambridge, MA: Harvard University Press.
Kaplan, H.I., & Sadock, B.J. (1995). *Comprehensive textbook of psychiatry/VI* (6th ed.). Baltimore: Williams & Wilkins.
Lowry, R.J. (Ed.). (1973). *Dominance, self-esteem, self-actualization: Germinal papers of A.H. Maslow.* Monterey, CA: Brooks-Cole.
Mahler, M. (1974). Symbiosis and individuation: The psychological birth of the infant. *Psychoanalytic Study of the Child, 29,* 89.
Maslow, A. (1970). *Motivation and personality.* New York: Harper & Row.
Murray, R.B., & Zentner, J.P. (1996). *Health assessment and promotional strategies* (6th ed.). Norwalk, CT: Appleton & Lange.
Pfafflin, S.M. (Ed.). (1990). Psychology: Perspectives and practice. *Annals of the New York Academy of Sciences.*
Spitz, R. (1965). *The first year of life.* New York: International Universities Press.

Influence of Family and Social Environment on the Individual

Behavioral Objectives

After reading this chapter the student will be able to:

- Describe the concept of personality disposition.

- Define **maladaptation**.

- Explain the concepts of **system, subsystem,** and **supersystem**.

- Describe the term **dynamic** and explain the dynamics in a closed versus an open family.

- Explain how the dynamics of a family are altered when one of its members is treated for mental illness.

- Explain why sibling position in a family can have an effect on personality development.

- Describe homeostasis in the family.

The family is the first social group experienced by a developing infant. The comfort of an individual with any social group during childhood and adulthood is shaped by his or her relationships with mother, father, siblings, and the extended family. The extended family includes grandparents, aunts, uncles, and cousins. Because of today's mobile society, some of the important roles usually performed by family members may be filled by friends, neighbors, teachers, ministers, and so on.

As described in the previous chapter, an infant is a unique being who is born with a certain disposition or temperament that is determined by his or her physical inheritance. For example, he or she may have a quiet, easy-going disposition, be irritable and difficult to please, or be very alert and inquisitive.

Just as the infant has his or her own unique disposition, so too do parents. Depending on the fit in disposition between a child and his or her parents, there may be a higher capacity for trust or for anxiety-producing tension or conflict. As an example, consider the experience of a cranky, irritable infant who is born to a frequently anxious mother versus an easy-going, confident mother. The psychological "fit" between a parent and child can be an important factor in the development of a child's self-esteem.

A family is a very complex social structure. There are countless factors that shape its development and that of each of its members. **Family system** is a term that describes the characteristics of a family. These characteristics include the roles in a family, such as mother, father, oldest child, and so on. Other characteristics include the ways that a family interacts, such as boundaries, open and closed patterns of communication, and so on. These characteristics will be described later in this chapter.

Maladaptation is the result of chronic ineffective coping on the part of one or both parents. Maladaptation can result in dysfunctional patterns of responses to stress within one or more family members. These dysfunctional social and communication patterns are usually acquired by children in their socialization within the family. Maladaptive characteristics in the family system can contribute to the development of mental disorders in one or more family members.

Socialization is the shaping of an individual to the communication style, beliefs, and emotional patterns of a social group. The growth and development of a child in the family is shaped by the internal and external stresses and forces that affect the child, the family, both parents, and every child in the family. Most of these family forces, stresses, and dynamics have been examined in order to understand the causes of mental illness.

Personality theorists generally believe that the usual cause of mental illness is the result of two factors: genetic physiologic inheritance and the effect of the family environment on the child during infancy and childhood. In order to understand the importance of the multiple forces and dynamics that occur in families, mental health theorists turned to the scientific field for the terminology to describe family processes. General systems theory has been adopted from the field of biology to explain family processes and their effects on personality development.

◆ GENERAL SYSTEMS THEORY

General systems theory is a concept that is helpful to nurses in the care of clients. The original concept of systems theory was developed by von Bertalanffy in the 1920s. In his field, biology, he was constantly impressed by the organization of organisms and the dependence of biological systems on one another. The metabolism and growth of one organism depends on another; for example, photosynthesis by trees requires carbon dioxide given off as a waste product by human metabolism. Conversely, humans use oxygen given off as a waste product by trees in their metabolic process.

As scientists from other fields began to apply von Bertalanffy's general systems concepts to their own disciplines, they began to see that there was, indeed, an interdependence of one system on another. This concept can be applied to the smallest microscopic life form or to the solar system and the interactions of the planets.

This idea of interdependence applies very well to the fields of psychiatry and psychology. No human being exists in complete isolation from all others. The infant, for example, depends on others for his or her physical care and nurturing. His or her personality is formed as the result of interactions, primarily with immediate family and later with teachers, peers, and others.

◆ SYSTEMS, SUBSYSTEMS, AND SUPERSYSTEMS

What is a system? A **system** is actually a collection of working parts that, when combined together, make up a more complex working object or abstract entity. These smaller components are called subsystems. They are essential to the overall functioning of a system. A **subsystem** is a concrete or abstract, essential part of a larger system and relates in specific ways with all parts of the larger entity. Without the subsystem, the system cannot function.

The human psyche is an example of an abstract system. It is made up of three major parts or subsystems. They are the id, ego, and superego. If one or more of these subsystems is not present, the psyche is unable to function. The cardiovascular system is a concrete example. This system is made up of several working subsystems—the heart, the arteries, veins, and so on.

The body itself is a very complex entity made up of a large number of systems. When a number of systems are essential for an entity to function, then it is called a supersystem. A **supersystem** is a large complex made up of many systems. A state's department of mental health is also a supersystem; it consists of many hospitals, departments, and groups of workers that are essential to its functioning.

THE HUMAN BEING AS A SYSTEM

The human being is a system made up of two main subsystems, the physiologic and the psychological. The physiologic subsystem includes many smaller subsystems, such as cardiovascular, neurologic, and musculoskeletal. If one of these subsystems fails, the result is that all the other subsystems will ultimately fail, and death will occur. The human psychological subsystem includes the id, ego, and superego subsystems.

As suggested above, a human being is part of larger systems that can be called supersystems. A person belongs to several social supersystems. His or her primary social system is the family. It is in the family that he or she acquires basic values, self-image, and the capacity for relating with others throughout his or her lifetime. In addition, a person belongs to social systems through school and work. A person is also a part of the ecologic supersystem; in the environment he or she lives interdependently with other animals, plants, gases, and water.

SYSTEMS THEORY AND MENTAL ILLNESS

The concept of systems is important for our purposes. It allows us to look for the cause of mental illness somewhere within one of a human's subsystems or supersystems. Identification of the cause, when possible, allows us to plan therapeutic interventions.

◆ MAJOR CONCEPTS IN FAMILY SYSTEM FUNCTIONING

FAMILY SYSTEM TERMINOLOGY

The immediate family into which a child is born is called the **nuclear family.** It is made up of mother, father, and siblings and is also known as the **family of origin.** The family members not in the nuclear family—grandparents, aunts, uncles, cousins, and so on—are known as the **extended family.**

DYNAMICS

A **dynamic** is a constantly operating force within a system that results in some type of action or observable result. If, for example, a person was orphaned as a young child or was born with a major handicap, it can be said that these factors lying deep within the experience of a person have a constantly operating effect on him or her. Dynamics are usually operating in all of us without our conscious awareness.

There are dynamics that occur within a person's psyche, such as unconscious impulses or drives of the id. In addition, there are social system dynamics that operate in families. These can include defensive avoidance of a family member with an explosive temper or schizophrenia.

OPEN AND CLOSED FAMILY SYSTEMS

Depending on the openness or closedness of the family, a child's needs will or will not be shaped or formed in such a way that is healthy and supports his or her continuing social and psychological development.

An **open family** is one in which the members, especially the parents, have had the opportunity to develop as healthy, active, members of society with positive self-esteem. They not only contribute to the society and to their families, but they are able to recognize their needs and have them met by others, when necessary. In other words, they know how to receive or to take from others, in a socially responsible manner, whatever they need to develop as actualized human beings. An open family allows for flexibility in the roles of its members.

A **closed family,** on the other hand, is rigid and allows little change in the roles and patterns in the family. Usually one of the parents (frequently both) has moderate to high levels of psychopathology. The climate in the home does not support the development and ultimate healthy separation of the child from the family when he or she reaches adulthood.

The majority of people we work with in psychiatric settings come from the latter type of family. The dynamics in the closed family frequently contribute to inadequate or pathologic personality development in the developing child. These traits evolve into the adult's personality. Remember that an individual's personality has been shaped over a long period of time. This usually happens to meet the family's needs but without their conscious awareness.

◆EFFECTS OF MENTAL ILLNESS ON FAMILY DYNAMICS

Accordingly, when this family member becomes mentally ill, it is a worsening of a mental state to which the family has become accustomed. If the person is treated in a mental health setting and his or her normally dysfunctional pattern is eliminated, the family's dynamics are changed significantly. A simple example of this is a woman who has a violent temper even when she is only mildly angry. Her family unconsciously knows her boiling point. They relate as a family in a way that will not upset her. Conversely, when the family is upset about something, she expresses the emotion that others feel, and it helps to clear the air.

For this particular family this is their normal communication style. Equilibrium in the family is maintained by the dynamic of the mother's anger. If her boiling point were to change permanently to a better, healthier level, it would dramatically change the way the family members interact. The other family members would unconsciously work to restore the communications to their former normal style.

All families, open or closed, relate in a way that maintains their normal communication patterns. When the behavior of one person is changed, it disrupts these patterns and causes increased anxiety in all the other members. Accordingly, if people admitted to a mental health facility are treated with no attention to the family, their chances for long-term recovery are diminished. Family patterns that may have contributed to the development of the client's dysfunctional symptoms must be examined and, if necessary, modified. This requires that the family meet with a family therapist, usually one or more times weekly, during the client's hospitalization. The types of patterns and dynamics that exist in families are described below.

SIBLING POSITION IN FAMILY OF ORIGIN

Studies of all types of families have found that birth order strongly influences the way a person communicates and behaves in a family. In addition, a person carries these interpersonal traits into adulthood, and they become part of the way he or she relates in any social setting. Generally, the oldest child is more responsive to criticism, is more responsible, achieves consistently, and functions behaviorally in a more rigid manner than younger brothers or sisters. These traits result from the parents' tendencies to demand more of oldest children and expect them to assist with the care of younger siblings.

The youngest child is frequently more dependent, less achievement-oriented, and often quite charming. This results from the love and attention received by the youngest child. If his or her needs were easily met, he or she did not learn to tolerate frustration in pursuit of goals.

The middle child, because of his or her position between the oldest and youngest children, frequently is more flexible and more independent. He or she also tends to be more easy-going than the oldest or youngest child. A client's interaction style in the hospital setting, both with caregivers and other clients, frequently reflects his or her sibling position.

FAMILY RULES

Family rules are the unwritten expectations about what types of roles or behavior will be acceptable or unacceptable to the family. Remember that most people behave in ways that will ensure approval by those they care about. As we grow older we tend to conform to the expectations of others in order to maintain their love and acceptance. These rules are often based on the value system that each partner brings into a marriage. Remember that we inherit many of our values from our families. Most people tend to marry individuals with similar values or expectations. It is in this way that family patterns, rules, and expectations tend to remain somewhat similar from one generation to the next.

BOUNDARIES

Within a family system, **boundaries** are the rules that keep the role of one family member separate from another. Staying within one's role in the family is often the key to acceptance in the family. Boundaries develop as the result of family rules. For example, if women in a family have traditionally been passive, a daughter from such a family may be passive as well. She will most likely marry a man who enjoys his role as sole decision maker. This type of family pattern of relationships teaches the children to go to the father automatically when a decision needs to be made. If the mother uncharacteristically makes a major decision, conflict usually will result. She has, in effect, overstepped her customary boundary and altered her normal role in the family.

When a mentally ill person is successfully treated and reenters the family, the role he or she filled before treatment is changed. Accordingly, his or her normal boundaries of functioning are also different. A family therapy process, in conjunction with inpatient psychiatric hospitalization, is designed to renegotiate and reestablish boundaries and role patterns so that the newly discharged person's different (and more healthy) style of functioning will not be reshaped by the family to his or her preadmission family role.

HOMEOSTASIS

The concept of a system is helpful when we look at homeostasis or equilibrium within a family. It can be helpful to visualize a mobile with a number of objects hanging from it as a symbol of homeostasis. Compare the mobile with a family system. When it is in balance it maintains perfect equilibrium. If one of the objects is tapped, what happens? All the other objects are affected and jostled. If one object is removed what happens? There is an even stronger effect. The entire mobile loses its balance.

Homeostasis is a dynamic, ever-changing state in which a system constantly works to maintain balance. As one subsystem or person changes, the other members alter their patterns of communication or behavior to maintain the balance of the family. When a person becomes mentally ill, the family struggles to counter the effects of his or her worsening symptoms. If admission to the hospital becomes necessary, it triggers a crisis. The removal of the person from the family can allow the family to work toward equilibrium or homeostasis. Remember, however, that without the return of the ill member to the family, true family homeostasis is disrupted.

The concept of general systems theory applies to all systems. It encourages us to view physically or mentally ill clients holistically. We are aware of the interaction of physical illness on the psyche, and conversely, of the psyche on physical illness. It also allows us to evaluate the interaction of the overall social system and family on the etiology, diagnosis, and treatment of illness.

CHAPTER 10 SUMMARY

- The family is the first social group that each person experiences. Patterns of behavior in a family that contribute to mental illness are referred to as the family system.

- A system is a collection of working parts that, when combined, make up a more complex working object or entity.

- A subsystem is a small but essential part of the system that relates to all parts of the larger system and is an integral part of it.

- A supersystem is a large complex made up of many systems.

- Human beings are made of two major interdependent systems, the physiologic and the psychological.

- Identifying the cause of mental illness within one of the human systems, subsystems, or supersystems helps caregivers plan therapeutic interventions.

- Major concepts in family systems functioning include the following:
  - *Family system terminology*—nuclear and extended family and family of origin
  - *Dynamics*—constantly operating forces within a system
  - *Open family system*—family members have flexible roles; helps produce healthy, active people
  - *Closed family system*—family members have rigid roles; does not support healthy development

- Treatment of a mentally disordered person needs to include attention to family dynamics. When the family is not considered, the client's chances for long-term improvement are diminished.

- Family dynamics that affect mental health and mental illness are sibling position in family of origin, family rules (expectations about roles and behavior), and boundaries (rules that keep one person separate from another).

- Homeostasis is a dynamic state in which a system constantly works to maintain balance. Families attempt to maintain homeostasis, or equilibrium, in response to changes in their system or subsystem.

CHAPTER 10 QUESTIONS

1. Which of the following is *not* a correct statement?
   a. No human being exists in isolation.
   b. Open family systems are less likely to support healthy development.
   c. Understanding the role of human systems in mental illness can help caregivers plan therapeutic interventions.
   d. A closed family system can produce maladaptive family patterns of communication that can contribute to mental illness.

2. It is important that caregivers assess the family of a person treated in mental health facility because
   a. it improves the person's long-term chances for recovery.
   b. family behavior patterns often contribute to the client's dysfunction.
   c. the way that the family interacts with the client may need to be modified.
   d. all of the above.

3. Maladaptation is
   a. the result of chronic ineffective coping mechanisms.
   b. not related to socialization.

    c. a healthy response to family stress.

    d. seldom seen in families of mentally disordered clients.

4. Homeostasis means that

    a. a family system constantly works to maintain balance.

    b. families need just one familiar mode of communication.

    c. each individual is separate, so a change in one family member does not affect another family member.

    d. mentally disordered people should be permanently removed from their families to maintain the family balance.

BIBLIOGRAPHY

Barry, P.D. (1996). *Psychosocial nursing: Care of physically ill patients and their families* (3rd ed.). Philadelphia: Lippincott-Raven.

Clemen-Stone, S., Eigsti, D.G., & McGuire, S.L. (1996). *Comprehensive family and community health nursing* (4th ed.). St. Louis: Mosby Year Book.

Freidman, M.M. (1997). *Family nursing: Theory and practice* (4th ed.). Norwalk, CT: Appleton & Lange.

Kaplan, H.I., & Sadock, B.J. (1995). *Comprehensive textbook of psychiatry/VI* (6th ed.). Baltimore: Williams & Wilkins.

Kaplan, H.I., & Sadock, B.J. (1994). *Synopsis of psychiatry: Behavioral sciences, clinical psychology* (7th ed.). Baltimore: Williams & Wilkins.

Minuchin, W. (1974). *Families and family therapy.* Cambridge, MA: Harvard University Press.

Schultz, D.P. (1995). *Theories of personality* (5th ed.). Pacific Grove, CA: Brooks-Cole.

Toman, W. (1976). *Family constellation: Its effects on personality and social behavior* (3rd ed.). New York: Springer.

Wilson, H.S., & Kneisl, C.R. (1996). *Psychiatric nursing* (5th ed.). Redwood City, CA: Addison Wesley.

11

The Structure and Development of Personality

Behavioral Objectives

After reading this chapter the student will be able to:

■ Name the three abstract structures of the personality identified by Freud and briefly describe the function of each.

■ Identify and define the three levels of consciousness in the mind described by Freud.

■ Name three causes of conflict in the personality.

■ List five factors that can influence a child's personality.

■ List the six stages of personality development described by Freud and indicate the age ranges of each.

■ Define sibling rivalry and give three examples that describe it.

■ List the eight stages of personality development described by Erik Erikson.

■ Explain the developmental tasks and challenges of each of the Erikson stages of personality development.

◆ STRUCTURAL THEORY OF PERSONALITY

Sigmund Freud, one of the founders of the field of study of human personality, proposed that the personality is formed by the interaction of environment and heredity. The personality consists of three abstract structures: the **id,** the **ego,** and the **superego.** It is the conflict among these abstract structures of personality and the resulting balance that produce behavior.

THE ID

The id is made up of the biological drives that are uniquely bestowed by heredity. At birth, the child's personality is driven by the id. The id, therefore, is that part of the personality that is inborn; it is ruled only by the **pleasure principle**—the concept that humans instinctually seek to avoid pain and discomfort and strive for gratification and pleasure. The id is the raw stuff of personality, consisting of the body's primitive, biological drives, which strive only for satisfaction and pleasure.

Shortly after birth the baby is frustrated because his or her needs are not immediately satisfied. The baby cries to be fed, moved, or held, or to have his or her diaper changed, but must often wait for a while. Crying is the baby's first form of protest; it is used as a tool to achieve needs. And so the second component of personality comes into being—the **ego** or **reality principle.**

The ego encompasses a large variety of functions that are essential to mental and physical well-being. They include the following:

Consciousness

Mastery of motor skills

Mobility

Perception

Judgment

Sense of reality

Regulation and control of emotions and impulses

Object relations

Memory

Thinking

Defense mechanisms

THE EGO

The ego is the part of the self that is most closely in touch with reality. Its job is to mediate between the urges of the id and the demands of the environment and to satisfy both in a way that coincides with physical and social reality. It is roughly equivalent to the terms "conscious awareness," or "the self." As it develops, the reality principle, or ego, overrules or operates in concert with the id, or pleasure principle, in guiding behavior.

By the age of 3, the average child has learned that there are many things he or she may not do and other things that he or she must do. The child is also learning to defer immediate satisfactions for anticipated or delayed satisfactions. For example, the child will stop doing something that feels good in order to obtain his or her mother's approval. During this time, the child has learned to accept the attributes and standards of his or her parents as his or her own. The child is not yet able to understand the reasons behind behavior, but readily accepts his or her parents' judgment about what is right or wrong to do or say.

The child tends to idealize and view himself or herself as close to perfection. Thus, his or her ego ideal is formed. The **ego ideal** is a high standard within the ego that motivates the individual to continued growth and self-actualization.

THE SUPEREGO

Slowly, the child begins to make judgments about the rightness or wrongness of things and to regulate his or her conduct on the basis of these judgments. By the time the child is 7 years old, this judgment process should be fairly well integrated into the personality. Freud called the judgment process the **superego** and labelled it as being social or cultural in origin. The superego is roughly equivalent to the **conscience**—the inner voice that judges whether thoughts and actions are good or bad.

The id, ego, and superego are involved in constant conflicts. These conflicts and frustrations give rise to our behavior and result in emotional growth. Without conflict and frustration, there would be no personality growth. Some conflicts are apparent to us; we are aware of some, consciously involved in many, but unaware of other conflicts. Because the conflicts that are unknown to us function at a deeper level, we cannot resolve them. Nevertheless, they act as strong motivators of our behavior.

◆ LEVELS OF CONSCIOUSNESS

One of Freud's greatest contributions to the understanding of human behavior was his concept of the **unconscious.** He saw the mind as consisting of three overlapping parts. These he labeled, from the one we are most aware of to the one we are least aware of, the **conscious mind,** the **subconscious mind,** and the **unconscious mind,** likening them to parts of an iceberg.

The **conscious mind** refers to that part of the mind that is focused in a here-and-now awareness (the part of the iceberg that is above the water level, freely visible).

The **subconscious mind** refers to that part of the mind just below immediate awareness—the storehouse for memories. These memories are either those that have ceased to be important to us or those that we suppressed because they are mildly uncomfortable. They can be brought back into awareness at will. (This is the part of the iceberg below the water level that can be seen by peering down into the water.)

The **unconscious mind** refers to that part of the mind that is closed to immediate awareness. It is a vast reservoir of memories, experiences, and emotions that cannot be recalled. (This is the part of the iceberg that cannot be seen at all and may extend a great distance down into the water, completely unknown to the observers above it.)

◆ CONFLICT

Conflicts among the three parts of the personality may result in behavior that is wholly conscious, partly conscious, wholly subconscious, or wholly unconscious. *The important aspect of behavior is that it usually resolves conflict.* Faced with an upsetting situation, people ordinarily do one of three things: (1) They become aggressive and oppose the situation. (2) They flee from it. (3) They compromise with it. This last way of handling a situation seems to be the most realistic one and the one most likely to resolve the conflict or anxiety.

Conflicts are resolved through the use of certain methods of thinking and acting that either eliminate the conflict or reduce its severity. These methods, commonly called **defense mechanisms** or **mental mechanisms,** are not always clear cut; in fact, they often overlap or may be used simultaneously. Many defense mechanisms have been identified; they will be described in Chapter 14, Stress: Ineffective Coping and Defense Mechanisms.

Why do people seem so different? Why is one person angry, aggressive, and ready to fight at the slightest provocation, whereas another is passive and gentle, always willing to compromise and bend in order to seek a peaceful solution?

The differences in basic personality style and energy level are apparent in any newborn nursery. One-day-old infants vary greatly in their amount of movement, crying vigor, sucking strength, and tolerance for discomfort. Any mother with more than one child will readily admit that each child exhibited definite differences throughout the neonatal period and infancy. One child was weaned more easily, another was more difficult to toilet train, and so forth.

◆ FACTORS IN PERSONALITY DEVELOPMENT

One can observe that even with the same parents, the genetic makeup of each sibling is different. One may "take after" his or her mother and the other "lean to the father's side of the family." One child may be significantly brighter than another. Literature is full of references to "the beautiful sister" and "the ugly sister," to the son who is "the dreamer" and the son who is "the doer."

The order of birth also plays a role in personality development. The first child is born into a home where childbearing is a new experience for the parents. Not only is the infant new at the job of being an infant, but the parents are new at the job of being parents. The second child is born into a different situation. His or her parents have had some experience at being parents. They may be practiced at limit setting. They have, perhaps, made the house more childproof so that the second child is less likely to break valuable possessions or stray into situations of physical danger.

The first child is an only child until his or her brother or sister is born. He or she has the parents' full attention until suddenly the parents have a new baby, and he or she is an only child no longer. The second child is never an only child.

Although they often deny it, parents have preferences among their children. The father may like boys or more aggressive children, while the mother may prefer girls or quiet, obedient children. Often the reverse is true, the mother favoring her sons and the father favoring his daughters.

With all of these variables, it is little wonder that a great number of theories (also referred to as **belief systems**) have evolved regarding the issue of how personality development occurs. That genetic factors play a part is virtually beyond dispute. The most universally accepted belief about heredity is that it is the background, the set, on which environmental factors play to form the personality.

For example, it is believed by some, although by no means proved, that an infant with a genetic predisposition to schizophrenia may develop in one family as a quiet, sensitive, artistic youth; in another as a person with schizoid personality (see Chapter 27, Personality Disorders); and in still another family as an acute schizophrenic with a clearly defined psychosis (see Chapter 23, Schizophrenia and Other Psychotic Disorders). Studies on identical twins, who have identical genetic structures, show that there is a very high likelihood of each twin developing the same mental disorder even when they are separated at birth and reared in different families.

Related to the heredity-as-cause belief system, but containing some of its own special concepts, is the **biochemical** (or neurotransmitter)

theory. There are subtle, but distinct, biochemical differences between people with no mental disorder and people with major mental illnesses. Which comes first, the biochemical disorder or the mental disorder, is still under dispute, but this area of investigation is among the most promising in psychiatric research today.

◆ THEORIES OF PERSONALITY DEVELOPMENT

Most belief systems, however, have little to do with heredity or bio- chemistry. They are concerned with one or another facet of the individ- ual person's development from birth on. They focus on the various forces that impinge on the child, such as the father, mother, siblings, family, or society; or the intrinsic developmental forces, such as the child's initial dependence and growth toward independence, the de- velopment of language, the development of motor skills, and bowel and bladder control.

It should be well understood by the student at the outset that no theory is entirely and absolutely correct. At the same time, there is no place for a negative attitude that says, "since nobody knows, there's no reason for listening to anybody." Each theory contains plausible ele- ments that assist in understanding the formation of personality.

Carl Jung emphasized concepts of the collective unconscious, in- dividuation (becoming an individual), and introversion and extrover- sion.

Harry Stack Sullivan believed that the individual could be studied only in relation to his or her social interactions with others. Sullivan de- veloped four basic postulates that underlie his theories:

1. The *biological postulate*, which states that man (as an animal) dif- fers from all other animals in his cultural interdependence.

2. *Man's essentially human mode of functioning*, which refers to those characteristics that distinguish man from all other animal life.

3. *Significance of anxiety*, which refers to the central role of anxiety in human development.

4. The *tenderness postulate*, in which Sullivan states that "the activ- ity of an infant which arises from the tension of his needs pro- duces tension in the mothering one which is felt by her as ten- derness." Man has a growing capacity for tenderness.

Gertrude Mahler described the important psychological develop- ment that occurs in children during the first 2¹/₂ years of life. She be- lieves that the availability of a consistent, loving caregiver, ideally the mother, is essential if the child is to avoid feeling abandoned and inse- cure during later life.

Erich Fromm's theories reflect the orientation of the social scientist. He emphasizes the role of society in mental disorders rather than the role of the individual, which is the classic psychoanalyst's concern. Fromm believes that "self-love" is really self-affirmation, which is the basis of the capacity to love others.

Alfred Adler influenced child psychiatry a great deal with his early considerations of organ inferiority and nervous character. He later became preoccupied with educational, social, and political issues as the causes of mental illness.

Karen Horney believed that specific cultural values and beliefs cause disturbances in human relationships leading to neuroses.

Jean Baker Miller describes the psychological development of women as a process in which they learn the value of being subordinate in order to gain acceptance from the larger social system, which includes men and authority figures. She also identifies several important traditional roles of women: the giver of care; the mediator, who avoids and mediates conflicts; and the avoider of power. She believes that these roles undermine women's ability to develop their full potential as human beings.

Wilhelm Reich made a valuable contribution to the understanding of how the character or personality style evident in adulthood is developed.

Otto Rank was primarily concerned with the application of psychoanalysis to mythology and literature.

Eugen Bleuler published a comprehensive study of schizophrenia (a term he coined).

Hermann Rorschach, who developed the ink blot test, was a pioneer in the elaboration of projective psychological testing.

Carl Rogers's theory of personality states that the values of a society and of a person living within that society may differ. If a person replaces his or her own values and choices regarding self-actualization with those of the social environment in order to gain acceptance and approval, conflict occurs in the form of anxiety.

◆ FREUD'S CONCEPT OF PERSONALITY DEVELOPMENT

Sigmund Freud (1856–1939) was a Viennese physician who made important contributions to our understanding of personality development. The contributions are a part of the system of psychology he named **psychoanalysis.** The word is obtained from the term *psyche,* or mind, and the process that Freud developed to analyze the way the mind works.

Freud emphasized an aspect of the personality that he termed **sexuality.** His selection of this term to express the pleasure-seeking component of the personality is unfortunate because it erroneously carries the implication that all forms of pleasure seeking are associated with genital sexuality and pleasure. Bear in mind that Freud's use of the term sexuality is quite broad and traces a step-by-step development of the psychosexual aspect of the personality from its earliest expression in the baby to maturity.

Freud divided the growth and development of the human body into phases, or stages. From birth to adulthood, he listed them as: (1) the oral stage; (2) the anal stage; (3) the phallic stage; (4) the latent stage; (5) the genital stage; and (6) adulthood.

THE ORAL STAGE

The first stage of psychosexual development lasts from birth until about the end of the first year. It terminates in weaning. Before birth, the infant is fed through the maternal bloodstream and never experiences the pleasure provided by the gratification of this first instinctual need. With birth, however, a biologic need for food arises, and the infant receives satisfaction through nursing. Not only is the discomfort from hunger relieved by sucking but, as other tensions arise, the infant may turn to the most available substitute as a source of security and satisfaction—sucking his or her thumb. The mouth becomes the part of the body in which interests, sensation, and activities are centered and through which gratification is secured. If a baby is seldom held or loved, if he or she is left lying untended for long periods of time, often uncomfortable at not being turned or changed, or if he or she is consistently allowed to go hungry beyond the first hunger pangs, the baby will probably enter childhood and, ultimately, adulthood with a disturbed capacity to trust in all relationships.

THE ANAL-EXPULSIVE STAGE

This phase starts toward the end of the first year. At that time, the mouth begins to share its pleasure-giving role with the organs of elimination. The child becomes as interested in discovering his or her excretory functions as the mother is in controlling them. This period covers the toilet training stage and usually terminates early in the third year. The small child does not have the same feeling of revulsion for urine and feces that an adult has. To him or her the process of elimination is pleasure giving.

In our culture, toilet training is often begun early and is usually rigidly enforced. Usually toilet training is not possible until the necessary development of the nervous system has taken place (around the age of 2 years) and until the child has acquired a sign language to communicate his or her wants. When harsh parental expectations and/or punishment occur during this period, the child may develop anxiety that persists into adulthood, primarily around the issue of control.

THE PHALLIC STAGE

This phase is characterized by the child's growing awareness of the differences between the male and the female body. This stage usually extends from late in the third or early in the fourth year until the sixth year. At this stage of personality development, there is increasing interest in the genitals, and the child discovers that he or she achieves a pleasurable sensation when the genitals are handled or rubbed. As the child fondles himself or herself, he or she is not at all aware of doing something socially unacceptable—masturbating—and it is only when parents express displeasure in his or her actions that it assumes an abnormal significance to the child.

Masturbation is not physically harmful in any way, but it does pose an emotional problem when conflicts set in. If the child's unhappiness intensifies, he or she will resort to masturbation in secret, and this will increase his or her guilt feeling and isolate the child even further from his or her parents. Obsessive masturbation can be avoided by a wise and tolerant attitude on the part of the mother and father. Parents should try to spend more time with the child during this period. A wholesome attitude in the home toward the human body will help the child pass through this phase with a minimum of difficulty.

Another problem that is frequently seen in children between 3 and 7 years of age (although this problem can also occur earlier and later in a child's life) is **sibling rivalry.** A sibling is a brother or a sister who is the offspring of the same parents. The phenomenon can also be observed in children with half-brothers or sisters, as well as adopted or step-siblings. The problem is most noticeable when a new brother or sister is born. At that time the older child is bound to feel dislodged from his or her previously secure position in the family circle. Because the parents, especially the mother, must spend extra time with the newborn, the older child feels neglected, unwanted, and jealous. He or she may actively hate the newcomer, or may even try to get rid of the baby. He or she resents his or her mother's limited attention and will try all kinds of attention-getting devices. If these fail, the child may resort to infantile behavior, such as thumb sucking or bed wetting. He or she may develop stuttering, or may lose his or her appetite. The child often misbehaves in the presence of guests. If parents perceive these difficulties appearing in their children and understand the causes, they can be sure to give each child his or her full share of attention and praise and divide their love equally among them.

THE LATENT STAGE

The **latent** phase refers to the child's 7th through 12th years. The term *latent* suggests that this is a quiet time in which little development is occurring. Actually, it is a time when the personality traits, sex role mannerisms, and values that will accompany children into adulthood are deeply ingrained.

THE GENITAL STAGE

The genital stage is marked by the beginning of **puberty.** Puberty usually begins during the 12th year. The first stage of the genital phase, also known as **adolescence,** is characterized by profound physical changes combined with growing awareness of sex and sexual attraction toward others. This is a significant time for girls, because menstruation begins. The secondary sex characteristics start to appear, and sexual urges arise. Children need the close support of their parents during this time, and they especially need a full and frank explanation about the many changes taking place in their bodies and in their emotions. Explanations of sexual functioning and assurances that sexual feelings are normal help to decrease their anxieties and fears of being abnormal.

This final phase of transition from childhood to adulthood occurs by about the 18th year. As a rule, adolescence manifests itself later in boys than in girls. It is an acute period of transition that includes many physical and emotional strains. Caught between the dependency of childhood and the independence of adulthood, the teenager is strongly ambivalent in his or her desires and emotions. He or she is torn between desire for emancipation from parental controls and fear of the consequences of his or her own actions and judgments.

In addition to severing the parental bonds, the adolescent must seek a satisfactory relation with the opposite sex. He or she must also choose a vocation and start preparing for it, and must develop a sense of mature responsibility for self and others.

◆ ERIKSON'S CONCEPT OF PERSONALITY DEVELOPMENT

Erik Erikson's concept of personality development does not stress the psychosexual aspect of the stages of development as Freud's does. Erikson compares the evolution of the personality to the evolution of tissues in the early stages of embryonic development. He believes that there is a timetable inherent in the development of various specialized tissues, organs, and systems in the physical body. Erikson proposes that during each stage of development there is a **developmental task** to be accomplished, and that each developmental task not only contributes some vital attribute of personality but lays the groundwork for the next task.

The stages of psychosocial development identified by Erikson and the developmental challenges of each stage are listed below:

1. Early infancy (birth to 1 year): Trust vs. mistrust

2. Later infancy (1 to 3 years): Autonomy vs. shame and doubt

3. Early childhood (4 to 5 years): Initiative vs. guilt

4. Later childhood (6 to 11 years): Industry vs. inferiority

5. Puberty and adolescence (12 to 20 years): Ego identity vs. role confusion

6. Early adulthood (20 to 40 years): Intimacy vs. isolation

7. Middle adulthood (40 to 60 years): Generativity vs. stagnation

8. Late adulthood (60 years and older): Ego integrity vs. despair

Upon this concept he builds the theory that a whole or partial failure at one step means that the personality will be deficient in the trait that should have arisen at that particular time. If succeeding stages are developed on too weak a foundation, the total personality may suffer as a result. Erikson points out that these successive stages of personality development should not be thought of as arising at exact time periods but, rather, at approximate age levels, with considerable individual variation, and that the developmental tasks of each stage overlap. According to Erikson, if a developmental task is not fully mastered during a particular stage of development, it is possible for the unresolved issues of that stage to be worked through during later stages. Following is a brief description of Erikson's stages of psychosocial development.

EARLY INFANCY

This period is characterized by **basic trust**. An infant is completely helpless and at the mercy of adults. The baby who is warmly accepted, wanted, and loved comes to know the world as a nice place and the people in it as friendly and helpful. He or she develops a cheerful confidence that his or her needs will be met. On the other hand, the baby who feels unloved and unaccepted will develop a diffuse anxiety, a distrust of his or her small world. The baby may become preoccupied with his or her own needs as a result of uncertainty over whether they will be met. Because the baby is given so little opportunity to respond positively to others, he or she is likely to become demanding, fearful, hostile, or simply cold and withdrawn.

Basic trust is the necessary foundation for the capacity to love. The histories of people with schizophrenia, the largest group of mentally ill individuals, all have a remarkable sameness; they felt unloved and unwanted in childhood, so unloved that they failed to develop the basic trust that enables them to build binding ties with other human beings. The schizophrenic is afraid to love, afraid to invest affection in others. Thus, he or she lives in a world of isolation.

LATER INFANCY

This period is characterized by **autonomy**. Between the ages of 2 and 4 years, the young child comes into contact with increasing restrictions. He or she must adapt to the family and its practices, and learn to adjust to social and moral norms. The child becomes fiercely rebellious at all these restrictions and impatient with routines and regulations. His or her favorite word is no. Because the child is still dependent on the very adults he or she defies, however, and because he or she desires their love and approval, the child usually will build a fine, but precarious, balance between independence and conformity.

EARLY CHILDHOOD

This period is characterized by **initiative** and occurs during the 4th and 5th years. As trust represents the first phase and independence the second, so the third is characterized by an outstanding attribute of personality—initiative. Early childhood is the period during which the child expands his or her imagination. He or she starts trying on, or identifying with, the role of the same-sex parent. The boy unconsciously adopts the mannerisms and attitudes of his father, while the girl adopts those of her mother. The underlying dynamic in the child who attempts new situations is positive self-esteem. Positive self-esteem is the internalization of the acceptance and approval the child received from his or her parents during the first years of life.

LATER CHILDHOOD

This period is characterized by **industry** and **accomplishment**. It is equivalent to the **latent** stage in Freud's classification. Children between 6 and 11 years of age have much energy that needs channeling into constructive accomplishments. The child is in school, and he or she learns to compete with peers in many areas. Pride in achievement develops as a result of praise and attention to his or her efforts. Group projects become absorbing; interests develop into hobbies. These are the joyous, exciting years of childhood, when the child learns to work beside and with others, when he or she begins to learn the skills, both intellectual and mechanical, necessary for a future role as a citizen in a complex society. It is the lull before the turbulent years of adolescence. Parents can assist the child's transition during latency by being actively involved in his or her activities and supporting his or her self-esteem.

PUBERTY AND ADOLESCENCE

This period can be a stormy one, characterized by a search for **identity.** The young boy or girl is usually ill-prepared for the great physiologic changes that must occur before the body becomes ready for reproduction. During the same period, emotions must stabilize in preparation for assuming the responsibility of a family. An adolescent's new surge of sexual feelings, striving for independence from family restrictions, self-doubt about his or her abilities, and a strong sense of ambivalence can cause confusion.

The teenager needs to choose a vocation or career but often has qualms about the selection of a life's work. He or she may be bewildered by the vast array of possibilities and uncertain about what course he or she really wishes to follow. Sympathetic and understanding parents and teachers can do much to lighten the emotional burdens of the adolescent. They must understand the adolescent's need to reject their standards and ideals temporarily and find security in identifying with the mannerisms, dress, speech, and activities of peers. If the teenager feels loved and knows his or her parents stand as safe ports in a storm who will provide temporary shelter when the going gets too rough, he or she will emerge from the turmoil with a renewed sense of identity and with good, fundamental human values intact. The teenager's redefined identity is founded on inner integrity—a conviction that he or she is truly a person worthy of respect in the adult world.

EARLY ADULTHOOD

The developmental challenge of the young adult between 20 and 40 years of age is to be capable of **intimacy.** Intimacy is the capacity to trust another in a deep and committed relationship. The challenge is to know and be known by another. This includes accepting one's own foibles, as well as those of another. Intimacy in a long-term sexual relationship is marked by love, concern, compassion, and commitment to the well-being of the other. A capacity for intimacy is also an essential characteristic of long-lasting, deep friendships. When a person is incapable of intimacy, he or she is aloof and isolated, shunning closeness with others.

MIDDLE ADULTHOOD

The middle-aged adult between 40 and 60 years is engaged in developing and guiding the next generation, be it children, grandchildren, coworkers, or young people in various types of social groups. The psychologically mature adult is productive rather than stagnant. The person who does not master this developmental hurdle is preoccupied with himself or herself to the exclusion of others' needs. The immature adult also exhibits a tendency toward hypochondriacal sickliness and general dissatisfaction with life.

LATE ADULTHOOD

This period is characterized by **integrity.** To Erikson, integrity sums up our ability to live out the later portion of our life with dignity and an assured sense of order and meaning in the total scheme of life. The facets of integrity are serenity, continual joy in living, a sense of accomplishment, and anticipation of worthwhile endeavors yet to be accomplished. These traits contrast with the despair that eventually develops in elderly adults who are unable to resolve the losses of later life or master this last stage of psychosocial development.

C H A P T E R   1 1   S U M M A R Y

- According to Freud, the personality consists of three abstract structures:
  - Id—the pleasure principle with which all infants are born
  - Ego—the reality principle, that mediates between the id and the environment
  - Superego—the conscience or inner voice that labels actions as good or bad

- The conflicts that arise between these parts of the personality give rise to behavior. Satisfactory resolution of the conflicts, usually through defense or mental mechanisms, results in emotional growth.

- According to Freud, the human mind consists of the conscious, the subconscious, and the unconscious.

- The major factors in personality development are genetic makeup and environmental impacts and influences.

- Most personality theories focus on the various forces that affect the child, such as heredity, family structure, societal expectations, and other developmental forces. A number of theories of personality exist, although no one theory is completely correct or completely incorrect.

- Sigmund Freud divided development into five stages:
  - 1. Oral—interest is focused on the mouth
  - 2. Anal-expulsive—interest is focused on the organs of elimination

— 3. Phallic—growing interest in differences between male and female bodies

— 4. Latent—personality traits, sex role mannerisms, and values are deeply ingrained

— 5. Genital—profound changes of puberty (around age 12) plus growing awareness of sex and sexual attraction toward others. Culminates in the final phase of transition to adulthood, at about age 18.

■ Erik Erikson's concept of personality proposes eight stages of development, from infancy to old age, each of which has a developmental task to accomplish. The stages and tasks are as follows:

— 1. Early infancy—trust vs. mistrust

— 2. Later infancy—autonomy vs. shame and doubt

— 3. Early childhood—initiative vs. guilt

— 4. Later childhood—industry vs. inferiority

— 5. Puberty and adolescence—ego identity vs. role confusion

— 6. Early adulthood—intimacy vs. isolation

— 7. Middle adulthood—generativity vs. stagnation

— 8. Late adulthood—ego integrity vs. despair

CHAPTER 11 QUESTIONS

1. According to Freud's structural theory of personality, the id
   a. is ruled by the pleasure principle.
   b. is not really involved with personality development because it is so primitive.
   c. develops after the superego and the ego are fully developed.
   d. is another term for the reality principle.

2. Freud's concept of the unconscious mind refers to
   a. the part of the mind just below immediate awareness.
   b. the storehouse for memories that are not important or are suppressed.
   c. the level of consciousness between conscious mind and the unconscious mind.
   d. all of the above.

3. The phallic stage of development described by Freud is characterized by a child's
   a. indifference to differences in male and female bodies.
   b. awareness that masturbation is not socially acceptable.

   c. discovery that touching his or her genitals is pleasurable.

   d. generous tolerance of siblings, especially newborn ones.

4. According to Erikson, which of the following characterizes late adulthood?

   a. Intimacy

   b. Integrity

   c. Identity

   d. Incoherence

BIBLIOGRAPHY

Barry, P.D. (1996). *Psychosocial nursing: Care of physically ill patients and their families* (3rd ed.). Philadelphia: Lippincott-Raven.

Combrinck-Graham, L. (1990). Developments in family systems theory and research. *Journal of the American Academy of Child and Adolescent Psychiatry, 29,* 501–512.

Erikson, E. (1987). The way of looking at things. In S. Schlein (Ed.), *Selected papers from 1930 to 1980.* New York: Norton.

Erikson, E. (1963). *Childhood and society* (2nd ed.). New York: Norton.

Freud, S. (1914). On the history of the psychoanalytic movement. In Freud, S. (1959). *Collected papers,* Vol. 1. New York: Basic Books (*The ego and the id.* [1928]. London: Hogarth Press).

Kaplan, H.I., & Sadock, B.J. (1995). *Comprehensive textbook of psychiatry/VI* (6th ed.). Baltimore: Williams & Wilkins.

Lego, S. (1996). *Psychiatric nursing: A comprehensive reference* (2nd ed.). Philadelphia: Lippincott-Raven.

Schultz, D.P. (1995). *Theories of personality* (5th ed.). Pacific Grove, CA: Brooks-Cole.

DEVELOPING CRITICAL THINKING SKILLS THROUGH CLASS DISCUSSION

UNIT THREE Case Study
Basic Concepts of Mental Health

Pablo is an 8-year-old who lives with his mother and father and five siblings in an inner-city housing project. When he was 2 years old his mother left him in the care of his aunt while she returned to Puerto Rico for a 1-week visit with her family. While there, Pablo's mother became seriously ill and did not return to this country for 7 months.

Pablo's father was overwhelmed by the demands of being a single parent and was rarely able to visit his son at the aunt's home. Pablo had been separated from his siblings because he was a "nervous" and "high-strung" youngster.

D I S C U S S I O N   Q U E S T I O N S

1. What do you think it was like for Pablo to be separated from his mother when he was 2 years old?

2. Based on the readings in this unit, what do you think would have been the most supportive emotional environment for him when his mother became ill?

3. What would you tell Pablo about his mother's absence?

4. How could you reassure him during the long absence?

5. What are some of the changes that might occur in the family as a response to the mother's illness and absence?

6. What emotional effects of his mother's absence would you expect to see in Pablo at his current age?

7. Is it possible that his self-esteem would be altered by the event of his mother's absence? How so?

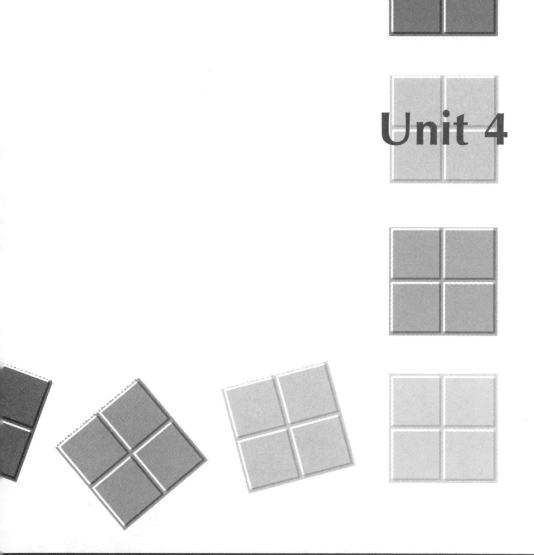

Unit 4

MENTAL HEALTH AND MENTAL DISORDER

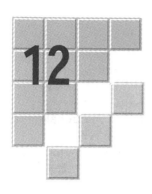

Human Emotions

Behavioral Objectives

After reading this chapter the student will be able to:

■ Describe the physiologic changes caused by emotions such as anger and fear and explain what is meant by the "fight or flight" syndrome.

■ Explain three ways that a child may handle or repress unacceptable feelings.

■ Describe anxiety and tell how it is experienced.

■ Describe how a small child expresses aggression and learns to control this feeling.

■ Identify the ways aggression can be expressed outwardly and inwardly.

■ List several types of behavior that are forms of self-destruction.

■ Describe the differences among the experiences of control, powerlessness, and hopelessness.

Emotions are **feeling states** that involve both physiologic and psychological changes. If a need is satisfied, the resulting emotion tends to be pleasant. For example, when babies are hungry, they make their needs known. When they are fed, they relax in satisfied, contented emotional states. Conversely, if a need is blocked, or ungratified, the resulting emotions are unpleasant. Thus, if babies are not fed when they make their needs known, they become tense and frustrated, usually showing their frames of mind by loud, angry crying.

◆ PHYSIOLOGIC RESPONSES

Emotional stress, whether it is pleasantly or unpleasantly experienced, is often accompanied by physical changes. When a person is angry, heart and pulse rates speed up, the face flushes, breathing quickens, and hands tremble. When struck by fear, some of the above symptoms may occur, as may blanching or turning pale; in addition, the mouth may become dry, lips may tremble, pupils may dilate, the breath may be held, the digestive tract may slow down (peristalsis may actually reverse itself), and small hairs on the body may stand erect. Even a feeling of delight tends to produce physiologic changes, although they are not usually as intense as those evoked by anger, hatred, fear, or anxiety.

The fight or flight response. These responses in the body are the result of sympathetic nervous system activation. As may be recalled from anatomy and physiology principles, the major division of the nervous system that controls all body functions is the autonomic nervous system. This system has two major branches, the parasympathetic and the sympathetic. The parasympathetic nervous system maintains the normal homeostasis of all organs and body systems. When the individual is threatened or challenged, the sympathetic nervous system overrides the parasympathetic nervous system physiology in order to prepare the body for "survival." The concept of "fight or flight" is the normal physiologic shift that gives the body the fullest potential strength to overcome the challenge or threat.

In the "fight or flight" syndrome, the physical reactions that accompany emotions of anger and fear are readying the body for addressing the challenge or threat by creative thinking, active aggression, or escape from what is feared (hence, the name fight or flight syndrome). The adrenal glands pour out adrenaline into the bloodstream. The result is extra strength or power available for quick or lifesaving action.

All people feel both pleasant and unpleasant emotions. Humans have needs they want filled; when a need is met they feel good, but an unmet need produces unpleasant emotions. Humans are creatures torn among many conflicting emotions, which run the range between the extremes of love and hate, childlike trust and paranoid suspiciousness, self-sacrificing bravery and lowly cowardice. Emotions are powerful motivators of behavior. It is important to note that unpleasant emotion is often the underlying cause of positive growth and change; unpleasant emotion usually results in an attempt by the individual to become free of the emotional distress by creating changes in behavioral response or the cognitive interpretation of the cause of the unpleasant emotion. The outcome can be a more adaptive form of coping.

◆ CONTROL OF EMOTIONS

One of every person's major struggles is learning to control his or her emotions. Even in early childhood, one learns ways to express emotions or repress them. Some emotions are acceptable in a social group; others are not. Each culture defines its own standards of behavior, and to be socially accepted, its citizens must conform to these standards.

Some cultures impose more control over emotions than others do. As an example of this, contrast the lack of emotionalism that is a valued personality characteristic in some ethnic groups with one that embraces a rich range of emotional responses. For example, a child raised in the former type of culture may be taught to repress expression of emotion, to become stoic. This is not to say that he or she is unemotional. He or she has the same strong urges to express joy, love, hatred, and fear as any other human being, but social acceptance by the immediate and extended family may depend in part on whether expression of emotion is controlled. Family custom may demand a deadpan facial expression even when experiencing intense fear, joy, or pain.

The child raised in an emotionally open culture may grow up in a highly charged atmosphere. He or she is highly verbal and is encouraged to express likes and dislikes freely; laughter and tears may succeed each other quickly. Surging anger often results in aggressive behavior.

All too often, a child learns that the expression of certain emotions is unacceptable. Since he or she feels these emotions, such as jealousy, hatred, anger, and fear, and since punishment may occur for showing them, repression may occur in one way or another. Repression is a defense mechanism that pushes unpleasant thoughts or feelings into the unconscious (see Chapter 14, Stress: Ineffective Coping and Defense Mechanisms).

Although a child may no longer be consciously aware of these repressed feelings, they can strongly influence his or her conscious choices. These buried feelings may cause a person to experience guilt, depression, hostility, or other negative feelings that are unexplainable. The child may displace these feelings onto toys, pets, or belongings; for example, he or she may break or destroy his or her possessions or mistreat a pet.

Mature, enlightened parents should encourage their children to feel their emotions fully and to verbalize their feelings when it is appropriate. They should help them find ways of expressing their feelings that damage neither society nor the child.

◆ COMMONLY EXPERIENCED EMOTIONAL STATES

The following list includes many of the emotional states experienced by human beings. As you are reading the names of each of the states below, notice if you experience the feeling associated with it. Where in your body do you experience the feeling? Is it in your mind or in your chest, stomach, or some other part? Feeling or emotion is usually experienced in the body, rather than in the mind. Feelings are very much intertwined with the body and somatic sensations, rather than in the head, thinking, or cognitive realm. Other names for feelings are **affect** and **mood**. Affect and mood are the internal or subjective feeling states. Affect is also used to describe the feeling state that can be seen by an observer making an objective assessment.

Aggression	Hate
Anger	Homesickness
Anxiety	Hopefulness
Bitterness	Hopelessness
Boredom	Jealousy
Complacency	Joy
Curiosity	Love
Cynicism	Peace
Depression	Powerlessness
Despair	Relief
Disillusionment	Resignation
Elation	Reverence
Enthusiasm	Shame
Envy	Shyness
Fear	Smugness
Fury	Spiritual distress
Grief	Trust
Guilt	Wistfulness

ANXIETY

Anxiety is a vague and unpleasant feeling that produces many somatic effects or physical sensations in the body: tenseness, tremors, cardiovascular excitation, gastrointestinal tightening, restlessness. It causes feelings of apprehension, helplessness, and general distress. Anxiety differs from the emotion of fear, in which there is a specific, identifiable cause. When a person is anxious, he or she is not able to identify the focus or reason for the emotional distress. Until the cause of anxiety is identified, the feeling will continue as an unspecific and unpleasant physical and mental state.

FEAR

Fear is a feeling of dread associated with a specific cause that is identifiable. The feeling is accompanied by a subjective experience of psychological distress. If the fear is acute, normal problem-solving abilities are often diminished. A person may feel overwhelmed about being able to engage in problem solving to address the cause of the fear and to modify or change the contributing conditions.

The physiologic responses to fear include an increase in heart rate and blood pressure; dilation of pupils; and vasoconstriction of peripheral blood vessels, resulting in whitening or blanching of the skin accompanied by a decrease in skin temperature. With acute fear, the person's neuromuscular responses may be "frozen," disorganized, or uncoordinated. The change in body coordination and organization is matched by a mental state of disorganization.

ANGER

Anger is an inborn emotional reaction to loss. In its most basic response, it stimulates the individual to retrieve or recover what was lost or to obtain what he or she wants to have. This can include the newborn infant who "loses" the nipple while nursing; the 6-month-old infant who drops his or her toy; the 2-year-old who wants a cookie; the adolescent who is angry about not being trusted to borrow the family car; the family that must go on welfare; or the individual who is forced into early retirement.

The physiologic responses to the emotion depend on the type of anger being experienced. There are two predominant patterns of anger: active, organized anger and helpless anger. Active anger is a physical and mental state in which the individual feels energized to use the angry feeling to correct the "wrong" or to retrieve what was lost. The person experiences the loss as a challenge that he or she has the power or strength to address. During the state of active or organized anger a person feels in mental control, there is a heightening of skin color, respirations become fuller, and the blood pressure and pulse are decreased.

Helpless anger, on the other hand, is a distressing feeling. The individual perceives that he or she is unable to address the cause of his or her anger and feels disempowered. This experience is similar to that of powerlessness described below. In the state of helpless anger, the individual feels emotionally overwhelmed and disorganized. Breathing becomes rapid and shallow; the pupils dilate; systolic and diastolic blood pressure are elevated; the person appears pale because skin temperature is decreased due to vasoconstriction of the peripheral capillaries.

AGGRESSION

Just what is aggression? Karl Menninger, in his book *Man Against Himself,* defines **aggression** as an emotion compounded of frustration and hate or rage. It is an emotion deeply rooted in every one of us, a vital part of our emotional being that must be either projected outward on the environment or inward, destructively, on the self.

Menninger likens hate to an ugly, gray stone wall that is softened in time by love. Love is compared to a creeping mantle of green ivy that covers the ugly starkness of the stone, turning it into a thing of beauty. He postulates that hate and frustration appear first in personality growth, followed by the appearance of love as we mature. Hate never completely disappears, however. It shows itself in various aggressive disguises and even, on occasion, in frankness when our controls slip.

Aggression becomes apparent in the infant shortly after birth. In the child's prenatal life, all of its needs are met, but with the advent of birth, its comfort is violently shattered. It is this birth trauma that supposedly sets the pattern for all subsequent frustration anxieties. As the infant becomes hungry, cold, wet, and uncomfortable, he or she exhibits rage by crying, stiffening, and contracting muscles. The skin flushes a deep red color, and the infant may hold his or her breath.

As the baby grows older, he or she exhibits increasing rage when needs are not met. He or she may have temper tantrums, scream, hold his or her breath, scratch, strike out, throw and smash toys and other articles within reach, bite, pinch, kick, whine, and refuse to comply with instructions or admonitions. Still later, he or she may run away, use angry or abusive language, spit, or soil himself or herself intentionally. The child is narcissistic and wants his or her own way. This is common, frequently encountered behavior in the normal small child. It is a display of frank, uninhibited aggression.

The ego begins to defend itself by using defense mechanisms that operate at an unconscious level to control the unpleasant feelings of anxiety and anger. Depending on the developing ego strength of the child, these mechanisms can either help or hinder further personality development.

Outward Aggression

Progressively, these manifestations of aggression will be met by environmental controls, such as parents, other family members, and caregivers who start curbing temper tantrums and destructive behavior. The child resents restrictions and demands and his or her hostility builds. This feeling of hostility is accompanied by, or followed by, a deep feeling of guilt.

In addition to guilt feelings, the child fears the loss of love and approval of the those who are significant to him or her. Additionally, the child expects to be punished when he or she is disobedient. The small child learns to modify his or her behavior to conform to the demands of family and, later, to conform to the expected norms of society. Slowly he or she learns to build up a set of inner controls, and as self-judgment or conscience develops in the child, he or she learns to differentiate between right and wrong.

HOPELESSNESS

Hopelessness is a self-perception in which individuals believe that they have no choices or alternatives in their current life situations. The belief that they are helpless to meet their own needs and change their circumstances continues to support the experience of hopelessness.

One of the adaptive needs of human beings is to feel that they have some measure of control over their own feelings as well as their functioning in the environment in which they live. Hopelessness is a state of perceiving that one has no control. It becomes a very limiting factor in having the energy to change or the belief that change from the current state is possible.

It is normal for all individuals to experience feelings of hopelessness occasionally. Usually, however, the perception motivates the person to view their current experience from a different perspective. The ability to change perspective in most cases will increase the level of energy to change, as well as the belief that change is possible.

When a feeling of hopelessness persists beyond 2 weeks, depression often results. The symptoms of depression are described in Chapter 24, Mood Disorders. Many of the factors described in the experience of hopelessness are also present in the state of powerlessness.

POWERLESSNESS

Powerlessness is a self-perception that one's own actions cannot change the outcome of a current negative life situation. Usually a person can recognize that change is needed, but feels incapable of making it happen. The feeling is often accompanied by a physical and mental experience of lacking the energy or strength to create a different outcome.

BOX 12-1. THE CONTINUUM OF CONTROL

PERCEPTIONS OF CONTROL

In Control
The perception that one has choices and is able to create change in his or
   her psychological state or current life circumstances

Powerlessness
The perception that one's actions cannot effect changes in outcome

Hopelessness
The perception that one's needs have no potential to be met

The differences between the subjective states of hopelessness and
powerlessness, showing the continuum from the experiences of control
to powerlessness and hopelessness, are shown in Box 12-1.

SPIRITUAL DISTRESS

Spiritual distress is a fundamental distress within the self that leads one
to question the meaning of one's life. As with other forms of emotional
distress, this type of deep personal questioning is a normal human response. Personal growth and development are often motivated by this
type of personal introspection. When the process consumes a significant amount of one's day and persists for a period beyond a few weeks,
it is possible that it can undermine effective coping and lead to prolonged spiritual distress.

When spiritual distress occurs, a person expresses concern about
the meaning of one's life, for example, the presence or absence of a belief in God, the meaning of suffering and pain, or the value of living.
The normal religious practices that may previously have been valuable
and meaningful may now be perceived as meaningless.

Prolonged spiritual distress that does not gradually move to
deeper understanding or acceptance can eventually lead to the experience of hopelessness, described earlier. As with hopelessness, if the experience of spiritual distress does not lead to a different level of understanding or insight, depression can occur.

C H A P T E R   1 2   S U M M A R Y

■ Emotions are feeling states that involve both physical and psychological changes. They are powerful motivators of behavior.

■ The fight or flight syndrome is a physical response to emotions related to challenge or threat. It prepares the body for aggression (fight) or to escape from the perceived danger (flight).

■ A major human task is learning to control emotions.

■ Children learn to repress emotions that they learn are unacceptable. Even though the emotion is no longer visible, it can continue to exert an influence on the child's behavior.

■ Anxiety is a vague, unpleasant feeling that produces physical sensations such as tension and increased heart rate. An anxious person often cannot identify the reason for the emotional distress.

■ Fear is the result of a specific, identifiable cause. The physiologic reactions may be very similar to anxiety.

■ Anger is an inborn, instinctive emotional reaction to loss.

■ Aggression is a combination of frustration and hate or rage. Outward manifestations of this emotion in children are usually met by the controls of family; children learn to modify the aggressive behavior.

■ Directing aggression inward is often the result of strong guilt feelings and is theorized to be a possible causative factor in both physical and psychological disorders.

■ Pathologic forms of inwardly directed aggression include antisocial behavior, sexual impotence and frigidity, criminality, and various forms of self-mutilation.

■ Three perceptions people have about control are in control (one has choices), powerlessness (one's actions cannot effect changes), and hopelessness (one's needs have no potential to be met).

■ All people occasionally have a sense of powerlessness. However, if these feelings persist, they often lead to depression.

CHAPTER 12 QUESTIONS

1. The fight or flight syndrome
   a. does not apply to humans.
   b. is a physical response that prepares a person for aggression or escape.
   c. drains the body of adrenaline.
   d. is caused by anger but not by fear.

2. Children who repress
   a. push unpleasant or unacceptable thoughts and feelings into the unconscious.

b. have behavior that can be strongly influenced by the repressed feelings.
c. are reacting to cultural or parental standards of socially acceptable behavior.
d. all of the above.

3. The primary difference between fear and anxiety is
   a. the degree of psychological distress.
   b. only fear causes a physiologic response.
   c. fear results from a specific, identifiable cause while anxiety is vague; its cause often cannot be identified.
   d. anxiety is a more serious concern.

4. Anger is an inborn emotional reaction to
   a. loss.
   b. birth.
   c. siblings.
   d. shame.

BIBLIOGRAPHY

Barry, P.D. (1991). An investigation of cardiovascular, respiratory, and skin temperature changes during relaxation and anger inductions. *Dissertation Abstracts International, 52-09-B,* 5012.

Barry, P.D. (1996). *Psychosocial nursing: Care of physically ill patients and their families* (3rd ed.). Philadelphia: Lippincott-Raven.

Freud, S. (1914). On the history of the psychoanalytic movement. In Freud, S. (1959). *Collected papers,* Vol. 1. New York: Basic Books (*The ego and the id.* [1927]. London: Hogarth Press).

Kaplan, H.I., & Sadock, B.J. (1995). *Comprehensive textbook of psychiatry/VI* (6th ed.). Baltimore: Williams & Wilkins.

Kubler-Ross, E. (1981). *Living with death and dying.* New York: Macmillan.

Lego, S. (1996). *Psychiatric nursing: A comprehensive reference* (2nd ed.). Philadelphia: Lippincott-Raven.

NANDA's definitions and classifications, 1995-1996. St. Louis: North American Nursing Diagnosis Association.

Shives, L.R. (Ed.). (1994). *Basic concepts of psychiatric mental health nursing* (3rd ed.). Philadelphia: J.B. Lippincott.

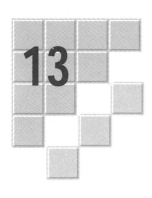

Stress: Effective Coping and Adaptation

Behavioral Objectives

After reading this chapter the student will be able to:

■ Define the words **stress** and **stressor**.

■ Define coping and name the three stages of the coping process described by Lazarus.

■ List the three ways the mind judges events or occurrences in its monitoring process.

■ Describe the action of neurotransmitters as they relate to stress.

■ Describe the three major realms of psychological functioning that are affected by stress and name five responses under each.

■ Define **adaptation**.

■ Explain why an event that causes a change in a person's life causes stress.

Stress is a word in common use today. Many people believe that the world is becoming increasingly stressful. Indeed, it seems that the rapid changes in the world have had a strong impact on social systems and the individuals who comprise them. The word **stress** is used in two ways. The first refers to the subjective feeling of tension experienced in the physiologic, intellectual, and emotional realms as a response to environmental events that are perceived as threatening. The second use of the word commonly refers to those environmental events that result in internal feelings of stress. Actually, the correct word to use when describing a threatening environmental event is **stressor.**

◆ THE COPING PROCESS

PSYCHOLOGICAL STRESS

Coping refers to the way the mind responds to awarenesses that are challenging or threatening. It is important to be aware that an event perceived as threatening by one person may be a challenge to another, and be perceived by a third person as quite normal. For example, an experienced pilot does not usually feel psychological distress when sitting at the controls. An experienced student pilot may feel the challenge of sitting behind the controls, whereas a neophyte student of flying may feel a high level of psychological distress when the time to solo arrives. It is the difference in these individuals that causes the differences in their responses. In addition to the psychological uniqueness of the meaning of flying a plane to the three pilots, there are differences in their physiologic responses to the event of piloting. These differences create an internal subjective reaction that can never be identical for any two people.

Because of the different subjective experiences of stress, it follows that coping responses are also uniquely different. Coping is the result of the exquisite interplay of perceptions of stressful events, the psychological meaning attributed to them, and the physiologic responses associated with that meaning.

At the same time that the mind is monitoring all of these external and internal awarenesses, it gradually uses a variety of mechanisms to adapt to the stress associated with them. Some of these are unconscious devices, called defense mechanisms; they operate automatically. (Defense mechanisms are described in Chapter 14.) The person also engages in active, conscious problem solving about the distress. These solutions, usually ones that have worked in the past, are called coping devices.

As a person adapts to his or her internal feelings of stress, the mind modifies its awareness of both internal and external steps that make up the coping process. The mind constantly monitors the environment in order to provide safety. Another word for monitoring is appraising.

Richard Lazarus has described the steps involved in the appraisal process. The three possible outcomes of **primary appraisal** are as follows:

1. The event is unimportant and can be ignored.
2. The event is good and contains no threat.
3. The event is potentially or already threatening owing to one or more causes:
   a. It is harming the psyche or has resulted in a significant change in self-esteem, relationships, role, or physical health.
   b. It contains a threat that one of the events described above could occur.
   c. It may be a challenging rather than a threatening event if mastery results in a positive outcome.

The next step in this process is called **secondary appraisal.** During this stage, the mind decides whether it is OK or in trouble. If the mind experiences anxiety about the situation, it will automatically use defense mechanisms to regulate the unpleasant emotion associated with the awareness. In addition, during this state the individual can ask, "What can I do to help myself?" This is the time when conscious coping strategies are used by the person. For example, a college freshman feeling overwhelmed by all the new experiences may decide on any one of several options to reduce stress—to begin jogging, drop one difficult course, talk it out with his or her parents over the telephone, or any number of other stress-relieving activities.

The mind is continuously evaluating the outcome of its coping efforts and is ready to develop new strategies if those currently in use are not working. This is called **reappraisal.**

PHYSIOLOGIC STRESS

Adaptation involves both a psychological and physiologic state of well-being. With increased research on the effects of neurotransmitters on the body, scientists are rapidly learning that it is impossible to separate the mind and body in assessing a person's health status. The most commonly known neurotransmitter is adrenaline. Think for a moment about what effects adrenaline causes in the body during an extremely angry moment or close call while driving. Awareness of the danger of a near-accident is experienced through the perceptual sphere of our psychological system. Anger is experienced through the emotional sphere of our psychological system. Both experiences, however, have strong physiologic effects. They include elevations in pulse and respirations, slowing of digestion, and so on.

Neurotransmitters are the bridge between the mind and body.

They are biochemical substances released in the central nervous system that send messages through the sympathetic nervous system to all body organs and muscles. Researchers in the field of neurobiochemistry have currently identified more than 100 such substances, all having different effects within the body. Scientists expect they will increasingly be recognized as significant players in the mediation of stress and the development of many, if not most, physical illnesses.

GENERAL ADAPTATION SYNDROME

When coping efforts are not successful, the result is a subjective feeling of anxiety and concurrent physiologic symptoms of stress. These phys-

---

BOX 13-1.   GENERAL RESPONSES TO STRESS

BODY RESPONSES

Increased heart rate	Headache
Increased blood pressure	Backache
Indigestion	Nausea
Diarrhea	Constipation
Decreased appetite	Increased appetite
Tightness in chest	Clenching of jaw, neck, shoulders, and arms
Prone to colds, flu	Difficulty breathing
Urinary frequency	Sneezing
Prone to accidents	Insomnia

MIND RESPONSES

Cognitive

Forgetfulness	Decreased concentration
Math and spelling errors	Blocking
Preoccupation	Decreased attention to details

Emotional

Anxiety	Being close to tears
Depression	Angry outbursts
Feelings of worthlessness	Suspiciousness
Self-criticism	Jealousy

SPIRITUAL RESPONSES

Decreased interest	Loss of sense of inner vitality
Decreased hope	Loss of sense of inner calm
Decreased connectedness with others	Loss of sense of connectedness to God or higher force
Decreased creativity	Loss of enthusiasm or motivation
Loss of capacity to feel joy	Withdrawal
Isolation	

ical symptoms occur as the result of neurotransmitter stimulation, described earlier. Hans Selye, known as the "father of stress research," described the physiologic responses to stress in a concept called the **general adaptation syndrome** (GAS). The GAS includes the following three stages:

1. The alarm reaction—the body responds to a stressor with a strong defensive response stimulated by hormones from the adrenal cortex. This decreases to a steady and consistent physiologic stress response. If the stressor is not withdrawn, the body moves to the next stage.

2. The stage of resistance—the body maintains resistance to the stressor until it disappears. If the stressor does not disappear, the body moves to the next stage.

3. The stage of exhaustion—the effects of the continuing stressor cause the body's resistance ability to fail. Ultimately, without medical intervention, death will occur.

The human psyche and body are well-designed to endure the effects of stress. Realistically, however, they are limited in their ability to tolerate severe, unremitting stress. Eventually a point arrives at which either the mind or the body is unable to continue providing resistance to either environmental or intrapsychic stress. When this happens, the person can become physically or mentally ill.

Box 13-1 presents the many responses that normal individuals experience when they are under stress. When people are under acute stress they often feel as though they are out of control. This is because normal functioning is altered in many ways.

◆ THE EFFECTS OF COPING ON MENTAL AND PHYSICAL HEALTH

As nursing examines the effects of stress on physical and mental disease processes, coping has been identified as a critical factor that influences the potential for wellness or disease. Coping is the response to a demand or threat.

In 1980, the American Nurses Association described nursing as "the diagnosis and treatment of human responses to actual or potential health problems." Since 1980, nursing philosophy and practice have been influenced by a greater elaboration of the science of caring and its integration with the traditional knowledge base for diagnosis and treatment of human responses to health and illness. The word *response* is a term that encompasses the concept of coping. Ideally, when a person is challenged or threatened by environmental stressors, he or she will have a variety of resources present that support healthy, effective coping. The resources that assist in an effective coping response include the following:

- Good problem-solving ability
- Prior experience with the stressor
- Adequate knowledge about the cause of the stressor
- Available support system, such as family, friends, and so on
- Adequate sleep, nutrition, and physical hygiene to support normal mental and physical functioning.

If an individual is challenged or threatened by a stressful event and is unable to cope, he or she experiences psychological stress. If the stressful feeling is severe, it is possible that a mental disorder can occur. The primary cause of many types of mental disorders is ineffective coping.

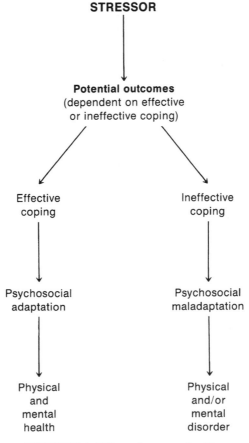

FIGURE 13–1. Effects of stress on health.

When mental or physical disease is present, the demands on an individual are greater. Effective coping becomes yet another demand on a person who is already weakened by the mental or physical condition. The role of a mental health nurse is to provide support that assists with effective immediate and long-term coping.

ADAPTATION

Adaptation is the process of coping effectively with one's social environment so that growth and development proceed in a way that supports healthy social relationships, good self-esteem, and ongoing positive challenge. Psychosocial adaptation, as described in Chapter 7, Building a Person-Centered Therapeutic Relationship, is the ability of an individual to perceive reality and respond to it in a way that supports his or her own emotional and physical well-being and that of others in the environment. All of these characteristics of adaptation are built on the foundation of effective coping. When ineffective coping occurs, it is the foundation of psychosocial maladaptation. Concepts relating to ineffective coping will be addressed in Chapter 14, Stress: Ineffective Coping and Defense Mechanisms. The relationship between stress, coping, and adaptation can be seen in Figure 13-1.

◆ LIFE EVENTS THAT CAUSE STRESS

An important factor in the level of stress a person feels is the number of events in his or her life that are causing change. A person whose life is more or less routine—whose personal life and working life are stable and without change or conflict—undergoes relatively low levels of stress. In the current world of frequent change in the structure of family and workplace, very few people find this to be so. In fact, it is not uncommon to find that one life change often precipitates other life changes.

With the knowledge that stress is experienced in direct relationship to the number of life changes one is undergoing, it is possible to understand that an accumulating series of changes can intensify until one more new change becomes "the straw that breaks the camel's back." For example, if a woman is promoted to a new position in another city, she will usually encounter the following changes:

- Leaving a workplace where she is secure and has many acquaintances
- Moving to a new workplace where she must take on new responsibilities, usually before she is fully oriented and before she knows her new supervisors, peers, or subordinates

◆ TABLE 13–1. Social Readjustment Rating Scale

Item Number	Life Event (Item Value)*
1	Death of spouse (100)
2	Divorce (73)
3	Marital separation (65)
4	Jail term (63)
5	Death of close family member (63)
6	Personal injury or illness (53)
7	Marriage (50)
8	Fired at work (47)
9	Marital reconciliation (45)
10	Retirement (45)
11	Change in health of a family member (44)
12	Pregnancy (40)
13	Sex difficulties (39)
14	Gain of a new family member (39)
15	Business readjustment (39)
16	Change in financial state (39)
17	Death of a close friend (37)
18	Change to a different line of work (36)
19	Change in number of arguments with spouse (35)
20	Mortgage over $10,000 (31)
21	Foreclosure of mortgage or loan (30)
22	Change in responsibilities at work (29)
23	Son or daughter leaving home (29)
24	Trouble with in-laws (29)
25	Outstanding personal achievement (28)
26	Spouse begins or stops work (26)
27	Begin or end of school (26)
28	Change in living conditions (25)
29	Revision of personal habits (24)
30	Trouble with boss (23)
31	Change in work hours or conditions (20)
32	Change in residence (20)
33	Change in schools (20)
34	Change in recreation (19)
35	Change in church activities (19)
36	Change in social activities (18)
37	Mortgage or loan less than $10,000 (17)
38	Change in sleeping habits (16)
39	Change in number of family gatherings (15)
40	Change in eating habits (15)
41	Vacation (13)
42	Christmas (12)
43	Minor violations of the law (11)

* Signifies the numerical point value assigned to each stressor.
Holmes, R., Rahe R.H. (1967). The social readjustment rating scale. *Journal of Psychosomatic Research 11*, 213–218.

- Leaving a home that she may need to sell or breaking a lease
- Hunting for a new home, which is usually more costly
- Moving her possessions
- Leaving her friends and moving to a new area with no immediate family or other sources of support
- Arranging for new telephone installation, changes of addresses to all friends, creditors, magazines, and so on

Can you see that what initially sounds like a positive event can actually cause an individual to experience increasing levels of stress? Holmes and Rahe, researchers in the field of stress, developed an assessment scale on which they established point values for the specific events the study participants reported as most stressful. The events and the points assigned to each appear in Table 13-1. The researchers found that when the study participants' stress points totaled more than 300, they frequently developed physical or mental illness.*

◆ EFFECTIVE COPING TECHNIQUES

Researchers on coping have identified a number of effective coping factors, which will be described later. The use of nursing skills that draw on these factors can be helpful to clients with mental disorders.

The value of worry. The experience of worrying about an upcoming threatening event can often be a trigger to effective coping. The important factor is how much worrying. A moderate level of worry is usually adaptive. For example, a person who is not worried about an upcoming serious event, such as coronary bypass surgery, may not be adequately prepared psychologically and may be overwhelmed just prior to surgery or during the immediate postoperative period.

The moderately worried person, on the other hand, engages in a variety of adaptive activities to decrease his or her mental distress. They include asking questions of the physician, talking with others who have had the surgery, problem solving about how to cope, and expressing concern about the surgery to family members and friends. Accordingly, they receive extra social support. The highly worried person is usually

---

*Although unvalidated, my own finding in using this scale in stress workshops is that many people today experience stress at the 300-point level without developing physical or mental illness. This may be the result of general adaptation to the increasing levels of stressors in our society during the 30 years since the original studies of Holmes and Rahe. A word of caution, however. Individuals who are experiencing stress at 300 or at a higher level should become familiar with events listed on the Holmes and Rahe scale. They would be wise to review future decisions carefully in order to reduce or delay current or anticipated changes that could introduce further stress and seriously compromise coping abilities.

overwhelmed with anxiety to the point that he or she does few or none of the steps described above.

Focusing on the objective, concrete aspects of a current or anticipated threatening event. Usually, when a person is undergoing a difficult time, it is helpful for him or her to gather as much information as possible about what to expect. The information includes specific elements, for example, answers to specific questions such as: How long will this last? What will be going on around me? What will I see, hear, taste, smell, and so on? What is causing this to happen? What do other people do to cope with this situation?

Generally, it can be helpful for the person to obtain objective, concrete, realistic answers to these questions. Long, involved answers are not necessary. Complicated answers sometimes can generate more anxiety. Brief answers that provide specific elements of information can regulate emotional responses or stimulate problem solving.

The nurse can provide information so that an individual can judge how well he or she can perform or respond to specific types of events. When individuals have information about how to take care of themselves, they usually feel more able to cope with new types of situations. Realistically, in new situations most people don't know what they don't know! Accordingly, an empathic caregiver may be able to anticipate the specific aspects of the new situation that are likely to be anxiety provoking and share that information.

Effective coping is essential to good health, both physically and mentally. The next chapter describes information about what happens when normal coping efforts are not successful.

CHAPTER 13 SUMMARY

- Stress refers to the subjective feeling of tension in response to environmental events that are perceived as threatening. These events are called stressors.

- Coping refers to how the mind responds to awareness of potential threats.

- An event perceived as threatening by one person may not be threatening to another person. Likewise, coping mechanisms vary from person to person.

- Defense mechanisms are unconscious and operate automatically. Coping devices are conscious and are usually based on successful previous experience.

- Neurotransmitters are chemicals released in the body that trigger physical responses such as elevated pulse and respiration and slowed digestion. The most commonly known neurotransmitter is adrenaline, which is released in response to anger or fear.

■ The general adaptation syndrome (GAS) developed by Hans Selye includes three progressive stages: alarm, resistance, and exhaustion.

■ Coping has been identified as a critical factor that influences the potential for wellness or disease. Ineffective coping mechanisms are the primary cause of mental disorders.

■ Resources that assist an effective coping response include the following:
— Good problem-solving ability
— Prior experience with the stressor
— Adequate knowledge of the stressor's cause
— Availability of a support system
— Adequate sleep, nutrition, and physical hygiene

■ Adaptation refers to coping effectively with one's environment, resulting in growth and development that support healthy social relationships and good self-esteem.

■ Stress is experienced in direct relationship to the number of life changes a person is currently undergoing and the availability of personal resources.

■ Effective coping mechanisms are a slight to moderate level of *worrying* and *focusing* on the objective or concrete aspects of a threatening event.

CHAPTER 13 QUESTIONS

1. The difference between stress and stressor is
   a. one is more severe than the other.
   b. stress is a feeling and stressor is the event that causes it.
   c. just a matter of adjustment.
   d. stressors are more emotionally based.

2. The ultimate effect of unrelieved stress is
   a. a lessening of the stress.
   b. periodic resistance.
   c. death.
   d. increased physical energy.

3. Which of the following contributes to an effective coping response?
   a. Available support system
   b. Good problem-solving ability and prior experience with the stressor

    c. Adequate sleep and nutrition

    d. All of the above

4. Worry is

    a. a way of rehearsing a reaction to an upcoming stressful event.

    b. seldom a trigger for effective coping.

    c. most useful if it is constant.

    d. usually a sign of serious neurosis.

BIBLIOGRAPHY

Barry, P.D. (1996). *Psychosocial nursing: Care of physically ill patients and their families* (3rd ed.). Philadelphia: Lippincott-Raven.

Holmes, R., & Rahe, R. (1967). The social adjustment rating scale. *Journal of Psychosomatic Research, 11,* 13.

Kaplan, H.I., & Sadock, B.J. (1995). *Comprehensive textbook of psychiatry/VI* (6th ed.). Baltimore: Williams & Wilkins.

McFarland, G.K., Wasli, E.L., & Gerety, E.K. (1996). *Nursing diagnoses and process in psychiatric mental health nursing* (3rd ed.). Philadelphia: Lippincott-Raven.

NANDA's definitions and classifications, 1995–1996. St. Louis: North American Nursing Diagnosis Association.

Nettina, S.M. (1996). *The Lippincott manual of nursing practice* (6th ed.). Philadelphia: Lippincott-Raven.

Nursing social policy statement. (1995). Kansas City, MO: American Nurses Association.

Standards of clinical nursing practice. (1991). Kansas City, MO: American Nurses Association.

Weisman, A. (1997). Coping with illness. In N.H. Cassem (Ed.). *Massachusetts General Hospital handbook of general hospital psychiatry* (4th ed.). St. Louis: Mosby Year Book.

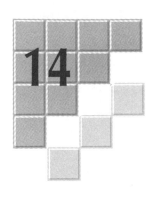

Stress: Ineffective Coping and Defense Mechanisms

Behavioral Objectives

After reading this chapter the student will be able to:

- Explain the American Nurses Association's definition of nursing practice.

- Describe the role of ineffective coping in the conditions included in nursing diagnosis categories.

- Name the feeling that triggers the use of **defense mechanisms**.

- List the four levels of defense mechanisms and the names of two defense mechanisms within each category.

- Explain the use of **denial** and give an example of ineffective denial.

- Describe the differences and similarities between **repression** and **suppression**.

The American Nurses Association has described nursing practice as the diagnosis and treatment of the human response to illness. The term **response** can be described as a reaction to a stimulus. It can also be generalized to include the concept of coping as a response to a stimulus or event. Effective coping has been identified as a factor that is essential to mental and physical health.

During the 1970s a group of nurses met to develop a list of the types of health problems that nurses are prepared to diagnose and treat in their clinical practices. The list they created was named the Taxonomy of Nursing Diagnosis. The nursing group, called the North American Nursing Diagnosis Association (NANDA), meets every 2 years to review the list and to add new diagnostic categories. Currently, the list includes 9 patterns and 128 conditions.

More than half of these conditions are psychosocial in nature. Most of the psychosocial category titles are very specific. They include such names as Social Isolation, Altered Parenting, Self-Esteem Disturbance, and so on. Additional categories include psychosocial factors, for example, Sleep Pattern Disturbance, Altered Health Maintenance, and Altered Sexuality Patterns.

In all of the NANDA categories that involve a problem with psychosocial adaptation, ineffective coping is occurring. Indeed, ineffective coping is an umbrella term or comprehensive concept that is a fundamental factor in all mental disorders and all psychosocial-related nursing diagnoses.

Coping is the combination of conscious problem-solving strategies and unconscious defense mechanisms that result in the cognitive and behavioral responses to challenging or threatening events. The factors that comprise effective coping were described in the previous chapter.

◆ THE USE AND PURPOSE OF DEFENSE MECHANISMS

The use of defense mechanisms by the mind is an unconscious process; that is, the mind automatically activates them when the conscious coping techniques are unable to manage the anxiety or threat of the threatening event.

Because adaptation is a fundamental requirement of coping with life's demands, it is natural that humans have developed unconscious defense mechanisms that increase their sense of security, protect their self-esteem, and assist in solving their emotional dilemmas. The self-conscious personality, with its intense need for security and self-esteem, evokes protective mental defenses as instinctively as self-preservation prompts protection against physical harm. Anxiety is part of life from the cradle to the grave. Everyone, to a greater or lesser degree, employs defense mechanisms to ensure comfort and defend against anxiety. A study of these mechanisms is essential to understanding human behavior and should lead to a clearer recognition of the forces operating in the psyche.

Some defense mechanisms, if employed within certain adaptive limits, may help to promote a sound or generally "healthy" personality. If used excessively, however, defense mechanisms may lead to a personality distortion. The maladaptive use of defense mechanisms can progressively disorganize the personality.

Defense mechanisms are unconscious and automatic mental maneuvers that decrease the unpleasant feeling of anxiety. These mechanisms begin operating in early childhood. Different types of these adaptive defense mechanisms appear as the child matures.

Depending on the level of stress a person is experiencing, the mind will shut out all or part of a painful awareness. Generally speaking, the defense mechanisms that develop early in life are used by adults only when severe stress occurs or when a person has a low tolerance for stress. The higher-level, more mature mechanisms develop as the personality matures. They are used when the level of stress being experienced is low to moderate.

◆ TYPES OF DEFENSE MECHANISMS

Defense mechanisms are classified by the age at which they appear in the child, the amount of reality they block, and the level of pathology they can cause if used excessively. In this section the defenses seen most commonly in the mental health care setting will be discussed. In addition, examples of maladaptive use of these defenses will be given to illustrate their effect on personality and their potential to cause mental disorder.

NARCISSISTIC DEFENSE MECHANISMS
(BIRTH TO 3 YEARS)

The term **narcissistic** is used to refer to a person who is self-centered in a very immature way. The word is derived from the Greek myth about Narcissus, a very handsome young man who fell in love with the reflection of his face in a pond. It is normal for toddlers and young children to be self-centered, but as the child develops, he or she should gradually develop the capacity to be aware of others as well as self. Narcissistic defense mechanisms develop as the earliest defense mechanisms. These defenses are denial, distortion, and delusional projection. They are employed by the healthy adult mind only during periods of extreme stress. When used routinely in the older adolescent or adult, they contribute to the development of severe forms of mental disorders, such as schizophrenia.

Denial is the first defense used in infancy. It remains available as the strongest defense for shutting out painful awareness in the environment. The person sees, hears, or perceives an event but the mind refuses to recognize it consciously. Denial and the other two defenses in this category are used when the ego senses a severe threat.

> Tom is a married, 53-year-old man with a high-level position in a large organization. He was told by the company president that his job would be ending in 2 months. He refused to discuss the matter further. Four weeks later he was continuing to refuse discussion of his termination with his boss. He became increasingly withdrawn. He did not disclose his situation to his wife and family. His superiors at work became increasingly concerned for his well-being as he continued to shut out the reality of his employment.

Distortion is an automatic unconscious defense mechanism used to reshape external reality to reduce anxiety and restore a feeling of emotional comfort. When present in a mental disorder, it is the basis for hallucinations and nonparanoid types of delusions.

> To continue with the story of Tom, he has not had a regular savings program and has limited monetary savings. During his career he continuously told himself that he could never lose his job and would receive a plentiful monetary settlement when he retired. In essence, he deluded himself with a belief that was untrue.

Delusional projection is a mechanism by which the mind forms conclusions and beliefs that are not based on reality. These beliefs, when firmly rooted, form the basis of paranoid delusions, in which a person believes that someone is out to get him or her.

> After several weeks of using denial and distortion to quiet his unconscious psychological terror about his circumstances, the mental pressure is causing yet another serious defense mechanism to occur. While at work, Tom increasingly believes that his superiors are plotting against him, plan to injure him and eventually kill him to get rid of him. Beliefs that have no basis in reality that someone is going to purposely injure another are called **paranoia**.

The effect of chronic use of narcissistic defense mechanisms to shut out reality is often a serious mental disorder. This disorder may require hospitalization when outpatient mental health intervention either does not occur or is not successful.

IMMATURE DEFENSE MECHANISMS
(AGES 2 TO 4 YEARS)

The immature defenses develop during the toddler stage and are used by healthy adults under moderate to severe stress and by people with all types of personality disorders. **Acting out** is the behavioral outcome of conflict between an unconscious need to express anger and a conscious need to deny it.

> Ann is a 19-year-old college student who is living away from home for the first time. She has a high level of unconscious anger about emotional abuse she experienced from her mother. In relationships with women authority figures at her school, such as her freshman advisor, one of her instructors, and the dormitory monitor, she is aggressive and unreasonable. She is acting out or expressing the anger she feels toward her mother but does not consciously acknowledge.

Avoidance causes an individual unconsciously to stay away from any person, situation, or place that might cause unwanted sexual or aggressive feelings to occur.

> Because of Ann's unresolved conflict with her mother she unconsciously avoids close relationships with all women. As a result Ann is increasingly isolated in her new college environment.

Projection is a less pathologic form of delusional projection, described earlier. It occurs when a person is unable to acknowledge his or her own thoughts or feelings and attributes them to others.

> When Ann's freshman advisor asks to meet with her, Ann is quiet and sullen. When her advisor asks what is wrong, Ann looks at her and angrily says, "I know you don't like me."

Regression occurs when the ego is unable to tolerate severe intrapsychic or environmental stress. As a way of reducing anxiety, a person's psychosocial functioning returns to an earlier developmental stage.

> In her family Ann was very dependent on her father and frequently acted childlike when she was with him. Now that she is away at college she has begun to visit a senior male student from her home town. He is becoming irritated with her frequent unexpected visits and her requests for assistance and counsel.

The chronic use of immature defense mechanisms, while not as seriously maladaptive as narcissistic defenses, indicates major developmental and adaptation problems. Without modification of the defenses that Ann is using, she is at risk for depression, anxiety disorder, or other types of mental disorders related to her inability to cope adaptively with her new living conditions.

NEUROTIC DEFENSE MECHANISMS

Neurotic defenses can cause a significant level of psychological distress, but usually do not result in the need for psychiatric hospitalization. If neurotic defenses cause some form of ineffective coping with a significant life event, it is possible that major forms of depression or anxiety may result. Descriptions of neurotic defenses appear below.

Displacement occurs when feelings about a person or thing are shifted to another, safer object. Although the feelings are shifted, their original cause remains the same. For example, when a person is angry at the boss he or she may go home and become angry with a family member or play an extra hard game of tennis. **Identification** is a defense mechanism that results in a person taking on the thoughts, feelings, or particular circumstances of another person as if they were his or her own. For example, an expectant father may develop symptoms of morning sickness similar to those of his pregnant wife.

Isolation is a defense mechanism that separates the emotion associated with a thought. The emotion is repressed, however. For example, a nurse may be working closely with a dying client and be able to acknowledge that the person's symptoms indicate he or she is near death. Although very attached to the client, the nurse may not experience the grief associated with this awareness until a later time. Other names for isolation are **intellectualization** and **rationalization.**

Reaction formation is a defense mechanism that is also known as **compensation.** It is used when a thought, feeling, or impulse is unacceptable to the conscious mind. As a result, the defense causes the person to behave in the exact opposite manner. A person who has had an amputation, for example, may feel deep rage toward the surgeon, but when the doctor enters the room, the client is very cordial. **Repression** is sometimes considered to be one of the most important defense mechanisms. It causes the anxiety associated with any distressing internal awareness to be stored away in the unconscious. Without the capacity to repress painful thoughts, feelings, and memories, humans could be overwhelmed by them.

MATURE DEFENSE MECHANISMS

These defense mechanisms are used by the healthy, mature ego when it is under minimal stress. These defenses have a larger conscious component than the defense mechanisms described previously. Because of their conscious component, mature individuals often use them as conscious coping devices when they recognize they are experiencing stress. These mechanisms develop during the middle and later years of childhood. They include **altruism,** which is a defense that channels the desire to satisfy one's own needs into the wish to meet the needs of others. **Anticipation** is a defense by which a person intellectually and emotionally acknowledges an upcoming situation that is expected to provoke anxiety. By acknowledging it and working through some of the anxiety in advance, the event will be less stressful when it occurs.

Humor is a defense used when a person cannot fully tolerate a difficult situation. It is used without expense to the self or another person. Humor differs from **wit,** in which the actual anxiety-provoking subject is avoided. **Sublimation** operates in association with the defense of repression. In sublimation, a repressed urge or desire is expressed in a socially acceptable or useful way. **Suppression** is a defense that is similar to repression; it stores thoughts or memories in the subconscious mind where they are easily retrievable. Repression stores thoughts or memories in the unconscious where they usually remain buried and are not retrievable.

CONVERSION—AN UNCLASSIFIED DEFENSE MECHANISM

Be aware of another defense mechanism that is actually a combination of elements of other defense mechanisms. **Conversion** is a mechanism by which emotional conflicts are channeled into physical symptoms or physical illness. An example is when an individual develops chronic diarrhea or constipation as the result of emotional conflict. In conversion, the symptoms are real. Doctors are baffled, however, to explain the cause. When a physiologic basis cannot be found despite a good diagnostic workup, it is important to assess the psychological stress the client has been and is currently experiencing. The interaction between mind and body is increasingly being recognized as an important etiology in the development of physical illness. The field of **liaison psychiatry** addresses the emotional outcomes of physical illness.

 ## TYPES OF BEHAVIOR

MALADAPTIVE BEHAVIOR

Maladaptive behavior is the result of ineffective coping and psychosocial maladaptation. When ineffective coping is caused by chronic use of narcissistic or immature defenses, there can be serious behavioral problems. Maladaptive behavior usually causes severe strain in family and social relationships. Consider, for example, the behavior of Ann, discussed earlier in the chapter.

PSYCHOTIC BEHAVIOR

Psychotic behavior is the most severe manifestation of ineffective coping. It is caused by psychosis. **Psychosis** is the mental state caused by a loss of contact with reality. Usually psychosis occurs when the actual external reality is too threatening or anxiety provoking to be acknowledged. The mind unconsciously uses every defense possible to deny, distort, and avoid reality when it does not have the strength to cope consciously and problem solve about the actual problem or sets of problems that are occurring. The story of Tom illustrates the potential for psychotic behavior because of his need to shut out totally the reality about his job loss. His behavior moves into the psychotic range when he begins to fear that his coworkers are plotting against him.

The cause of mental disorder is usually related to ineffective coping. The reason why individuals with mental disorders are admitted to the hospital is to provide an environment that supports effective coping. The primary purpose of nursing care is to provide an environment where individuals can be restored to their prior effective coping level, receive medications that support coping, or learn new coping methods. The next unit describes how the nursing process in mental health care can assist clients in returning to states of mental health.

CHAPTER 14 SUMMARY

- Ineffective coping is a fundamental factor in all mental disorders and in all psychosocial-related nursing diagnoses.

- Excessive use of defense mechanisms may lead to personality distortion.

- Defense mechanisms are classified by the age at which they appear, the amount of reality they block, and the level of pathology they can cause. Major groups of defense mechanisms are narcissistic, immature, neurotic, and mature.

- Narcissistic defense mechanisms include denial, distortion, and delusional projection.

- When used routinely, narcissistic defense mechanisms cause severe forms of mental disorders such as schizophrenia.

- Immature defense mechanisms include acting out, avoidance, projection, and regression.

- Neurotic defense mechanisms include displacement, identification, rationalization, reaction formation, and repression.

- Mature defense mechanisms, used by the healthy, mature ego when it is under minimal stress, include altruism, anticipation, humor, sublimation, and suppression.

- Conversion is a mechanism in which the ego channels emotional conflict into physical symptoms.

CHAPTER 14 QUESTIONS

1. The purpose of defense mechanisms is to
   a. manage an anxiety-producing event.
   b. increase the sense of security.
   c. protect self-esteem.
   d. all of the above.

2. Which of the following is true about narcissistic defense mechanisms?
   a. They develop after the age of 4.
   b. They include distortion and denial.
   c. They are never employed by healthy adults, even under extreme stress.
   d. They never lead to serious forms of mental disorders.

3. An example of an immature defense mechanism would be
   a. rationalization.
   b. regression.
   c. repression.
   d. displacement.

4. The most severe manifestation of ineffective coping mechanisms is
   a. altruism.
   b. conversion.
   c. psychotic behavior.
   d. repression.

BIBLIOGRAPHY

Barry, P.D. (1996). *Psychosocial nursing: Care of physically ill patients and their families* (3rd ed.). Philadelphia: Lippincott-Raven.

Brooke Army Medical Center. (1973). *Interpersonal skills.*(Videocassette). Fort Sam Houston, TX: Academy of Health Sciences.

Kaplan, H.I., & Sadock, B.J. (1995). *Comprehensive textbook of psychiatry/VI* (6th ed.). Baltimore: Williams & Wilkins.

Kaplan, H.I., & Sadock, B.J. (1994). *Synopsis of psychiatry: Behavioral sciences, clinical psychology* (7th ed.). Baltimore: Williams & Wilkins.

Lazarus, R.S. (1992). Coping with the stress of illness. *WHO Regional Publication, European Series, 44*, 11–31.

McFarland, G.K., Wasli, E.L., & Gerety, E.K. (1996). *Nursing diagnoses and process in psychiatric mental health nursing* (3rd ed.). Philadelphia: Lippincott-Raven.

Nettina, S.M. (1996). *The Lippincott manual of nursing practice* (6th ed.). Philadelphia: Lippincott-Raven.

Nursing social policy statement. (1995). Kansas City, MO: American Nurses Association.

Weisman, A. (1997). Coping with illness. In N.H. Cassem (Ed.). *Massachusetts General Hospital handbook of general hospital psychiatry* (4th ed.). St. Louis: Mosby Year Book.

Woods, N.F., Habaerman, M.R., & Packard, N.J. (1993). Demands of illness and individual, dyadic, and family adaptation in chronic illness. *Western Journal of Nursing Research, 15*(1), 10–25.

Mental Status Exam

After reading this chapter the student will be able to:

- List the categories of mental status functioning.

- Name the three spheres of **orientation.**

- Describe three types of facial expressions, posture, and dress.

- Define **apraxia, akathisia, akinesia,** and **dyskinesia**.

- Name four categories of affect and give an example of one emotion in each category.

- Define thinking.

- Describe the differences between **thought content** and **thought process**.

- Name and define five types of **thought disorders.**

- Define perception.

- Name and define two types of perception disorders.

- Define **judgment.**

To work with clients who are mentally ill, it is important to understand the various ways in which the psyche can dysfunction and to be able to identify the specific symptoms that the client is displaying. First, the symptoms of mental dysfunctioning must be recognized; only then is it possible to determine the category of mental disorders the client is displaying. The treatment plan of individuals with mental disorders will be based on interventions designed to reduce or eliminate the specific symptoms described in this chapter.

A person displays his or her mental state or mental status in many ways. In our normal dealings with people, when we notice something unusual about their behavior, we may actually be seeing symptoms of an abnormal mental state. For example, when we see a person whose speech is slow and unclear, whose eyes do not focus, whose clothes are dirty and disheveled, and whose thoughts are confused, we know that something is wrong. If a person smells like alcohol, then we may begin to form an opinion about the cause of his or her abnormal mental status. If, on the other hand, there is no such odor, then we can eliminate it from a wide range of other possible causes of the person's behavior. In the psychiatric setting, it is important to view mental functioning as comprising many different categories of behavior. **Behavior** is the observable or objective sign of mental functioning.

The categories of mental status functioning are listed below.

Level of awareness and orientation

Appearance and behavior

Speech and communication

Mood or affect

Thinking

Perception

Memory

Judgment

◆ LEVEL OF AWARENESS AND ORIENTATION

Level of awareness describes the client's wakefulness or consciousness. The levels of awareness range on a continuum from unconsciousness/coma → drowsiness/somnolence → normal alertness → hyperalertness → suspiciousness → mania.

Orientation is closely related to level of awareness. Depending on a client's level of awareness, he or she may be more or less oriented. Orientation is the person's ability to identify *who* he or she is, *where* he or she is, and the date and approximate time. These three categories of orientation are known as "orientation to time, person, and place" and are often abbreviated to "oriented × 3" to describe the person who is oriented.

Orientation is a major criterion in determining a person's mental status. However, a client, particularly an elderly client, can be cognitively impaired even though he or she is oriented. Orientation by itself does not provide a complete picture of mental status.

◆ APPEARANCE AND BEHAVIOR

This category includes observable characteristics of a person, which can also be termed objective data. These include **facies** or facial expression, posture, dress, physical characteristics, motor activity, and reaction to caregiver.

Facies or facial expression includes the following types of characteristics. Pay close attention to whether or not the facies matches the emotions and content expressed by the client during his or her interactions with others. The most common types of facial expressions are as follows:

Animated

Fixed and immobile (also called masked)

Sad or depressed

Angry

Pale or reddened, and so on (coloration of face)

Gestures are the subtle physical cues that can indicate what a person is feeling. These can include a flick of a finger or hand that can indicate annoyance, anger, discouragement, and so on; a shrug of the shoulders; a firm shake of the head; and other signs that signify meaning to the observer.

Posture is the way a person holds his or her body, and it often indicates how he or she is feeling. Some posture characteristics include the following:

Relaxed

Tense

Erect

Slouching, leaning away from the caregiver

Sitting, lying, and so on

Dress refers to the way a person clothes and cares for himself or herself. The way the person dresses usually reflects the appropriateness of his or her social judgment. Some dress characteristics include the following:

Neat

Careless

Eccentric

Foul-smelling, soiled, and so on

Physical characteristics, especially the unusual appearance of any part of the body, should be described. For example, the person may have had his or her foot amputated and may have long, unkempt hair and a beard.

Motor activity, the way a person moves his or her body, is another important indication of mental status. The various types of movement include the following:

Agitation, restlessness, and so on

Tremors

Motor retardation (slow movement)

Apraxia, or inability to carry out purposeful movement to achieve a goal

Abnormal movement

> **Akathisia:** extreme restlessness
>
> **Akinesia:** complete or partial loss of muscle movement
>
> **Dyskinesia:** excessive movement of mouth, protruding tongue, facial grimacing (a common side effect of the major tranquilizers)
>
> **Parkinsonian movement:** fine tremor accompanied by muscular rigidity
>
> **Reaction to caregiver,** the way that a client relates with or responds to a caregiver; can include:

Friendly

Hostile

Suspicious

◆ SPEECH AND COMMUNICATION

In this category we are evaluating *how* the client is communicating, rather than *what* he or she is telling us. What the client is telling us is actually a reflection of his or her thinking process, which is described below. The ways in which a person's speech should be evaluated are as follows:

Rate—usually consistent with overall psychomotor status

Volume—quietness or loudness

Modulation and flow—lively or dispirited

Production—ability to produce words

Also included in this section are nonverbal forms of communication. These include facial expression, gesture, and posture, described in the previous section. It is a matter of choice whether they are described under communication or behavior.

◆ MOOD OR AFFECT

Affect refers to a person's display of emotion or feelings he or she is experiencing. **Mood** is the subjective way a client explains his or her feelings. Actually, the two words can be used interchangeably to describe the feelings associated with thoughts about situations. The following list with accompanying descriptions includes only those emotional states that are considered beyond the normal range.

Inappropriate affects

Unexpected responses to a given situation

Discussion content that does not fit with accompanying emotions

Pleasurable affects

Euphoria—excessive and inappropriate feeling of well-being

Exaltation—intense elation accompanied by feelings of grandeur

Unpleasurable affects (**dysphoria**)

Depression—hopeless feeling of sadness; grief or mourning; prolonged and excessive sadness associated with a loss

Anxiety—feeling of apprehension that is caused by conflicts that the client is unable to identify

Fear—excessive fright of consciously recognized danger

Agitation—anxiety associated with severe motor restlessness

Ambivalence—alternating and opposite feelings occurring in the same person about the same object

Aggression—rage, anger, or hostility that is excessive or seems unrelated to a person's current situation

Mood swings (also called **lability**)—alternating periods of elation and depression or anxiety in the same person within a limited time period

Lack of affect

Blunted or **flat affect**—normal range of emotions is missing; commonly seen in people with depression, some forms of schizophrenia, and some types of organic brain syndrome; can be seen in people whose personalities are tightly controlled, where it is termed **constricted** to describe both feeling and the whole personality

La belle indifference—of French derivation, meaning "the beautiful lack of concern" and used to describe lack of worry in a difficult situation that ordinarily warrants it

◆ THINKING

A person's thinking ability is the way he or she functions intellectually. It is his or her process or way of thinking; his or her analysis of the world; his or her way of connecting or associating thoughts; and his or her overall organization of thoughts. Some of the major disorders in thinking are outlined below.

I. Disturbance in thought process (how a person thinks)

A. **Loose associations**—poorly connected or poorly organized thoughts

1. **Circumstantiality**—frequent digressions on the way to eventual conclusion

2. **Tangentiality**—frequent digression until initial reason for beginning a discussion is forgotten

B. **Flight of ideas**—rapid speaking with quick changes from one thought to another connected thought; frequently seen in manic clients

C. **Perseveration**—repetition of the same word in reply to different questions

D. **Blocking**—cessation of thought production for no apparent reason

II. Disturbance in thought content (what a client is thinking)

A. **Delusion**—inaccurate belief that cannot be corrected by reasoning

1. **Delusion of grandeur**—exaggerated belief about own abilities or importance

2. **Delusion of reference**—client's false belief that he or she is the center of others' attention and discussion

3. **Delusion of persecution**—client's false belief that others are seeking to hurt or in some other way damage him or her either physically or by insinuation

B. **Preoccupation of thought**—connecting all occurrences and experiences to a central thought, usually one with strong emotional overtones

C. **Obsessive thought**—unwelcome idea, emotion, or urge that repeatedly enters the consciousness

D. **Phobia**—strong fear of a particular situation

1. **Claustrophobia**—fear of being in an enclosed place

2. **Agoraphobia**—fear of being in an open place, such as outdoors or on a highway

3. **Acrophobia**—fear of high places

E. Other disturbances of thought, or memory impairment— any type of change in ability to recall thoughts from the unconscious into consciousness in an accurate manner

1. **Amnesia**—complete or partial inability to recall past experiences

2. **Confabulation**—filling in gaps in memory with statements that are untrue

3. **Déjà vu**—feeling of having experienced a new situation on a previous occasion (Note: this can normally occur in all individuals when they are fatigued or stressed.)

◆ PERCEPTION

Perception is the way that a person experiences his or her environment and how he or she perceives his or her frame of reference within that environment. It is equivalent to the person's sense of reality. Perception derives from the senses of vision, hearing, touch, smell, and taste. The information perceived through the senses is monitored by the mind and its defenses. Mental dysfunction can result in distortion of reality that can range from mild to severe.

A hallucination can be the result of serious mental dysfunction. **Hallucinations** are false sensory perceptions that do not exist in reality. The most common types of hallucinations are as follows:

Visual hallucination—seeing object(s) not present in reality

Auditory hallucination—hearing sounds not present in reality

Hypnagogic hallucination—sensing any type of false sensory perception during the twilight period between being awake and falling asleep

Another type of sensory dysfunction, called an **illusion,** is a misinterpretation or distortion (by the ego) of an actual stimulus. Two other terms relating to perception of self or the environment are used to describe mental status dysfunctioning:

Depersonalization—feeling detached from one's surroundings

Derealization—ranging from a mild sense of unreality to a frank loss of reality about one's environment

◆ MEMORY

Memory is the mind's ability to recall earlier events. The two types of memory are **recent**, for events that happened during the previous few days, and **remote**, for events that occurred from the first recollections of childhood through adolescence, adulthood, and up until the current week.

Memory loss is one of the most important signs of cognitive disorders. The two types of cognitive disorders are delirium and dementia. Memory loss occurs both in delirium, which is an acute brain disorder that is usually reversible, and in dementia, a chronic, usually irreversible brain disease (see Chapter 21, Delirium, Dementia, and Amnestic and Other Cognitive Disorders).

◆ JUDGMENT

Judgment is the final outcome of the processes described above. It is a person's ability to form conclusions and behave in a socially appropriate manner. If the psyche is functioning properly in the thinking and feeling spheres and a person has good awareness of his or her surroundings, then he or she will form valid conclusions about appropriate conduct.

◆ MENTAL STATUS EXAM IN OUTPATIENT CARE

An increasing number of clients are treated as outpatients and monitored by home health or community-based nurses. This means the nurses must make critical assessments of the client's mental status, without the supervision or consulting resources available in a hospital setting. In the case of an elderly client, the nurse may also need to consider the mental status of the client's caregiver (often an elderly spouse) and his or her ability to accurately report on the client's status or be responsible for medications and other care. In addition, the time the nurse spends with clients is brief, which may make assessing mental status more challenging.

A key component of the mental status exam is the nurse's subjective assessment of the mental status categories noted above. These subjective assessments should be backed up by careful observation and charting of specific behaviors. In addition, the nurse should listen carefully to and document the changes reported by the primary caregiver, and try to verify those behaviors as part of the mental status exam. (The mental status exam can also be given to members of the caregiver group.) Finally, all medications, past and present, need to be carefully charted, since medications or interactions between medications can significantly affect mental status.

CHAPTER 15 SUMMARY

- Behavior is the observable sign of mental functioning. Nurses can observe a client's behavior to assess his or her mental status.

- Level of awareness refers to the client's wakefulness or consciousness. Orientation is closely related to level of awareness and is measured by clients' ability to identify who they are, where they are, and the date and approximate time (person, place, time).

- Appearance and behavior that can be observed include facial expression, gestures, posture, dress, physical characteristics, motor activity, and response to caregiver.

- Evaluating speech and communication means noting how the client is communicating. This includes rate of speech, its volume, whether it is lively or dispirited, and the client's ability to produce words.

- Nurses can observe clients' affect, or display of emotions or feelings. Generally, the nurse is looking for affect that is outside the range of normal emotion, such as lack of or inappropriate affect; euphoria; depression, anxiety, fear, aggression; or la belle indifference.

- The client's thinking process reveals how the client is functioning intellectually. A nurse can observe disorders in thought process (loose associations, flight of ideas, blocking) and disorders in thought content (delusions, obsessive thoughts, phobias).

- Perception, how clients experience their environment, derives from the five senses. A false sensory perception, or a perception of something that does not exist in reality, is called a hallucination.

- Memory is the mind's ability to recall earlier events. Recent memory is for events that happened in the past few days. Remote memory is for events that occurred from childhood up until the current week.

- A common feature of two major cognitive disorders, dementia and delirium, is loss of memory.

- Judgment is the person's ability to form conclusions and behave in a socially appropriate manner. It is the result of level of awareness, affect, thinking, perception, and memory.

CHAPTER 15 QUESTIONS

1. A person who is oriented is able to recognize
   a. time, date, and current events.
   b. phone number and most recent address.
   c. time, person, and place.
   d. immediate family members.

2. Which of the following statements is *not* true?
   a. A client's gestures can indicate what he or she is feeling.
   b. A nurse can observe whether facial expression matches emotions expressed.
   c. Clients seldom relate with or respond to caregivers.
   d. Facial expression, gestures, and posture are nonverbal ways of communicating.

3. A person's ability to form conclusions and behave in a socially appropriate manner is
   a. remote memory.
   b. judgment.
   c. euphoria.
   d. la belle indifference.

4. The symptom shared by dementia and delirium is
   a. memory loss.
   b. judgment.
   c. déjà vu.
   d. dyskinesia.

BIBLIOGRAPHY

Barry, P.D. (1996). *Psychosocial nursing: Care of physically ill patients and their families* (3rd ed.). Philadelphia: Lippincott-Raven.

Bauer, J., Roberts, M.R., & Reisdorff, E.J. (1991). Evaluation of behavioral and cognitive changes: The mental status examination. *Emergency Medicine Clinics of North America, 9,* 1–12.

Carpenito, L.J. (1995). *Nursing diagnosis: Application to clinical practice* (6th ed.). Philadelphia: J.B. Lippincott.

Dellasega, C., & Cutezo, E. (1994). Strategies used by home health nurses to assess the mental status of homebound elders. *Journal of Community Health Nursing, 11*(3), 129–38.

Kaplan, H.I., & Sadock, B.J. (1995). *Comprehensive textbook of psychiatry/VI* (6th ed.). Baltimore: Williams & Wilkins.

Kaplan, H.I., & Sadock, B.J. (1994). *Synopsis of psychiatry: Behavioral sciences, clinical psychology* (7th ed.). Baltimore: Williams & Wilkins.

McFarland, G.K., Wasli, E.L., & Gerety, E.K. (1996). *Nursing diagnoses and process in psychiatric mental health nursing* (3rd ed.). Philadelphia: Lippincott-Raven.

Stuart, G.W., & Sundeen, S.J. (Eds.). (1994). *Principles and practice of psychiatric nursing* (5th ed.). St. Louis: Mosby Year Book.

Wilson, H.S., & Kneisl, C.R. (1996). *Psychiatric nursing* (5th ed.). Redwood City, CA: Addison-Wesley.

DEVELOPING CRITICAL THINKING SKILLS THROUGH CLASS DISCUSSION

UNIT FOUR Case Study
Mental Health and Mental Disorder

John is a 48-year-old engineer whose job has been eliminated in the aerospace industry. He does not believe he can locate another position in his geographic area. He also believes that his boss "had it out for him" and that is why his position was eliminated. He is married and has two children ages 19 and 17. His family is accustomed to a comfortable middle-class lifestyle. His wife does not cope well with stress. His 19-year-old son is a sophomore in college. His 17-year-old daughter has already submitted college applications to five private universities. John is angry and bitter.

D I S C U S S I O N   Q U E S T I O N S

1. What are some of the emotions that John may be experiencing at this time?

2. Since John is experiencing anger at this time, what is the likelihood that he is feeling helpless anger? Why?

3. If John's coping patterns are ineffective, what types of symptoms would you expect him to manifest?

4. What would you identify as the causative factors in his ineffective coping?

5. What types of activities would you encourage John to engage in at this time in order to support effective coping?

6. Can you describe the different categories of mental status you would expect to see in John 1 week after his job termination?

Unit 5

NURSING THE CLIENT WITH A MENTAL DISORDER

16

Nursing Process in the Mental Health Setting

Behavioral Objectives

After reading this chapter the student will be able to:

- Name the four steps of the nursing process.

- List the different questions that are asked in collecting data for use in developing a nursing care plan.

- Describe how problem solving is used in the second step of the nursing process.

- Explain why contracting with the client is a part of the nursing care plan.

- Use systems theory to explain why a nursing care plan is essential to a therapeutic outcome for the client.

- Tell why the last step of the nursing process is important.

Interacting therapeutically with clients demands a capacity for relating well with people. In addition, the nurse must understand nursing theories, physical and psychosocial assessment, and specific nursing tasks. Nurses must also possess the cognitive skills of analyzing, decision making, and evaluating—indeed, a nearly limitless number and range of skills. Caring for clients is a complex process.

It is important to give structure to this process in order to be able to practice nursing skills in an organized manner. The term **nursing process** has been coined as a title for the steps involved in organizing and implementing client care. The four steps are as follows:

1. Assessment and diagnosis
2. Planning
3. Implementation/intervention
4. Evaluation

These steps are the same whether the nurse is in the home, community, or hospital setting. Increasingly, mental health care is occurring out of the hospital as alternative care sites provide positive client outcomes and more cost-effective care.

◆ ASSESSMENT

Assessment is the first step of the process. It includes gathering all the information needed to diagnose the specific problems that require nursing care and to develop a care plan. The care plan is specifically designed to meet the client's unique needs and will result in a therapeutic outcome. This type of information seeking includes an initial interview session with the client in which the information listed below should be obtained. Frequently it may take more than one session to complete the collection of data. Depending on the information given in response to questions, additional questions might be useful in order to reach a good comprehension of the client's situation. In addition, while talking, the areas of mental functioning described earlier (see Chapter 15, Mental Status Exam) can be observed. The evaluation of mental status should be included under this section. The types of questions to be asked are as follows:

1. *Tell me what was going on that caused you to feel this way?* This information helps the nurse to understand the client's perception of his or her problem. A client commonly misinterprets the actual reason for admission and will relate the problem differently.

2. *Was there something specific that caused things to come to a crisis?* Frequently, the client's level of emotional stress has been increasing for a number of days, weeks, or months. There has been an accompanying deterioration in his or her ability to cope with this stress. There is usually a precipitating event that causes the client to go into crisis (see Chapter 28, Crisis Intervention).

3. *With whom do you live?* This information describes the client's immediate support system or lack of it. He or she could be living with family or friends or may live alone. Watch emotional responses as the question is answered; it can give clues as to the quality of the client's living situation. If a quick answer is given and eye contact is avoided, it could be an indication to explore this subject to obtain more information.

4. *How have things been for you with them?* One of the greatest factors in successful coping is the availability of a support system. Frequently, the members of the client's support system, whether family, friends, or some other type of support person or group, have been under stress or, for some reason, have been unavailable during the critical period before the crisis.

5. *What type of work do you do?* The answer to this question can give many types of information including his or her capacity for role functioning in a job, psychosocial status, and level of education.

6. *Have you been working up until this admission?* If the answer is no, then determine how recently the client was able to work and what happened to lead him or her to stop working.

7. *Have you and your family (or whomever the client lives with) been under any unusual stress during the past year?* Describe the type of stress being asked about. For example, *Has anyone in the family died? Been very sick? Has there been a divorce in the family?* Review the life-change events in the Holmes and Rahe scale that appears in Chapter 13, Stress: Effective Coping and Adaptation, in order to be aware of the significant events that impose stress on individuals.

8. *When you are under stress, what do you usually do to help yourself?* This indicates the client's level of coping ability, as well as his or her problem-solving capacity and current reality orientation.

The answers to these questions will provide an understanding of the issues concerning the client. Other important sources of information during the assessment step are family members, current and former charts, and the reported observations of caregivers from nursing and other disciplines.

◆ NURSING DIAGNOSIS AS THE FINAL STEP IN NURSING ASSESSMENT

When an adequate amount of data has been collected, it can be used to formulate nursing diagnoses as the basis for the planning of care. The use of nursing diagnoses in planning care has been defined as an essential part of the practice of nursing by the American Nurses Association Social Policy Statement. It has also been included in nurse practice acts written into law in many states. One of the implicit expectations of the diagnostic and treatment process is that the goal of the specific interventions designed in the planning stage must be identified so that a basis for evaluating nursing care outcomes is established.

The formal selection of a nursing diagnosis is done by a registered nurse, using the criteria developed by the institution in which he or she works. The information gathered by members of the nursing care team and given to the registered nurse further expands the information known about the client. Effective care planning depends on a reliable data base and on proper identification of problems appropriate for nursing intervention. These nursing problems are then classified into nursing diagnoses. The process of selecting and using nursing diagnoses in the mental health setting is described in Chapter 17, Nursing Diagnosis in the Mental Health Setting.

The most frequently used classification of diagnoses has been developed by the North American Nursing Diagnosis Association (NANDA). The list of classifications appears in Chapter 17, page 190. They are classified by the categories of normal human functioning.

◆ PLANNING

The planning stage involves a problem-solving process. The steps are as follows:

1. Analyze the data.
2. Identify and rank the significant problems (stated in Nursing Diagnosis terminology).
3. Examine the possible causes of each.
4. Consider the possible interventions for each.
5. Rule out the interventions that are not possible to implement.
6. Consider the possible outcome of each of the possible interventions.
7. Choose one or more interventions for the identified nursing di-

agnosis. The identified problems and the interventions that will help resolve the client's problem are then discussed with the client. Usually he or she will agree with the plan. The client may also request that the plan be modified. In either case, the nurse and client should agree about the final plan. This is also known as a contract.

A written nursing care plan that is based on nursing diagnosis of client problems is the guide used by all members of the nursing staff so that the client receives consistent care. The use of such a plan ensures that all nursing members of the multidisciplinary team are working toward common goals on a full 24-hour basis. The plan can also indicate the direction of the therapeutic plan of nursing to the other clinical team members from psychiatry, social work, psychology, and so on. The development of a nursing care plan is described in Chapter 18, Nursing Care Planning With Specific Types of Disordered Mental States.

◆ IMPLEMENTATION/INTERVENTION

In this step, the nursing care plan is put into practice. It is the *action* part of the nursing process in which interventions are begun. The goal is to decrease or eliminate the symptoms of the specific problems that have been identified. A critical aspect of the implementing step is that the care plan should be used consistently by all members of the nursing care team. If not, the client's progress toward wellness will be undermined by inconsistent care approaches.

Another important aspect of the implementing stage is that ongoing assessment of the client's problem or problems should be part of daily nursing care. In addition, the data base can be further refined by obtaining more detailed information about the client's life, relationships, experiences, and so on. As more specific information about the client's problem is gathered, it may be necessary to alter the plan and at the same time notify other nursing colleagues about the change in approach and the new knowledge leading to the modification in the care plan.

To promote a systems approach, the care plan should be shared with the other members of the nursing staff and, in most instances, with the family. If a family therapist is working with the family, review the plan with him or her in case there are differences in the care approaches of nursing and the family therapist. The family therapist is usually aware of complex family dynamics that may have been detrimental to the hospitalized family member.

When clients and family members receive conflicting messages from two different care disciplines they become confused. Accordingly, they may be noncompliant with the recommendations they receive. Ultimately, the client may lose the social support that could contribute toward more rapid resolution of his or her problems.

When the nursing care plan is shared with the family, they experience a greater sense of security about their family member's prognosis. In addition, it is an opportunity to explain the interventions designed to support their loved one's mental disorder and to model a beneficial type of caregiving behavior. Specific interventions for the various psychiatric disorders are described in Unit 6, Categories of Mental Disorders.

◆ EVALUATION

Evaluation is the final step of the nursing process. During and after the intervention step, the outcome of nursing care can usually be observed. Is there a decrease in the symptoms that originally caused the plan to be implemented?

Evaluating involves obtaining feedback, verbal or nonverbal, from the client about the results of interventions. Verbal feedback is also known as subjective information; the client is directly describing how he or she feels. Nonverbal feedback includes those clues the client is giving, frequently without conscious awareness. These include facial or body gestures and observable emotional states, such as tenseness, anger, sadness, depression, and so on. This type of information is called objective; in a way, the client is the object being observed.

The nurse's objective observations can, on occasion, differ from the subjective comments the client makes about himself or herself. For example, the client may say that he or she is feeling much better and more cheerful. On several occasions throughout the day, however, the client may be observed sitting alone, silently weeping.

The evaluation stage is actually similar to the original step in the nursing process. The final step of the nursing process involves collecting data that will determine whether the goals of the nursing care plan were achieved. When an evaluation of any type of intervention process occurs, it is important to base the evaluation on criteria or standards that determine whether the goal was reached. This means that the symptoms of the problems originally identified should be decreased or entirely relieved. When the evaluation determines that some or all of the symptoms remain, the nursing process should be reinitiated. A reassessment of the *current* symptoms should occur, and a new or modified care plan should be instituted.

CHAPTER 16 SUMMARY

- Psychiatric nurses need the following skills and knowledge: interpersonal communication, nursing theory, and the nursing process.

- **Nursing process** refers to the four steps involved in organizing and implementing client care. The steps are assessment and diagnosis, planning, implementation or intervention, and evaluation.

- Assessment includes gathering all information needed to diagnose a client's specific problems. When an adequate amount of information has been gathered, a nursing diagnosis can be formed. This diagnosis serves as the basis for planning the client's care.

- Nursing care planning is a problem-solving process that includes seven steps:
  — 1. Analyze data
  — 2. Identify significant problems and rank them
  — 3. Examine possible causes of each problem
  — 4. Consider possible interventions for each problem
  — 5. Rule out interventions that cannot be implemented
  — 6. Consider the outcome of each possible intervention
  — 7. Choose one or more interventions for the identified diagnosis

- The result of the nursing care planning process is a written care plan that guides all the nursing care and is compatible with the plan of the unit mental health team.

- The goal of the implementation or intervention stage is to decrease or eliminate the symptoms of the specific problems that have been identified.

- Evaluation involves gathering data (subjective and objective feedback) about whether the goals of the plan have been met.

CHAPTER 16 QUESTIONS

1. The nursing process includes assessment and diagnosis, planning, implementation, and
   a. hourly cost estimate.
   b. confirmation of drug therapy.
   c. evaluation.
   d. reality orientation.

2. Which of the following is *not* true about assessment?
   a. It includes gathering as much information as possible.
   b. It does not include evaluation of mental status.
   c. It may take more than one session to get adequate data.
   d. Answers to questions will provide understanding of issues that concern the client.

3. A contract with a client means that
   a. if the client does not cooperate, he or she will be dismissed.
   b. the client sets his or her own treatment plan after speaking with the nurse.
   c. the information is not shared with anyone other than the client and nurse.
   d. the client and nurse agree with the nursing care plan.

4. Evaluation is important because
   a. it determines whether nurses get pay raises.
   b. data collected determine if nursing care goals were met.
   c. it means the client is ready to be released.
   d. none of the above

BIBLIOGRAPHY

Barry, P.D. (1996). *Psychosocial nursing: Care of physically ill patients and their families* (3rd ed.). Philadelphia: Lippincott-Raven.

Carpenito, L.J. (1994). *Nursing care plans and documentation: Nursing diagnosis and collaborative problems* (2nd ed.). Philadelphia: J.B. Lippincott.

Diagnostic and statistical manual of mental disorders (4th ed.). (1994). Washington, DC: American Psychiatric Press.

Johnson, B. (1996). *Psychiatric mental health nursing* (4th ed.). Philadelphia: Lippincott-Raven.

Kaplan, H.I., & Sadock, B.J. (1995). *Comprehensive textbook of psychiatry/VI* (6th ed.). Baltimore: Williams & Wilkins.

McFarland, G.K., Wasli, E.L., & Gerety, E.K. (1996). *Nursing diagnoses and process in psychiatric mental health nursing* (3rd ed.). Philadelphia: Lippincott-Raven.

NANDA's definitions and classifications, 1995-1996. St. Louis: North American Nursing Diagnosis Association.

Nettina, S.M. (1996). *The Lippincott manual of nursing practice* (6th ed.). Philadelphia: Lippincott-Raven.

Nursing's Social Policy Statement. (1995). Washington, DC: American Nurses Association.

Potter, P.A., & Perry, A.G. (1996). *Fundamentals of nursing: Concepts, process, and practice* (4th ed.). St. Louis: Mosby Year Book.

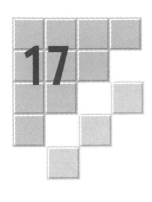

17

Nursing Diagnosis in the Mental Health Setting

After reading this chapter the student will be able to:

■ Name the number of nursing diagnoses identified by the North American Nursing Diagnosis Association.

■ Name three reasons why the use of nursing diagnoses in clinical practice was developed.

■ Describe why the use of a formal assessment tool is important in reviewing the range of potential health problems of a newly admitted client.

■ Describe five of the patterns of human functioning that are used in assessing and diagnosing clinical problems that nursing is prepared to diagnose and treat.

■ Explain why the assessment review of these patterns can assist the nurse in developing a comprehensive care plan.

In 1973 a group of nurses met in St. Louis in order to identify the types of health problems that nurses are clinically prepared to diagnose and treat. Their guiding principles in selecting a list of nursing diagnoses included the following:

1. Identify all clinical problems that nurses identify and diagnose in clients.
2. Develop specific and consistent names for the different problems that nursing care can address.
3. Classify the different diagnoses into groups and subgroups in order to study the relationships between the different diagnoses, as well as the specific patterns that contribute to the clinical problem.
4. Develop a numeric code for the various diagnoses, groups, and subgroups of diagnoses so that the codes can be entered into computer systems.

The original number of nurses that met in 1973 has expanded to include an international group of nurses from clinical, academic, and research settings. They meet every 2 years to review, analyze, and add to the list of nursing diagnoses. The list of approved nursing diagnoses is called Taxonomy I—Revised. Taxonomy is a word that describes the laws and principles covering the classification of items into natural and related groups.

◆ Categories of Nursing Diagnosis

The most recent meeting of the North American Nursing Diagnosis Association (NANDA) was held in 1996. The approved list of 128 nursing diagnosis categories appears below. The nursing diagnosis categories commonly seen in mental health settings are preceded by an asterisk (*).

Pattern 1: Exchanging
Altered Nutrition: More than body requirements
Altered Nutrition: Less than body requirements
Altered Nutrition: Potential for more than body requirements
Risk for Infection
Risk for Altered Body Temperature
Hypothermia
Hyperthermia
Ineffective Thermoregulation

Dysreflexia

Constipation

Perceived Constipation

Colonic Constipation

Diarrhea

Bowel Incontinence

Altered Urinary Elimination

Stress Incontinence

Reflex Incontinence

Urge Incontinence

Functional Incontinence

Total Incontinence

Urinary Retention

Altered (Specify Type) Tissue Perfusion (renal, cerebral, cardio-
pulmonary, gastrointestinal, peripheral)

Fluid Volume Excess

Fluid Volume Deficit

Risk for Fluid Volume Deficit

Decreased Cardiac Output

Impaired Gas Exchange

Ineffective Airway Clearance

Ineffective Breathing Pattern

Inability to Sustain Spontaneous Ventilation

Dysfunctional Ventilatory Weaning Response (DVWR)

*Risk for Injury

Risk for Suffocation

Risk for Poisoning

*Risk for Trauma

Risk for Aspiration

Risk for Disuse Syndrome

Altered Protection

Impaired Tissue Integrity

Altered Oral Mucous Membrane

Impaired Skin Integrity

Risk for Impaired Skin Integrity

Decreased Adaptive Capacity: Intracranial

Energy Field Disturbance

Pattern 2: Communicating
*Impaired Verbal Communication

Pattern 3: Relating
*Impaired Social Interaction
*Social Isolation
*Risk for Loneliness
*Altered Role Performance
*Altered Parenting
*Risk for Altered Parenting
*Risk for Altered Parent/Infant/Child Attachment
*Sexual Dysfunction
*Altered Family Processes
*Caregiver Role Strain
*Risk for Caregiver Role Strain
*Altered Family Process: Alcoholism
*Parental Role Conflict
*Altered Sexuality Patterns

Pattern 4: Valuing
*Spiritual Distress (distress of the human spirit)
*Potential for Enhanced Spiritual Well Being

Pattern 5: Choosing
*Ineffective Individual Coping
*Impaired Adjustment
*Defensive Coping
*Ineffective Denial
*Ineffective Family Coping: Disabling
*Ineffective Family Coping: Compromised
*Family Coping: Potential for Growth
*Potential for Enhanced Community Coping
*Ineffective Community Coping
*Noncompliance (Specify)
*Ineffective Management of Therapeutic Regimen: Families
*Ineffective Management of Therapeutic Regimen: Community
*Ineffective Management of Therapeutic Regimen: Individual

*Decisional Conflict (Specify)

*Health Seeking Behaviors (Specify)

Pattern 6: Moving

Impaired Physical Mobility

Risk for Peripheral Neurovascular Dysfunction

Risk for Perioperative Positioning Injury

Activity Intolerance

*Fatigue

Risk for Activity Intolerance

*Sleep pattern Disturbance

Diversional Activity Deficit

*Impaired Home Maintenance Management

*Altered Health Maintenance

Feeding Self Care Deficit

Impaired Swallowing

Ineffective Breastfeeding

Interrupted Breastfeeding

Effective Breastfeeding

Ineffective Infant Feeding Pattern

Bathing/Hygiene Self Care Deficit

Dressing/Grooming Self Care Deficit

Toileting Self Care Deficit

Altered Growth and Development

*Relocation Stress Syndrome

Risk for Disorganized Infant Behavior

Disorganized Infant Behavior

Potential for Enhanced Organized Infant Behavior

Pattern 7: Perceiving

*Body Image Disturbance

*Self Esteem Disturbance

*Chronic Low Self Esteem

*Situational Low Self Esteem

*Personal Identity Disturbance

*Sensory/Perceptual Alterations (Specify) (Visual, auditory, kines-
   thetic, gustatory, tactile, olfactory)

Unilateral Neglect

*Hopelessness

*Powerlessness

Pattern 8: Knowing

*Knowledge Deficit (Specify)

*Impaired Environmental Interpretation Syndrome

*Acute Confusion

*Chronic Confusion

*Altered Thought Processes

*Impaired Memory

Pattern 9: Feeling

Pain

Chronic Pain

*Dysfunctional Grieving

*Anticipatory Grieving

*Risk for Violence: Self-directed or directed at others

*Risk for Self-Mutilation

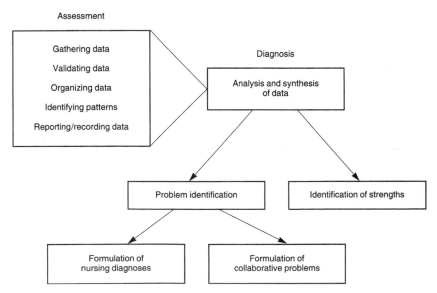

FIGURE 17–1. The diagnostic process. (In Alfaro-Lefevre, R. (1994). Applying nursing diagnosis and nursing process: A step-by-step guide (2nd ed.). Philadelphia: J.B. Lippincott. Used with permission.)

*Post-Trauma Response

*Rape-Trauma Syndrome

*Rape-Trauma Syndrome: Compound reaction

*Rape-Trauma Syndrome: Silent reaction

*Anxiety

*Fear

The assessment of a newly admitted mental health client leads to the formation of nursing diagnoses. The process is illustrated in Figure 17–1.

◆ PATTERNS OF HUMAN RESPONSES

Whenever nursing assessment occurs and a nursing diagnosis assessment model is used, there are specific patterns of human functioning that are evaluated. They include the following:

Exchanging—This pattern includes the clinical problems present when normal physical functioning is altered.

Communicating—This pattern includes the clinical problems present when the capacity for verbal communication is altered.

Relating—This pattern includes the clinical problems present when normal, effective interpersonal processes are altered.

Valuing—This pattern includes the clinical problems associated with the meaning of significant personal events such as illness and death.

Choosing—This pattern includes the clinical problems present when there is ineffective coping, compliance, decision-making, or health-seeking behavior.

Moving—This pattern includes the clinical problems present when health status is altered by changes in physical mobility or body coordination.

Perceiving—This pattern includes the clinical problems present when perception of the self or the environment is altered because of acute or chronic psychological or physical distress.

Knowing—This pattern includes the clinical problems present when cognitive processes are altered because of a psychiatric disorder, organic brain deficit, knowledge deficit in an otherwise well-functioning individual, or knowledge deficit due to below-normal intellectual functioning.

Feeling—This pattern includes the clinical problems present when distressing affect or mood results in ineffective coping.

These patterns can be assessed by using a questionnaire format that covers a broad range of psychosocial and physical functions. The Barry Psychosocial Assessment Interview Schedule in Appendix A demonstrates the types of questions that provide adequate assessment data.

◆ HOW NURSING DIAGNOSES ARE CHOSEN

The nursing diagnosis categories are described in a manual published by NANDA. Information about the categories can also be found in a variety of nursing textbooks. Some of these are listed in the bibliography at the end of the chapter. (See also holistic health care priorities discussed in Chapter 3.)

Definitions accompany each of the nursing diagnoses. These definitions have been developed and researched in clinical practice by nurses across the United States and Canada. Each nursing diagnosis category contains sections that describe the elements of the nursing problem or diagnosis. These sections are the **etiologic contributing risk factors** and the diagnosis' **defining characteristics.**

The **etiologic risk factors** of an actual nursing diagnosis such as Ineffective individual coping may be losing a job, getting a divorce, or moving to new city. These same risk factors may *potentially* place the person under increased stress and require psychosocial nursing interventions.

The **defining characteristics** of a nursing diagnosis are the signs or symptoms that the person is manifesting or describing related to the nursing problem. There are two categories of criteria that must be met for the diagnostic label to be applied. **Major** signs or symptoms *must* be present in order to use a particular nursing diagnosis. For example, for the nursing diagnosis Impaired adjustment, at least one major defining characteristic must be present in order for the diagnostic criteria to be met: "verbalization of nonacceptance of health status change or inability to be involved in problem-solving or goal-setting."

Minor signs or symptoms *may* be present. In the diagnosis of Impaired adjustment, minor defining characteristics are "lack of movement toward independence; extended period of shock, disbelief, or anger regarding health status change; lack of future-oriented thinking."

◆ THE DEVELOPMENT OF A NURSING DIAGNOSIS

Following the assessment step of the nursing process, the assessment data are analyzed by the nurse and a nursing diagnosis statement is developed. The statement describes the specific clinical problem that can be addressed by nursing intervention. Usually a client will have at least three specific problems. A nursing diagnosis statement also includes the cause of the problem. This statement then guides the nursing care plan for all members of the nursing staff on a 24-hour basis.

The following are examples of nursing diagnosis statements that may be seen in the mental health setting. The actual nursing diagnosis category is printed in italics. It is followed by the words "related to." The causative factor, which can be different for different clients, is indicated in bold type. The sample diagnoses are:

> *Social isolation* related to **death of father and beginning college away from home.**

> *Sensory perceptual alterations*: auditory hallucinations related to **psychosis.**

> *Impaired social interaction* related to **hallucinations.**

> *Noncompliance* related to **not taking psychotropic medication.**

The diagnosis states the problem and primary cause around which nursing care planning and interventions will be developed. It is important that the nursing diagnosis and resulting care plan are in agreement with the client's admitting diagnosis and the therapeutic goals of the multidisciplinary mental health team. The use of nursing diagnosis in care planning is described in Chapter 18, Nursing Care Planning with Specific Types of Disordered Mental States.

◆ COLLABORATIVE PROBLEMS

The nursing diagnosis is always developed in conjunction with a medical diagnosis and related treatment plan. The nursing diagnosis rounds out and completes the care ordered by a physician. In psychiatric settings the diagnostic codes developed by the American Psychiatric Association are used to describe the condition for which a client is admitted to the inpatient setting. These are the same codes used in outpatient mental health care. All nursing diagnoses should be developed in conjunction with the identified mental disorder admitting diagnosis. These diagnostic codes are published in the *Diagnostic and Statistical Manual of Mental Disorders*, fourth edition (DSM-IV).

The nursing care plan is always developed to address the specific nursing diagnosis, as well as the added nursing interventions that are standard accepted nursing roles in the mental health setting. These include nursing assessment for physical safety, administration of medications, and so on.

The nursing diagnosis statements are presented in the multidisciplinary team meetings attended by all members of the unit clinical staff. By discussing the nursing diagnoses in these meetings, all members of the team are aware of the specific problems that nursing will be addressing that are unique for each client on the unit. The use of nursing diagnoses assists the nurse in organizing the nursing care plan so that therapeutic and time-effective nursing care is ensured. The nursing diagnosis step of the nursing process is essential to therapeutic nursing care. Properly selected nursing diagnoses provide the foundation of stating client problems so that therapeutic clinical outcomes can be achieved.

CHAPTER 17 SUMMARY

- Guiding principles for the North American Nursing Diagnosis Association (NANDA) for selecting and approving nursing diagnoses include:
  - — Identify all clinical problems that nurses identify and diagnose.
  - — Develop specific and consistent names for these problems.
  - — Classify diagnoses to study the patterns that contribute to clinical problems.
  - — Review research findings related to proposed diagnostic categories.
  - — Develop a numeric code for the diagnoses, to be used in computer data entry.

- The approved list of nursing diagnosis categories, issued by the North American Nursing Diagnosis Association (NANDA), contains 128 entries.

- In nursing assessment, specific patterns of human functioning that are evaluated include exchanging, moving, communicating, perceiving, relating, knowing, valuing, feeling, and choosing.

- Each nursing diagnosis category contains etiologic contributing risk factors and the defining characteristics of the diagnosis.

- Etiologic contributing risk factors are those factors that may potentially place the person under increased physical and psychosocial stress and require nursing interventions.

- Defining characteristics of a nursing diagnosis are the signs or symptoms a person is manifesting or describing related to the nursing problem. These characteristics are categorized as major or minor.

- A nursing diagnosis statement describes the specific clinical problem to be addressed and the cause of the problem. The statement is used to guide all nursing staff members in client care.

- The nursing diagnosis is always developed in conjunction with a medical diagnosis and related medical treatment plan.

CHAPTER 17 QUESTIONS

1. The NANDA nursing diagnosis categories were developed to
   a. identify all clinical problems that nurses identify and diagnose in clients.
   b. provide specific, consistent names for the different problems.
   c. classify the diagnoses and study their relationships and patterns.
   d. all of the above

2. Which of the following are patterns of human responses?
   a. Valuing, choosing, and perceiving
   b. Etiology, contributing factors, and risk
   c. Assessment, diagnosis, and investigation
   d. None of the above

3. Defining characteristics of a nursing diagnosis are
   a. the way a client describes his or her physical condition.
   b. the signs and symptoms a client is manifesting or describing.
   c. completely arbitrary.
   d. merely a formality for record keeping.

4. Which of the following is *not* a component of a nursing diagnosis statement?
   a. Statement of the specific clinical problem to be addressed
   b. The cause of the problem
   c. A 24-hour nursing care plan guide for the entire staff
   d. Recommendations for treatment for the clinical psychologist only

BIBLIOGRAPHY

Barry, P.D. (1996). *Psychosocial nursing: Care of physically ill patients and their families* (3rd ed.). Philadelphia: Lippincott-Raven.
Carpenito, L.J. (1995). *Handbook of nursing diagnosis* (6th ed.). Philadelphia: Lippincott-Raven.
Diagnostic and statistical manual of mental disorders (4th ed.). (1994). Washington, DC: American Psychiatric Press.
Johnson, B. (1996). *Psychiatric mental health nursing* (4th ed.). Philadelphia: Lippincott-Raven.
Kaplan, H.I., & Sadock, B.J. (1995). *Comprehensive textbook of psychiatry/VI* (6th ed.). Baltimore: Williams & Wilkins.
McFarland, G.K., Wasli, E.L., & Gerety, E.K. (1996). *Nursing diagnoses and process in psychiatric mental health nursing* (3rd ed.). Philadelphia: Lippincott-Raven.
NANDA's definitions and classifications, 1995-1996. St. Louis: North American Nursing Diagnosis Association.
Nettina, S.M. (1996). *The Lippincott manual of nursing practice* (6th ed.). Philadelphia: Lippincott-Raven.
North American Nursing Diagnosis Association. (1993). *Classification of nursing diagnosis: Proceedings of the tenth conference*. Philadelphia: J.B. Lippincott.
Tucker, S.M., Canobbio, M.M., Paquette, E.V., & Wells, M.F. (Eds.). (1996). *Patient care standards: Nursing process, diagnosis, and outcome* (6th ed.). St. Louis: Mosby Year Book.

18

Nursing Care Planning With Specific Types of Disordered Mental States

Behavioral Objectives

After reading this chapter the student will be able to:

■ Name the three preliminary steps to effective nursing care planning.

■ Describe the five elements of a nursing care plan.

■ Explain the association between a nursing goal and the interventions designed to address the nursing diagnoses.

■ Give one example of a nursing intervention used with clients who demonstrate the following mental states: psychotic, depressed, manic, anxious, confused, and violent.

The nursing process is a way of organizing nursing care that provides a comprehensive overview of the mental health problems that contribute to the need for hospitalization or community intervention. The planning of inpatient nursing care in mental health nursing is based on three preliminary steps:

1. Admission to an inpatient psychiatric setting with a diagnosed mental disorder selected from the *Diagnostic and Statistical Manual of Mental Disorders,* fourth edition (DSM-IV)

2. Nursing assessment of all mental and physical patterns so that specific problematic or illness patterns can be identified that are within the diagnostic and intervention scope of nursing practice

3. Development of nursing diagnosis statements to describe the unique ineffective coping patterns that are causing the client's current problem or problems

This chapter includes information on how to develop a nursing care plan using a consistent care planning format. Many types of care planning formats are currently in use in this country. The most important criterion for selection of a specific format is that the client receives therapeutic care. Other important criteria for selection of a nursing care planning format include its ease of communication and comprehension by all nurses involved in the ongoing 24-hour client care.

◆ MENTAL STATES REQUIRING SPECIFIC TYPES OF NURSING PLANNING

Most clients who are admitted to inpatient mental health care settings are diagnosed with a particular type of mental disorder prior to their admission. For example, a person may have a diagnosis of Major depressive disorder, recurrent. A nurse can expect that this client will demonstrate symptoms of this disorder as described in the DSM-IV. The nurse can prepare to assess and treat these symptoms of depression. It is possible, however, that there may be a variety of other mental states that are also subtypes of behavior associated with depression; for example, there could also be anxiety and confusion that require different types of nursing assessment and care planning than those associated specifically with depression.

To assist in comprehensive care planning for the most frequently seen mental states in psychiatric care settings, this chapter will present a nursing care planning format[1] with clinical case presentations based on the following mental states:

[1] The hypothetical cases described in this chapter were prepared in consultation with Nancy Jarasek, a clinical nurse specialist at the Institute of Living in Hartford, Connecticut.

Psychosis

Depression

Mania

Anxiety

Confusional state

Violence

These mental states will be presented in association with a case description in which the mental state is prominent. The nursing care planning format presented below uses fundamental concepts in presenting the nursing care problems and their associated nursing diagnosis with each of the mental states. The format includes the following components:

Nursing diagnosis—A statement of a nursing problem selected from the list of North American Nursing Diagnosis Association (NANDA)–Approved Nursing Diagnoses. The nursing diagnosis also includes a brief statement about the cause of the nursing problem.

Nursing goal or priority—A statement about the expected measurable client behavior that will demonstrate that the original clinical problem has been resolved or is decreased so that discharge is possible.

Nursing intervention—A statement about the nursing behavior/action that can alter the client's clinical problem and achieve the nursing goal or priority.

Nursing rationale—A statement developed in conjunction with each nursing intervention that provides the reasoning to support the nursing plan for each diagnosis.

Evaluation—A statement that describes the change in behavior that can be used as a measure of whether the nursing intervention is effective.

The nursing care plan format can be structured as shown in Table 18–1.

It should be noted that the care plan examples used in this chapter are not complete. A partial listing of nursing diagnoses associated with the care plans in boxes 1 and 2 is included so that the student can learn about how nursing diagnoses are phrased. The care plan for each diagnosis is specifically related to that diagnosis only. Following the first two case examples, only one nursing diagnosis and care plan are developed for each case example. The diagnosis and accompanying care plan are based on a clinical problem that commonly accompanies that type of mental state.

◆ TABLE 18–1. Nursing Care Plan Format

Nursing Diagnosis:

Nursing Goal:

Nursing Interventions	Rationale
1.	1a.
2.	2a.
3.	3a.
4.	4a.
5.	5a.
6. etc.	6a. etc.

Evaluation:

BOX 18–1 CARE PLANNING FOR A PSYCHOTIC CLIENT

Anna is a 30-year-old single female. She is a chronic schizophrenic whose first schizophrenic episode occurred when she was a college sophomore. Since that time her social development has been markedly affected by her ongoing schizophrenia. In the past, she frequently did not take her medication; her noncompliance with medications resulted in frequent hospitalizations. She eventually became a homeless person.

During the past year she has taken her medication on a regular schedule, as demonstrated by laboratory blood testing of medication levels. Despite her compliance with medication, attendance at a medication group, and blood testing, her mental condition has deteriorated. She is admitted in order to (1) begin a new medication regimen on a new form of medication that requires close supervision of potentially health-threatening side effects and (2) restore reality testing. Her DSM-IV diagnosis is schizophrenia. The nursing diagnoses should be listed by highest priority first.

NURSING DIAGNOSIS #1
Sensory-Perceptual Alteration (Auditory) related to schizophrenia.

NURSING GOAL
To monitor effects of psychotropic medication for therapeutic effects on mental and physical state.

NURSING INTERVENTIONS	RATIONALE
1. Assess and report level of symptoms, including changes in mental state and physical responses.	1a. If symptoms do not decrease, medication level may be reassessed.
2. Decrease social stimulation until paranoid symptoms subside.	2a. Overstimulation can result in more severe symptoms, as well as possible risk of violence to self and others.
3. Document mental state responses, every 2 hours	3a. Shift-to-shift monitoring will be easier to perform.

EVALUATION
Documentation will describe decrease in auditory hallucinations and paranoid symptoms.

(continued)

BOX 18–1 (continued)

NURSING DIAGNOSIS #2
Impaired Social Interaction related to schizophrenia with paranoid ideation. Moderate Risk for violence: Self-directed or directed toward others related to schizophrenia with paranoid ideation.

NURSING GOAL
To protect client from mental or physical injury to self or others because of her paranoid and aggressive behavior.

NURSING INTERVENTIONS	RATIONALE
1. Restrict client to own room rather than have her participate in group activities until paranoid behavior decreases.	1a. Client could injure others or be injured because of her severe suspiciousness of others.
2. Monitor client in room every ½ hour.	2a. Determine if medication effects are sedating her activity level and paranoid ideation.
3. Spend brief periods of time (2–3 minutes) interacting with client to assess current mental status.	3a. Excessive interaction with client will stimulate paranoid ideation.

EVALUATION
Aggressive behavior is nonexistent or minimal without causing interpersonal confrontation.

NURSING DIAGNOSIS #3
Ineffective Thermoregulation related to being newly medicated with clozapine.

NURSING GOAL
To maintain body temperature below 100°F.

NURSING INTERVENTIONS	RATIONALE
1. Take body temperature using noninvasive technique every hour.	1a. Elevated temperature can occur rapidly as negative side effect of clozapine drug therapy.
2. Record body temperatures and report a temperature in excess of 100˙F.	2a. Immediate action is necessary to prevent hyperthermia crisis.

(continued)

BOX 18–1 (continued)

EVALUATION
Temperature is regulated below 100°F.

NURSING DIAGNOSIS #4
Self-Care Deficit (Feeding).

NURSING GOAL
To provide adequate nutrition to maintain admission body weight.

NURSING INTERVENTIONS	RATIONALE
1. Review diet choices on daily hospital menu.	1a. Give client choice and control over food choices.
2. Obtain list of favorite foods.	2a. Client will be more likely to eat favorite foods.
3. Monitor client briefly while eating and record observations.	3a. Client may be throwing away food because of paranoid ideation about poisoned food.
4. Observe and record percentage of ingested food from tray.	4a. See 3a.
5. Request consultation for client with dietitian if meals are not 60% eaten.	5a. Dietitian is experienced in consulting regarding paranoid food ideations.

EVALUATION
Weight will not decrease below current level. Client will gain 2 pounds per week during hospital admission period.

BOX 18-2 CARE PLANNING FOR A DEPRESSED CLIENT

Tom is a 21-year-old college junior who is a music major in a local college. The precipitating event of this admission is the break-up of a 2-year relationship with his girlfriend. The relationship had begun at the same time his parents divorced. He has not yet addressed the emotional issues regarding the divorce. In addition, he is experiencing increased academic stress because final exams are 1 week away. He is sleep deprived because of extra hours spent completing term papers and studying for finals.

NURSING DIAGNOSIS #1
Dysfunctional Grieving related to break-up with girlfriend, as well as the ending of his parents' marriage.

NURSING GOAL
To monitor effects of verbalization about loss of girlfriend, as well as adjustment to parents' divorce.

NURSING INTERVENTIONS	RATIONALE
1. Encourage discussion of loss of girlfriend and parents' divorce in individual and group sessions.	1a. Discussion can allow release of painful emotion and support the development of insight.
2. Observe family visits and recommend discussion about feelings with family members.	2a. Increased communication with family can potentially increase his experience of support and decrease his feelings of isolation.

EVALUATION
Documentation will record summary of his discussions about loss. In addition, family visits and follow-up comments will be recorded. Comments will reflect increased insight about his responses and his choices.

NURSING DIAGNOSIS #2
Ineffective Individual Coping related to approaching final exams.

(continued)

BOX 18–2 (continued)

NURSING GOAL

To problem-solve with Tom about effective study habits while hospitalized; to provide a suitable environment for studying.

NURSING INTERVENTIONS	RATIONALE
1. Meet with Tom in morning to decide study plans for the day.	1a. Tom's coping ability is decreased because of the crisis that precipitated his admission. Accordingly, his problem-solving skills are decreased.
2. Provide quiet, suitable environment for effective study skills.	2a. Tom's level of concentration is decreased due to admission crisis.
3. Encourage Tom to invite fellow students to study with him on unit.	3a. Companionship can increase Tom's social support, decrease isolation, and maintain his interest in studying.

EVALUATION

Tom's study times will be documented. He will study at least 3 hours a day.

NURSING DIAGNOSIS #3

Sleep Pattern Disturbance related to difficulty falling asleep associated with depression.

NURSING GOAL

To stabilize sleep patterns so that 6 hours minimum of sleep is obtained.

NURSING INTERVENTIONS	RATIONALE
1. Observe and report sleep patterns.	1a. The documentation of evening and night staff regarding sleep patterns can assist selection of effective interventions.
2. Teach effective sleep hygiene, e.g., no caffeine, no TV/ratio, no conversation for ½ hour before bedtime.	2a. The reduction of stimulants and stimulation can provide assistance in returning to predepression sleep patterns.

EVALUATION

Day, evening, and night staff will document teaching, as well as hours of recorded sleep. Six hours of apparent sleep will be recorded.

BOX 18–3 CARE PLANNING FOR A MANIC CLIENT

Barbara is a 30-year-old single female. She has had a bipolar disorder since age 21. She is currently living in a homeless shelter. She has a mental status that includes flight of ideas, religious delusions, loose associations, and grandiosity. She is admitted for stabilization of her thought disorder.

NURSING DIAGNOSIS

Altered Thought Processes related to mania phase of bipolar disorder.

NURSING GOAL

To reduce the behavioral responses associated with the client's altered thought processes.

NURSING INTERVENTIONS	RATIONALE
1. Reduce external stimuli, e.g., limit presence and participation in unit activities, as well as access to radio and TV.	1a. Excessive stimulation will enhance the content of the delusions.
2. Maintain consistent caregivers.	2a. Exacerbation of thought disorder and excitability can occur with excessive clinician interactions.
3. Assess and record thought content and behavior every 2 hours.	3a. Effectiveness of medications can be more closely monitored on a shift-to-shift basis.
4. Maintain fair but firm limit-setting, e.g., schedule 2 hours' time in room, ½ hour out of room.	4a. A consistent set of limits will increase the client's sense of control.

EVALUATION

Documentation will demonstrate a reduction in behavioral responses to altered thought processes.

BOX 18–4 CARE PLANNING FOR AN ANXIOUS CLIENT

Angie is a 24-year-old female who has been married for 4 years. She is employed as a computer programmer. She is the adult child of an alcoholic father. Within the last week she saw a made-for-TV movie on incest that resulted in nightmares of being raped. Within the past 2 days she has begun to have memory flashbacks of smelling alcohol and being sexually abused by her father. She was admitted to the hospital because of acute anxiety accompanied by frequent episodes of tachycardia (rapid heartbeat) and hyperventilation (rapid breathing).

NURSING DIAGNOSIS
Post-Trauma Response related to remembering of childhood sexual abuse by father.

NURSING GOAL
To provide client with safe, nonjudgmental environment while memories of incest are entering into conscious awareness.

NURSING INTERVENTIONS	RATIONALE
1. Remove client from daily responsibilities at home and work.	1a. Allow client to re-experience memories in quiet, nondemanding environment.
2. Ask client to record flashbacks and dreams of trauma memories.	2a. Recording by client can assist with reality testing and problem solving about responses.
3. Assess level of anxiety and record.	3a. Recording by staff will document the progression of trauma symptoms.
4. Intervene when anxiety symptoms are moderate to severe.	
a. Hyperventilation: Ask client to breathe into paper bag.	4a. Acidosis will decrease.
b. Tachycardia: Encourage client to talk then exercise.	4b. Ventilation can reduce anxiety symptoms. Exercise reduces the physical causes of tachycardia caused by anxiety.
c. Agitation	4c. Same as 4b.
d. Check on availability of medication.	4d. Medication can effectively reduce all symptoms discussed above.

EVALUATION
Documentation will describe that anxiety responses will decrease each day.

BOX 18–5 CARE PLANNING FOR A CONFUSED CLIENT

Anthony is an 84-year-old male who was the head of his own construction business. His wife died 1 month ago. He was found yesterday wandering in traffic. He was confused and dressed in his pajamas. Apparently his wife compensated for his failing mental state. Since her death, his four children have avoided facing the reality of his dementia. His safety is severely compromised by his living alone.

NURSING DIAGNOSIS
Ineffective Family Coping: Disabling, related to father's dementia.

NURSING GOAL
To increase reality testing and problem solving with family to ensure Anthony's safety.

NURSING INTERVENTIONS	RATIONALE
1. Meet with all children and their spouses to discuss father's condition.	1a. Meeting with only one child can increase potential for conflict in family if other members continue to deny the reality of parent's condition.
2. Ask family to select one member who will serve as liaison between family and nurse.	2a. Communication and decision making can be severely compromised by multiple, independent decision makers.
3. Contact liaison person every day with update on father's condition.	3a. Reality testing of family will be increased.
4. Report evidence of family dissension to mental health team leader.	4a. Administrative intervention may be necessary if family denial persists.
5. Discuss and assess current plans of family for father's care following consultation with Social Service.	5a. Level of denial vs. effective problem solving can be assessed.

EVALUATION
Discharge plan that supports father's physical, mental, and spiritual well-being will be developed with family liaison person.

Discharge plan will be communicated to family in conjunction with nursing and Social Service.

Family will demonstrate agreement to coordinate this plan of care during planning meeting.

Roles of responsible family members will be clarified.

Communication plan for case coordinator and caregivers will be developed by consensus in family.

BOX 18–6 CARE PLANNING FOR A VIOLENT CLIENT

David is a 26-year-old male with an explosive, angry personality. He has had repeated hospitalizations. This hospitalization was necessary because he was angry with his parents because of their pending divorce. He became suicidal and took an overdose of antidepressants. After hospitalization and following a visit from his mother, he became violently angry, threw a chair in the day room, and threatened the staff when they attempted to subdue him.

NURSING DIAGNOSIS
Risk for Violence: Self-directed and directed toward others related to explosive personality.

NURSING GOAL
To reduce risk of injury to self or staff.

NURSING INTERVENTIONS	RATIONALE
1. Maintain client's and staff members' safety.	
*a. Four-point restraints for 24 hours using following method:	Each arm and leg must be restrained before safety of other clients and the staff is ensured.
1. Check cuffs for pressure every 15 minutes	Injury to client can occur if cuffs prevent normal blood flow.
2. Release alternate links once an hour and do range-of-motion exercises.	Injury to client can occur when stationary position is enforced.
3. Examine skin for evidence of chafing, edema, or other signs of distress.	Decreases risk of injury from restraints.
b. Document status of client every 15 minutes.	Legally required.
c. One-to-one staff: client monitoring at all times	Decreases risk of injury to self.
d. Discuss with client when he is subdued why he is on restraint and what he plans to do when the restraints are removed.	Increases reality testing and allows client to problem solve regarding his options.

*Restraint methods should follow specific institutional requirements that adhere to legal restraint guidelines.

EVALUATION
At the time of discharge, no injury has occurred to client or staff as a result of client's violence.

CHAPTER 18 SUMMARY

- Planning inpatient nursing care in mental health nursing is based on three steps:
  — Admission to inpatient setting with DSM-IV diagnosis
  — Nursing assessment of all physical and mental patterns
  — Development of nursing diagnosis statements

- The nursing care plan format consists of five parts:
  — 1. Nursing diagnosis—statement of nursing problem and its cause.
  — 2. Nursing goal or priority—expected measurable client behavior showing the original clinical problem has been resolved or decreased enough for the client to be discharged.
  — 3. Nursing intervention—nursing behavior action that can alter the client's clinical problem and achieve the nursing goal or priority.
  — 4. Nursing rationale—the reasoning to support the nursing plan for each diagnosis, used in conjunction with each nursing intervention.
  — 5. Evaluation—describes the change in behavior that can be used to measure whether the nursing intervention is effective.

CHAPTER 18 QUESTIONS

1. Which of the following statements best defines the nursing intervention phase of the nursing process?
   a. A statement about the nursing action that can alter the client's clinical problem
   b. A statement that describes the change in behavior
   c. A statement about expected measurable client behavior
   d. A statement about the reasoning supporting the nursing plan

2. The planning of inpatient nursing care in mental health nursing is based on
   a. admission to an inpatient psychiatric setting with a diagnosed mental disorder from the *Diagnostic and Statistical Manual of Mental Disorders*.
   b. nursing assessment of all mental and physical patterns.
   c. development of nursing diagnosis statements to describe the ineffective coping mechanisms causing the client's current problems.
   d. all of the above.

3. Which of the following is *not* a part of the nursing care format?
   a. Nursing rationale
   b. Nursing intervention
   c. Evaluation
   d. Nursing estimate of length of inpatient stay

4. In a nursing care plan, each nursing rationale is developed in conjunction with
   a. local union rules.
   b. the anticipated resistance of the client.
   c. nursing intervention.
   d. weekly staff meetings.

BIBLIOGRAPHY

Barry, P.D. (1996). *Psychosocial nursing: Care of physically ill patients and their families* (3rd ed.). Philadelphia: Lippincott-Raven.

Carpenito, L.J. (1994). *Nursing care plans and documentation: Nursing diagnosis and collaborative problems*. Philadelphia: J.B. Lippincott.

Diagnostic and statistical manual of mental disorders (4th ed.). (1994). Washington, DC: American Psychiatric Press.

Fortinash, K.M., & Holoday-Worret, P.A. (1995). *Psychiatric nursing care plans* (2nd ed.). St. Louis: Mosby Year Book.

Kaplan, H.I., & Sadock, B.J. (1995). *Comprehensive textbook of psychiatry/VI* (6th ed.). Baltimore: Williams & Wilkins.

Lederer, J.R., Marculescu, G.L., Mochik, B., & Seaby, N. (Eds.). (1995). *Nursing diagnosis and intervention pocket guide* (5th ed.). Redwood City, CA: Addison-Wesley Nursing.

Lego, S. (1996). *Psychiatric nursing: A comprehensive reference* (2nd ed.). Philadelphia: Lippincott-Raven.

Nettina, S.M. (1996). *The Lippincott manual of nursing practice* (6th ed.). Philadelphia: Lippincott-Raven.

19

Nursing Care of the Older Adult With a Mental Disorder

After reading this chapter the student will be able to:

- Name the percentage of older Americans who are institutionalized.

- Describe why general systems theory is important in assessing the health status of the older adult.

- List the types of losses older adults can experience.

- Name the most common types of mental distress in the elderly and describe each condition and the types of nursing intervention that can reduce the distress.

Advances in health care and government involvement in ensuring adequate care for older adults have resulted in large numbers of people living into their 70s, 80s, and 90s. A great majority of the elderly are self-sufficient and live in their own homes. They are able to maintain an independent lifestyle, often with the involvement of family members who assist them in a variety of supportive ways.

Indeed, although there is a prevalent misconception that the majority of old people are institutionalized, it is not true. It is estimated that 11.7% of the U.S. population—25 million people—are over 65. The number of institutionalized Americans over age 65 is approximately 1,126,000, or only 0.4% of the total population. With few exceptions, the majority of those people were no longer able to live independently or with their families because their mental or physical condition was progressively worsening. The inability of the family system to continue coping with the increasing strain of the infirmity, rather than the severity of the infirmity, determines when institutionalization occurs in most cases.

In considering the nursing care of the elderly with mental disorders, we must remain constantly aware of general systems theory, discussed in Chapter 10, Influence of Family and Social Environment on the Individual. All aspects of our functioning are constantly interacting: physical, psychological, and social systems. In children and younger adults, the interactions of these three realms of our being are occurring at all times, although they may not be completely evident. In aged people, it is the effects of these interactions that create the difficulties that they encounter as time progresses.

The majority of older people remain intellectually aware and are capable of independent living until very old age. Despite the losses they encounter, they remain remarkably adaptable and resilient. Their long life experience has prepared them to flow with the currents of change that accompany aging rather than be overwhelmed by them.

◆ EFFECTS OF LOSS ON THE OLDER ADULT

People of all ages experience losses brought about by physical illness and disabilities. The losses are accompanied by a grieving process in which a variety of mental changes occur as the grief is resolved. The grieving process can take up to 1 year when a significant loss occurs. For the elderly, the number of losses they experience can occur in a succession that does not allow them time to adequately resolve one loss before another occurs. Examples of losses frequently encountered in the aging process are as follows:

Loss of employment through retirement

Loss of self-image, if job was a strong source of self-gratification

Loss of physical health

Loss of good body image as a result of declining health

Loss of independence as infirmities increase

Loss of mobility

Loss of spouse, friends, or other family members owing to death

Loss of opportunities for social contact with others

Loss of home

Loss of income

Needless to say, these losses strain a person's coping abilities. The mastery of this strain requires well-functioning intellectual and emotional resources. But age slowly degenerates these resources.

As we age, our bodies, minds, and social systems begin to change at an increased rate. Brain tissue is not immune to these physiologic changes that are occurring throughout the body. The changes in the brain affect our intellectual and emotional capabilities, including our abilities to cope.

◆ THE MOST COMMON PSYCHOSOCIAL DISORDERS OF THE AGED

It is important to distinguish between the terms **psychiatric** and **psychosocial** when referring to mental disorders in the aged. In order to be termed a psychiatric disorder, a person's mental status must meet the criteria of the *Diagnostic and Statistical Manual of Mental Disorders,* fourth edition, (DSM-IV) categories of mental disorders (see Chapters 20 to 27). Many people who experience mental distress and emotional pain do not meet these formal criteria. The quality of their lives and that of their families can be severely disrupted, however, because of the impact of their decreasing mental abilities on their psychosocial functioning. The following are the most common types of mental distress in the elderly:

Depression

Insomnia

Cognitive impairment

Stress reactions

Decrease in social and daily living skills

◆ Nursing Care of the Older Adult With Depression

The incidence of depression in the elderly has never been well-documented by research. The number of people of all ages with depression who meet the DSM-IV criteria of major affective illness is approximately 4% to 6%. As described above, the elderly experience a number of losses as aging progresses. Because unresolved loss is a major factor in many depressive reactions, it is possible that the amount of depression in the elderly is higher than that in the general population.

Remember that two of the symptoms of depression are slowing of cognitive functioning and decrease in memory. These are also the symptoms of progressive dementia, a form of cognitive disorder. Unfortunately, primary health caregivers often do not take the time to obtain more information from their clients in order to differentiate between the possible causes of decreased intellectual functioning. Depression is treatable and reversible; generally, dementia is not. Too often, the symptoms of depression are assumed to be the signs of dementia; no treatment occurs, and the person's emotional discomfort continues. The symptoms that are present in older people who meet the criteria of depression are at least 2 weeks of experiencing the following symptoms:

Dysphoric feelings of sadness and hopelessness

Changes in appetite

Changes in sleep patterns

Loss of energy

Lack of interest or pleasure in normal activities

Increased feelings of guilt

Slowed or agitated physical activity

Decreased thinking, concentration, and memory

The most common treatments for depression in the elderly are psychotherapy and antidepressant medication.

The nursing care recommendations given in this chapter should be used as a basis for nursing care planning with depressed older adults. Another nursing care approach that can be considered is nurse-led support groups. This type of group is not the same as a psychotherapy group in which there is more intensive probing and interpretation of a person's statements. Rather, it is a group in which the depressed person has the opportunity to relate with other people who have similar problems.

Often, older people, whether living in their own home, with family members, or in institutions, are isolated from other people. The opportunity to engage in discussion with others in a formal group can provide them with a sense of support and understanding that may have been lacking in their lives. Caring family members, despite their best intentions, cannot provide for all of the psychosocial needs of their aging relative. The sharing of feelings and thoughts with others who are experiencing similar changes can be reassuring and fulfilling.

Nursing care of a depressed older person who is taking antidepressant medication also involves careful observation for the many physical side effects caused by antidepressants (see Chapter 31, Psychopharmacology and Electroshock Treatment of Mental Disorders). These medications can have negative effects on each of the body's major systems. If there is a previously existing physical disorder, these drugs could worsen it. Furthermore, these medications can cause physical symptoms that can be confused with newly emerging illnesses. Elderly individuals often experience a mix of these conditions, which leads to variations in the severity and duration of the distress. Evaluating and determining cognitive abilities may be complicated by age-related changes, such as poor eyesight or hearing, slowed responses, or chronic illness, that make the client's participation in the assessment process more difficult. Remember to document routinely mental and physical status, noting and reporting changes in either. This will assist the physician in evaluating the therapeutic effects of the medication. (See Chapter 15, Mental Status Exam and Appendix A, Barry Psychosocial Assessment.)

◆ NURSING CARE OF THE OLDER ADULT WITH COGNITIVE IMPAIRMENT

Cognitive impairment is a decrease in the intellectual aspect of mental functioning; it includes a decrease in problem-solving ability, reasoning, judgment, concentration, and memory. The two most common causes (mentioned in the preceding section) are depression and cognitive disorders.

Remember that some organic brain syndromes are reversible. Ideally, all people suspected of having a dementia type of cognitive disorder should receive a thorough physical examination and laboratory tests to rule out any other physical condition that could cause a toxic brain syndrome and could be reversed with treatment (see Chapter 21, Delirium, Dementia, and Amnestic and Other Cognitive Disorders). Toxic brain syndromes can be caused by medication side effects, nutritional deficiencies, different types of physical illness such as metabolic disorders, infection, trauma, and so on.

The clients should also be examined by a psychiatrist. Within the field of psychiatry a new subspecialty, geriatric psychiatry, has developed specifically to care for the older adult with mental disorders. Whenever possible, someone trained in this specialty, who has a systems perspective of the multiple causes of geriatric mental disorders, should perform the psychiatric evaluation.

People with cognitive impairment experience a number of other changes in mental functioning as an outcome of their decreased intellectual ability. Their capacity to cope with stress is decreased, because their ability to solve problems and think through the various events they are encountering is hampered. In addition, they experience a decrease in self-esteem because they can no longer rely on their minds. As a result, they may gradually withdraw from relationships and stop attending social functions, because they do not want others to notice their decreased mental functioning.

STRESSFUL EFFECTS ON THE FAMILY OF THE AGED PERSON

Cognitive impairment in an elderly family member places a strain on the entire family system as its members try to adapt. For example, an elderly woman who lives alone may have a physician's appointment, which her son calls to remind her of on the morning of the appointment. When he arrives after a half-hour drive to discover that his mother has forgotten about it and is not ready to leave, he may become frustrated and angry. With the increase in the elderly population also comes an increase in the number of elderly caregivers; in these situations, the person providing the care is experiencing the same kinds of losses and stresses as the identified patient.

As these types of events increase and concern rises about the aging couple's ability to care effectively for one another, or for the safety of the aging person living alone, many families elect to bring the elderly relative into their home. The immediate solution can be positive for all concerned. If the cognitive impairment worsens, however, the level of strain on the family increases.

The children of the aging relative, sometimes called the "sandwich generation," experience increased stress as they attempt to balance the needs of their parents with those of their own children. Communication within the immediate family can become rigid and closed as negative emotions are avoided. Communication in the extended family network of relatives can be equally affected if there is resentment by the person who assumes the caretaking role.

As the mental impairment of the older person increases, it is not unusual for the stress within the family to rise to a critical point, at which a decision is made to institutionalize the older adult rather than risk what feels like or actually is family disintegration.

Increasingly, support services are being developed in the community to assist families before they reach a crisis point. These include adult daycare programs or programs designed to relieve the primary caregiver. In addition, programs for the primary caregiver are beginning to include group or individual counseling, giving them a chance to relieve themselves of unpleasant feelings such as sadness, anger, or guilt that frequently accompany the care of a cognitively impaired person. Home-based care is another option that is increasingly available. Mental health interventions conducted in the home allow caregivers and family members to participate in these counseling sessions. In-home sessions are particularly useful for clients who find it difficult to get to a doctor's office or mental health clinic. Other helpful programs support coping by increasing knowledge of resources and problem-solving skills for both the older adult and his or her caregivers.

The nursing care of the institutionalized older adult with cognitive impairment is described in Chapter 21, Delirium, Dementia, and Amnestic and Other Cognitive Disorders, under the sections on dementia or delirium, depending on the cause of the mental disorder.

◆ Nursing Care of the Older Adult With Insomnia

Another condition that causes mental distress for many elderly people is **insomnia**, a disturbance in a person's normal sleeping pattern. Insomnia can be due to many causes: pain caused by physical conditions, stimulant or diuretic medications, effects of excessive coffee or nicotine, sleeping at other times during the day, poor sleeping environment, or depression or anxiety.

Nearly one fourth of healthy adults over age 65 report sleeping difficulties. In fact, many people overestimate their need for sleep. It should be noted that as a person ages, metabolic rate declines and the need for sleep decreases. In addition, as a person grows older, there are changes in brain wave activity during the various stages of sleep that contribute to increased wakefulness.

Many times, people who experience sleep disturbances of varying levels of difficulty further contribute to the problem by worrying about not sleeping in advance of going to bed. Gradually, they condition themselves so that the thought of not sleeping is accompanied by anxiety.

Generally, it can be helpful to remember that the body maintains regulating mechanisms to ensure its own well-being. Sleep occurs when it is necessary to maintain physical and mental equilibrium. An important fact for nurses to know is that hypnotic medications—chronically overused in this country—are effective for no more than 2 weeks, in most cases.

The majority of people with insomnia are not in institutions and are not recipients of nursing care. Appropriate nursing intervention, regardless of the setting, includes sharing accurate information, providing an environment that is conducive to sleep, and using the therapeutic nursing approaches recommended in Chapter 26, Dissociative, Sexual, and Other Disorders.

◆ NURSING CARE OF THE OLDER ADULT WITH DECREASE IN SOCIAL AND DAILY LIVING SKILLS

An aging person may experience a decrease in his or her normal relationship abilities and living skills. Often, this is the result of cognitive impairment, decreased opportunities for social relationships, and other types of deprivation. Accordingly, as older adults become less able to maintain relationships and to care adequately for nutritional and hygiene needs, it becomes necessary for them to be cared for by relatives, agencies, or institutions.

An innovative program designed by clinicians at the Florida Mental Health Institute seeks to address the needs of two populations: institutionalized clients for whom the goal is discharge, and people who are not institutionalized, but whose poor self-care will soon lead to admission if there is no intervention. The programs they designed are aimed at teaching skills—hygiene; self-maintenance skills, such as laundering, meal planning, and money management; normal communication skills; and so on.

Nurses can teach these skills to institutionalized people who lack them and can reinforce their accomplishments with warmth and approval. Also, nurse-led groups that address the topics discussed above are helpful in teaching social and daily living skills and promoting a supportive group environment in which skill acquisition can take place.

◆ NURSING CARE OF THE OLDER ADULT WITH STRESS REACTIONS

As described early in the chapter, biopsychosocial assessment of older people allows appropriate intervention to be developed. The number of life stressors experienced in old age is usually high. In most cases, adults maintain the same style of coping in old age that they have used throughout their lifetime, but now, a series of life stressors can pile up, undermining coping abilities and overloading coping strength.

A mild form of cognitive impairment, added to this scenario, can further reduce tolerance for stress. Coping strength is greatly dependent on a person's intellectual capacity. As it diminishes, so too can tolerance for stress.

The most important external factor in a person's capacity to deal with stress is the availability of support people. Ideally, this support is available from family members or friends. Community support services are hard-pressed to meet the needs of the ever-increasing number of elderly clients.

Some of the primary factors that determine an older person's stress tolerance are as follows:

Perception of the stressful incident. Does the person view this event as significantly threatening? Why?

History of other stressful incidents during the previous year. Is the current incident the "straw that breaks the camel's back"?

Degree of cognitive impairment due to organic causes.

Availability of support people.

RETIREMENT

The level of stress tolerance for older adults is often related to the issue of retirement. The partner of the retired person can be equally affected. Reichard, Livson, and Peterson have proposed the following three basic personality types that adapt well to retirement:

1. The mature type. Emotionally well adjusted; life is satisfying for them.
2. The "rocking chair" type. Easygoing natures; relieved to be free of responsibilities of work and active family.
3. The "armored" type. Actively involved in life to avoid feelings of uselessness; probably have many type A personality characteristics; goal oriented.

They also believe that there are two personality types who may not cope well with retirement:

1. The angry type. Resentment about unfulfilled goals causes them to resist acceptance of retirement.
2. The self-hating type. Feelings of failure cause ongoing guilt and poor self-esteem.

CATASTROPHIC REACTION

On occasion, if an older person is severely stressed, he or she may be subject to a catastrophic reaction. A **catastrophic reaction** occurs when there is a sudden, unexpected stressor, and the person's normal coping mechanisms fail. The result is severe anxiety accompanied by disruption of equilibrium in the physical, intellectual, and emotional realms (see Chapter 13, Stress: Effective Coping and Adaptation). This response is also known as a panic reaction. Frequently it is due to organic impairment that decreases a person's intellectual capacity to think through and adapt to the stressor.

When an older person is demonstrating decreased tolerance for stress, it often is an indication that his or her problem-solving and decision-making capacities are decreased. Caregivers can help by initiating a discussion of the person's current life situation, with the intention of identifying situations that are problematic. In addition, it is wise to have the person describe potentially stressful circumstances he or she is anticipating. Often, by using the following problem-solving process, solutions can be found that decrease the stress he or she is experiencing.

PROBLEM-SOLVING PROCESS

1. Identify the problem. Describe why it is a problem and what factors are feeding into it.
2. Describe the possible solutions.
3. Choose the best solution.
4. Implement it.
5. Evaluate the outcome. If not successful, analyze why, choose an alternative from item 2 above, and implement and evaluate it.

Often, this process relieves the person's distress because it gives him or her the opportunity to describe it. The person then has a stronger sense of mastery of the problem. Recommend the use of this process to the client's family, whether the client is in a hospital or living independently.

If the person is unable to actively participate in this process, it may be necessary to assume a more custodial role. Problem solving by the nurse, in consultation with the family, if available, can provide the client with a stronger sense of security.

Generally, it is unwise to routinely administer minor tranquilizers to institutionalized people experiencing chronic stress reactions due to organic impairment. Instead, whenever possible, control the environment to minimize the potential for such reactions.

For older people living independently and experiencing increasing amounts of stress, individual counseling is often helpful. This can assist them in identifying both causes and solutions for their stress. In addition, it can help to reduce their anxiety levels. Minor tranquilizers should be avoided, except in the transition period immediately following a severe stressor, such as the unexpected loss of a spouse.

Another stress reliever in the healthy adult is a regular exercise regimen, such as daily walking. The tension-relieving benefits of exercise can have therapeutic effects in chronically stressed individuals.

CHAPTER 19 SUMMARY

- Only a small percentage of older adults are institutionalized. Institutionalization often has more to do with lack of family resources for care than with the severity of the elderly person's impairment.

- The losses experienced by an elderly person can occur without time for recovery between losses. This can lead to a strain on the person's coping abilities.

- The most common psychosocial disorders of the elderly are depression, insomnia, cognitive impairment, stress reactions, and decrease in social and daily living skills.

- Slowing of cognitive function and decrease in memory can be caused either by depression or by progressive dementia.

- Elderly clients suspected of having a dementia type of cognitive disorder should receive a physical examination to rule out a treatable physical cause.

- Cognitive impairment and other factors of aging place increased strain on the family unit.

- Factors that determine an older person's stress tolerance are perception of the stressful incident, history of other stressful incidents, degree of cognitive impairment, and available support system.

- Three basic personality types that adapt well to retirement are mature (well adjusted), "rocking chair" (relieved to be free of responsibilities), and "armored" (actively involved).

- Two personality types that do not adapt well to retirement are the angry and self-hating types.

- A catastrophic reaction occurs when there is a sudden, unexpected stressor and the person's normal coping mechanisms fail. The response is severe anxiety and disruption of equilibrium, also known as a panic attack.

- Using a problem-solving process (identify the problem, describe possible solutions, choose the best solution, and implement it) can help decrease stress.

CHAPTER 19 QUESTIONS

1. Which of the following is *not* a common type of mental distress in the elderly?
   a. Cognitive impairment
   b. Extended manic episodes
   c. Decrease in social and daily living skills
   d. Stress reactions

2. All older adults suspected of having a dementia type of cognitive disorder should receive
   a. immediate psychiatric hospitalization.
   b. a thorough physical exam and laboratory tests.
   c. no further treatment since there is no cure.
   d. an immediate increase in sedating medication.

3. Nursing care to improve social and daily living skills includes teaching
   a. nutrition and meal planning.
   b. hygiene and self maintenance.
   c. communication skills.
   d. all of the above.

4. The three personality types that adjust well to retirement are
   a. "armored," angry, and "rocking chair."
   b. mature, "armored," and angry.
   c. mature, "rocking chair" and "armored."
   d. angry, self-hating, and paranoid.

BIBLIOGRAPHY

Barry, P.D. (1996). *Psychosocial nursing: Care of physically ill patients and their families* (3rd ed.). Philadelphia: Lippincott-Raven.

Hogstel, M.O. (1995). *Practical guide to health assessment through the lifespan* (2nd ed.). New York: Davis Co.

Hughes, C.P. (1992). Community psychiatric nursing and depression in elderly people. *Journal of Advanced Nursing, 17,* 34–42.

Kaplan, H.I., & Sadock, B.J. (1995). *Comprehensive textbook of psychiatry/VI* (6th ed.). Baltimore: Williams & Wilkins.

McFarland, G.K., Wasli, E.L., & Gerety, E.K. (1996). *Nursing diagnoses and process in psychiatric mental health nursing* (3rd ed.). Philadelphia: Lippincott-Raven.

Nettina, S.M. (1996). *The Lippincott manual of nursing practice* (6th ed.). Philadelphia: Lippincott-Raven.

Reichard, S., Livson, F., & Peterson, P. (1980). In L. Stein (Ed.). *Aging and personality: A study of 87 older men.* Salem, NJ: Ayer Company Publications.

Stuart, G.W., & Sundeen, S.J. (Eds.). (1994). *Principles and practice of psychiatric nursing* (5th ed.). St. Louis: Mosby Year Book.

Timby, B.K., & Lewis, L.W. (1996). *Fundamental skills and concepts in patient care* (6th ed.). Philadelphia: Lippincott-Raven.

Wilson, H.S., & Kneisl, C.R. (1996). *Psychiatric nursing* (5th ed.). Redwood City, CA: Addison-Wesley.

DEVELOPING CRITICAL THINKING SKILLS THROUGH CLASS DISCUSSION

UNIT FIVE Case Study
Nursing the Client With a Mental Disorder

Peter is a 79-year-old widower who has early dementia related to Alzheimer's disease. Since the death of his wife 2 years ago, he has been living with his 82-year-old brother, Andrew. Andrew, who had been in good health, died suddenly 3 days ago of a cerebral vascular accident. Andrew's daughter, Marilyn, lives in the same community and is the only relative within a several hundred mile radius. She is divorced, works full time, and has four children, aged 11 to 17.

D I S C U S S I O N   Q U E S T I O N S

1. Using Maslow's Hierarchy of Human Needs in Chapter 9 as a guide, can you determine and prioritize Peter's needs during the next week?

2. Discuss the reasons for your priorities.

3. Can you name the different types of challenges to a family when suddenly confronted with the care of a mentally disordered loved one?

4. If you were Marilyn, how would you begin to examine your options for Peter's care?

5. Can you select five nursing diagnoses that you might expect Peter to experience as the result of the sudden loss of his caregiver and home environment? Why?

6. Can you name five nursing diagnoses that may occur in Marilyn or in her family as a response to the loss of her father and the sudden care burden of her uncle. Why?

7. If you were Marilyn's friend, what are some methods you would use to give her emotional support during this period of time?

Unit 6

CATEGORIES
OF MENTAL DISORDERS

As human beings begin to experience changes in mental state and behavior on the continuum from mental health to mental disorder, a cluster of unusual mental symptoms usually occurs. This cluster of mental symptoms frequently falls into certain patterns that fit a specific type of mental disorder. Such clusters of mental symptoms and patterns of mental changes are described in lists of the various categories of mental disorders that are published in a book by the American Psychiatric Association (APA) titled *The Diagnostic and Statistical Manual of Mental Disorders,* more commonly known as the DSM.

In early 1994, the APA published the categories of mental disorders, fourth edition (DSM-IV), to replace the third edition, revised (DSM-III-R). All chapter headings and diagnostic criteria are based on the DSM-IV.

20

Disorders Usually First Diagnosed During Infancy, Childhood, or Adolescence

Behavioral Objectives

After reading this chapter the student will be able to:

■ Name five major categories of mental disorders first evident in infancy, childhood, or adolescence.

■ List two conditions in each category.

■ Explain five possible causes of mental retardation.

■ Name the four categories of mental retardation and the IQ levels of each.

This chapter presents the clinical symptoms manifest in a variety of disorders that are primarily developmental in etiology. These conditions usually are evident during infancy, childhood, or adolescence and may diminish as the child matures or as the result of therapeutic intervention with the child and his or her family.

Often, however, these disorders continue to manifest themselves in the adult personality. Usually they are of a mild nature, so that the adult is able to engage in the normal roles of adulthood. When severe, they contribute toward lifelong difficulties that decrease the person's quality of life and that of his or her family. Such disorders, if not treated early, become deeply ingrained and are difficult, if not impossible, to reverse.

A wide variety of conditions are included in this category of mental disorders. Most are rarely seen in inpatient psychiatric facilities because the preferred method of treatment is in the outpatient setting. Accordingly, the nursing care of each condition is not included here. Exceptions in types of conditions that are nondisruptive and allow the client to live at home are those of mental retardation and pervasive developmental disorders. The specific care recommended for these conditions can be found in textbooks written about the disorders.

◆ Mental Retardation

The most universally accepted definition of mental retardation in use today is that adopted by the American Association on Mental Deficiency.

The terms **idiot, imbecile,** and **moron** are still in common use in Europe. **Feeblemindedness** was used in the past in the United States to refer to the mild forms of mental retardation and continues to be used in Great Britain. **Oligophrenia** is still commonly used in the former Soviet Union and some other Western European countries. None of these terms is currently popular in the United States.

Approximately 3% of the population of the United States (nearly 7 million people) are said to be mentally retarded. The vast majority (87%) of the mentally retarded are classified as borderline or mildly retarded, whereas the remainder (13%) are classified as moderate, severe, or profound. Approximately 60,000 to 90,000 of the mentally retarded population, those in the severe or profound categories, require lifetime custodial care. A disproportionately large number of the mildly retarded group of nearly 6 million come from the lower socioeconomic levels of society. Table 20–1 describes the developmental characteristics of the mentally retarded.

◆ **TABLE 20–1. Developmental Characteristics of the Mentally Retarded**

Degree of Mental Retardation	Preschool Age 0–5 Maturation and Development	School Age 6–20 Training and Education	Adults 21 and Over Social and Vocational Adequacy
Profound IQ 0–25	Gross retardation; minimal capacity for functioning in sensorimotor areas; needs nursing care	Some motor development present; may respond to minimal or limited training in self-help	Some motor and speech development; may achieve very limited self-care; needs nursing care
Severe IQ 20–40	Poor motor development; minimal speech; generally unable to profit from training in self-help; little or no communication skills	Can talk or learn to communicate; can be trained in elemental health habits; profits from systematic habit training	May contribute partially to self-maintenance under complete supervision; can develop self-protection skills to a minimal useful level in controlled environment
Moderate IQ 35–55	Can talk or learn to communicate; poor social awareness; fair motor development; profits from training in self-help; can be managed with moderate supervision	Can profit from training in social and occupational skills; unlikely to progress beyond second grade level in academic subjects; may learn to travel alone in familiar places	May achieve self-maintenance in unskilled or semi-skilled work under sheltered conditions; needs supervision and guidance when under mild social or economic stress
Mild IQ 50–70	Can develop social and communication skills; minimal retardation in sensorimotor areas; often not distinguished from normal until later age	Can learn academic skills up to approximately sixth grade level by late teens; can be guided toward social conformity	Can usually achieve social and vocational skills adequate to minimal self-support but may need guidance and assistance when under unusual social or economic stress

Adapted from *Mental Retardation Activities of the U.S. Department of Health, Education, and Welfare.* Washington, DC: U.S. Government Printing Office, and *Diagnostic and Statistical Manual* IV (1994). Washington, DC: American Psychiatric Association.

CAUSES OF RETARDATION

Retardation may be present at birth or it may begin during childhood. Its causes are many and, in some cases, as yet unknown. Some forms are familial or genetic (ie, they are transmitted through parental genes from generation to generation, or parental genes may become damaged or rearranged by accident or radiation). Other forms are thought to be caused by damage to the embryo's developing nervous system while in the mother's uterus. This damage may result from a variety of causes.

It is also possible that injuries from the stress of birth cause some types of retardation. The baby's head molds under great pressure as it advances through the birth canal; in rare instances, damage can occur to the delicate blood vessels in the brain. Anoxia, or lack of sufficient oxygen to the brain, can also cause retardation. This oxygen starvation can occur prenatally, perinatally, or postnatally.

Childhood diseases with high fever and toxicity can result in brain damage, especially in the very young; glandular imbalances may prevent normal central nervous system growth; chemical imbalances in the blood may result in brain damage; and accidents and falls may seriously injure the brain.

Many of the most common causes of mental retardation can be ascribed to social, cultural, and economic factors. These are classed as environmental factors; we are becoming more aware of the impact the environment has on our learning processes. A child functioning at a lower level than normal as a result of cultural deprivation can achieve normal intellectual growth, provided he or she receives early and adequate help. Other forms of retardation, however, appear to be self-limiting; it is possible to develop a mind to its full potential, but it is not possible to change its innate intelligence level.

◆ TABLE 20–2. Nursing Care Needs of the Mentally Retarded

Level of Retardation	Nursing Care Needs
Mildly retarded	Coping skills are limited during periods of moderate to heavy stress, needs extra support; preventive health care teaching should be developed to meet the level of understanding
Moderately retarded	Dependent on caregivers for assistance with activities of daily living; can follow simple instructions
Severely retarded	Constant supervision is required owing to level of functioning at the infant or early childhood level
Profoundly retarded	Complete care is required

NURSING CARE OF THE MENTALLY RETARDED

It is unusual to see mentally retarded individuals in the psychiatric setting unless they also have a psychiatric disorder. In such cases, the nursing care plan for the specific psychiatric disorder can be modified to meet the needs of the person based on the degree of mental retardation. Table 20–2 describes nursing care needs based on the level of retardation.

◆ PERVASIVE DEVELOPMENTAL DISORDERS: AUTISTIC DISORDER

One of the most profound mental disorders in a person of any age is autistic disorder. This is a condition that most commonly manifests itself in infancy but may begin as late as 36 months of age. It usually does not change significantly over the lifespan. Individuals with this disorder are usually institutionalized in long-term facilities. The autistic person is markedly dysfunctional in most realms of human functioning. The aspects of impaired functioning are as follows:

1. Interpersonal relations
   a. Lack of awareness of the presence of other people; lack of awareness of others' emotions or their need for privacy
   b. No comfort-seeking when distressed
   c. Limited or no imitation, social play, or capacity to form peer friendships
2. Verbal and nonverbal communication
   a. Abnormal eye-to-eye contact
   b. Abnormal speech patterns
   c. Abnormal conversational ability
3. Activity level and interests
   a. Repetitive body movements
   b. Preoccupation with objects
   c. Very low range of interests
   d. Adherence to nonfunctional routines or rituals

NURSING CARE OF CLIENTS WITH AUTISTIC DISORDERS

The care of an autistic person requires nearly 24-hour monitoring. Accordingly, they are most often institutionalized in long-term facilities. They usually cannot be left alone because of their lack of judgment. Depending on the level of impairment, they may require full assistance with all the normal activities of daily living (ADLs). ADLs include bathing, eating, dressing, and toileting. Their environments should be secure to ensure safety. People with autistic disorders may become combative and can pose a safety risk to themselves and others. Accordingly, a high level of nursing vigilance is necessary.

LEARNING DISORDERS (FORMERLY ACADEMIC SKILLS DISORDERS)

These disorders include three educational areas in which children may have problems:

1. Mathematics disorder
2. Disorder of written expression
3. Reading disorder

These conditions fall into the functional developmental disorder categories when the skill level within one or all of these domains is markedly below the individual's normal expected level of performance. This is determined by standardized, individual testing. The deficit causes interference in the child's or adult's normal ADLs that require the skill or skills. These deficits are not due to a defect in hearing or vision or to a neurologic disorder.

COMMUNICATION DISORDERS

PHONOLOGICAL DISORDER (FORMERLY DEVELOPMENTAL ARTICULATION DISORDER)

The criterion that determines this category is a consistent failure to use developmentally expected speech sounds. As in all of these disorders, the symptoms are not due to a pervasive developmental disorder.

EXPRESSIVE LANGUAGE DISORDER

This category includes the criterion of lack of correlation between a standardized test of expressive language and the person's nonverbal IQ, determined by an individually administered test; the expressive language score is substantially lower than the IQ score. In addition, the disturbance significantly interferes with academic achievement or ADLs.

MIXED RECEPTIVE-EXPRESSIVE LANGUAGE DISORDER

This category includes the criterion that the score received on a standardized test of receptive language does not correlate with a standardized, individually administered IQ test. The deficit also interferes significantly with academic achievement or ADLs.

STUTTERING

This category includes the criterion that speech patterning is inappropriate for the person's age and is characterized by frequent repetitions, sound prolongations, broken words, or words produced with an excess of tension. The disturbance interferes with academic achievement or ADLs.

◆ Motor Skills Disorder

The disorder in this category is **developmental coordination disorder.** In this condition, the person is significantly unable to perform academic functions or ADLs requiring motor coordination at a level similar to other children or adults of the same age. This condition is not caused by a physical disorder, such as cerebral palsy, hemiplegia, or muscular dystrophy.

◆ Attention-Deficit and Disruptive Behavior Disorders

ATTENTION-DEFICIT/HYPERACTIVITY DISORDER

The child with **attention-deficit/hyperactivity disorder** displays a majority of the behaviors listed below. They occur more frequently than in other children in the same age group. The behaviors are fidgeting; difficulty remaining seated; distractibility; difficulty waiting turn, following instructions, sustaining attention, remaining task-focused, and playing quietly; blurting out answers prematurely; excessive talking; interrupting; inattention; excessively losing things; and engaging in dangerous activities. In addition, these behaviors begin to manifest themselves before age 7, and they are not related to a pervasive personality disorder. The various diagnostic categories can be further classified as mild, moderate, or severe.

CONDUCT DISORDER

A child with a **conduct disorder** shows a repeated, persistent pattern of behavior that demonstrates little recognition or consideration of other people's basic rights or that violates social norms expected of a child of his or her age. The diagnostic criteria for conduct disorder require that at least three of the following symptoms be present. The person:

- Often bullies, threatens, or intimidates others
- Often initiates physical fights
- Has used a weapon in more than one fight

- Has been physically cruel to animals or people
- Has stolen with confrontation of a victim (for example, mugging, purse snatching)
- Has forced someone into sexual activity
- Has deliberately destroyed others' property
- Has deliberately set fires
- Has broken into someone else's house, building, or car
- Lies
- Has stolen items (for example, shoplifting) or forged without confrontation of a victim
- Has run away from home at least twice
- Often stays out all night despite parental prohibitions
- Is frequently truant[1]

Conduct disorders can be further classified as mild, moderate, or severe.

OPPOSITIONAL DEFIANT DISORDER

The **oppositional defiant disorder** is a disturbance that has been present for at least 6 months. The symptoms used as criteria should be present more frequently than they are in other children of the same age. The disturbance in behavior significantly impairs functioning in school, at home, and in social settings. The symptoms include frequent episodes of loss of temper, arguing with adults, defying or refusing adults' requests or rules, deliberately annoying others, blaming others for own mistakes, becoming easily aggravated, becoming resentful or angry, swearing, and being spiteful or vindictive. This category is further classified as mild, moderate, or severe.

◆ FEEDING AND EATING DISORDERS OF INFANCY OR EARLY CHILDHOOD

This category of disorders covers major disturbances in eating behavior and includes the following:

- Pica
- Rumination disorder
- Feeding disorder of infancy or early childhood

---

[1] Adapted from *Desk Reference to the Diagnostic Criteria from DSM-IV* (1994). Washington, DC: American Psychiatric Association, pp. 66–67.

Pica is an eating disorder seen most frequently in toddlers between 12 and 24 months of age. The youngster persistently eats nonnutritive substances such as paint, sand, plaster, and so on. It usually disappears spontaneously.

Rumination disorder is a condition in which an infant, usually between 3 and 12 months of age, repeatedly regurgitates partially digested food without nausea or other gastrointestinal illness. In order to meet the criteria for this diagnosis, the condition must follow a period of normal functioning and occur for 1 month. The infant experiences weight loss or fails to gain weight at a normal rate for his or her age.

Feeding disorder of infancy or early childhood is a category for eating disorders that do not meet the criteria of the conditions described above. For example, if a child experiences severe emotional trauma that involves some aspect of eating, such as being unreasonably disciplined for not completely eating all the food on the plate, he or she may demonstrate some aberration of normal eating behavior at the time or during a later stage of development.

Two other eating disorders are **anorexia nervosa** and **bulimia**. Although these disorders most frequently become evident during adolescence and into adulthood, it is believed that they are rooted in childhood.

Anorexia nervosa is a condition seen primarily (95%) in females between 12 and 18 years of age. The young woman develops a strong fear of becoming obese; this fear does not decrease as weight loss occurs. She has a distorted body image and views herself as being fat, even when she is emaciated. The diagnosis of anorexia nervosa is made when the weight loss is more than 15% of ideal body weight for height, body build, and age, and there is no physical cause for the weight loss. If not reversed, this condition can be fatal.

Bulimia is an eating disorder that occurs predominately in adolescent or young adult females. The person indulges in eating binges of high-calorie food. She is aware of the abnormal eating pattern. The binge eating may be pleasurable, but it is followed by a depressed mood. The binge episode ends abruptly with abdominal pain, self-induced vomiting, or sleep. The young woman repeatedly attempts to lose weight by self-induced vomiting, laxatives or diuretics, or severely restrictive diets. She also has rapidly fluctuating weight changes of over 10 pounds due to the alternating dieting and bingeing. She is fearful that she will not be able to stop eating voluntarily.

NURSING CARE OF CLIENTS WITH EATING DISORDERS

Clients with eating disorders are primarily seen in the outpatient setting. Those who receive care in the inpatient setting are usually in a life-threatening state due to long-term and extreme nutritional deficiencies and starvation. In the majority of hospitalized cases the person is diagnosed with anorexia nervosa. Bulimia may not produce the extreme symptoms requiring hospital intervention.

The nursing care of hospitalized individuals with eating disorders will include supportive nursing attitudes and behaviors, including an empathic approach that avoids the nurse's disbelief or displeasure regarding the appearance or behavior of the client. In addition, the nurse

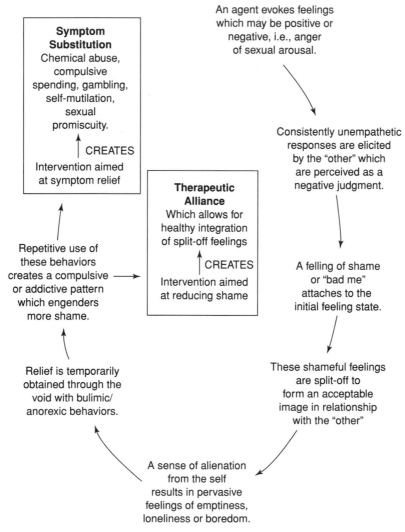

FIGURE 20–1. Development of bulimic/anorexic behaviors as a response to shame. (Conant, M. (1966). *Psychiatric nursing: A comprehensive reference.* (2nd Ed.) Philadelphia: Lippincott-Raven p. 229. Used with permission.)

supports the eating plan devised by the client in consultation with the clinical team leader. It is possible that tube feedings or intravenous hyperalimentation may also be ordered for this client. The client will often be put off by these treatments. The sensitive attitude of the nurse and readiness to communicate with the client about his or her feelings can help the client master the shame and anxiety that often accompany these procedures.

Figure 20–1 depicts the effects of shame on the development of anorexia and bulimia. These dynamics can provide important background knowledge for the nurse in monitoring his or her own therapeutic responses to the client's behavior.

Another important dimension of nursing care is to observe for signs of suicidal risk. These symptoms are described in Chapter 24, Mood Disorders. As the person with a severe eating disorder gradually begins to gain weight, it is not uncommon for significant depression to occur. Encouraging discussion of the client's feelings at all times during the hospitalization will be an important part of nursing care and can provide specific information about the client's response to the care regimen.

The client's readiness to talk about feelings will indicate responsiveness to the therapeutic plan. Accordingly, refusal or consistent reluctance to communicate feelings can be an important sign that noncompliance or severe emotional blocking are occurring. An important aspect of care of people with eating disorders is daily care planning meetings with the clinical care team. The observations of all members of the team are taken into consideration as the daily plan of care is developed.

◆ TIC DISORDERS

The disorders included in this category all include an abnormality of gross motor movement called tics. A **tic** is a rapid, involuntary movement of a related group of muscles or the involuntary production of words or noises.

The subcategories of this classification are as follows:

- Tourette's disorder
- Chronic motor or vocal tic disorder
- Transient tic disorder

Tourette's disorder occurs before the age of 18 and usually has a chronic lifelong course. The person experiences multiple vocal and motor (body) tics in many muscle groups. The intensity of the symptoms varies over months and the condition is present over 1 year in order to be diagnosed as Tourette's disorder.

Chronic motor or vocal tic disorder includes the presence of either motor or vocal tics, but not both, in someone under age 18. They occur very frequently for a period of over a year. There is no other neurologic condition causing the tics.

◆ ELIMINATION DISORDERS

Encopresis is a disorder in which a child over 4 years of age passes feces voluntarily or involuntarily in socially inappropriate places at least once a month. Approximately 1% of 5-year-olds demonstrate this behavior. There are two other subclassifications of this disorder: **with constipation and overflow incontinence**, in which history or physical examination reveals evidence of constipation before the disturbance; and **without constipation and overflow incontinence**, in which there is no evidence of constipation before the dysfunction.

Enuresis is a condition in which a child of at least 5 years voids into clothing or bed during the daytime or nighttime. The child has at least two events per week for at least three consecutive months.

Approximately 10% of all 5-year-old children experience this condition. It usually disappears as the child matures physically and mentally. It is not caused by a physical disease. Within this category it is important to specify the pattern of enuresis: **nocturnal only** (at night), **diurnal only** (during the daytime), or **nocturnal and diurnal.**

◆ OTHER DISORDERS OF INFANCY AND CHILDHOOD

SEPARATION ANXIETY DISORDER

The youngster with a **separation anxiety disorder** experiences anxiety at or near the panic level when separated from a major attachment figure, such as a parent, sibling, and so on. The reaction exceeds what would be expected of a child of his or her age. The child demonstrates clinging behavior and is unable or finds it difficult to be away from home independently, at camp or on school outings, for instance. Physical signs of anxiety appear in anticipation of separation. These include stomach aches, nausea, vomiting, diarrhea, headaches, and so on. Cardiovascular symptoms such as dizziness and palpitations may occur in older children and adolescents. Their separation from significant others may cause morbid fears about death or accidents that might happen to themselves or their parents. (For more detailed information on the phenomenon of anxiety in adolescents refer to Chapter 25, Anxiety and Somatoform Disorders.)

SELECTIVE MUTISM (FORMERLY ELECTIVE MUTISM)

Selective mutism is a condition in which a person has the ability to speak and understand language but consistently fails to talk in one or more major social situations. These symptoms are unrelated to a communication or pervasive developmental disorder.

REACTIVE ATTACHMENT DISORDER OF INFANCY OR EARLY CHILDHOOD

This condition affects a child's ability to bond with or attach to others in a trusting manner. The child either is aloof and uninterested in social relations or is inappropriately familiar with unknown people. These symptoms are unrelated to mental retardation or to a pervasive developmental disorder.

The child has been improperly cared for with a history of persistent lack of concern about the child's basic emotional needs for comfort, stimulation, and protection; continual disregard of the child's basic physical needs including adequate housing, nutrition, and protection from danger; or continuous change of primary caregiver, reducing the potential for attachment. The course of the disorder usually begins with improper care, leading to the incapacity of the child to form attachments.

STEREOTYPIC MOVEMENT DISORDER (FORMERLY STEREOTYPE/HABIT DISORDER)

Stereotypic movement disorder involves repetitive intentional behaviors such as head banging, body weaving, self-biting or hitting, and hand shaking or waving. The activity either causes or risks physical injury or interferes with normal ADLs.

CHAPTER 20 SUMMARY

- Mental retardation may be caused by hereditary factors, nervous system damage before birth, injury during birth, childhood diseases or injuries, or social, cultural, and economic factors.

- Autistic disorder is a profound mental disorder usually beginning from infancy to 36 months. Characteristics include significant impairment in interpersonal relationships, verbal and nonverbal communication, and activity levels and interests.

- Learning disorders, motor skills disorders, and communication disorders are characterized by a child's skill level that is markedly below what is expected for his or her age group and that interferes with normal activities of daily living.

- Attention-deficit and disruptive behavior disorders include the following:
  - Attention-deficit/hyperactivity disorder—fidgeting, distractibility, interrupting, inattention, difficulty remaining task-focused
  - Conduct disorder—aggression to people and animals, destruction of property, deceitfulness or theft, and serious violations of rules
  - Oppositional defiant disorder—loss of temper, frequent fighting or arguing, deliberately annoying others, being spiteful or vengeful

- A child with separation anxiety disorder experiences panic-level anxiety when separated from a major attachment figure.

- Feeding and eating disorders include pica, rumination disorder, anorexia nervosa, and bulimia.

- Tics are rapid, involuntary movements of a related group of muscles or the involuntary production of words or noises. Tourette's disorder is a major tic disorder.

- Age-inappropriate incontinence is encopresis (feces) and enuresis (urine).

- Other disorders of infancy, childhood, and adolescence include the following:
  - Selective mutism—failure to speak in specific social situations
  - Reactive attachment disorder—unable to respond appropriately to social interactions
  - Stereotypic movement disorder—repetitive motor behavior not caused by tic or autistic disorder

CHAPTER 20 QUESTIONS

1. Which of the following is true about autistic disorder?
   a. It manifests between 4 and 5 years of age.
   b. It improves markedly with community-based treatment.
   c. Characteristics include lack of awareness and repetitive body movements.
   d. It causes minimal dysfunction.

2. Possible causes of mental retardation include genetic factors and
   a. birth injury.

b. childhood illness.

c. social, cultural, or economic factors.

d. all of the above.

3. Which of the following behaviors is associated with oppositional defiant disorder?

a. Frequent episodes of loss of temper

b. Extreme shyness with adults and other children

c. Consistent cooperation with rules and regulations

d. Accepting constructive criticism

4. Tourette's disorder is characterized by

a. morbid fear of separation from parents.

b. involuntary body and vocal tics.

c. frequent regurgitation.

d. engaging in dangerous activities.

BIBLIOGRAPHY

Barry, P.D. (1996). *Psychosocial nursing: Care of physically ill patients and their families* (3rd ed.). Philadelphia: Lippincott-Raven.

Conant, M . (1996). The client with an eating disorder. In S. Lego (Ed.). *Psychiatric nursing: A comprehensive reference*. Philadelphia: Lippincott-Raven.

Delaney, K.R. (1992). Nursing in child psychiatric milieus. Part I. What nurses do. *Journal of Child and Adolescent Psychiatry and Mental Health Nursing, 5*(1), 10–14.

Diagnostic and statistical manual of mental disorders (4th ed.). (1994). Washington, DC: American Psychiatric Press.

Finke, L.M. (1994). Child psychiatric nursing. Moving into the 21st century. *Nursing Clinics of North America, 29*(1), 43–48.

Hogstel, M.O. (1995). *Practical guide to health assessment through the lifespan* (2nd ed.). New York: Davis Co.

Kaplan, H.I., & Sadock, B.J. (1995). *Comprehensive textbook of psychiatry/VI* (6th ed.). Baltimore: Williams & Wilkins.

Lego, S. (1996). *Psychiatric nursing: A comprehensive reference* (2nd ed.). Philadelphia: Lippincott-Raven.

Lewis, M.L. (Ed.). (1996). *Child and adolescent psychiatry: A comprehensive textbook* (2nd ed.). Baltimore: Williams & Wilkins.

McFarland, G.K., Wasli, E.L., & Gerety, E.K. (1996). *Nursing diagnosis and process in psychiatric mental health nursing* (3rd ed.). Philadelphia: Lippincott-Raven.

21

Delirium, Dementia, and Amnestic and Other Cognitive Disorders

Behavioral Objectives

After reading this chapter the student will be able to:

■ List the causes of cognitive disorders and describe one condition under each category.

■ Define **psychosis, delirium,** and **dementia.**

■ Describe the nursing care of clients with delirium.

■ Describe the nursing care of clients with dementia.

■ Identify the basic causes that underlie cognitive disorders.

■ Explain the difference between acute organic psychoses and chronic organic psychoses.

■ Identify the most common degenerative condition that results in significant dementia.

■ List the symptoms associated with the form of alcoholic psychosis called delirium tremens.

Cognitive disorders are caused by dysfunctions in brain anatomy or physiology. These disorders can cause marked change in intellectual functioning, judgment, and memory. Cognitive mental disorders can also result in a severe disruption of mental status called **psychosis**.

A psychosis is the most serious form of mental disorder. A person who is psychotic temporarily loses contact with reality. There are two main types of organic psychosis: delirium and dementia. Generally, **delirium** is an acute condition that develops rapidly and subsides spontaneously or when the underlying physical cause is treated. **Dementia** is caused by a chronic, irreversible physical deterioration of anatomic parts of the brain. Accordingly, dementia usually cannot be reversed. Delirium and dementia are discussed later in this chapter.

Psychoses caused by cognitive disorders with an organic or physiologic etiology are different from functional psychoses such as those caused by schizophrenia. Functional psychoses are not associated with any known physical abnormality (although researchers in the field of neuropsychiatry believe that there is a basic defect in the biochemistry of the brain that causes functional psychoses). Cognitive psychotic conditions have a variety of causes or etiologies. The following "mend a mind" mnemonic aid can assist in recalling the various biologic causes of cognitive disorders:

M Metabolic disorder

E Electrical disorder

N Neoplastic disease

D Degenerative disease

A Arterial disease

M Mechanical disease

I Infectious disease

N Nutritional disease

D Drug toxicity

The types of conditions that belong to the various categories are outlined below.

Metabolic

Endocrine gland disorders

Electrolyte imbalances

Electrical

Epileptic disorders

Neoplastic

Benign or malignant tumors of the brain or elsewhere

Degenerative
  Alzheimer's disease
  Huntington's chorea
Arterial
  Cerebrovascular accident (CVA)
  Degenerative changes of cerebral arteries
  Vascular dementia (formerly multiple infarct dementia)
Mechanical
  Head injury
Infectious
  Encephalitis
  Meningitis
  Cerebral abscess
  General systemic infections
  AIDS
Nutritional
  Nicotinic acid
  Vitamin B_{12}
  Thiamine
  Folic acid
Drugs
  Alcohol
  Controlled substances
  Prescribed drugs

The conditions listed above can produce a variety of acute psychiatric symptoms including acute confusion, hallucinations, and delusions. Generally speaking, one of the differences between the psychotic episodes of people with cognitive disorders and those of people with functional psychiatric illness is that the hallucinations of the client with cognitive disorder tend to be primarily visual, whereas those of the functionally ill client are usually auditory. Some of the conditions, for example, epileptic disorders, do not routinely cause psychiatric disturbance. On occasion, depending on the types of neurologic dysfunction in the different parts of the brain, psychiatric symptoms of various types and severity may occur. In addition, the neurologic disorder can cause the basic personality tendencies of the person to be magnified. For example, a person who has always been mildly suspicious may become paranoid.

◆ **TABLE 21-1. Symptoms of the Two Types of Cognitive Disorders**

Categories	Delirium	Dementia
Onset	Usually rapid: waxes and wanes abruptly	Usually slow: 1 month or more
Level of awareness	Increased or decreased	Normal or decreased
Orientation	Disoriented	Usually not affected until late in course
Appearance and behavior	May be semicomatose; agitated	Usually slowed responses
Speech and communication	Incoherent; degree of change based on severity of delirium	Usually slowed because of cognitive deficits
Mood	Labile; anxiety or panic common	Constricted affect or depression
Thinking process	Markedly altered	Mildly altered decreased intellectual ability
Memory	Partial or full loss of recent memory; remote memory intact	Partial loss of both recent and remote memory
Perception	Usually markedly altered	Usually intact or mildly affected
Abstract thinking and judgment	Markedly decreased	Mildly decreased
Sleep-wake cycle	Disrupted	Not affected
Treatment	Identify and remove underlying cause; symptomatic treatment	Symptomatic treatment
Prognosis	Reversible in most cases	Usually irreversible

Kaplan H., Sadock, B. (1994); Lishman (1978). In Barry, P. (1996) *Psychosocial nursing assessment and intervention.* Philadelphia: Lippincott-Raven.

Table 21–1 presents the symptoms seen in delirium and dementia. Development of a nursing care plan for the client with a cognitive disorder should include nursing assessment of the mental status categories in this chart. The planning and intervention steps of the nursing process can be developed more easily when the specific types and symptoms of mental dysfunction are identified.

◆ DELIRIUM

Delirium is an acute cognitive disorder that produces a marked change in mental status. A toxic condition related to one of the categories described in the mnemonic above causes delirium. To determine its cause and prevent its occurrence, an immediate assessment of physiologic status is needed: a physical examination, diagnostic workup including laboratory tests and other tests as indicated, and review of all medications. Once the underlying cause is diagnosed and treated, the person usually returns to his or her previously existing mental status and personality style.

NURSING CARE OF CLIENTS WITH DELIRIUM

A client who is developing a toxic cognitive disorder, whether he or she is on a psychiatric, medical, or surgical unit, often demonstrates symptoms of changing mental status before full-blown delirium occurs. Regardless of mental status on admission, the client becomes more restless and agitated. There may be physiologic changes such as increased temperature, blood pressure, and pulse and facial flushing. Such changes indicate that the client's status is changing: you should check frequently to determine how quickly the client's mental or physical state is deteriorating. Notify the physician as soon as you determine the specific changes. Ideally, a delirious episode can be avoided if a diagnostic evaluation is performed with little delay and proper medication is ordered.

The drug of choice for many clients with cognitive disorder is haloperidol (Haldol). It is a major tranquilizer of the butyrophenone group, which is chosen over the major tranquilizers of the phenothiazine group because it has fewer anticholinergic effects on the other body systems. Remember that a client with an organic brain syndrome suffers from an illness in one or more of the many physiologic systems; therefore, you do not want to give this client a medication with anticholinergic effects, since it likely will further disrupt the body's homeostasis. One of the side effects of haloperidol is the risk of tardive dyskinesia (see Chapter 31, Psychopharmacology and Electroshock Treatment of Mental Disorders). Because of this risk, it is wise to discontinue this medication as soon as the acute delirious episode has passed. If one of your clients continues to be on this medication, double check with the charge nurse to be sure that it is still indicated. Generally speaking, once the underlying physical cause of the cognitive disorder is treated, and if the client has had no prior history of major psychiatric illness, the medication can be discontinued or replaced by a minor tranquilizer that has fewer toxic effects.

Caring for a client experiencing a delirious episode can be frightening. Maintain your own composure during the time you are with the client. Although out of control, the client with cognitive disorder will remember what happened. Avoid saying or doing anything that could further alarm the client or cause him or her to remember you in an unpleasant light. Caring firmness and honesty are the most therapeutic behaviors you can display.

Restraints

The use of restraints is an area of nursing care that **must** conform with the hospital policy and procedure manual. Using the hospital guidelines, safeguard the client's safety during such an episode. If the client is totally out of control, use whatever mechanism your hospital has devised to gather enough people to restrain him or her. Remember, these may include non-nursing personnel who are afraid and may use stronger restraint than absolutely necessary. Your composure and quiet directions can calm them and strongly affect their handling of the client. Watch that their physical restraint does not unnecessarily injure the client.

Do not leave the client alone during an acute psychotic episode. Restraints may or may not be used depending on the policies of the institution, the orders of the physician, and the circumstances of the client's cognitive disorder. Although medication decreases the acute state, it may still be necessary to restrain the client for his or her own safety.

Restraints are frightening to a client who is confused as the result of delirium. They should be used only after careful assessment of the client's problem. The need for restraints should be explained quietly to the client, even if he or she does not appear to be able to understand. It is important to obtain the order of a physician or to know what the *written* policy of the institution states about the use of restraints. The use of restraints and their abuse is an important legal issue for nurses. Liability can result in lawsuits if the nurse using restraints is not legally covered by such a policy or if the guidelines are modified in any way.

The types of restraints available include wrist and ankle restraints and camisoles. Make sure the wrist and ankle restraints are properly padded to safeguard the integrity of the skin. Restraints should be released at least every 2 hours to allow for freedom of movement and to check the condition of the skin. Also check that good body positioning is maintained when restraints are used.

Another important point to remember when you are caring for a client who has had a delirious episode is that the terror experienced during delirium remains repressed in his or her unconscious. The client may demonstrate increased levels of anxiety or experience frightening nightmares after the psychotic episode. If you gently ask what the client remembers feeling and thinking while it was happening, he or she may be relieved to describe it to you. As the painful thoughts and feelings are released, anxiety and nightmares should diminish. Your caring and knowledge in listening to the details of the experience can comfort and reassure the client.

◆ Dementia

Dementia is a change in mental status that is due to physical changes in the brain. It usually is a chronic condition that progresses slowly and is not reversible. Dementia is frequently associated with the elderly and is often incorrectly assumed to be a part of the aging process. Actually, many elderly people retain their intellectual functioning into their 80s and 90s. Important factors determining whether dementia occurs are genetic predisposition, family history, nutritional status, and general level of health.

NURSING CARE OF CLIENTS WITH DEMENTIA

Often people who are hospitalized in nursing homes have varying levels of dementia, as do elderly people in the acute hospital setting. When dementia progresses to an advanced stage, psychosis can occur. When psychosis is present, the nursing care outlined earlier for the psychotic client with delirium should be followed. Most clients with early or moderate dementia will require the nursing care described later. Table 21–1 can help you identify the various symptoms of dementia the client is experiencing. Chart the severity of these symptoms and take them into consideration as you develop the nursing care plan. The participation of family members, whenever possible, is valuable, because the client's altered mental status, including impaired memory, may result in an inaccurate or incomplete data base. The following should be considered when completing the remaining steps of the nursing process.

- Give good basic physical care.
- Give simple verbal directions in a calm voice.
- Avoid sensory overload.
- Provide a regular toileting schedule. Clients may forget to void and are embarrassed by their incontinence.
- Monitor and document bowel activity.
- Monitor and document nutritional intake.
- Maintain reality orientation by mentioning the day of the week and discussing seasonal and current events.
- Provide night light. Clients with cognitive disorders are susceptible to **sundowning,** a decrease in orientation at night.
- Provide some type of enjoyable activity.
- Avoid using physical restraints unless indicated.

- Avoid placing intravenous lines in the lower arm. They are often displaced by the confused client.

Elderly people who are mildly confused, forgetful, and listless should not automatically be assumed to have dementia. Remember that elderly people have experienced a profound number of losses, and they may be acutely depressed. Nutritional deprivation, a possible cause of cognitive disorder, can also cause depression. The symptoms of acute depression and mild dementia can appear similar. If you suspect depression, obtain a psychiatric consultation if the client is in a nonpsychiatric institution.

◆OTHER COGNITIVE DISORDERS

All of the following mental disorders have an organic etiology, which can be discovered in the client's history, physical exam, or laboratory tests, but they do not meet the specific criteria of delirium and dementia.

Amnestic disorder is a cognitive disorder in which the level of consciousness is not affected as it is in other organic brain disorders. Short-term and long-term memory are impaired, and the client is in an amnestic state. It is a rare condition.

◆SUBSTANCE-INDUCED DELIRIUM

This section will concentrate on the most frequently seen substance-related mental disorders in the clinical setting. In the event that you are caring for a client whose condition is not described in this section, it may be helpful to refer to the *Diagnostic and Statistical Manual of Mental Disorders*, fourth edition (DSM-IV) on your clinical unit or in the library. It will describe the specific symptoms of the condition.

Substance intoxication delirium is a separate syndrome unlike those caused by other cognitive disorders. It is caused by recent intake of one or more psychoactive substances. The result is abnormal behavior, such as impairment of judgment, occupational functioning, or social functioning. These behavioral changes are due to the effects of the substance on the central nervous system. **Substance withdrawal delirium** is caused by the reduction or cessation of ingestion of a psychoactive substance following its regular use.

DSM-IV categories of substance-induced cognitive disorders include a large number of syndromes. These conditions present a wide variety of symptoms. The full presentation of symptoms for all conditions can be found in the DSM-IV. Here, the symptoms of intoxication and withdrawal are described for each of the major drug-induced cognitive disorders. In each case, none of the physical or mental symptoms are caused by any other type of medical condition. The names of other conditions that can develop with prolonged drug use appear under each major drug abuse group.

ALCOHOL-INDUCED COGNITIVE DISORDERS

Alcohol intoxication is a condition in which recent ingestion of alcohol causes negative behavioral effects, including at least one of the following signs: slurred speech, lack of coordination, unsteady walking, nystagmus, or flushed face. In addition, at least one of the following psychological symptoms appears: mood change, irritability, excessive talking, or impaired attention.

AMPHETAMINE (OR AMPHETAMINE-LIKE SUBSTANCE)-INDUCED COGNITIVE DISORDER

The drugs included in this category are those of the substituted phenethylamine: amphetamine, dextroamphetamine, and methamphetamine (speed). Other differing drugs such as methylphenidate or appetite suppressants (diet pills) are also included. **Intoxication** in this category includes the same physical and psychological symptoms as those of cocaine intoxication. **Abrupt or gradual withdrawal** from the drug induces depression and two or more of the following symptoms: increase in dreaming, disturbed sleep, and fatigue. Those who abuse these drugs can also develop delirium and delusional disorders.

CANNABIS-INDUCED COGNITIVE DISORDER

The symptoms in **cannabis** (marijuana, hashish, or THC) **intoxication** are tachycardia and at least one of the following psychological symptoms that occur shortly after use: perception of slowed time, intensified subjective perceptions, apathy, and elation. In addition, one or more of the following physical symptoms appear: dry mouth, increase in appetite, and redness of the eyes. Disruption in social and occupational functioning and suspiciousness can result. A more severe form of cannabis-related mental disorder is **cannabis intoxication delirium**. There are no changes in level of consciousness and intellectual abilities, no major symptoms of depression, and no hallucinations or delusions.

COCAINE-INDUCED COGNITIVE DISORDER

Cocaine intoxication occurs within 1 hour of using the drug and includes at least two of the following psychological symptoms: euphoria, grandiosity, excessive wordiness, excessive vigilance, and psychomotor agitation. In addition, at least two of the following physiologic conditions are present: dilated pupils, elevated blood pressure, tachycardia, nausea and vomiting, and chills or perspiration. There also are symptoms of antisocial behavior.

HALLUCINOGEN-INDUCED COGNITIVE DISORDER

The drugs included in this category are substances related to 5-hydroxytryptamine (for example, LSD), dimethyltryptamine (DMT), and catecholamine (for example, mescaline). The hallucinogenic drugs are not categorized by intoxication or withdrawal. Rather, they markedly alter the mental status of those who use them and can cause hallucinosis, delusional disorder, and affective disorder.

INHALANT-INDUCED COGNITIVE DISORDER

Inhalant intoxication follows the use of an inhalant that results in abnormal changes in behavior such as assaultiveness, impaired judgment, belligerence, and impaired occupational or social functioning. At least two of the following signs must be present: dizziness, nystagmus, lack of coordination, slurred speech, unsteady gait, lethargy, depressed reflexes, psychomotor retardation, tremor, generalized muscle weakness, blurred vision, stupor or coma, and euphoria.

OPIOID-INDUCED COGNITIVE DISORDER

The drugs included in this category are heroin, morphine, and the morphine-like drugs, such as meperidine (Demerol) and methadone. The diagnostic criteria for **opioid intoxication** are recent use of an opioid; constriction of pupils, or dilation if there is a major overdose; and the presence of one or more emotional or neurologic signs: euphoria, dysphoria, apathy, or psychomotor retardation.

Symptoms of **opioid withdrawal** include at least four of the following signs: tachycardia, mild hypertension, fever, lacrimation, dilated pupils, rhinorrhea (running nose), piloerection (hairs of skin standing on end), sweating, diarrhea, and yawning.

PHENCYCLIDINE (PCP) (OR PHENCYCLIDINE-LIKE SUBSTANCE)-INDUCED COGNITIVE DISORDER

The most common drugs in this category are known by the following names: Ketalar, TCP, PCP, angel dust, THC, crystal, and peace pill. These substances are usually ingested by inhaling or smoking. The symptoms of **intoxication** shortly following ingestion include at least two of the following physiologic symptoms: decreased pain response, tachycardia and elevated blood pressure, dysarthria, decrease in voluntary muscle coordination, and horizontal or vertical nystagmus. In addition, there should be at least two of the following psychological symptoms: severe anxiety, mood swings, elation, grandiosity, psychomotor agitation, and sensation experienced in a different part of the body than where pressure is applied. Abuses of this class of drugs can also cause delirium and mixed mental disorder.

SEDATIVE, HYPNOTIC, OR ANXIOLYTIC-INDUCED COGNITIVE DISORDER

Intoxication within this category can be caused by any of the following drugs: sedatives, including pentobarbital sodium (Nembutal), secobarbital (Seconal), and a combination of secobarbital sodium and amobarbital sodium (Tuinal); the minor tranquilizers; and benzodiazepines, including chlordiazepoxide (Librium), diazepam (Valium), and oxazepam (Serax). The common hypnotics are ethchlorvynol (Placidyl), flurazepam hydrochloride (Dalmane), glutethimide (Doriden), methyprylon (Noludar), chloral hydrate, and methaqualone. The symptoms of intoxication are the same as those for alcohol. Any differences are due to differences in basic personality structures of different people.

    Withdrawal symptoms following prolonged, heavy use of these drugs are also similar to alcohol withdrawal symptoms. At least three of the following physical symptoms are present in this brain syndrome:

    Coarse tremors of the hands, eyelids, and tongue

    Nausea and vomiting

    Malaise or weakness

    Autonomic hyperactivity

    Anxiety

    Depressed or irritable mood

    Orthostatic hypotension

    Other syndromes that can develop in abusers of this family of drugs are withdrawal delirium and amnestic disorder.

◆ PHYSICAL CONDITIONS THAT CAN CAUSE MENTAL DISORDERS

The physical conditions that can cause mental disorders follow our "mend a mind" mnemonic. The following section has been added to this chapter, although it is not one of the DSM-IV classifications. Its purpose is to familiarize you with physical conditions that can disrupt the anatomy or physiology of the brain. Such disruption can cause changes in mental status.

PSYCHOSIS ASSOCIATED WITH METABOLIC DISORDERS

This category of cognitive disorders includes those caused by endocrine disorders: complications of diabetes (other than cerebral arteriosclerosis) and disorders of the thyroid, pituitary, adrenals, and other endocrine glands.

Hyperactivity or hypoactivity of the thyroid gland often results in mental disturbances. If the secretion of the gland is insufficient, a condition known as **myxedema** develops. In addition to a well-known syndrome of physical symptoms (lowered blood pressure, temperature, pulse rate, and respiration rate; chilliness of the body, especially cold hands and feet; slowed down physical activity; and dullness of facial expression) such clients become slow in their thinking and in their ability to grasp ideas. Their memory becomes impaired, and their speech becomes slow and listless. Some are irritable, fretful, fault-finding, or even paranoid in their ideas and attitudes. Congenital insufficiency of the thyroid gland results in a condition called **cretinism,** in which there are both mental and physical defects.

An overactive thyroid gives rise to a condition known as **exophthalmic goiter** or **Graves' disease.** The client's symptoms are the exact opposite of those seen in clients suffering from insufficient thyroxine. The client is nervous, high strung, irritable, very active, anxious, and apprehensive. In acute thyroid intoxication, he or she may go into acute delirium, accompanied by incoherence, hallucinations, and great restlessness. This intoxication may lead to coma and death.

An undersecretion of the islands of Langerhans in the pancreas causes **diabetes mellitus.** Diabetes is characterized by a hyperglycemia (or excessive amount of sugar in the blood) due to a deficiency of insulin that helps the cells burn up sugars. When the hyperglycemia mounts too high, the client goes into diabetic coma. He or she becomes irritable, anxious, and confused, hallucinates, and may even become delirious before reaching the convulsion state. Without treatment, coma usually results.

In addition to the disorders of the endocrine system, another type of metabolic disturbance is related to **electrolyte imbalance**. The brain is accustomed to functioning in homeostatic balance. Owing to illness or other factors, the body's electrolytes may be out of balance. Sensitive brain tissue that is bathed in the body fluids of blood and cerebrospinal fluid is affected by excessively high or low levels of electrolytes. Table 21–2 lists the electrolytes and their generally accepted normal ranges as

◆ TABLE 21-2. Electrolytes That Can Alter Mental Status

Electrolyte	Normal Range	Abnormal Levels
Calcium	8.5–10.5	Hypocalcemia, hypercalcemia
Sodium	135–145 MEq/liter	Hyponatremia, hypernatremia
Phosphorus	2.6–4.5	Hypophosphatemia, hyperphosphatemia
Potassium	3.5–5.0 MEq/liter	Hypokalemia, hyperkalemia
Base bicarbonate	Blood pH 7.38–7.42 Bicarb level 24 MEq/liter	Acidosis, alkalosis

a guideline for recognizing electrolyte imbalance as the cause for mental status changes in a general hospital client.

Be aware, however, that when clients have been chronically physically ill, their body tissues have had a period of time to allow for a gradual adjustment to altered electrolyte levels. Accordingly, their electrolyte levels may extend above or below the ranges shown above with no toxic effects on brain tissue.

PSYCHOSIS ASSOCIATED WITH ELECTRICAL DISORDERS

In certain clients with idiopathic epilepsy, the epileptic attack may take the form of an episode of excitement with hallucinations, fears, and violent outbreaks. Most commonly, clouding of consciousness occurs before or after a convulsive attack or, instead of a convulsion, the client may show only dazed reaction with deep confusion, bewilderment, and anxiety. There are no psychiatric disorders directly related to epilepsy, however, and this type of occurrence is relatively rare.

PSYCHOSIS ASSOCIATED WITH NEOPLASTIC DISORDERS

Tumors that develop in the brain can produce psychotic reactions. Such tumors may be benign or malignant. The benign tumors are usually encapsulated. If diagnosed before their growing pressure has done much damage and if located in an area where surgery is feasible, they are often successfully removed. Angiomas, or blood tumors, although benign, do not lend themselves well to surgical removal. Malignant tumors spread rapidly and usually result in severe mental imbalance. Surgery is of little avail, and although radiation therapy is usually tried, it merely slows down the spreading of the tumor. Chemotherapy may or may not help. An additional type of neoplasm that frequently results in acute depression is carcinoma of the pancreas. The cause of this acute change in mental state is not known.

PSYCHOSIS ASSOCIATED WITH DEGENERATIVE DISORDERS

Alzheimer's disease is the most common degenerative condition that results in significant dementia, which is now categorized as **dementia of the Alzheimer's type**. It is a condition that begins with gradual decrease in memory, emotional stability, and general functioning. The initial symptoms usually appear between the ages of 40 and 60. Intellectual ability and personality functioning gradually decrease. Memory fails markedly. There are muscular and gait changes. Within a year, profound dementia accompanied by hallucinations and delusions usually occurs. Complete nursing care is required.

Another example of this type of disorder is **Huntington's chorea,** a hereditary, sex-linked form of psychosis. It appears chiefly in men, usually in their early 30s, and progresses rapidly so that the client ages mentally in a very short time and becomes helplessly psychotic in a few years.

PSYCHOSIS ASSOCIATED WITH ARTERIAL DISORDERS

The brain must receive a rich supply of oxygen in order to function normally. Anoxia, from whatever cause, can seriously affect the nervous tissue and result in brain damage. **Cerebral arteriosclerosis** (hardening of the arteries of the brain) is a frequent cognitive disorder. The number of clients admitted to public mental hospitals with this disorder is exceeded only by schizophrenics. The onset of arteriosclerotic mental disorder varies widely but, in general, may appear between the years of 50 and 65. Among the early symptoms are headaches, dizziness, inability to sustain concentration, short attention span, emotional instability, memory impairment, and episodes of confusion. Some clients develop paranoid delusions; some develop epileptiform convulsions; others show fluctuations in orientation and memory.

When this disease becomes advanced, small thromboses may form in small intracranial blood vessels, and the client will have a series of minor strokes. Following the rupture of such a vessel and until the small blood clot is absorbed again, the client will be confused and have difficulties in speech, memory will ramble back into youth, and he or she will, perhaps, show some small degree of muscular paralysis. This is called **vascular dementia.**

Also included in this category are circulatory disturbances such as cerebral thrombosis, cerebral embolism, arterial hypertension, cardiorenal disease, and cardiac disease (particularly in decompensation). When a large blood vessel becomes occluded by a large clot, or ruptures, the symptoms are much more severe, and we say the client has had a **stroke** or a **cerebrovascular accident** (CVA).

In about half of these vascular accidents, consciousness is either lost or greatly disturbed. If a coma develops, it may be only a brief episode or it may terminate in death. Paralysis of the muscles on the opposite side of the body from the site of the cerebral hemorrhage usually results (**hemiplegia**), or there may be **monoplegia** (paralysis of just one extremity), **paraplegia** (paralysis of both legs), or **quadriplegia** (paralysis of all four extremities or the entire body). **Aphasia** (the inability to correctly say the words one is thinking) is frequently present, swallowing may be difficult or impossible, and bladder and bowel control may be lost.

PSYCHOSIS ASSOCIATED WITH MECHANICAL DISORDERS

These disorders include injury or trauma to the brain from an external force. Oddly enough, relatively few head injuries result in permanent brain damage. The brain tissue, although extremely delicate, is very well protected by its meningeal coverings and the bony case of the cranium. However, some injuries *do* result in extensive brain damage. In this event, scar tissue usually develops in the injured area.

Three types of acute psychoses due to trauma are **concussion, traumatic coma,** and **traumatic delirium.** Concussion very commonly results from a head injury. Its symptoms are amnesia (the client will have a memory loss from just before the time of the accident up until awakening from unconsciousness), unconsciousness (which may be momentary or continue for several hours), and nausea (the client may vomit while regaining consciousness). He or she may regain consciousness suddenly or may pass through a variable period of clouded consciousness and confusion. The client usually recovers fully in a short time, but if the brain damage is more pronounced, coma may develop or the concussion may be followed by a chronic state of deterioration, personality change, or chronic emotional invalidism.

Traumatic delirium may follow emergence from a traumatic coma or stupor. If the delirium is mild, the client acts more or less bewildered, irritable, and restless. If it is severe, he or she may be noisy, belligerent, demanding, and verbally abusive. Delirium or coma of more than a month's duration usually indicates severe brain damage.

In the event the client does not recover from the concussion (ie, the brain damage becomes chronic), he or she may show mental enfeeblement accompanied by epileptic seizures, paralysis, and other neurologic disturbances. The client may develop a definite personality change, becoming unstable, aggressive, quarrelsome, and destructive; or he or she may become depressed, apprehensive, easily fatigued and, in short, a chronic, complaining invalid.

DEMENTIA ASSOCIATED WITH INFECTIOUS DISORDERS

AIDS dementia complex is a mental state that can occur in the advanced stage of HIV-1 infection. The symptoms that appear in this condition are a decrease in cognitive, emotional, behavior, and motor abilities. There are three stages of progression associated with this condition. They are as follows:

1. Symptom occurrence related to disease development
2. Concurrent involvement of different levels of the neurologic system
3. Development of multiple pathologic processes within one part of the nervous system

The nursing care of AIDS complex is symptom specific. Emotional distress is addressed by supporting effective coping. As the neuropathology progresses, issues of safety may become the most important problem to address. Delirium may occur as an outcome of the acute neurologic deterioration. The management of delirium associated with AIDS is described in the next section.

PSYCHOSIS ASSOCIATED WITH INFECTIOUS DISORDERS

AIDS and intracranial infections such as encephalitis, meningitis, and cerebral abscess can result in hallucinations, delusions, and other psychotic symptoms. Once the acute episode has passed, there usually are no ongoing psychiatric side effects. On occasion, there can be some ongoing changes in personality traits, such as increased stubbornness, that become part of a person's permanent personality style.

In addition, systemic infections (eg, pneumonia, typhoid, malaria, acute rheumatic fever) are very often associated with acute mental disturbances. Toxins produced by viral and bacterial invasion of the bloodstream may involve the central nervous system, and delirium is frequently seen. The higher the fever, usually the more intense is the delirium.

PSYCHOSIS ASSOCIATED WITH NUTRITIONAL DISORDERS

Certain vitamins are essential to a well-functioning neurologic system. Often, inadequate nutrition can result in deterioration of neurologic functioning within the tissues of the brain. When this occurs, psychiatric symptoms may develop. Deficiencies in several B vitamins can cause these changes in mental status. The vitamins are nicotinic acid, B_{12}, thiamine, and folic acid.

Although **pellagra** is not common today, it may occur in the chronic alcoholic whose diet has consisted chiefly of alcohol over a period of several months, in poverty areas where residents are very restricted in their choice of foods, and in people suffering from intestinal diseases that prevent the absorption of food. Clients with advanced pellagra exhibit symptoms of mental confusion and delirious states.

Irritability, distrust, anxiety, and depression are also common. The disorder is due to a lack of vitamin B (especially the nicotinic acid factor).

Pernicious anemia, although seldom reaching the frank psychotic state, does exhibit the milder symptoms of mental fatigue, memory loss, irritability, depression, and apprehension.

Thiamine deficiency can result in Wernicke's encephalopathy, most commonly seen in chronic alcoholic clients. It also may be present in clients with carcinomas of the digestive tract, tuberculosis, or toxemia.

Folic acid deficiency is an important *and* reversible cause of dementia symptoms in the elderly. The symptoms are progressive dementia, depression, and, in some cases, epilepsy. When given therapeutic doses of folic acid, the client's mental status improves in many cases. It can take several months, however, for improvement to occur.

PSYCHOSIS ASSOCIATED WITH DRUG SIDE EFFECTS

A significant cause of drug-related cognitive disorders are the side effects of medications used in physical illness. Many cardiac drugs cause psychiatric symptoms, such as anxiety, depression, short-term memory loss, disorientation, emotional lability, and hallucinations. In addition, synergistic effects of two or more medications may result in a toxic level of medication that affects neurophysiologic functioning. **Synergism** is the effect of separate entities that, when combined, have a greater effect than the sum of their individual actions. It is similar to a $1 + 1 = 3$ result. Any good drug reference lists the reported psychiatric side effects that can occur with use of specific medications.

CHAPTER 21 SUMMARY

- Possible causes of cognitive disorders include the following:
  - Metabolic disorder—endocrine gland disorder, electrolyte imbalance
  - Electrical disorder—epileptic disorders
  - Neoplastic disease—tumors
  - Degenerative disease—Alzheimer's disease, Huntington's chorea
  - Arterial disease—CVA, vascular dementia
  - Mechanical disease—head injury
  - Infectious disease—meningitis, encephalitis, abscess, systemic infections
  - Nutritional disease—vitamin deficiency or toxicity
  - Drug toxicity—alcohol, prescribed medications

■ Delirium is an acute cognitive disorder that produces a marked change in mental status. Once its cause is determined and treated, mental status usually returns to its previous state.

■ Dementia is a change in mental status due to physical changes in the brain. It progresses slowly and is not reversible.

■ Intoxication is caused by the intake of one or more psychoactive substances.

■ Withdrawal is a syndrome that results when a person reduces or stops ingesting a psychoactive substance that he or she has been using regularly.

■ Both alcohol intoxication and alcohol withdrawal can cause delirium.

■ Other substances that can cause substance-induced cognitive disorders include amphetamines, cannabis, cocaine, hallucinogens, inhalants, opioids, phencyclidines, sedatives, and hypnotics.

■ Some medications for physical conditions can create psychiatric symptoms. In addition, the combined effects of medications may create more symptoms than the two medicines would if taken separately. This is called synergism.

CHAPTER 21 QUESTIONS

1. The difference between delirium and dementia is
   a. delirium produces no marked change in mental status, whereas dementia causes sudden marked change in mental status.
   b. delirium usually subsides when the underlying cause is found, whereas dementia is not reversible.
   c. delirium occurs only in people under age 40, whereas dementia occurs after age 55.
   d. there is no difference; the terms are interchangeable.

2. Which of the following can cause a substance-induced cognitive disorder?
   a. Cocaine
   b. Inhalants
   c. Opioids
   d. All of the above

3. Delirium tremens is
   a. a "flashback" from cocaine or amphetamine intoxication.
   b. characterized by an irresistible need to sleep.
   c. not a serious medical or psychological condition.
   d. alcohol withdrawal accompanied by delirium.

4. Degenerative diseases that can result in significant dementia are
   a. diabetes mellitus and gout.
   b. myxedema and Graves' disease.
   c. Huntington's chorea and Alzheimer's disease.
   d. concussion and traumatic coma.

BIBLIOGRAPHY

Barry, P. (1996). The physical causes of cognitive mental disorders. In P. Barry (Ed.). *Psychosocial nursing assessment and intervention* (3rd ed.). Philadelphia: Lippincott-Raven.

Barry, P.D. (1996). *Psychosocial nursing: Care of physically ill patients and their families* (3rd ed.). Philadelphia: Lippincott-Raven.

Carpenito, L.J. (1995). *Nursing diagnosis: Application to clinical practice* (6th ed.). Philadelphia: Lippincott-Raven.

Diagnostic and statistical manual of mental disorders (4th ed.). (1994). Washington, DC: American Psychiatric Press.

Frazier, A., Molinoff, P.B., & Winokur, A. (Eds.). (1994). *Biological bases of brain function and disease*. New York: Raven Press.

Kaplan, H.I., & Sadock, B.J. (1995). *Comprehensive textbook of psychiatry/VI* (6th ed.). Baltimore: Williams & Wilkins.

Kaplan, H.I., & Sadock, B.J. (1994). *Synopsis of psychiatry: Behavioral sciences, clinical psychiatry* (7th ed.). Baltimore: Williams & Wilkins.

McFarland, G.K., Wasli, E.L., & Gerety, E.K. (1996). *Nursing diagnoses and process in psychiatric mental health nursing* (3rd ed.). Philadelphia: Lippincott-Raven.

Murray, G.B. (1997). Confusion, delirium, and dementia. In N.H. Cassem (Ed.). *Massachusetts General Hospital handbook of general hospital psychiatry* (4th ed.). St. Louis: Mosby Year Book.

Nettina, S.M. (1996). *The Lippincott manual of nursing practice* (6th ed.). Philadelphia: Lippincott-Raven.

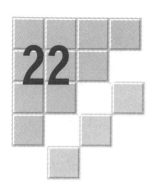

Substance-Related Disorders

Behavioral Objectives

After reading this chapter the student will be able to:

■ Draw up an outline using the following drug or drug categories: opioids; barbiturates, sedatives, tranquilizers, or other hypnotics; amphetamines; cannabis. Under each of these drug headings, list the following information:
  - □ Names of the most commonly used forms of the drug
  - □ Basic physical effects of each
  - □ Withdrawal symptoms
  - □ Treatment and nursing care for withdrawing the client from the drug

The diagnosis **substance-related disorder** is now used in place of psychoactive substance-use disorder and the term *drug addiction*. It is used for clients whose mental states are altered by alcohol, drugs, tobacco, and ordinary caffeine-containing beverages. Included are changes in mental status caused by the side effects of medically prescribed drugs taken as medically indicated.

This chapter includes information on the behavioral aspects of the maladaptive use of substances. The changes in mental status caused by such use are described in the previous chapter on cognitive disorders.

There are 12 major categories of substances that are abused under this classification.

Alcohol

Amphetamine or similarly acting sympathomimetic

Caffeine

Cannabis

Cocaine

Hallucinogen

Inhalant

Nicotine

Opioid

Phencyclidine (PCP) or similarly acting arylcyclohexylamine

Sedative, hypnotic, or anxiolytic

Polysubstance abuse

The classification also includes other substance-related disorders, such as changes in mental state caused by side effects of medications prescribed for medical conditions.

◆ Substance Use Disorders

SUBSTANCE DEPENDENCE AND SUBSTANCE ABUSE

The diagnostic criteria for each of these disorders fall under two terms: **substance dependence** and **substance abuse.**

Substance dependence describes a condition in which the individual's symptoms (listed later) have persisted for at least 1 month or occurred at the same time in the same 12-month period. The individual must manifest three of the following symptoms:

1. Tolerance: as defined by either:
   a. Need for markedly increased amounts of the substance to achieve intoxication or desired effect

b. Markedly diminished effect with continued use of the same amount of the substance

2. Withdrawal, as manifested by either:

a. Characteristic withdrawal syndrome for the substance

b. The same (or a closely related) substance is taken to relieve or avoid withdrawal symptoms

3. The substance is often taken in larger amounts or over a longer period than was intended.

4. There is a pattern of persistent desire or unsuccessful efforts to cut down or control substance use.

5. A great deal of time is spent in activities necessary to obtain the substance, use the substance, or recover from its effects.

6. Important social, occupational, or recreational activities are given up or reduced because of substance use.

7. The substance use is continued despite knowledge of having a persistent or recurrent physical or psychological problem that is likely to have been caused or exacerbated by the substance.[1]

Psychoactive **substance abuse** is a maladaptive pattern of substance use leading to clinically significant impairment or distress, as manifested by one (or more) of the following, occurring within a 12-month period.

1. Recurrent substance use resulting in a failure to fulfill major role obligations at work, school, or home

2. Recurrent substance use in situations in which it is physically hazardous

3. Recurrent substance-related legal problems

4. Continued substance use despite having persistent or recurrent social or interpersonal problems caused or exacerbated by the effects of the substance[2]

◆ALCOHOL-RELATED DISORDERS

Alcohol use disorder includes the two categories of substance abuse and substance dependence. The criteria for alcohol substance abuse follow:

1. A pattern of pathologic alcohol use is noted.

[1]Adapted from *Desk Reference to the Diagnostic Criteria from DSM-IV*. (1994). Washington, DC: American Psychiatric Association, pp. 108–109.
[2]Adapted from *Desk Reference to the Diagnostic Criteria from DSM-IV*. (1994). Washington, DC: American Psychiatric Association, p. 112.

  a. Daily use of alcohol is necessary to function.
  b. Person is unable to cut down or stop drinking.
  c. Binges last longer than 2 days.
  d. Person occasionally consumes as much as a fifth of liquor
     per day.
  e. Amnesia occurs during periods of intoxication (blackouts).
2. Social or occupational functioning is impaired.
3. Disturbance lasts longer than 1 month.

Alcohol dependence includes either a pattern of pathologic alcohol use or impairment in social or occupational functioning. In addition, there is evidence of tolerance or withdrawal symptoms as well as continued use despite knowledge that alcohol consumption causes or worsens a physical or psychological problem.

TREATMENT APPROACHES TO ALCOHOLISM

Before treatment can begin, the client's body must be detoxified of alcohol. With the physiologic dependency that results from alcoholism, detoxification usually must be medically supervised to ensure the client's physical and mental well-being. This most frequently takes place in a general hospital medical-surgical setting or in an alcohol rehabilitation center, not on a general psychiatric unit. Refer to any standard text on alcoholism treatment for specific information about the treatment and nursing care of this complex physiologic condition. Once detoxification is completed, three major treatment options are most frequently presented to recovering alcoholics—Alcoholics Anonymous, aversive therapy with disulfiram (Antabuse), or an inpatient rehabilitation treatment program.

Alcoholics Anonymous

Alcoholics Anonymous (AA) is a peer-support, self-help program that has helped millions of recovering alcoholics to achieve a life of sobriety. It was begun in 1935 by two recovering alcoholics who banded together to help each other. They were Bill Wilson, a stockbroker, and Dr. Bob Smith, a physician. By supporting each other as peers, they were able to remain sober. Wilson and Smith decided to share this support with others and developed a series of steps to help the alcoholic recover. In this way AA was founded.

AA is an organization that exists worldwide and is readily available in most communities. Its simple, free approach has brought hope to millions of alcoholics and their families. AA has also developed a related organization for the families of alcoholics called Al-Anon. There is also a group available for adolescent children of alcoholics called Alateen.

Antabuse

Disulfiram or Antabuse therapy is considered a useful adjunct treatment for some types of alcoholics. It is a form of behavior therapy (see Chapter 29) that uses learning principles to cause the client to associate the thought of drinking with an unpleasant stimulus; in this way the client can be motivated to avoid drinking.

Disulfiram (Antabuse) is a drug that causes the metabolism of alcohol to be blocked. The result is a buildup of acetaldehyde, which is a toxic by-product of alcohol metabolism in the body. Acetaldehyde produces a variety of very unpleasant physical symptoms, such as flushing, sweating, palpitations, dyspnea, hyperventilation, tachycardia, hypotension, nausea, and vomiting.

The body's reaction to even a small amount of alcohol can be violent and, indeed, can be physiologically threatening to the body's homeostasis. Accordingly, this treatment should be used only with a compliant, motivated individual in order to avoid serious complications.

Inpatient Treatment Programs

Some people with alcoholism and other types of substance-related disorders need more structure in their return to sobriety. A treatment program that has met with increasing success is an inpatient treatment approach in which a therapeutic environment (see Chapter 29, Milieu Therapy and Behavior Modification) is used. In many institutions, alcohol and drug abuse clients are treated in the same setting. Following the detoxification period, there is intensive emphasis on individual, group, and family therapy. Counselors in the individual and group therapy sessions frequently are recovered substance abusers. Many of these programs include intensive education and behavior modification to teach new coping skills to these individuals who have previously turned to alcohol because of their inability to cope. The major emphasis of this teaching is on communication skills and stress management.

Outpatient Treatment Programs

Outpatient treatment programs are increasingly an option for treating alcohol use disorders. After the detoxification period (usually inpatient), individuals follow the therapeutic and coping-skills focus outlined earlier, but this treatment takes place in an outpatient setting, generally with the client returning to his or her home in the evening.

NURSING CARE OF CLIENTS WITH ALCOHOLISM

Nursing care planning includes prioritizing the areas of functioning that are most threatening to the client's physical or mental well-being.

For example, during episodes of acute cognitive disorder, such as intoxication, withdrawal, or withdrawal delirium, follow the guidelines presented under the nursing care of clients with delirium in Chapter 21, Delirium, Dementia, and Amnestic and Other Cognitive Disorders.

Treatment with the benzodiazepines (minor tranquilizers) or barbiturates is effective in managing the life-threatening and distressing effects of alcohol withdrawal during detoxification. If the drug is administered and its effects are monitored and titrated (balanced) carefully, the nurse can maintain the client in a calm and wakeful state. The sedative usually needs to be administered over a 24- to 48-hour period and is reduced to smaller doses over 2 to 3 days until it is discontinued.

Maintain adequate fluid and nutritional needs. The client, because of nutritional deprivation, usually has inadequate electrolyte and vitamin levels.

Once the acute detoxification stage is over, the client's long-term needs should be more actively addressed in the nursing care plan. Alcoholic people are at risk for many types of dysfunction. Evaluate the potential risks in the following list in assessing your client and planning your nursing intervention. Base your plans, including counseling and preventive teaching, on positive findings in any of the areas described below.[3]

Physical State

Increased susceptibility to infection

Altered nutritional status

Interference with sleep activity

Interference with sexual activity

Impairment of vital organs

Diminished energy

Increased risk of accident and injury

Substantial reduction in lifespan

Insufficient exercise

Psychosocial State

Low self-concept

Feelings of alienation, guilt, depression, anger

Increased risk of suicide

Increased consumption of other drugs that interact with alcohol

[3]Adapted from Estes, N., & Heinemann, M. (1986). *Alcoholism: Development, consequences, and interventions.* St. Louis: C.V. Mosby.

Interferences with interpersonal relationships, including family, friends, co-workers

Lack of creative diversion such as hobbies, recreational activities

Thwarted personal growth, learning, and maturity

Delayed development of potential

Lack of philosophical or spiritual pursuits

Economic State

Possible loss of job or demotion

Indebtedness

Legal Entanglements

Increased incidence of arrest for driving while intoxicated or for assaults, including child abuse, spouse battering, and tavern fights

**Factors Associated With the Diagnosis
of Alcoholism**

Social stigma with regard to alcoholism

Lack of acceptance of the diagnosis by all involved

◆ AMPHETAMINE-RELATED DISORDER

The drugs included in this category of drug disorder are amphetamines, dextroamphetamine sulfate (Dexedrine), methamphetamine (speed), and others that have amphetamine-like action, such as methylphenidate or other substances used as appetite suppressants (diet pills). The abuse and dependence subcategories include the symptoms listed earlier in this chapter. In addition, there is a frequent drug use pattern of taking the drug for 10 to 14 days at a time.

Amphetamines are frequently used to treat obesity; they are used by students to stay alert and study, by truck drivers to stay awake, and by soldiers to decrease fatigue and increase aggression. Evidence today suggests that tolerance *does* develop to their use, they produce both dependency and withdrawal states, and they are clearly among the most dangerous drugs presently available. In the most mentally stable person, amphetamines are able to produce a toxic psychosis that is clinically indistinguishable from paranoid schizophrenia. Death from overdosage is usually associated with hyperpyrexia, convulsions, and cardiovascular shock. The intravenous use of these drugs since the 1960s has resulted fairly often in cases of severe serum hepatitis, lung abscess, and endocarditis. In 1970, necrotizing angiitis was first reported as a result of intravenous amphetamine abuse. Necrotizing angiitis is the destruction of the lining of blood vessels due to a toxic substance.

In most cases, amphetamine-induced psychotic disorder clears in a matter of days or weeks following withdrawal of the drug, differentiating it from paranoid schizophrenia. Antipsychotic agents (phenothiazines or haloperidol) often help. The withdrawal depression, which may reach suicidal proportions, may be treated with tricyclic antidepressants.

◆ CANNABIS-RELATED DISORDER

The substances included in this category are marijuana, hashish, and, occasionally, purified delta-9-tetrahydrocannabinol (THC). Marijuana is the most commonly used substance in this category. It has been a subject of controversy since 500 BC in China. During the 19th century, cannabis was widely prescribed for a variety of ailments and discomforts (coughing, fatigue, migraine, asthma, delirium tremens, etc.). It remained in the U.S. *Pharmacopeia* until 1941.

Its ability to cause euphoria has been of principal interest throughout history. The effects last 2 to 4 hours from smoking marijuana and 5 to 12 hours from ingestion of the drug. Marijuana also has a tendency to produce sedation. There is no substantial evidence in the world literature, however, that cannabis induces either mental or physical deterioration, at least not in well-integrated, stable people.

Adverse reactions to cannabis appear to be dose related and depend on the setting in which the drug is used. Although rare, anxiety states, with or without paranoid thinking, panic states, and toxic psychosis, have been reported.

An amotivational syndrome has been discussed in association with cannabis use, but careful studies fail to prove that this syndrome does, in fact, follow the use of the drug. It may be a sociocultural phenomenon that happens to coincide with the regular use of marijuana.

◆ COCAINE-RELATED DISORDER

This category includes the general symptoms of substance abuse listed earlier in the chapter. In addition, during periods of intoxication, there are delusions and hallucinations with an otherwise clear sensorium.

Cocaine is an alkaloid derived from the leaf of the plant *Erythroxylon coca*, a shrub indigenous to Bolivia and Peru. Its leaves have been chewed by natives of these countries for many years, producing central nervous system stimulation. The "high" is similar to that achieved by amphetamines (ie, euphoria, exhilaration, and a powerful sense of well-being and confidence).

Cocaine abuse is a problem of almost epidemic proportions in our society today. The pattern of cocaine use has altered from snorting the cocaine intranasally to intravenous injection or smoking. The commonly abused form of cocaine has changed to "freebase." Freebase is available in a product called "crack," an inexpensive, very potent, and readily available substance. Crack has significantly increased the number of cocaine abusers. Cocaine intoxication is marked by excitement, euphoria, restlessness, stereotyped movement, and gnashing, grinding, or clenching the teeth.

Tolerance develops, as does physical dependency. Acute toxic effects may be treated with a short-acting barbiturate administered intravenously. A toxic psychosis with visual, auditory, and tactile hallucinations and a paranoid delusional system may develop as with amphetamines. When psychosis develops, it is classified as a cocaine-induced psychotic disorder.

◆HALLUCINOGEN-RELATED DISORDER

This subcategory includes abuse of substances structurally related to 5-hydroxytryptamine. These are lysergic acid diethylamine (LSD), dimethyltryptamine (DMT), and substances related to catecholamines (for example, mescaline). The abuse symptoms are those described earlier. In addition, episodes of hallucinogen persisting perception disorder (flashbacks) can occur at unpredictable times for years following termination of the drug.

◆NICOTINE-RELATED DISORDER

Tobacco use continues in this country despite widespread knowledge that it is an important factor in the development of cardiovascular disease, cancer, and severe forms of lung disease. In severe cases of tobacco dependence, several signs of nicotine withdrawal symptoms include the following:

Depressed mood

Insomnia

Irritability, frustration, or anger

Anxiety

Difficulty concentrating

Restlessness

Decreased heart rate

Increased appetite or weight gain

◆ OPIOID-RELATED DISORDER

The client with an opioid-related disorder experiences the same symptoms as described for barbiturates. Taken in normal, medically supervised doses, the barbiturates and opioids mildly depress the action of the nerves, skeletal muscles, and heart muscle. They slow down heart rate and breathing and lower blood pressure. In higher doses, however, the effects resemble alcoholic drunkenness, with confusion, slurred speech, and staggering. The client finds it difficult to think, concentrate, and work, and emotional control is weakened. Users may become irritable and angry and want to fight someone. Sometimes, they fall into a deep sleep from which it is difficult to arouse them. In addition, episodes of intoxication involve impairments of attention, speech, memory, respiration, and consciousness. The opioid drugs include heroin, morphine, and synthetics with morphine-like action, such as meperidine (Demerol) and methadone.

References to opium smoking can be found so far back in Oriental history that we do not know the date of its first use as a producer of pleasant dreams. It is still smoked in some areas in Asiatic countries, but in Western countries, the alkaloids of opium are preferred. Morphine is one of the main alkaloids of opium, and heroin is a derivative of morphine. **Heroin** is the narcotic most widely used by addicts today. Because of its strong addictive power, it has been outlawed in the United States and cannot be made, imported, or sold legally.

When a person becomes dependent on heroin, his or her body craves repeated and larger doses of the drug. Once the habit starts, larger and larger doses are required to get the same effects. This happens because the body develops a tolerance for the drug.

One of the signs of heroin addiction is **withdrawal sickness.** When the user stops the drug, he or she sweats, shakes, gets chills and diarrhea, vomits, and suffers sharp stomach pain. In addition to physical dependence on narcotics, there is also a strong psychological dependence.

Typically, the first emotional reaction to heroin is an erasing of fears and a relief from worry. This is usually followed by a state of inactivity bordering on stupor. Heroin, which is a fine white powder, is usually mixed into a liquid solution and injected into a vein. It tends to dull the edges of reality. Addicts report that heroin "makes troubles roll off the mind," and makes them feel more sure of themselves. This drug also reduces feelings of pain.

The drug depresses certain areas of the brain and reduces hunger, thirst, and the sex drive. Because addicts often do not feel hungry, usually they must be treated for malnutrition when hospitalized.

◆ PHENCYCLIDINE (PCP)-RELATED DISORDER

Drugs included in this category are ketamine (Ketalar) and the thiophene analogue of phencyclidine (TCP). This subcategory includes the general symptoms of abuse referred to earlier. In addition, with phencyclidine-induced intoxication, the person experiences delirium associated with the drug or a mixed cognitive disorder.

◆ SEDATIVE–HYPNOTIC-RELATED DISORDER

The drugs that are most commonly abused in this category are the anxiolytic drugs, including chlordiazepoxide (Librium), diazepam (Valium), and oxazepam (Serax). The sedatives that are regularly abused are pentobarbital sodium (Nembutal), secobarbital (Seconal), phenobarbital (Luminal), and amobarbital (Amytal). Commonly abused hypnotics are ethchlorvynol (Placidyl), flurazepam (Dalmane), glutethimide (Doriden), methyprylon (Noludar), chloral hydrate, paraldehyde, and methaqualone.

The symptoms of the abuse and dependence subcategories are listed earlier in the chapter. The person with this disorder uses the equivalent of 600 mg or more of secobarbital (Seconal) or 60 mg or more of diazepam and experiences amnestic periods during intoxication. The person in the dependence category experiences an increasing need or withdrawal symptoms of cognitive disorder occur.

BARBITURATES

The sedative category includes **barbiturates,** which belong to a large family of drugs manufactured for the purpose of relaxing (depressing) the central nervous system. They are synthetic drugs made from barbituric acid (a coal-tar product). Doctors prescribe these drugs widely to treat insomnia, high blood pressure, and epilepsy. They are occasionally used in the treatment of mental illness and to sedate clients before and during surgery. They are often used in combination with other drugs to treat many other types of illness and medical conditions. The symptoms of barbiturate abuse are discussed in the section on opioid abuse.

Often barbiturates are obtained illegally. Because doctors prescribe these drugs so frequently, many people consider them safe to use freely. They are not safe drugs. Overdoses can cause death. They are a leading cause of accidental poisoning deaths in the United States. These drugs distort the way that people see things and slow down their reactions and responses. They are an important cause of automobile accidents. When taken with alcohol, they tend to potentiate (enhance) the effects of the alcohol.

Because they are so easily obtained and produce sleep readily, barbiturates are frequently used in suicide attempts. Barbiturates range from the short-acting but fast-starting pentobarbital sodium (Nembutal) and secobarbital (Seconal) to the long-acting but slow-starting phenobarbital (Luminal), amobarbital (Amytal), and butabarbital (Butisol). The short-acting preparations are the ones most commonly abused. In the doses ordinarily taken by the drug abuser, barbiturates produce mood shifts, restlessness, euphoria, excitement, and, in some individuals, hallucinations. The users become confused and may be unable to walk or perform tasks requiring muscular activity.

The barbiturates cause physical dependence. The body needs increasingly higher doses to feel the effects. True dependence, however, requires taking large doses of the drug for more than a few weeks.

Sudden withdrawal of barbiturates from someone dependent on them is extremely dangerous because it may result in death. A physician will hospitalize the person and withdraw the drug slowly in order to alleviate the cramps, nausea, delirium, and convulsions that attend withdrawal. Some experts consider barbiturate dependence more difficult to cure than a narcotic dependency. It takes several months for a barbiturate user's body chemistry to return to normal.

METHAQUALONE

A nonbarbiturate sedative-hypnotic, methaqualone (Quaalude), was first introduced in the United States in 1966. Marketed as having little potential for abuse and no effect on dream-stage sleep, it rapidly became used as a recreational chemical. It was found, however, to suppress REM sleep (rapid-eye-movement sleep associated with dreaming). Tolerance to the drug may develop. It is capable of producing both considerable psychological and physical dependence.

A withdrawal syndrome has been observed in people using over 600 mg per day for prolonged periods of time. The withdrawal syndrome begins within 24 hours of cessation of use of the drug, persists for 2 to 3 days, and consists of insomnia, headache, abdominal cramps, anorexia, nausea, irritability, and anxiety. Hallucinations and nightmares have also been reported.

The nursing care of this client and clients with the other substance-use disorders in this chapter is essentially the same as for the alcoholic client described earlier. The side effects of drug withdrawal that are most threatening to health and require the greatest vigilance occur during the detoxification period. The cognitive disorders and the nursing care required during withdrawal and detoxification are described in Chapter 21.

BENZODIAZEPINES

Chlordiazepoxide (Librium) and diazepam (Valium) are widely used as minor tranquilizers for the control of anxiety. They produce less euphoria than the preceding two hypnotics, but a withdrawal syndrome may occur when large doses (several hundred milligrams per day) are abruptly stopped. Convulsions may be delayed by several weeks and are managed as with meprobamate withdrawal, described later.

MEPROBAMATE

Introduced as an antianxiety drug in 1954, meprobamate's therapeutic usefulness is in considerable doubt, but it is still widely prescribed and popular. Tolerance develops, and withdrawal symptoms can occur. Abrupt withdrawal causes tremors, ataxia, headache, insomnia, and gastrointestinal disturbances lasting for several days. Occasionally, convulsions occur (usually upon withdrawal from 3 g or more daily). A delirium–tremens-like state may occur in 36 to 48 hours. Diphenylhydantoin sodium (phenytoin) IV is useful in controlling convulsions.

◆ NURSING CARE OF CLIENTS WITH SUBSTANCE-RELATED DISORDERS

Because of the wide variety of side effects of substance withdrawal, this chapter will not attempt to recommend nursing actions for each of the nursing care problems that can result from both substance overdose and withdrawal. In addition, the nursing care in each of these types of substance dependence and their acute side effects will be different depending on whether the client is in the inpatient or community setting. The reader is referred to textbooks that address the specific care setting and specific nursing problems associated with different types of substances.

FAMILY AND SOCIAL SYSTEM RESPONSES TO SUBSTANCE-RELATED DISORDERS

A frequent issue for family members and loved ones of people with substance-related disorders is the loss of self-autonomy. Self-autonomy is the capacity of an individual to have a clear sense of his or her identity while also respecting the autonomy of others. *Co-dependence* is the term that describes relationships in which the role of one individual is highly related to the dysfunction of another. When co-dependence is occurring within one relationship, it often occurs in all important relationships, such as in the immediate family, social relationships, and at work. A family in which co-dependence is occurring often has unwritten, unspoken rules with which family members are expected to comply.

The nurse who observes these behaviors can gently present other options that support the autonomy of each family member. Because of the strength of co-dependent characteristics, it is possible that the family member may avoid addressing these options; these characteristics have often been present in succeeding generations. The continuum of co-dependence is present in many individuals and can affect well-being in many ways. Because of the importance of this issue and its effects on relationships, the reader is encouraged to seek further information on co-dependence, the subject of many books available to the general public.

CHAPTER 22 SUMMARY

- A person with substance dependence displays at least three of the following symptoms:
  - Tolerance (need for markedly increased amounts or diminished effect with use)
  - Withdrawal (experiencing characteristic symptoms or taking a related substance to avoid withdrawal)
  - Substance often taken in larger amounts or over a longer period than was intended
  - Persistent desire or unsuccessful efforts to cut down or control substance use
  - Great deal of time spent in obtaining, using, or recovering from effects of the substance
  - Important social, occupational, or recreational activities given up or reduced owing to substance use
  - Continued substance use despite persistent or recurrent physical or psychological problem caused or exacerbated by the substance

- Substance abuse is more severe than dependence and includes recurrent substance use that results in a failure to fulfill major role obligations at work, school, or home; continues in situations in which it is physically hazardous; and continues despite recurrent substance-related legal, social, or interpersonal problems caused or exacerbated by the effects of the substance.

■ Treatment approaches to alcoholism include Alcoholics Anonymous, Antabuse therapy, and inpatient treatment programs. Nursing care of clients must cover the acute detoxification stage *and* the long-term recovery stage.

■ Substances can produce psychiatric symptoms even in a mentally stable person, for example, toxic psychosis (amphetamines), delusions and hallucinations (cocaine), and flashbacks (hallucinogens).

■ Opioid drugs include heroin, morphine, methadone, and synthetic morphine-like drugs such as Demerol. Withdrawal sickness (sweating, shaking, chills, diarrhea, vomiting) occurs when the regular user stops taking heroin.

■ Barbiturates are physically addictive, requiring larger and larger amounts to create the same effect. Withdrawal, which causes cramps, nausea, delirium, and convulsions, should be medically supervised.

CHAPTER 22 QUESTIONS

1. Substance abuse is characterized by
  a. ongoing use of a substance despite its potential for creating a hazardous situation.
  b. recurrent substance-related legal problems such as arrest.
  c. failure to fulfill major role obligations because of substance use.
  d. all of the above.

2. Which of the following is *not* characteristic of pathologic alcohol use?
  a. Blackouts (amnesia during bouts of drinking)
  b. Daily use of alcohol is needed for person to function.
  c. The person can stop drinking at will.
  d. Binges last longer than 2 days.

3. "Withdrawal sickness," characterized by sweating, shaking, chills, diarrhea, and vomiting, is a sign of withdrawal from
  a. nicotine.
  b. heroin.
  c. LSD.
  d. PCP.

4. Which of the following is *not* true about barbiturates?
  a. They depress the central nervous system and their effects are enhanced by alcohol.
  b. They are a leading cause of accidental poisoning in the United States.

    c. They cause physical addiction, meaning larger doses are required to feel the effects.

    d. Those dependent on barbiturates can withdraw easily, with no harmful effects.

BIBLIOGRAPHY

Barry, P.D. (1996). General systems theory applied to individual and family coping responses. In P. Barry (Ed.). *Psychosocial nursing assessment and intervention*. Philadelphia: Lippincott-Raven.

Barry, P.D. (1996). *Psychosocial nursing: Care of physically ill patients and their families* (3rd ed.). Philadelphia: Lippincott-Raven.

Diagnostic and statistical manual of mental disorders (4th ed.). (1994). Washington, DC: American Psychiatric Press.

Estes, N., Smith DiJulio, K., & Heinemann, M. (1980). *Nursing diagnosis of the alcoholic person*. St. Louis: Mosby Year Book.

Frances, R.J. (1994). Substance abuse in the general hospital: A priority area for evaluation and treatment. *General Hospital Psychiatry, 16*, 71.

Kaplan, H.I., & Sadock, B.J. (1995). *Comprehensive textbook of psychiatry/VI* (6th ed.). Baltimore: Williams & Wilkins.

Lego, S. (1996). *Psychiatric nursing: A comprehensive reference* (2nd ed.). Philadelphia: Lippincott-Raven.

McFarland, G.K., Wasli, E.L., & Gerety, E.K. (1996). *Nursing diagnoses and process in psychiatric mental health nursing* (3rd ed.). Philadelphia: Lippincott-Raven.

Naegle, M.A. (1992). Nursing strategies with the client with alcohol and drug problems. *NLN Publication 15-2464*, 355–402.

Nettina, S.M. (1996). *The Lippincott manual of nursing practice* (6th ed.). Philadelphia: Lippincott-Raven.

Talashek, M.L., Gerace, L.M., & Starr, K.L. (1994). The substance abuse pandemic: Determinants to guide interventions. *Public Health Nursing, 11*(2), 131–139.

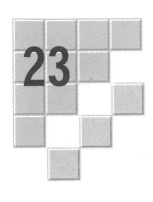

23

Schizophrenia and Other Psychotic Disorders

Behavioral Objectives

After reading this chapter the student will be able to:

■ List five major criteria necessary for a diagnosis of schizophrenia and describe them.

■ Name the five types of schizophrenia and explain the main characteristic of each.

■ Define the terms **hallucination, delusion,** and **loosening of associations.**

■ Describe the possible causes of schizophrenia using the psychoanalytic theory and the physiologic theory.

The functional group of psychoses, of which schizophrenia is the most prevalent, is divided into five types: schizophrenia, major mood disorders, paranoid states, other nonorganic psychoses (primarily psychotic depressive reaction), and psychoses with origin specific to childhood (see Chapter 20, Disorders Usually First Diagnosed During Infancy, Childhood, or Adolescence). The term **dysfunctional mental states** describes the specific mental states that occur in each of these conditions.

A person's basic type of personality will be the predisposing factor as to which form of psychosis he or she will develop. It occasionally happens that a person with recurrent psychosis *may* show a different form than the one evidenced earlier. As a rule, however, if psychosis occurs several times in the life of a person, it tends to follow the same behavioral pattern each time.

◆SCHIZOPHRENIC DISORDERS

The behavioral patterns of **schizophrenic** clients are characterized by much disorganization and discord of the personality. Schizophrenia comes from two Greek words—one meaning *to split,* and the other, *mind.* Schizophrenia includes a large group of disorders characterized by disturbances of thinking, mood, and behavior. Disturbances of thinking are shown by changes in concept formation that often lead to misinterpretation of reality and, on occasion, to delusions and hallucinations. These delusions and hallucinations often appear to be psychologically self-protective.

Accompanying mood changes may include ambivalent, constricted, and inappropriate emotional responsiveness and loss of empathy with others. Behavior may be withdrawn, regressive, and bizarre. In the schizophrenias, the mental status is primarily due to a thought disorder. These states must be distinguished from the major affective disorders, which are disorders of mood. In paranoid states, psychotic symptoms, other than a narrow but deep distortion of reality, are absent.

THEORIES OF CAUSES OF SCHIZOPHRENIA ⊬

Today's researchers are probing into body and brain chemistry to see if there is, perhaps, some chemical substance affecting the nervous tissues of these disorganized people. The biochemical substances released in the brain are known as neurotransmitters. The purpose of the neurotransmitters is, as their name implies, to transmit or send messages within the brain or between the brain and various parts of the body. There are many known neurotransmitter substances in the brain, and perhaps others that have not yet been identified by neurobiologists. The neurotransmitter that is most frequently mentioned as a possible factor in the development of schizophrenia is **dopamine**. Research has demonstrated that there is a possible association between the behavioral symptoms of schizophrenia and the presence of elevated levels of dopamine in schizophrenic clients.

One of the factors that contributed to the research into the relationship between neurotransmitters and schizophrenia was the recognition that the mental status that resulted from the use of lysergic acid diethylamine (LSD) was similar in many ways to the mental status changes experienced by people with schizophrenic illness.

Should research bear out the theory that perhaps the schizophrenic has a chemical or physiologic basis for his or her psychosis, we shall have to classify this large group of psychoses as organic rather than functional. An alternate finding may be that the schizophrenic has both a physiologic and a psychological cause for his or her psychotic state.

According to psychoanalytic theory, the schizophrenic person appears to have a childhood deprived of meaningful relationships with the important people in his or her family circle. An outstanding fact is that most of these people have felt that as children they were unloved, unwanted, and unimportant to their families. This lack of good, firm interpersonal relationships at an early age results in immature adult personalities that find it difficult to adjust socially or to relate intimately with other people.

SYMPTOMS OF SCHIZOPHRENIA

Thought disorder is evidenced by behavior or spoken thoughts that are disorderly, unrealistic, and often irrational. **Autism** is common.[1] People with thought disorders disregard external reality to a large extent. When expressing thought in words, the schizophrenic shows a loss of orderly progression of thought by using unconnected words. This is termed **fragmentation,** or **word salad.** He or she may also coin new words that have no meaning to the listener. We call these new words **neologisms.** The schizophrenic client's speech lacks unity, clearness, and coherence, reflecting the confusion of his or her mind.

The schizophrenic client is often given to eccentric, unexplained, and sudden activities. Undirected restlessness, fitful behavior, and impulsive, apparently unpremeditated acts are frequent. To sum up, the schizophrenic client's behavior is **autistic** (ie, actions, thoughts, feelings, ideas, and experiences are inappropriate, distorted, and not easily understood by other people). He or she may laugh or show pleasure as the result of a painful experience, or may weep when the occasion would call for laughter (inappropriate emotional responses).

---

[1]Autism is a mental state in which a person seems unaware of external reality.

A **lack of affect,** or emotional **blunting,** is coldness of emotional response to others. The client fails to relate to others in a meaningful way. He or she is emotionally shallow, and any emotion shown is often inappropriate.

Withdrawal is a progressive shutting out of the world. There is reduction in interest, initiative, and spontaneity. Many clients seem to have withdrawn behind barriers, which if they could be penetrated, would reveal loneliness, hopelessness, hatred, and fear. The client may build a shell of indifference in self-defense. The withdrawal may vary from a mild degree of isolation to one so profound that the client seems to be completely unaware of his or her surroundings. However, these severely withdrawn people, in spite of appearances, are sometimes acutely aware of all that goes on in the environment.

Regression varies in degree from slight to profound. There is a tendency for the schizophrenic client to retreat to a more primitive and infantile level of thinking and behaving.

A **delusion** is a fixed, false belief based on a misinterpretation of fact. Since the ideas, or mental content, of the schizophrenic client are so often delusional, and since the client's needs are so often disguised by symbolism, his or her thought content often appears complicated and difficult to understand. Delusions tend to center around themes of persecution, grandiosity, sex, and religion. The client dramatizes problems, strivings, and conflicts in fantastic delusional beliefs.

Hallucinations are another common symptom of schizophrenia. Hallucinations are sensory perceptions that have no basis in fact. They come, instead, from troublesome material from the client's inner life. They are very real to the client. Sometimes they are terrifying, sometimes accusing, sometimes pleasurable.

DIAGNOSTIC CRITERIA OF SCHIZOPHRENIA

When unresolved anxiety mounts too high, the schizophrenic person tends to meet problems by turning away from the real world and withdrawing into a dream world that is produced through fantasy, projection, delusions, and hallucinations. In other words, he or she becomes psychotic.

Although there are five major subdivisions of schizophrenia, each with distinguishing characteristics, there are several overall characteristics common to all subgroups.

◆ SCHIZOPHRENIA

Characteristic symptoms would include two (or more) of the following, each of which would be present for a significant portion of time during a 1-month period (or less if successfully treated):

1. Delusions
2. Hallucinations
3. Disorganized speech (eg, frequent derailment or incoherence)
4. Grossly disorganized or catatonic behavior
5. Negative symptoms, (ie, affective flattening, alogia, or avolition)[2]

MAJOR SUBTYPES OF SCHIZOPHRENIA

The subtypes of schizophrenia are defined by the prominent symptoms at the time of evaluation. They are as follows:

Paranoid type

Disorganized type

Catatonic type

Undifferentiated type

Residual type

Paranoid Type

The **paranoid schizophrenic** adds suspiciousness, projection, and delusions of persecution to his or her other basic schizophrenic traits. Delusions occupy a prominent place in his or her mental concepts, and hallucinations are tied in with these delusions.

Voices issue commands to the client from the air or out of the walls; he or she may refuse medications or food for fear of being poisoned. The paranoid schizophrenic client is usually highly verbal and will tell you about the detectives who are following him or her everywhere, or about unseen instruments that are reading his or her mind. At times, the paranoid schizophrenic client may become quite aggressive and even combative, and utterances may become disconnected and fragmentary.

The paranoid schizophrenic does **not** demonstrate the following traits normally associated with other forms of schizophrenia: incoherence, marked loosening of associations, catatonic behavior, grossly disorganized behavior, or flat or very inappropriate affect.

Disorganized Type

The **disorganized type**, formerly known as the **hebephrenic type,** has an insidious onset that usually begins in adolescence. The client's emotions become shallow and inappropriate. He or she withdraws from so-

[2]Adapted from *Desk Reference to the Diagnostic Criteria from DSM-IV*. (1994). Washington, DC: American Psychiatric Association, pp. 147–148.

cial contacts, appears preoccupied, and smiles and giggles frequently in a silly manner. The client's speech becomes badly fragmented, often to the point of incoherence. Bizarre delusions and hallucinations, often of a pleasant type, if present, are transient and not well organized. Hypochondriacal complaints are frequent. There is more disorganization of personality and habits in the disorganized type than in any of the other types of schizophrenia, but it is rarely seen today because of early intervention, the use of the powerful phenothiazine drugs, and the end of the era of long-term institutionalization of clients.

Catatonic Type

The **catatonic type** appears primarily in two major forms. One form is characterized by apparent stupor, immobility, mutism, and negativism; the other phase is characterized by unorganized, excessive, impulsive, and sometimes destructive behavior. The diagnosis can be made if any of the symptoms described below are present.

In **catatonic stupor,** or withdrawal, the client shows no interest in the environment. The client's facial expression is vacant; he or she may stare into space, frequently with head bowed, and may lie, sit, or stand very still for long periods of time. The client often must be tube fed and given complete physical care when in this state. While apparently unheeding and insensible, the client's consciousness is actually very clear, and after recovery he or she will often relate minute details of what went on. The client lives in an unreal world and seems oblivious to the external environment. Occasionally, the client may be seen whispering and smiling slightly; at other times, he or she may exhibit odd mannerisms and strange positioning of the head and extremities.

If someone raises the client's arm into an upright position, he or she will maintain this position for an amazingly long time. The term **waxy flexibility** is used to describe this phenomenon. Two other peculiar mannerisms are occasionally seen: **echolalia,** in which the client repeats the words or phrases of others but offers no conversation of his or her own, and **echopraxia,** in which the client mimics all actions of the person who is addressing him or her, but makes no answer at all.

Catatonic negativism is marked by resistance to instructions of others or to purposeful action. **Catatonic rigidity** is the holding of a particular posture for long periods of time and resistance to being moved.

In **catatonic excitement,** the client's behavior is characterized by impulsive and stereotyped activities, poorly coordinated, and often lacking apparent purpose. Hostility and feelings of resentment are common; unprovoked outbursts of violence and destructiveness may occur; hallucinations are frequent. The flow of speech may vary from mutism to a rapid speech, also known as pressured speech, suggesting flight of ideas. Some excitements are in the form of short panic reactions.

The characteristic symptoms of catatonia are withdrawal, regression, repetitive stereotyped actions, odd mannerisms, strange positioning of parts of the body, waxy flexibility, mutism, and hallucinations.

Undifferentiated and Residual Types

Schizophrenia, undifferentiated type refers to less severe psychotic symptoms that cannot be classified in the types described previously or to symptoms that meet the criteria for more than one of the other schizophrenia categories.

Schizophrenia, residual type is a classification used when the client has had at least one episode of schizophrenia but does not display acute psychotic symptoms. Other symptoms of schizophrenia are present, however. They include the following:

Eccentric behavior

Emotional blunting or blunted affect

Social withdrawal

Disordered thinking

Loosening of associations

Loosening of associations is a type of thinking in which the normal connectedness between ideas or thoughts seems haphazard. The thinking process does not flow in a normal pattern.

NURSING CARE OF CLIENTS WITH SCHIZOPHRENIC DISORDERS

The schizophrenic client admitted to a psychiatric institution is out of control. His or her thoughts and feelings are bizarre. The schizophrenic client may be terrified or overwhelmed with grief or rage, or may seem to be falling apart psychologically (also known as **disintegrating**). **Disintegration** is the disruption of the normal influence of the ego on combining our thoughts, feelings, memories, and perceptions into a realistic view of ourselves and our environment. When the ego loses its ability to maintain these psychological functions in balance, the client feels as though he or she really is falling apart.

The client who is experiencing an acute schizophrenic episode appears to have indeed lost the ability to function psychologically. For nurses new to the psychiatric setting, observing this can be a frightening experience. Seeing a fellow human in the rawest emotional state touches our own vulnerability as human beings. Our own safety can be threatened. In addition, we may wonder whether this could ever happen to us. As a result, we can be flooded with anxiety as we imagine the terror of losing control.

You may have a family member or friend who has experienced a psychotic disorder. Memories associated with their psychotic episodes may also create fear, anxiety, or sadness in you. It is important to realize that these feelings are common in all people new to the psychiatric unit, regardless of their caregiving discipline: nursing, medicine, social work, and so on. As you learn more about the nature of the illness, its treatment, and prognosis and discuss your feelings with peers, supervisors, or instructors, these feelings can gradually diminish.

Assessment

A basic rule governs those who work with psychiatric clients: a consistent nurse should be assigned to the care of each client. This is essential, especially for the psychotic client whose level of functioning is, in some way, severely regressed. As a young child benefits from the security of a consistent caregiver and is disturbed by frequent changes in caregivers, so, too, is the client with a psychotic disorder.

The assessment of the newly admitted schizophrenic client is a slow process that requires obtaining information from many people, including the client. Despite the psychotic episodes the client is experiencing, he or she may be able to give reliable information at certain times. The family or friends of the client are important because they can often give facts that validate the client's statements or fill in the many gaps of knowledge that are important in understanding the client's current illness. It is also possible to discern maladaptive family relationship patterns that may have contributed to the person's current disorder. In addition, if these dynamics are not addressed in the treatment setting, they can undermine the client's ability to function independently once he or she is discharged from the hospital.

When talking with the client early in the admission process, always remember his or her need for safety. Accordingly, maintain a non-threatening, calm communication style, observing for signs of increasing anxiety and agitation. Rather than continuing an interview with an increasingly anxious psychotic client, tell him or her gently that you will return later. The types of questions you can ask appear in Chapter 7, Building a Person-Centered Therapeutic Relationship. They should be modified to accommodate the client's level of functioning.

The assessment of the psychotic client will include the data obtained by members of other disciplines on the treatment team. Depending on the particular treatment philosophy of the institution in which you are working, this information may be pooled and used in a unified team approach to provide a positive therapeutic care plan. The nursing diagnoses that are determined in reviewing the data will form the basis of the planning step. Essentially, the symptoms or problems the client demonstrates should ultimately diminish during the treatment process.

Planning

The planning step of the nursing process should be integrated with the overall plan of the multidisciplinary treatment team as developed by the client's primary therapist. The recommendations in Chapter 18, Nursing Care Planning With Specific Types of Disordered Mental States, should be used in developing the care plan according to the nursing process model. The discussion on the nursing care of the psychotic client will be limited to specific recommendations for interventions with this type of client. It is important to remember that the treatment process of the psychotic client may be lengthy. Accordingly, planning should include both short-term and long-term goals. In this way, the client and caregivers will have realistic, achievable goals to minimize discouragement if progress is slow.

Implementation

First, be concerned with the client's safety and physical well-being. The psychotic client who experiences loss of contact with reality is at particular risk of inflicting self-harm and harm to others. The assessment process should include this major consideration. Intervention includes active steps to ensure the safety of the client and all others with whom he or she comes in contact. This includes careful monitoring of the environment by the nurse. It may be necessary for the high-risk client to be secluded until medication reduces the level of risk. Limits and controls that you carry out in a therapeutic and supportive manner promote the client's sense of control and security. These should be outlined carefully in the nursing care plan so that they are carried out in a consistent manner by other nurses in your absence.

The psychotic client is often unable to care for himself or herself. Nursing intervention includes ensuring that bathing, dressing, eating, and toileting are adequately maintained. If you need to encourage the client to undertake self-care, or if you must provide assistance in self-care, make sure your attitude and actions will preserve the client's self-esteem and dignity.

Know how to intervene therapeutically when the client is experiencing hallucinations or delusions. These periods can be very frightening to the client. Because one aspect of the client's ego is aware of the loss of contact with reality, he or she becomes highly anxious. When a nurse sits quietly, accepting and understanding the client's distress, the client's sense of trust can slowly develop. The nurse will gradually come to understand the cause of the client's emotional distress and can respond to the client's statements about his or her perceptions, thoughts, or feelings in ways that can gently restore a stronger sense of reality.

Do not agree with or in any way enter into the client's misperceptions. Rather, repeat the client's statements to show that he or she is being heard, and then gently tell the client that you do not hear the same voices or feel the same things. Reality-based statements by the client can be validated, and you can encourage reality orientation by the nature of questioning used in discussion with the client.

It is especially important with the families of schizophrenic clients to use a family therapy approach. Nurses can sometimes actively participate in this process. Attend treatment team meetings in which the family patterns are discussed so that, regardless of your level of involvement, you will understand the issues that the client has faced and will continue to face in his or her family. Your interventions should be supportive to the overall family system of which the client is an integral member.

Evaluation

Evaluation of the nursing intervention should be based on whether or not there is a decrease in the original symptoms observed in the assessment process. Evaluation of both short-term and long-term goals should be an ongoing process. When revision is indicated, the nursing process should be reinstituted.

Outpatient Nursing Care

Over the past several years, there has been a trend toward "deinstitutionalization" and increased community-based outpatient care of people with psychiatric disorders, including people with schizophrenia and other psychotic disorders. People with these disorders may be hospitalized for a time. But after being stabilized, they are often released to be treated primarily in an outpatient setting.

The basic needs of the outpatient client with schizophrenia—medication, physical safety, and general well-being—remain the same as for the client being treated as an inpatient. However, the very nature of these disorders may make consistent client care difficult to attain, and a client most in need of medication or other care may "fall through the cracks." This reality is reflected in the increasing incidence of people with schizophrenia among the homeless population. Responding to the needs of these clients is an ongoing challenge for the community-based psychiatric nurse.

◆ DELUSIONAL DISORDERS

The behavioral pattern in these disorders is characterized by a firm, fixed system of delusion in an otherwise well-balanced personality.

This delusional system centers around feelings of persecution and grandiosity. The major areas of activity most frequently involved are those of religion, politics, or another person. The delusional system slowly develops after a false interpretation of an actual occurrence. There are no hallucinations. The client simply becomes convinced that a certain thing or situation is true, and will accept no proof, regardless of how convincing it is, that he or she has a wrong concept of the thing or situation.

The types of delusional disorders are as follows:

Erotomanic

Grandiose

Jealous

Persecutory

Somatic

Mixed

Unspecified

In the **erotomanic** disorder, the individual believes that someone, usually of higher status, is in love with him or her. In the **grandiose** type, the person has an inflated sense of self-worth, power, identity, knowledge, or special relationship to a famous person or to God. In the **jealous** form, the individual believes incorrectly that his or her sexual partner is unfaithful.

In the **persecutory** type, the person becomes increasingly suspicious of people and situations, and feels that people are spying on him or her with harmful intentions. The client with a persecutory disorder assumes anything other people are talking about concerns him or her. As this persecution complex enlarges, the client becomes grandiose. This increased sense of self-importance is reflected in statements such as "a foreign government is after me," or "an international ring is pursuing me."

In the **somatic** type, the individual believes he or she has some physical disease, disorder, or defect. In the **mixed** type, delusions of the above types appear but no one theme predominates. The **unspecified** type does not fit any of the previous categories, but does have a general delusion that is not grounded in reality.

NURSING CARE OF CLIENTS WITH DELUSIONAL DISORDERS

The general principles for nursing care of the client with schizophrenia should be employed with the delusional client. Depending on the level and type of delusion, the client can be a risk to himself or herself and to others. The delusions will continue until the effects of medication and hospitalization gradually diminish the level of psychosis. Until that time, you must frequently monitor the client and, if indicated, use physical and pharmacologic restraints to ensure his or her safety and that of others.

When institutionalized, a client's suspiciousness often involves food and medications, and persuading him or her to eat or take medications often poses a real problem. The paranoid person is well oriented to person, place, and time, and speaks and acts rationally outside of his or her special delusional system. Thus, the paranoid client is frequently able to convince acquaintances that his or her "idea" is true. and may be able to convince a group that he or she is a great reformer, leader, or prophet, until finally the fallacy of the client's claims becomes clearly evident to them and they turn away in disillusionment.

The outstanding symptoms of paranoia are a well-developed delusional system involving feelings of persecution and grandiosity, strong projection, and suspiciousness; there are no hallucinations. These people may become dangerous. So great is their fear of being harmed by others that they may strike out first in self-defense. Therapy has not been especially effective in changing these delusional concepts. Phenothiazine medication, electroconvulsive therapy (ECT), or a combination of the two may be helpful.

◆ OTHER PSYCHOTIC DISORDERS

This category includes the following disorders:

Brief psychotic disorder

Schizophreniform disorder

Schizoaffective disorder

Shared-Induced psychotic disorder

Atypical psychosis

Brief psychotic disorder is a condition that can occur as the result of an acutely stressful episode before which the person functioned normally and had no other type of physical or mental disorder. The person experiences severe emotional distress and one or more of the following signs of psychosis: delusions, hallucinations, loose associations or incoherence, and severely catatonic or disorganized behavior. The symptoms disappear within 1 month, and the individual returns to his or her previous level of functioning.

Schizophreniform disorder meets some of the criteria of schizophrenia; however, the condition lasts less than 6 months, disallowing the schizophrenia diagnosis. There are two subclassifications of this type: the first is labeled **with good prognostic features.** These features include no flat affect, good pre-illness social and work role functioning, confusion or perplexity at the height of the psychotic episode, and onset of psychotic symptoms within 4 weeks of the first noted changes in normal behavior or functioning. The second subcategory is **without good prognostic features**. It includes the classic schizophrenia symptoms.

Schizoaffective disorder is a condition that manifests a mixture of symptoms of a major depressive episode or a manic episode of bipolar disorder, as well as some of the symptoms that meet the criteria of schizophrenia. There is a history of delusions or hallucinations during the period of the disturbance, but no permanent mood symptoms. The disorder does not meet all the criteria for schizophrenia. It is unknown whether there is an underlying organic cause.

Shared psychotic disorder (formerly induced psychotic disorder) is a condition in which a second person takes on a delusion similar to that of another who has a delusional (paranoid) disorder. The affected individual has no prior history of psychosis or schizophrenia.

Psychotic disorder not otherwise specified is a category for those conditions that involve the symptoms of psychosis but do not meet the full range of criteria of the other categories of functional psychotic mental disorders.

CHAPTER 23 SUMMARY

- Schizophrenia, the most prevalent of the functional group of psychoses, is characterized by disturbances of thinking, mood, and behavior.

- A person's basic personality will be the predisposing factor as to which form of psychosis he or she will develop. Repeated incidences of psychosis in a person's life tend to follow the same behavioral pattern each time.

- Current biomedical research links brain chemistry (especially the neurotransmitter dopamine) and the development of schizophrenia. According to current psychoanalytic theory, persons with schizophrenia were deprived in childhood of meaningful relationships with important members of the family circle.

- The main symptoms of schizophrenia are thought disorder, fragmented speech, autism, inappropriate or absent emotional affect, withdrawal, regression, delusion, and hallucination.

- Major subtypes of schizophrenia and their characteristics are as follows: catatonic (stupor, rigidity, unorganized or impulsive behavior); disorganized (inappropriate emotions, withdrawal, delusions); and paranoid (suspiciousness, projection, delusions of persecution).

■ Effective nursing care of clients with schizophrenia includes consistency of caregiver; a calm, nonthreatening communication style; intervention to ensure client safety; listening to client's statements without validating misperceptions; and basing evaluation on the observable decrease in symptoms.

■ Delusional disorders are characterized by a firm, fixed system of delusion in an otherwise well-balanced personality. Major types of delusional disorders are erotomanic, grandiose, jealous, persecutory, and somatic.

■ Shared psychotic disorder is when a second person takes on a delusion similar to that of another person who has a delusional disorder.

CHAPTER 23 QUESTIONS

1. The behavioral patterns of clients with schizophrenia include
   a. disorganization of the personality.
   b. disturbances of thinking.
   c. inappropriate emotional responses.
   d. all of the above.

2. Which of the following is *not* a symptom of schizophrenia?
   a. Hallucinations
   b. Word salad
   c. Improved interaction with others
   d. Lack of affect

3. Which of the following would *not* be appropriate nursing care of the schizophrenic client?
   a. A consistent nurse assigned to the care of each client
   b. Attention to client's need for safety
   c. Intervention to prevent self-harm when client loses contact with reality
   d. Agreeing with the client's misperceptions to help calm the client

4. Clients with an erotomanic delusional disorder believe that
   a. they are being spied on by other people who intend to harm them.
   b. a famous or important person is in love with them.
   c. their sexual partner is unfaithful.
   d. they have a terminal disease.

BIBLIOGRAPHY

Barry, P.D. (1996). *Psychosocial nursing: Care of physically ill patients and their families* (3rd ed.). Philadelphia: Lippincott-Raven.

Buccheri, R., & Underwood, P. (1993). Symptom management: Inpatient nursing care of persons with schizophrenia. *New Directions in Mental Health Services, 58*, 23–31.

Diagnostic and statistical manual of mental disorders (4th ed.). (1994). Washington, DC: American Psychiatric Press.

Kaplan, H.I., & Sadock, B.J. (1995). *Comprehensive textbook of psychiatry/VI* (6th ed.). Baltimore: Williams & Wilkins.

Kaplan, H.I., & Sadock, B.J. (1994). *Synopsis of psychiatry: Behavioral sciences, clinical psychiatry* (7th ed.). Baltimore: Williams & Wilkins.

Krach, P. (1995). Nursing implications: Functional status of older persons with schizophrenia. *Journal of Gerontological Nursing, 19*(8), 21–27.

Lego, S. (1996). *Psychiatric nursing: A comprehensive reference* (2nd ed.). Philadelphia: Lippincott-Raven.

Nettina, S.M. (1996). *The Lippincott manual of nursing practice* (6th ed.). Philadelphia: Lippincott-Raven.

Wilson, H.S., & Kneisl, C.R. (1996). *Psychiatric nursing* (5th ed.). Redwood City, CA: Addison-Wesley.

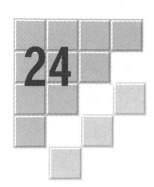

Mood Disorders

After reading this chapter the student will be able to:

■ List the major symptoms of the client with a major depressive episode and the client with a manic episode.

■ Tell the difference between the symptoms of a person with a bipolar disorder and a person with a cyclothymic disorder.

■ Name the medication most commonly prescribed for people with a bipolar disorder.

■ Describe five symptoms of a person who is acutely suicidal.

The affective mental disorders include those mental conditions that cause a change in a person's mood (also known as affect) or emotional state for a prolonged period of time. The changed emotional state may be depression, elation, or a combination occurring in alternative cycles. These conditions are not caused by another physical or mental disorder. It is important to note that a variety of physical illnesses or disorders and side effects of medication can result in depressive symptoms. Such physiologically induced conditions are not included in this category; rather, they are classified under the cognitive disorders category (see Chapter 21, Delirium, Dementia, and Amnestic and Other Cognitive Disorders).

The major categories of disorder under this classification are **mood episodes, depressive disorders,** and **bipolar disorders.** They include the following major categories:

   I.   Mood episodes
        A. Major depressive episode
        B. Manic episode
        C. Other
   II. Depressive disorders
        A. Major depressive
        B. Dysthymic disorder
   III. Bipolar disorders
        A. Bipolar I and II disorder
        B. Cyclothymic disorder

◆ Mood Episodes

The following criteria have been developed by the American Psychiatric Association for major depressive episodes and manic episodes:

MAJOR DEPRESSIVE EPISODE

For a diagnosis of a major depressive episode, five (or more) of the following symptoms have been present during the same 2-week period and represent a change from previous functioning; at least one of the symptoms is either (1) depressed mood or (2) loss of interest or pleasure.

   1. Depressed mood most of the day, nearly every day, as indicated by either subjective report or observation made by others
   2. Markedly diminished interest or pleasure in all, or almost all, activities most of the day, nearly every day

3. Significant weight loss when not dieting, or weight gain

4. Insomnia or hypersomnia nearly every day

5. Psychomotor agitation or retardation nearly every day

6. Fatigue or loss of energy nearly every day

7. Feelings of worthlessness or excessive or inappropriate guilt nearly every day

8. Diminished ability to think or concentrate, or indecisiveness, nearly every day

9. Recurrent thoughts of death, recurrent suicidal ideation without a specific plan, or a suicide attempt or a specific plan for committing suicide.

MANIC EPISODE

A manic episode is characterized by a distinct period of abnormally and persistently elevated, expansive, or irritable mood, lasting at least 1 week (or any duration if hospitalization is necessary). During the period of mood disturbance, three (or more) of the following symptoms have persisted and have been present to a significant degree:

1. Inflated self-esteem or grandiosity

2. Decreased need for sleep

3. More talkative than usual or pressure to keep talking

4. Flight of ideas or subjective experience that thoughts are racing

5. Distractibility

6. Increase in goal-directed behavior and psychomotor agitation

7. Excessive involvement in pleasurable activities that have a high potential for painful consequences.[1]

At the beginning of a manic episode, the client's physical appearance becomes increasingly disheveled as he or she speeds up physically, intellectually, and emotionally. The client becomes increasingly restless and aggressive. The id seems to take over, and the superego loses all control over the self. The client's thoughts speed up so that he or she becomes easily distractible. This gives rise to flight of ideas, as the client's mind darts from subject to subject, and accelerated speech flits from one idea to another. The client's mood becomes euphoric, then shifts into exaltation, and finally, at the peak of the half-cycle, into frenzy. The client in this state sleeps and eats very little, losing weight rapidly. He

[1]From *Desk Reference to the Diagnostic Criteria from DSM-IV*. (1994). Washington, DC: American Psychiatric Association, pp. 161–164.

or she frequently smashes or breaks things unintentionally. If prevented from doing something, he or she may become angry.

Because manic clients are so easily distracted, however, they can usually be managed fairly well. As a matter of fact, manic clients are usually happy-go-lucky, friendly, bossy, and highly verbal. They have delusions of grandeur and feel possessed of great charm, power, abilities, and wealth. If one or two of these hyperactive people are placed on a ward with a group of hypoactive clients, they actually have a stimulating effect on the latter by causing them to interact better. However, they also tend to offend other clients on the ward, since their language and actions are often coarse, lewd, and suggestive. With the gradual subsiding of their hyperactivity, moral values again settle into place, and behavior becomes more and more acceptable.

OTHER MOOD EPISODES

Other categories of mood episodes include mixed episode and hypomanic episode. In the mixed episode, criteria are met for both a manic episode and a major depressive episode. The hypomanic episode is a distinct period of elevated mood that is clearly different from the usual nondepressed mood but does not classify as a manic episode.

◆ DEPRESSIVE DISORDERS

MAJOR DEPRESSIVE DISORDER

The person with major depressive disorder demonstrates the presence of a major depressive episode (symptoms outlined previously) and has not exhibited a manic episode. A major depressive disorder may be recurrent or a single episode or recurrent. It can also be further specified according to other features displayed such as with catatonic or melancholic features or with postpartum onset.

For a client experiencing a major depressive episode, speech becomes slow, halting, and anxious as the superego takes over, and the client becomes increasingly self-accusative. In a typical depressive episode, the client paces slowly, later sits on a chair, rocking back and forth and moaning dejectedly, and finally takes to bed or the floor, where he or she slowly and restlessly moves in a small, circumscribed area. The client is very dejected, has a fixation about his or her worthlessness, the magnitude of his or her sins, and the need for punishment. The client is directing all aggression inward and eventually takes the blame for all the sins and crimes in the world. His or her misery is very great. Just before or immediately after reaching the bottom of this cycle, the client may attempt suicide.

DYSTHYMIC DISORDER

In past editions of the *Diagnostic and Statistical Manual of Mental Disorders*, this condition was called depressive neurosis or neurotic depression. This condition is marked by depressed mood for most of the day, more days than not, that has existed for at least 2 years for adults and 1 year for children and adolescents. The symptoms are not as severe, however, as those of a major depressive episode. Two or more of the following symptoms of depression are present: poor appetite or overeating, low energy level or fatigue, insomnia or excessive sleeping, low self-esteem, poor concentration or difficulty making decisions, and feelings of hopelessness.

◆ BIPOLAR DISORDER

The person with bipolar disorder demonstrates strong, exaggerated, and cyclic mood swings. All normal people are subject to a moderate degree of mood swing. The form found in this type of mental illness is, however, a very exaggerated form lasting for weeks or months at a time. There is a slow but steady increase in mood elevation and hyperactivity up to a climax of frenzy, then a slow decrease in activity down to normal behavior again. Then, as a rule, the client will start into the opposite cycle of hypoactivity, accompanied by depression, only to swing slowly through this cycle and back to balance once more (Figure 24–1).

These episodes tend to recur several times within the client's lifetime. It is not unusual for a client to experience only one half of the cycle, that is, only the hyperactive (manic) phase of behavior or recurrent episodes of hypoactive (depressive) behavior. Whether the client shows the entire cycle or only half of it, he or she will, even without treatment, return to normal and may be normal for several years, then repeat the cycle (or half-cycle) again. Modern therapy helps speed up the rate of recovery greatly. Currently, bipolar disorders are categorized according to whether the predominant characteristic is the presence of manic behavior (type I) or depressive behavior (type II).

BIPOLAR I AND II DISORDERS

Bipolar I disorder is characterized by the presence of manic episodes, although a client with this type of disorder can experience a depressed episode. Categories of bipolar I disorder are the single manic episode, most recent episode hypomanic, most recent episode manic, most recent episode mixed, most recent episode depressed, or most recent episode unspecified. Bipolar II disorder is characterized by recurrent

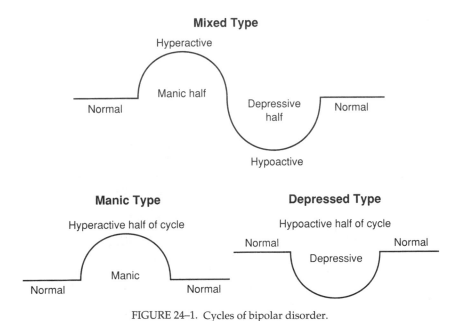

FIGURE 24–1. Cycles of bipolar disorder.

major depressive episodes with hypomanic (but not manic or mixed) episodes.

◆CYCLOTHYMIC DISORDER

A person with cyclothymic disorder tends to swing between moods of exhilaration and depression, but not to pathologic extremes. However, he or she may develop manic-depressive psychosis in stressful life situations or, in some cases, for no apparent reason. (Changes in brain chemistry have been postulated.) Two subforms are often seen, in which the person shows one of the moods much more than the other. The client who shows exhilaration much of the time is classified as a hypomanic person. Typically, hypomanic clients are outgoing and cheerful and thoroughly enjoy life; they are vivacious, buoyant, confident, aggressive, and optimistic. Many would make excellent salespeople, because they are gregarious, with a high energy level and few inhibitions. Sometimes, however, they are too easily swayed by new impressions. A few of this type are blustering, argumentative, and hypercritical. They all seem to have ready excuses for their failures and can usually talk themselves out of their difficulties. When these people become psychotic, they tend to become manic.

A client who shows a depressed pattern is classified as a melancholic person. This is the cyclothymic personality at the opposite pole from the hypomanic. The melancholic client tends to be easily depressed, though he or she is often kindly, quiet, sympathetic, and even-tempered. He or she is seldom eccentric. In moody periods, the melancholic client is a lonely person, solemn, submissive, gloomy, and self-deprecating. He or she often has feelings of inadequacy and hopelessness, becomes discouraged easily, suffers in silence, and weeps readily, though not in the presence of others. The melancholic client tends to be overly meticulous, conscientious, and preoccupied with work. He or she is fearful of disapproval and feels responsibility keenly. Indecisiveness and caution indicate feelings of insecurity. Under stress, the melancholic client tends to develop a psychotic depression of the manic-depressive type.

◆Nursing Care of Clients With Mood Disorders

BIPOLAR DISORDER, MANIC EPISODE

The client with bipolar disorder may be seen in the hospital during either an acute manic or depressive episode. During the manic phase of the illness, the client openly and sometimes aggressively tests the limits imposed by the therapeutic milieu and by specific caregivers. The client's critical tendencies and fault finding challenge the vulnerable aspects and the self-esteem of others. Although many of the mental status changes of the manic client may be similar to those of clients with schizophrenia, the personality traits of each have different qualities. The manic client is generally more engaging and warm than the schizophrenic client, who is detached and emotionally cold. Ideally, a primary nursing approach should be implemented.

Major areas of assessment and intervention include attention to the client's hyperactive state and monitoring of medication. Additional nursing interventions should be based on the client's mental status and physical and nutritional needs. The energy level of the manic client is almost limitless. The strain on his or her physical well-being, if not appropriately managed, is severe. The major tranquilizers are frequently used to decrease hyperactive status and to reduce the delusions, hallucinations, and disorientation that accompany the peak of manic excitement.

In addition to the major tranquilizers, lithium carbonate therapy is used to reduce the cyclic effects of the disorder. It is very effective in the treatment of bipolar disorder. This drug is described in more detail in Chapter 31, Psychopharmacology and Electroshock Treatment of Mental Disorders. Of particular importance to the client's treatment is the monitoring of serum lithium levels and titration of dosage, based on mental status and physical symptoms. Lithium promotes a therapeutic response in 6 to 10 days. Accurate and descriptive charting of the client's mental and physical signs is important in arranging the dose of lithium at an optimum therapeutic level. While the medication is gradually decreasing the frantic activity level of the client, other nursing measures can assist in maintaining his or her well-being.

Limit setting, when reasonable, increases the client's sense of control and trust in the caregiving system. Note the specific approach to limit setting in the nursing care plan so that all caregivers will be consistent and effective. Communication with other members of the care team about nursing interventions can assist in the overall therapeutic effectiveness of your plan. The client needs frequent showering because hyperactivity will increase perspiration. He or she will be motivated to eat if you provide foods that can be eaten while standing or moving. Ideally, the environment should not further stimulate the client's level of excitement. Keep noise and light levels low. Provide opportunities for physical activity so the client will have an outlet and purpose for his or her hyperactivity.

BIPOLAR DISORDER, DEPRESSED EPISODE OR MAJOR DEPRESSIVE DISORDER

The depressed client feels hopeless and helpless. He or she is vulnerable and suffers from feelings of worthlessness and futility. The depressed client lacks the mental or physical energy to restore himself or herself or to feel hope for the future. Because of these factors, the depressed client is dependent on the nurse for a number of needs. It is important to prioritize these needs in the assessment and intervention process.

Assessment for Suicide Risk

If the client is acutely depressed, suicide risk should be constantly monitored. According to Dubin, the following populations have been found to have higher risk of suicide:

Older, single, divorced, or widowed males

Caucasians

Protestants

Unemployed people

People in poor physical health

People living alone

People with an anniversary of death or loss

People with sudden changes in life situation

People who leave suicide notes

Older homosexual men

Table 24–1 shows the assessment of suicidal risk factors that can be determined by a comprehensive psychiatric history.

When talking with a client admitted for acute depression or who appears acutely depressed, assess the degree of hopelessness he or she is feeling with a question such as, "Tom, you seem very discouraged today. Can you tell me how you feel?" If he acknowledges feeling very depressed or in any way raises your concerns about suicide potential,

◆ **TABLE 24–1. Assessing the Degree of Suicidal Risk**

Behavior or Symptom	Intensity of Risk		
	Low	*Moderate*	*High*
Anxiety	Mild	Moderate	High or panic state
Depression	Mild	Moderate	Severe
Isolation withdrawal	Vague feelings of depression; no withdrawal	Some feelings of helplessness, hopelessness, and withdrawal	Hopeless, helpless, withdrawn, and self-deprecating
Daily functioning	Fairly good in most activities	Moderately good in some activities	Not good in any activities
Resources	Several	Some	Few or none
Coping strategies/ devices being used	Generally constructive	Some that are constructive	Predominantly destructive
Significant others	Several who are available	Few or only one available	Only one, or none available
Psychiatric help in past	None, or positive attitude toward	Yes, and moderately satisfied with	Negative view of help received
Lifestyle	Stable	Moderately stable or unstable	Unstable
Alcohol/drug use	Infrequently to excess	Frequently to excess	Continual abuse
Previous suicide attempts	None, or of low lethality	None to one or more of moderate lethality	None to multiple attempts of high lethality
Disorientation/ disorganization	None	Some	Marked
Hostility	Little or none	Some	Marked
Suicidal plan	Vague, fleeting thoughts but no plan	Frequent thoughts, occasional ideas about a plan	Frequent or constant thought with a specific plan

Reproduced with permission from Hatton, D., Valente, S., & Rink, A. (1997). Assessment of suicide risk. In *Suicide assessment and intervention.* New York: Appleton-Century Crofts, p 56.

ask him, "Tom, when things seem so difficult for you, do you ever wonder about ending your life?" When a person is having suicidal thoughts it can be a relief to acknowledge them. If the client acknowledges suicidal thoughts, report it immediately to the nurse in charge or to the client's physician. Follow the policy of your nursing unit regarding suicide precautions. If a client acknowledges suicidal thinking, other questions may further determine suicidal risk, including "Have you thought about how you would end your life?" A client who has developed a suicide plan is at increased risk. Another question that can help to determine increased risk is "Tom, are there any reasons keeping you from going ahead with your plan?" The client who has no reason for staying alive may see suicide as the easiest way out of his or her situation.

The actively suicidal client must be monitored at all times. Keep the client's room free of any items that could be used to injure self or others. Items such as eating utensils, belts, and nail files, which you would not normally think of as dangerous, can be dangerous in the hands of a severely depressed client.

A person who is acutely depressed usually demonstrates slowed thought processes, speech, movement, and so on. He or she may not be able to engage in conversation. Therapeutic intervention may simply involve just sitting quietly with the client. Your presence may be very supportive.

When the client is able to talk with you, allow his or her statements and answers to your earlier questions to be the guide as to what is on the client's mind. Ask further questions based on his or her previous statements. Avoid making reassuring comments that may seem superficial and cause the client to feel even more alone.

Accurate Documentation of Mental Status

Another aspect of nursing care of the depressed client is accurate documentation of his or her mental and physical states. The antidepressant medications usually take about 2 to 3 weeks to elicit a therapeutic response. Some of them also have sedative and hypnotic effects, as well as physiologic side effects. By accurately charting the client's changes in mental and physical status, you will help the physician determine when a therapeutic level of medication is reached or when the medication regimen needs to be reevaluated.

CHAPTER 24 SUMMARY

- Mood disorders are mental conditions that cause a change in a person's affect or mood for a prolonged period of time. The changed state may be depression, elation, or a cyclical combination of the two.

- A person with bipolar disorder demonstrates strong, exaggerated mood swings.

- Characteristics of a manic episode include grandiosity, decreased need for sleep, racing thoughts, psychomotor agitation, and excessive involvement in activities with negative consequences.

- Characteristics of a major depressive episode include markedly diminished pleasure in daily activities, significant weight loss or gain, sleep disturbances, fatigue or energy loss, feelings of worthlessness, diminished ability to concentrate, and recurrent thoughts of death.

- Clients with cyclothymic disorder exhibit mood swings without the pathologic extremes of bipolar disorder.

- Major areas of nursing assessment and intervention for manic clients include attention to the client's hyperactive state, monitoring of medication and serum lithium levels, and limit setting to increase the client's sense of control and trust.

- Major areas of nursing assessment and intervention for depressed clients include assessment for suicide risk and accurate documentation of mental status. Actively suicidal clients should be monitored at all times.

- Lithium carbonate is the medication most frequently used to reduce the cyclic effects of bipolar disorder.

CHAPTER 24 QUESTIONS

1. A client in the manic phase of a cycle exhibits
   a. increased appetite.
   b. apathy.
   c. restlessness and aggression.
   d. slowed thought processes.

2. The major difference between bipolar disorder and cyclothymic disorder is
   a. the disorders occur at different times of the year.
   b. people with cyclothymic disorders must be hospitalized.
   c. people with bipolar disorder function better from day to day.
   d. cyclothymic disorder exhibits less extreme mood swings.

3. The medication most commonly used to reduce the cyclic effects of bipolar disorder is
   a. lithium carbonate.
   b. dopamine.

c. adrenaline.

d. none of the above.

4. Suicide risk is considered higher

a. in older males, unemployed people, and people living alone.

b. when alcohol or drug abuse is present.

c. if the person thinks frequently of suicide and has a plan.

d. all of the above.

BIBLIOGRAPHY

Barry, P.D. (1996). *Psychosocial nursing: Care of physically ill patients and their families* (3rd ed.). Philadelphia: Lippincott-Raven.

Diagnostic and statistical manual of mental disorders (4th ed.). (1994). Washington, DC: American Psychiatric Press.

Kaplan, H.I., & Sadock, B.J. (1995). *Comprehensive textbook of psychiatry/VI* (6th ed.). Baltimore: Williams & Wilkins.

Kaplan, H.I., & Sadock, B.J. (1994). *Synopsis of psychiatry: Behavioral sciences, clinical psychiatry* (7th ed.). Baltimore: Williams & Wilkins.

Lego, S. (1996). *Psychiatric nursing: A comprehensive reference* (2nd ed.). Philadelphia: Lippincott-Raven.

McFarland, G.K., Wasli, E.L., & Gerety, E.K. (1996). *Nursing diagnoses and process in psychiatric mental health nursing* (3rd ed.). Philadelphia: Lippincott-Raven.

Shives, L.R. (Ed.). (1994). *Basic concepts of psychiatric mental health nursing* (3rd ed.). Philadelphia: J.B. Lippincott.

Stuart, G.W. (1994). *Detection and treatment of depression: The nursing perspective.* Washington, DC: American Nurses Association.

Wilson, H.S., & Kneisl, C.R. (1996). *Psychiatric nursing* (5th ed.). Redwood City, CA: Addison-Wesley.

25

Anxiety and Somatoform Disorders

After reading this chapter the student will be able to:

■ Define **dysphoria** and **anxiety.**

■ Describe the difference between anxiety and fear.

■ List several possible causes of anxiety.

■ Name five subjective and five objective signs of anxiety.

■ List the four levels of anxiety and describe the mental state accompanying each of them.

■ Name three categories of anxiety disorders and describe one condition in each category.

■ Name three categories of somatoform disorders and describe the psychological process that is occurring in each type.

One of the most common dysphoric emotions known to mankind is anxiety. **Dysphoria,** or **dysphoric** feeling, is an unpleasant emotion that causes psychological distress or conflict. The Tenth National Conference on Nursing Diagnosis described anxiety as "a vague, uneasy feeling, the source of which is often unspecific or unknown to the individual." As described in Chapter 12, Human Emotions, anxiety is different from fear. Fear is an uneasy feeling due to a *known* cause. The basic cause of anxiety is an unconscious conflict between the psyche and the environment or within the psyche itself. Intrapsychic conflicts are related to conflict between two or more of the intrapsychic structures of id, ego, and superego. For example, the id may cause a person to feel sexually attracted to another. The superego may judge the desire to be immoral. If the desire continues, anxiety can result.

The following are some of the specific causes of anxiety which have also been described in the nursing diagnosis category of anxiety: unconscious conflict about essential values or goals of life; threat to self-concept; threat of death; threat to or change in health status; threat to or change in role functioning; threat to or change in environment; threat to or change in interaction patterns; situational/maturational crises; interpersonal transmission/contagion; unmet needs.

Hildegard Peplau, a psychiatric nurse theorist, has proposed four levels of anxiety:

1. **Mild**—Person is hyperalert and is sharply aware of the environment. His or her perceptual abilities of vision, hearing, and smell are increased.

2. **Moderate**—Person's perceptual abilities are decreased. The person can maintain his or her concentration on one activity, however (selective inattention).

3. **Severe**—Person's perceptual abilities are markedly diminished. His or her attention span is scattered.

4. **Panic**—Person is either paralyzed or severely agitated. He or she is filled with terror. The object of anxiety is overwhelming in its intensity.

Peplau also describes the intellectual capacity of an individual to learn from anxiety and adapt his or her behavior accordingly. For people in the mild-to-moderate range, Peplau believes that if individuals have well-developed coping abilities, they are able to observe the situation causing the anxiety, describe and analyze it, formulate meanings and relations, discuss it with another person to obtain feedback and validation, and benefit from the experience by adapting.

A person with severe anxiety (panic level) is unable to apply the intellectual skills described above. Instead, he or she seeks immediate relief in the easiest way possible to reduce anxiety. This initially easy escape from anxiety may not prove adaptive in the more distant future, however.

The behavior exhibited by a person in flight from anxiety usually falls into one of four categories:

- "Acting out" behavior, for example, projecting anger and blame onto others

- Somatization (converting the stress into actual, physical symptoms or illness)

- Immobilization or paralysis, for example, depression or withdrawal

- Use of energy generated by anxiety to seek other solutions

Peplau believes that anxiety is a normal part of the human condition. It is the necessary impetus to change and develop better coping skills. Her recommendations for nursing care of the client with anxiety appear later in this chapter.

The North American Nursing Diagnosis Association (NANDA) has described the characteristics of anxiety using two types of criteria: subjective, which includes symptoms described by the client; and objective, which lists the symptoms that can be observed by the nurse. They appear in Table 25–1.

◆ **TABLE 25–1. Symptoms Experienced by the Client With Anxiety**

Subjective Symptoms	Objective Symptoms
1. Increased tension	1. Sympathetic stimulation cardiovascular excitation, superficial vasoconstriction, pupil dilatation
2. Apprehension	
3. Painful and persistent increased helplessness	2. Restlessness
4. Uncertainty	3. Insomnia
5. Fearful	4. Glancing about
6. Scared	5. Poor eye contact
7. Regretful	6. Trembling hand tremors
8. Overexcited	7. Extraneous movement (foot shuffling, hand/arm movements)
9. Rattled	
10. Distressed	8. Facial tension
11. Jittery	9. Voice quivering
12. Feelings of inadequacy	10. Focus on "self"
13. Shakiness	11. Increased wariness
14. Fear of unspecific consequences	12. Increased perspiration
15. Expressed concerns re: change in life events	

◆ ANXIETY DISORDERS

Many of the categories of anxiety disorder were formerly called neuroses or neurotic disorders. The term **neurosis** was discontinued in 1987 and replaced with the new category of **anxiety disorder**. The subcategories of anxiety disorder are as follows:

1. Panic disorder
   a. With agoraphobia
   b. Without agoraphobia
2. Agoraphobia without history of panic disorder
3. Social phobia
4. Specific phobia
5. Obsessive–compulsive disorder
6. Posttraumatic stress disorder
7. Generalized anxiety disorder
8. Anxiety disorder not otherwise specified

PANIC DISORDER

Panic disorders are conditions in which the person experiences intense fear or discomfort in which four (or more) of the following symptoms developed abruptly and reached a peak within 10 minutes:

Palpitations, pounding heart, or accelerated heart rate

Sweating

Trembling or shaking

Sensations of shortness of breath or smothering

Feeling of choking

Chest pain or discomfort

Nausea or abdominal distress

Feeling dizzy, unsteady, lightheaded, or faint

Derealization (feelings of unreality) or depersonalization (being detached from oneself)

Fear of losing control or going crazy

Fear of dying

Paresthesias (numbness or tingling sensations)

Chills or hot flushes[1]

According to the DSM-IV, subtypes of panic disorder are **with agoraphobia** and **without agoraphobia.** Panic disorder **with agoraphobia**

---

[1]From *Desk Reference to the Diagnostic Criteria from DSM-IV.* (1994). Washington, DC: American Psychiatric Association, pp. 199–200.

describes a person who is fearful of being in open areas or public places or of being alone where escape is difficult or help is unavailable. He or she avoids the feared locations.

The next category of panic disorder is **without agoraphobia**. A person with this condition meets the criteria for panic disorder but does not experience agoraphobia. **Agoraphobia without history of panic disorder** is another category. An individual with this form of panic disorder experiences agoraphobic symptoms but has no history of panic symptoms.

The treatment for each type is individual psychotherapy in which the therapist and client gradually explore developmental experiences that may have contributed to the disorder. Frequently, these experiences have been repressed for many years. As the traumatizing events are uncovered, the symptoms gradually disappear. Special phobia clinics, operating in a number of metropolitan areas, report limited success treating the problem using behavior modification techniques.

Frequently, people with anxiety are given minor tranquilizers by well-intentioned medical physicians. Unless there is a specific, identifiable cause related to a major loss, such as threat of death or loss of job or some other stressful event, such medication only prolongs the client's difficulty. When chronic, persistent anxiety is undermining a person's ability to fulfill normal role functions, he or she should seek psychiatric or counseling assistance. These people, despite the disabling nature of their conditions, are rarely treated in the inpatient setting. However, nursing care of those who are hospitalized will be covered later in the chapter.

SOCIAL PHOBIA AND SPECIFIC PHOBIA

Social phobia is a condition in which a person experiences excessive anxiety when exposed to the scrutiny of others—in a classroom, while speaking publicly, or in a social setting. **Specific phobia** is a condition in which a specific object (for instance, snakes or spiders) or a situation (such as flying, receiving an injection, or seeing blood) stimulates overwhelming anxiety.

OBSESSIVE–COMPULSIVE DISORDER

The word **obsessive** refers to the repetitive thoughts that a person has. For example, a woman may have the intrusive and recurring thought that she wants to injure her mother. The word **compulsive** refers to the repetitive, stereotyped act that the person finds himself or herself unable to resist performing. In this example, the woman may need to wash her hands every time she thinks about hurting her mother in order to neutralize the obsession. This obsessive–compulsive client could find both the thoughts and the actions repugnant, but her attempts to stop the pattern result in extreme anxiety. With this disorder, the obsessions or compulsions are time consuming (take more than 1 hour a day) and significantly interfere with normal routine or with occupational and social functioning.

Some clients experience relief from this condition by taking antidepressant medication. Psychoanalytic psychotherapy, when started early in the disorder process, may help. Treatment of fully developed obsessive–compulsive disorder is quite difficult. An alternative treatment is behavior therapy (see Chapter 29, Milieu Therapy and Behavior Modification), which aims to stop the unwanted thoughts, urges, or actions of the client.

POSTTRAUMATIC STRESS DISORDER

A person with a posttraumatic stress disorder (PTSD) has experienced a catastrophic event—a plane crash, hurricane, or war—that anyone would perceive as very stressful. Although it is common for a person recovering from such an event to experience marital stress, illness, or difficulties functioning at work, a person who develops this disorder is unable to work through dysphoric feelings and unpleasant thoughts that follow the trauma, and instead suppresses them in his or her unconscious.

The person with this disorder continues to experience unpleasant feelings and fears about the catastrophe that do not follow the usual course of diminishing with the passing of time. He or she experiences decreased interest in relationships and external events; lack of control over distressing memories or dreams of the event; sudden sensations of the event beginning again; survival guilt; sleep disorder; or difficulties with memory or concentration. Some Vietnam veterans experience this disorder, as do victims of childhood incest and abuse.

When symptoms persist for 3 months or longer, the disorder is considered to be **chronic**. When symptoms do not occur until 6 months after the event, it is a **delayed onset** PTSD.

NURSING CARE OF CLIENTS WITH PTSD

Because of the prevalence of PTSD in the general public, the nursing care of this condition is described here.

Nursing intervention includes providing social support interventions such as group and individual counseling. Actively listening to clients' recollections and encouraging them to identify aspects or details of the traumatic event that are troubling is important. By talking about the traumatic event, clients begin to gain some control over their reactions to the troubling memories.

The nurse should avoid judgmental statements that tell the clients how or what to think, feel, or do. Instead, his or her role is to help clients sort out the traumatic events as well as to assist them with strategies for managing anxiety and anger.

GENERALIZED ANXIETY AND OTHER ANXIETY DISORDERS

A **generalized anxiety disorder** is a condition in which a person experiences excessive and unrealistic worry and anxiety about two or more life circumstances for at least 6 months or longer. During the 6-month period, the individual experiences more days of unrealistic worry than days without the worry and finds it difficult to control the worry. At least three of the following six symptoms are present when the person is anxious:

1. Restlessness or feeling keyed up or on edge
2. Being easily fatigued
3. Difficulty concentrating or mind going blank
4. Irritability
5. Muscle tension
6. Sleep disturbance (difficulty falling asleep or staying asleep, or restless unsatisfying sleep)[2]

The category termed **anxiety disorder not otherwise specified** includes anxiety or phobic avoidance symptoms that do not fit the criteria of the anxiety disorders described previously.

◆NURSING CARE OF CLIENTS WITH ANXIETY DISORDERS

When a person is hospitalized for anxiety, he or she initially is relieved to be in a safe environment. Because these clients do not customarily require hospitalization, their admission is an indication of how acutely they are terrorized by feeling out of control.

The nursing care of these clients should follow the treatment plan of the multidisciplinary care team. Hildegard Peplau has proposed that people with excessive anxiety lack the capacity to decrease it because they do not possess the same abilities to cope that others have. She recommends incorporating into the nursing care plan a process that teaches these coping skills.

The person who has a mild-to-moderate level of anxiety continues

[2]From *Desk Reference to the Diagnostic Criteria from DSM-IV*. (1994). Washington, DC: American Psychiatric Association, p. 213.

to retain intellectual ability. During the counseling process, this client can use intellectual skills to define the problem, analyze it, and begin the problem-solving process. Your role as nurse counselor is to listen actively and ask perceptive questions that will help the client analyze and solve his or her problem. You should not recommend solutions, because that would ultimately take control away from the client and promote his or her dependence on you. The goal of hospitalization is to encourage independence.

The client whose anxiety is at the severe-to-panic level initially requires anxiety relief. A counseling approach that encourages intellectual reasoning may cause further anxiety. Instead, let him or her describe the "here and now" of what is happening. The client may be so emotionally scattered that he or she cannot make simple decisions. Give simple directions in a calm, reassuring manner; do not touch the client or give advice or encouragement about the future. Document observations about his or her fluctuating anxiety state so that appropriate medication management is ensured.

Antianxiety medication is an important aspect of caring for people with high levels of anxiety. The minor tranquilizers listed in Chapter 31 are the drugs of choice when there are no symptoms of psychosis accompanying the anxiety. The major tranquilizers are used only when psychotic thinking is present. In both instances, the dosage of these drugs should be gradually decreased and discontinued as soon as the person's anxiety becomes tolerable. Both classes of drugs can cause drug dependence.

◆ SOMATOFORM DISORDERS

Somatoform disorders are mental conditions that cause physiologic symptoms. They occur through an unconscious mental process. The conditions in this category are as follows:

Body dysmorphic disorder

Conversion disorder

Hypochondriasis

Somatization disorder

Pain disorder

Undifferentiated somatoform disorder

Somatoform disorder not otherwise specified

BODY DYSMORPHIC DISORDER

Body dysmorphic disorder is a condition in which a normal-appearing person is preoccupied with an imagined defect. It can also occur in an individual who grossly exaggerates a slight physical defect. This disorder is not as severe as a delusional disorder, somatic type, which was described in Chapter 23, Schizophrenia and Other Psychotic Disorders.

CONVERSION DISORDER

Conversion disorders frequently mimic neurologic disorders. The most common symptoms are paralysis of one or more body parts, anesthesia (loss of feeling) or paresthesia (abnormal sensations, such as tingling, numbness, or heightened sensation), blindness, and so on. Frequently, the body part affected is related to an inner psychological conflict the client is experiencing. For example, a couple may have serious marital discord. The husband can possibly be denying his awareness of the difficulties, but may be experiencing deep hatred at an unconscious level and want to kill his wife. He could experience a paralysis of his right arm, without any idea of its cause. These people are usually seen initially by medical physicians; a very thorough diagnostic process should rule out any physical etiology before a psychogenic cause is suspected.

A person with a severe conversion disorder develops a rigid denial defense, having been denying inner conflict most of his or her lifetime. When such a client is hospitalized, he or she requires special care. Attempts to crack through the denial will result in higher levels of denial and increased anxiety. Consult with the clinician in charge of directing the client's care to learn the exact approach he or she is using and to obtain specific recommendations about nursing interventions so that your efforts are not countertherapeutic.

As the client's level of denial gradually diminishes, you will observe increased anxiety. When this occurs, follow the recommendations for nursing care of anxious clients described earlier in the chapter.

HYPOCHONDRIASIS

People with **hypochondriasis** magnify mild, vague physical symptoms into more severe symptoms of potentially serious illnesses. The person is preoccupied, over a period of 6 months or more, with thoughts about his or her imagined disease. Although physical examination finds no evidence of physical pathology, the client remains preoccupied with his or her fears.

SOMATIZATION DISORDER

Somatization disorder is a condition that usually strikes a person before the age of 30. The person has a history of vague symptoms related to a specific body system. These occur as chronic illnesses that cause him or her to see a variety of physicians. Often the client is hospitalized for diagnostic workup and may also have a pattern of multiple surgeries. The most common symptom complexes are related to gastrointestinal, sexual/reproductive, and neurologic body systems. The client may also have vague, unexplained pain in these organs, or in the head, chest, or back. Sexual dysfunction may also be present. Depression and anxiety frequently accompany these symptoms. No physical cause can be found for these conditions.

PAIN DISORDER

Pain disorder is a condition in which a client is consistently preoccupied with pain for a period of over 6 months. Thorough physical examination reveals no physiologic basis for the pain or finds that although there is some pathology, the pain is beyond what should normally be expected.

SOMATOFORM DISORDERS NOT OTHERWISE SPECIFIED

Conditions in this category fit the general criteria of somatoform disorders, but lack the distinct symptom presentation of the other disorders in this category. Symptoms are of less than 6 months' duration.

◆ NURSING CARE OF CLIENTS WITH SOMATOFORM DISORDERS

People with these disorders are rarely seen in inpatient psychiatric settings. Instead, they are much more commonly admitted to medical units where their persistent physical symptoms and lack of physical findings frustrate the medical and nursing staffs. These clients strongly resist understanding the psychological basis for their difficulties. When presented with the suggestion that there may be a psychogenic cause, they frequently become angry and change physicians, only to begin anew their search for care.

CHAPTER 25 SUMMARY

- Dysphoria is an unpleasant emotion that causes psychological distress or conflict.

- Anxiety is a vague, uneasy feeling whose source is either unspecific or unknown to the individual. Its basic cause is an unconscious conflict between the psyche and the environment or within the psyche it-self.

■ Fear is an uneasy feeling due to a known cause.

■ The four patterns of behavior a person exhibits while trying to flee from anxiety are acting out, somatization, depression or withdrawal, and using energy generated by anxiety to seek other solutions.

■ Panic disorder is a category of anxiety disorder in which the person experiences intense fear or discomfort followed by symptoms such as shaking, faintness, shortness of breath, accelerated heart rate, and sweating.

■ A person with social phobia exhibits excessive anxiety when exposed to scrutiny by others, such as during public speaking, in a classroom, or in a social setting.

■ With specific phobia, a particular object, such as a snake or spider, stimulates overwhelming anxiety.

■ A person with obsessive–compulsive disorder experiences intrusive, recurring thoughts combined with repetitive, stereotyped action, such as hand washing. Attempts to stop the pattern of thought or ac-tion result in extreme anxiety.

■ Posttraumatic stress disorder results from experiencing a catas-trophic event, then being unable to work through the dysphoric feel-ings or thoughts and suppressing them into the unconscious. Symptoms include decreased interest in relationships, flashbacks, survival guilt, sleep disorders, and difficulty concentrating.

■ Mental disorders in which one or more aspects of physical function-ing are misperceived or distorted include somatoform disorders, body dysmorphic disorder, conversion disorders, hypochondriasis, pain disorder, and somatization disorder.

CHAPTER 25 QUESTIONS

1. The difference between fear and anxiety is that
   a. fear is more painful than anxiety.
   b. anxiety has an unspecific or unknown source.
   c. fear is caused by an unconscious conflict.
   d. anxiety is seldom seen by the psychiatric nurse.

2. A person who frequently washes his or her hands to neutralize painful or unacceptable thoughts probably has
   a. hypochondriasis.

   b. obsessive–compulsive disorder.

   c. social phobia.

   d. agoraphobia.

3. A person experiencing a panic disorder will feel intense fear or discomfort plus

   a. accelerated heartbeat or palpitations.

   b. shortness of breath.

   c. shaking or trembling.

   d. all of the above.

4. Mental conditions that cause physiologic symptoms are called

   a. somatoform disorders.

   b. autonomic hyperactivity.

   c. generalized anxiety disorder.

   d. flashbacks.

BIBLIOGRAPHY

Badger, J.M. (1994). Calming the anxious patient. *AJN, 94*(5), 46.

Barry, P.D. (1996). *Psychosocial nursing: Care of physically ill patients and their families* (3rd ed.). Philadelphia: Lippincott-Raven.

Diagnostic and statistical manual of mental disorders (4th ed.). (1994). Washington, DC: American Psychiatric Press.

Kaplan, H.I., & Sadock, B.J. (1995). *Comprehensive textbook of psychiatry/VI* (6th ed.). Baltimore: Williams & Wilkins.

Lego, S. (1996). *Psychiatric nursing: A comprehensive reference* (2nd ed.). Philadelphia: Lippincott-Raven.

Lehman, L., & Kelley, J.H. (1993). Nursing interventions for anxiety, depression, and suspiciousness in the home care setting. *Home Healthcare Nurse, 11*(3), 35–40.

Minarik, P. (1996). Psychosocial intervention with ineffective coping responses to physical illness: Anxiety-related. In P.D. Barry (Ed.). *Psychosocial nursing: Care of physically ill patients and their families* (3rd ed.). Philadelphia: Lippincott-Raven.

Nettina, S.M. (1996). *The Lippincott manual of nursing practice* (6th ed.). Philadelphia: Lippincott-Raven.

Peplau, H. (1983). *Living and learning* [Lecture]. Hartford, CT: Institute of Living, October 28.

Teasdale, K. (1995). The nurse's role in anxiety management. *Professional Nurse, 10*(8), 509–512.

Whitley, G.G. (1994). Expert validation and differentiation of the nursing diagnoses anxiety and fear. *Nursing Diagnosis, 5*(4), 143–150.

Wilson, H.S., & Kneisl, C.R. (1996). *Psychiatric nursing* (5th ed.). Redwood City, CA: Addison-Wesley.

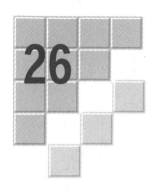

26

Dissociative, Sexual, and Other Disorders

Behavioral Objectives

After reading this chapter the student will be able to:

■ Define the terms **sexuality** and **ego-dystonic**.

■ List the developmental factors that affect adult psychosexual functioning.

■ Describe the characteristics of gender identity disorder.

■ Name and define three paraphilias and four categories of sexual dysfunctions.

■ Name three areas of emotional distress associated with adjustment disorders.

■ Name one condition from each of the following categories and describe the symptoms it presents: (1) dissociative disorders; (2) factitious disorders; and (3) impulse-control disorders.

◆ DISSOCIATIVE DISORDERS

A person with a **dissociative disorder** experiences a sudden loss of association and integration of self-identity, consciousness, or motor control. He or she is unaware that this change has occurred. These disorders are rare and, because of their profound and unpredictable nature, are traumatizing to families as well as to the person involved. In all cases, the possibility of an organic or other type of mental disorder is ruled out. The disorders in this category include the following:

Dissociative identity disorder (formerly multiple personality disorder)

Dissociative fugue (formerly psychogenic fugue)

Dissociative amnesia (formerly psychogenic amnesia)

Depersonalization disorder

Dissociative disorder not otherwise specified

Dissociative identity disorder is a complex mental state that was described in a novel by Corbett Thigpen and Hervey Cleckley, *The Three Faces of Eve*. The fictional character of Dr. Jekyll and Mr. Hyde described by Robert Louis Stevenson is another example of this disorder. The condition exists in a person who assumes two or more completely distinct identities and personalities during alternating times. The original personality has no knowledge or awareness of the concurrently existing personalities. Its course may begin in late adolescence or early adulthood.

One of the primary causes of this disorder is chronic physical, mental, or sexual abuse in childhood and adolescence. Its chronic nature distinguishes dissociative identity disorder from dissociative amnesia and dissociative fugue, which are usually brief episodes.

Dissociative fugue is a mental state that results in a person suddenly and unexpectedly traveling to a new location and assuming a new identity. He or she is unable to recall his or her former identity. The person with dissociative fugue experiences mild disorientation as the transition from one identity to the other is occurring, because of a inability to make any association with his or her former life. As the fugue state passes, the person resumes his or her former identity with no recollection of the interim fugue identity.

Dissociative amnesia is a condition in which a person is unable to recall commonly known types of personal information.

Depersonalization disorder is a condition in which a person experiences periods of unreality about who he or she is or about various aspects of his or her body. At times, the person may seem removed, as though observing from a distance. Such experiences may occur to a mild degree in anyone, for example, someone who is hypoglycemic (low in circulating blood sugar). However, in depersonalization disorder, the symptoms are severe enough to cause dysfunction in the person's normal role or occupation.

A **dissociative disorder not otherwise specified** is a condition that contains some of the symptoms of the other conditions in this category but does not meet the full criteria for any of them.

◆ Nursing Care of Clients With Dissociative Disorders

Nursing care of these clients requires a strong and consistent team approach so that short-term goals are therapeutic and gradually lead to a better long-term outcome. Good collaboration is essential among all team members. When accompanying symptoms of depression or anxiety occur, it can be helpful to follow the guidelines for nursing care of clients with depression (see Chapter 24, Mood Disorders) or with anxiety (see Chapter 25, Anxiety and Somatoform Disorders).

◆ Sexual Disorders

Sexuality is an aspect of personality and interpersonal functioning that cannot be separated from a person's basic feelings about himself or herself and relationships with others. **Sexuality** can be defined as those aspects of the personality determined by a person's view of his or her sexual functioning, body image, and relatedness with other people of the same or opposite sex. It is affected by factors such as self-esteem, value formation, and id, ego, and superego functioning. In a psychologically healthy adult, sexuality is integrated or blended into the self-image in a way that is ego-syntonic. **Ego-syntonic** is a term that describes thoughts, perceptions, or actions that are acceptable to the ego and do not cause it to experience conflict.

The sexuality of an adult is the result of a long developmental process that begins at birth. Studies have found that parents and other authority figures relate differently with female infants than with male infants. Parents respond favorably to baby girls when they are sweet and verbal and to baby boys when they are physically active and aggressive. Children have a firm sense of their sexual role by the time they are 1½ to 2 years of age.

A child's self-image is the result of his or her own uniqueness, which includes both an inherited physiologic and neuroendocrine base and inherited personality characteristics. This unique self then interacts and is shaped by interactions with parents and other people of importance in the child's life, as well as by moral training, experiences in school and with peers, and the media and environment at large.

Essentially, the child is seeking acceptance from others. The way in which the child's self-image is formed will be strongly affected by the attitudes, beliefs, and psychological health of those people whose approval is important to him or her. Because of the complexity of this process, it is possible for his or her sexual view of himself or herself to be altered in a way that does not fit expected social norms. **Norms** are society's expectations that a person should behave within limits that it considers to be "normal."

Ego-dystonic is a term that describes conflict within the ego. The conflict can be between the ego and the environment or within the psyche itself. When a person's sexual functioning is ego-dystonic, he or she feels mental distress and may seek psychiatric treatment.

It is also possible for a person's sexual behavior to be ego-syntonic, but to cause conflict in society at large. For example, a person may be homosexual and be comfortable with himself or herself. Ego-syntonic homosexuality is not considered to be a mental disorder.

Two major categories of psychosexual disorders are paraphilias and sexual dysfunctions. **Paraphilia** is a sexual disorder in which a person requires unusual or bizarre fantasies in order to be sexually aroused. A **sexual dysfunction** is a disorder in which sexual arousal is negatively affected by some physical or emotional cause. The two categories include the following diagnostic groups:

A. Paraphilias
   1. Exhibitionism
   2. Fetishism
   3. Frotteurism
   4. Pedophilia
   5. Sexual masochism
   6. Sexual sadism
   7. Transvestic fetishism
   8. Voyeurism
   9. Paraphilia not otherwise specified
B. Sexual dysfunctions
   1. Sexual desire disorders
      a. Hypoactive sexual desire disorder
      b. Sexual aversion disorder
   2. Sexual arousal disorders
      a. Female sexual arousal disorder
      b. Male erectile disorder
   3. Orgasmic disorders
      a. Female orgasmic disorder (formerly inhibited female orgasm)

      b. Male orgasmic disorder (formerly inhibited male orgasm)
      c. Premature ejaculation
    4. Sexual pain disorders
      a. Dyspareunia
      b. Vaginismus
    5. Other sexual dysfunction not otherwise specified
  C. Other sexual disorders not otherwise specified

PARAPHILIAS

Exhibitionism is sometimes combined with pedophilia, but ordinarily the (often) male exhibitionist prefers to expose his genitals to more mature girls or women. This is a very common sexual disorder. These men rarely rape. They take their sexual enjoyment from exhibiting themselves sexually to an unsuspecting stranger and may achieve orgasm at the height of this pleasure.

    Fetishism is another sexual disorder that is more common in men than women. The fetishist becomes attached to some object or body part. Perhaps this can be compared with the fetishistic attachment of small children to a toy, blanket, or other object that will satisfy their love instincts in the absence of their mothers. Some theorists consider the fetishistic attachment to be an effort to gain ego identification with a substitute object. This object attains a highly exaggerated value, becomes the main source of erotic gratification, and relieves both psychic and sexual tension as contact with it leads to orgasm. **Frotteurism** is a sexual disorder that results in intense sexual urges and fantasies that involve touching or rubbing against a nonconsenting person.

    Pedophilia is a disorder in which sexual strivings are directed toward children. This is almost exclusively a male disorder. It occurs largely in impotent and weak men. The pedophile seems to be functioning at an immature psychosexual level, and psychologists sometimes ascribe his actions to fear and doubt concerning his own maleness. Because he expects rejection of and failure in adult sexual advances, he expresses himself to children. He may actually rape children, but much more often he may fondle their sexual organs or expose his own to them with a request that they fondle his. **Child molestation** is very rarely homosexual. The usual case history involves an adult, adolescent, or mentally retarded male with a prepubescent female.

    Sexual sadism and **sexual masochism** are, respectively, the desire to inflict upon and the desire to receive from the sexual partner physical or mental pain. In milder forms, these desires are entirely compatible with normal sexual foreplay. In extreme forms they act as a substitute for normal sex and are considered disorders.

    In **transvestic fetishism**, a heterosexual male has recurrent, intense, sexually arousing fantasies, sexual urges, or behaviors involving cross-dressing. **Voyeurism** is another common sexual disorder. Voyeurs are "peeping Toms" who find sexual pleasure in secretly looking at others undressing or engaging in sexual activity. When these pursuits cause the person discomfort or become an exclusive sexual outlet, they are called disorders.

Paraphilia not otherwise specified is used to classify paraphilias that do not meet the criteria for any of the specific categories listed previously. Examples include, but are not limited to, telephone scatologia (obscene phone calls), necrophilia (corpses), and zoophilia (animals).

ORGASM DISORDERS

Orgasmic disorders include **female orgasmic disorder** and **male orgasmic disorder.** They occur when a person has sexual desire and normal physiologic signs of sexual excitement but fails to experience orgasm as the culmination of sexual activity.

Premature ejaculation is a condition in which the male releases semen and experiences orgasm with little or no control in delaying its occurrence.

SEXUAL PAIN DISORDERS

Dyspareunia occurs when intercourse is consistently accompanied by genital pain in either males or females. The disorder has no physical cause. **Vaginismus** is a condition in which the outer third of the vagina consistently develops spasms that prevent or interfere with intercourse. The last two categories, **sexual dysfunction not otherwise specified** and **other sexual disorders not otherwise specified,** do not meet the criteria of the other categories.

◆ GENDER IDENTITY DISORDERS

These disorders include conditions in which a person feels emotional distress about his or her sexual identity. The first major characteristic of **gender identity disorder** is strong, persistent cross-gender identification. In children, this is characterized by a repeatedly stated desire to be the opposite sex; insistence or persistent fantasies of being the opposite sex; strong and persistent preferences for cross-dressing or cross-sex roles in make-believe play; and strong preference for playmates of the other sex. In adolescents and adults, the disorder is characterized by stated desire to be the other sex, frequently passing as the other sex, and conviction of having the typical feelings and reactions of the other sex.

The second major characteristic of **gender identify disorder** is persistent discomfort with his or her sex. A boy with this disorder asserts that his penis or testes are disgusting or that it would be better not to have a penis, or shows aversion to stereotypical male games and activities. A girl with gender identity disorder insists that she has or will grow a penis or that she does not want to grow breasts or menstruate, or shows aversion to normative female clothes and activities. An adolescent or adult with this disorder is preoccupied with getting rid of secondary sex characteristics and believes that he or she was born the wrong sex.

 # OTHER MENTAL DISORDERS

These mental disorders do not usually require hospitalization. Their symptoms and course of illness are usually not as complex as other mental conditions previously described. An overview of the classification follows.

SLEEP DISORDERS

Dyssomnias

Insomnia disorders include difficulty in falling asleep, remaining asleep, or obtaining restful sleep at a rate of at least 3 times a week. **Primary insomnia** is sleep loss that causes mental distress and significant impairment in functioning but is not related to other dyssomnias or another mental disorder. **Primary hypersomnia** is a condition that causes excessive sleep or results in a prolonged transition to being fully awake after sleeping.

Other sleep disorders in this category include narcolepsy, breathing-related sleep disorder, and circadian rhythm sleep disorder.

Narcolepsy is characterized by irresistible attacks of sleep that occur daily over at least 3 months. The person with narcolepsy usually also experiences brief episodes of sudden, uncontrolled loss of muscle control during these periods of sleep. **Breathing-related sleep disorder** is sleep disruption due to a breathing condition such as apnea or other obstructive breathing syndrome.

Circadian rhythm sleep disorder (formerly sleep–wake schedule disorder) occurs when a person's internal sleep–wake schedule does not fit with the schedule of his or her environment, resulting either in insomnia or hypersomnia. This disorder may be caused by a persistent pattern of late sleep onset and awakening, repeated travel across time zones, or frequent changes of work shifts.

Parasomnias

Parasomnia is any type of disordered sleep. There are a number of such parasomnias. **Nightmare disorder** (formerly dream anxiety disorder) is a condition in which a person experiences anxiety-provoking dreams that cause him or her to waken fearfully. He or she quickly becomes oriented. However, **sleep terror disorder** is a condition in which a person experiences extreme anxiety, wakens abruptly from sleep, is confused for several minutes, and cannot be comforted by others.

Sleepwalking disorder is a condition in which a person experiences episodes of walking during sleep. He or she is not aware of the presence of others during these episodes, can be awakened only with extreme difficulty, and does not remember the episode when awake.

FACTITIOUS DISORDERS

Factitious disorders are psychological states in which a person pretends that he or she is experiencing some form of distress. A **factitious disorder with predominantly physical signs and symptoms** is one in which a person creates a physical problem or pretends that he or she has one in order to obtain the psychological benefit of the attention of others.

A **factitious disorder with predominantly psychological signs and symptoms** is one in which a person pretends that he or she has psychological distress. **Secondary gain** is a term that describes the sense of psychological well-being derived by a person when he or she receives care and attention from others as a response to his or her problems. A **factitious disorder not otherwise specified** is one that does not fit into either of the other categories.

IMPULSE-CONTROL DISORDERS

This category includes a number of psychological conditions, not classified elsewhere, in which a person experiences a loss of control of certain impulses or urges. He or she lacks the ability to inhibit these urges.

Intermittent explosive disorder is a condition in which a person loses control of his or her aggressive energy and seriously assaults other people, animals, property, and so on. This loss of control is out of proportion to the original stressor. **Kleptomania** is a condition in which a person cannot control the impulse to steal. **Pathologic gambling** is a condition in which a person cannot control the impulse to gamble. The pathological gambler is preoccupied with acquiring the money to gamble, wagers increasingly larger amounts of money, creating financial hardship, and is unsuccessful in stopping his or her gambling.

Pyromania is deliberate fire-setting on more than one occasion, preceded by emotional tension or arousal. Extreme pleasure is experienced when lighting the fire or observing its aftermath. It is not associated with setting fires for monetary gain.

Trichotillomania is a condition in which a person pulls out his or her own hair. The act of pulling out the hair is preceded by emotional tension and is followed by emotional relief. **Impulse-control disorder not otherwise specified** includes any impulse-control disorder not described previously.

ADJUSTMENT DISORDERS

Adjustment disorders are conditions that occur within 3 months after a known psychosocial stressor. The emotional symptoms are more distressing than would be expected from such a stressor and they impair normal role functioning. The following list of adjustment disorders are named for the emotional distress associated with each.

Adjustment disorder with anxiety

Adjustment disorder with depressed mood

Adjustment disorder with disturbance of conduct

Adjustment disorder with mixed disturbance of emotions and conduct

Adjustment disorder with mixed anxiety and depressed mood

Adjustment disorder unspecified

These adjustment disorders can be further classified as **acute** (less than 6 months' duration) or **chronic** (more than 6 months' duration).

PSYCHOLOGICAL FACTORS AFFECTING PHYSICAL CONDITION

Psychological factors affecting physical condition is a mental disorder in which environmental causes are temporarily related to the development or worsening of a specific physical disorder. An example would be a person who has an abnormal cardiac pattern that is aggravated by chronic anxiety.

C H A P T E R   2 6   S U M M A R Y

- Dissociative disorders are characterized by loss of association and integration of self-identity, consciousness, or motor function. This category includes dissociative identity disorder, dissociative fugue, dissociative amnesia, and depersonalization disorder.

- Two major categories of sexual disorders are paraphilia (bizarre or unusual fantasies are required to achieve sexual arousal) and sexual dysfunction (arousal is negatively affected by some physical or emotional cause).

- The categories of paraphilias are exhibitionism (exhibiting genitals to strangers); fetishism (attachment to an object or body part); frotteurism (touching or rubbing against a nonconsenting person); pedophilia (sexual attention directed toward children); sadism (desire to inflict pain); masochism (desire to receive pain); and voyeurism (secretly looking at others undressing or engaging in sexual activity).

- Gender identity disorder is characterized by a strong and persistent identification with the other gender, such as a repeatedly stated desire to be the other sex and persistent discomfort with gender.

- Sleep disorders include disturbances of normal patterns of sleep that cause mental distress and significant impairment. These include insomnia, hypersomnia, narcolepsy, and circadian rhythm sleep disorder.

- Other types of disordered sleep include nightmare disorder, sleep terror disorder, and sleepwalking disorder.

- A psychological state in which a person pretends he or she is experiencing some form of distress is called a factitious disorder. It may have predominantly physical or predominantly psychological symptoms.

- An impulse-control disorder is a psychological condition in which a person experiences a loss of control of certain impulses or urges and lacks the ability to control these urges. These disorders include intermittent explosive disorder, kleptomania, pathologic gambling, pyromania, and trichotillomania.

CHAPTER 26 QUESTIONS

1. A person with a dissociative disorder experiences
   a. a gradual loss of association.
   b. an awareness that the dissociative process has occurred.
   c. loss of self-identity, consciousness, or motor control.
   d. relatively little trauma as a result of the disorder.

2. Which of the following is true about dissociative identity disorder?
   a. A person assumes two or more distinct identities during alternating times.
   b. The original personality has no awareness of the concurrently existing personalities.

c. A primary cause is chronic mental, physical, or sexual abuse in childhood and adolescence.
d. All of the above

3. A mental state that results in a person suddenly and unexpectedly traveling to a new location and assuming a new identity is called
a. dissociative identity disorder.
b. dissociative amnesia.
c. dissociative fugue.
d. depersonalization disorder.

4. Paraphilia is
a. a compulsive desire to assume another identity.
b. a sexual disorder in which a person requires unusual or bizarre fantasies to be sexually aroused.
c. an obsession with the paranormal or occult.
d. deliberate fire setting.

BIBLIOGRAPHY

Barry, P.D. (1996). *Psychosocial nursing: Care of physically ill patients and their families* (3rd ed.). Philadelphia: Lippincott-Raven.
Diagnostic and statistical manual of mental disorders (4th ed.). (1994). Washington, DC: American Psychiatric Press.
Eisendrath, S.J. (1994). Psychiatric problems. In F.S. Bongard & D.Y. Sue (Eds.). *Current critical care diagnosis and treatment.* Norwalk, CT: Appleton & Lange.
Kaplan, H.I., & Sadock, B.J. (1995). *Comprehensive textbook of psychiatry/VI* (6th ed.). Baltimore: Williams & Wilkins.
Kaplan, H.I., & Sadock, B.J. (1994). *Synopsis of psychiatry: Behavioral sciences, clinical psychiatry* (7th ed.). Baltimore: Williams & Wilkins.
Lego, S. (1996). *Psychiatric nursing: A comprehensive reference* (2nd ed.). Philadelphia: Lippincott-Raven.
McFarland, G.K., Wasli, E.L., & Gerety, E.K. (1996). *Nursing diagnoses and process in psychiatric mental health nursing* (3rd ed.). Philadelphia: Lippincott-Raven.
Nettina, S.M. (1996). *The Lippincott manual of nursing practice* (6th ed.). Philadelphia: Lippincott-Raven.
Stafford, L.L. (1993). Dissociation and multiple personality disorder: A challenge for psychosocial nurses. *Journal of Psychosocial Nursing and Mental Health Services, 31*(1), 15–20.
Wilson, H.S., & Kneisl, C.R. (1996). *Psychiatric nursing* (5th ed.). Redwood City, CA: Addison-Wesley.

27

Personality Disorders

Behavioral Objectives

After reading this chapter the student will be able to:

■ Explain the differences between people who have a mental illness and those who have a personality disorder.

■ List the 11 personality disorders discussed and identify the maladaptive characteristics of each.

■ Compare and contrast the antisocial and narcissistic personalities.

In prior units human needs were discussed, including psychological needs for tenderness in infancy, participation with others in childhood activities, sharing experiences with peers in the juvenile period, and close friendships and relationships in adolescence. Chapter 14, Stress: Ineffective Coping and Defense Mechanisms, discusses how a person erects defenses against aggressive and sexual tendencies and experiences socially unacceptable feelings and attitudes about important people in his or her life, particularly during childhood. These adaptive defenses allow a person to channel excessive anxiety and balance his or her needs; this person will have a healthy personality.

However, a person who builds up too many such defenses cannot reduce tension and anxiety, and his or her personality may become rigid, narrow, and nonspontaneous. If a person's defenses become pathologically exaggerated or disorganized, he or she can eventually develop a **personality disorder.**

A person's basic personality forms during the early years, depending largely on the way he or she learns to adjust to situations, and it tends to remain identifiable throughout life. If a person develops mental illness, his or her basic personality traits will be similar before, during, and after a psychotic episode, even though his or her behavior tends to be more bizarre during the period of mental illness. The kind of mental disorder a person tends to develop when coping mechanisms fail depends largely on the basic personality structure that developed during his or her childhood.

Up to this point, we have discussed mental health and mental illness in considerable detail. We will now look at the vast number of people who seem to fit between the classifications of mentally healthy and mentally ill. These are the people whose behavior indicates they have **maladapted to life stressors**. Because their ego functioning and reality testing remain intact, most of them can adapt socially. These people have **personality disorders**.

The disorders included in this category are as follows:

Paranoid

Schizoid

Schizotypal

Antisocial

Borderline

Histrionic

Narcissistic

Avoidant

Dependent

Obsessive–compulsive

Not otherwise specified

◆ Paranoid Personality Disorder

These people tend to be hypersensitive, rigid, suspicious, jealous, and envious. They may have an exaggerated sense of their own importance and generally tend to blame others and ascribe evil motives to them. These characteristics quite often interfere with their ability to maintain satisfactory interpersonal relationships.

◆ Schizoid Personality Disorder

This behavior pattern manifests emotional coldness, sensitivity, fearfulness, inability to socialize well with others, and a tendency to daydream and withdraw from reality. A wide range of behaviors is included in the schizoid group. Most people with a schizoid personality disorder are very sensitive people who feel lonely, imperfectly understood, and isolated. Many of them are timid, shy, self-conscious, and dissatisfied with themselves; others are more secretive, suspicious, and sometimes stubborn. Their feelings are very easily hurt. A child of this type is often teased by playmates who look upon him or her as strange or a sissy. He or she is shy, cries easily, seldom participates in rough play, talks little, and makes no close friendships. Under acute stress he or she may retreat into fantasy and become autistic.

In adolescence, many of these youngsters show patterns of willfulness, disobedience, moodiness, passive stubbornness, and resentfulness. They resent advice, supervision, or correction. Such youngsters are often loners who prefer to get along without strong ties to other people. Although they may be disobedient and moody, they tend to do superior work in school.

In the upper grades and in college, they usually do very well, but tend to be quiet and unsociable. Their love of books may be a substitute for human companionship. They are often imaginative and idealistic and frequently are interested in plans for bettering humanity. They study abstract or philosophical courses in preference to concrete or objective types. Some of these people become artists, poets, or musicians.

Others, while retaining an imaginative attitude toward life and its experiences, lack the fine sensitivity of the above group. These people, while kindly and honest, are unsociable, dull, and taciturn; their personalities lack color and sparkle.

Many people have schizoid personalities—the overly sensitive person, the extremely shy person, the recluse, and the dreamer. Often, a sensitive and tender nature hides beneath a cold and unresponsive exterior, or a deeply kind person hides behind a gruff, apparently hostile facade. These types, fearful of hurt and intrusion into their inner world, camouflage their innate tenderness and kindness by erecting barriers that hold people at a distance.

SCHIZOTYPAL PERSONALITY DISORDER

A person with this type of personality disorder demonstrates many symptoms related to those of schizophrenia but of a less severe nature. He or she tends to be a loner and has an unusual pattern of talking that is vague and abstract. His or her emotions often do not match the content of a discussion and seem inappropriate for the circumstances. This person may seem preoccupied by his or her thoughts and is superstitious. The person may believe he or she can read the minds of others or that others are reading his or her mind. He or she may be suspicious or paranoid and is unusually sensitive to criticism.

 ## ANTISOCIAL PERSONALITY DISORDER

People with this disorder are unable to form any significant attachment or loyalty to other people, groups, or society. They are controlled by their ids and are given to immediate pleasures. They have no sense of responsibility, and in spite of punishment and repeated humiliations, they fail to learn to modify their behavior (i.e., they fail to learn by experience). They are lacking in social judgment and tend to turn their frustrations upon society. They are able to rationalize their antisocial actions and consider them warranted, reasonable, and justified. Their character traits seem to be fixed expressions of conflict, and there is a certain compulsiveness to their antisocial acts.

The defect in their character structures is their failure to develop a socialized superego and ego ideals; if these do exist, they are directed toward personal acquisition of money and material goods and the control of others for immediate pleasures and satisfactions. The factor, or factors, that produce such an individual are unknown.

As a group, these clients probably cause the most problems in society. They are frequently in trouble with the law, and might first be seen in psychiatric consultation on the recommendation of the court or probation office. They are unable to tolerate frustration, are easily enraged, and can act out violently without feeling remorse. They sometimes describe themselves as cold-blooded and are often described by others as such. They can be ruthless and vindictive and tend to blame others for their behavior.

People with an antisocial personality disorder demand much and give little. They are typically affectionless, selfish, ungrateful, and self-centered, and may be exhibitionistic. They are unable to judge their behavior from another's standpoint. Even though such people are inadequate and hostile from a social standpoint, they are quite satisfied with their behavior. To such people, routine is intolerable. They show few feelings of anxiety, guilt, or remorse, and demand immediate and instant gratification of their desires with no concern for the feelings or interests of others. Some use alcohol or drugs. They may react to alcohol poorly and when under its influence become noisy, quarrelsome, and destructive. Their behavior prevents psychosocial adjustment. The personality defect may be limited to a single form of misbehavior, such as stealing, running away, or promiscuity.

BORDERLINE PERSONALITY DISORDER

A person with a borderline personality disorder demonstrates unpredictability and instability in many areas of interpersonal and intrapsychic functioning. For instance, he or she may have intense interpersonal relationships that alternate between extremes of love, hate, and dependency. His or her emotional stability is also unpredictable. He or she is impulsive and displays major and inappropriate mood shifts. He or she can experience profound identity disturbances relating to self and body image, sexual identity, life goals, and the nature of relationships and others. In addition, he or she engages in self-harmful activities, such as fighting, self-mutilation, and suicidal gestures.

HISTRIONIC PERSONALITY DISORDER

This type of personality disorder is characterized by traits of vanity, self-indulgence, and a flair for dramatization or exhibitionism. These people are immature, self-centered, often vain, and prone to emotional outbursts. Sexual behavior can be provocative and seductive. Actually, most of these people are fearful of sex. Their provocative, attention-getting behavior appears to overlie dependency that is demanding of others. There is reason to suspect that many of these people were spoiled and overprotected in early years. Although they are usually actively engaged in the social world, they respond badly to the frustrations of reality.

Although this disorder is more common in women, the "Don Juan" character represents this personality type in men. His drive for sexual conquest and exhibitionism often hides a feeling of masculine inadequacy. His repeated conquests prove his lack of satisfaction in each successive affair.

NARCISSISTIC PERSONALITY DISORDER

These people are egocentric. **Egocentricity** describes a person's attitude and inner feeling that the world exists to meet his or her needs. The egocentric person is grandiose and requires constant attention, although in fact his or her self-esteem is actually poor. When this person's self-esteem is threatened, he or she responds with marked anger or feelings of shame. As could be expected, his or her interpersonal relationships are strongly affected by these personality traits. The egocentric person tends to manipulate and exploit other people in order to meet his or her own needs, and is lacking in empathy to understand the feelings of others.

◆ AVOIDANT PERSONALITY DISORDER

People with this type of disorder are basically afraid of rejection. They consciously and unconsciously make choices that will help them avoid conflict, humiliation, or shame. They tend to avoid social situations, although they desire affection and close relationships that will enhance their sense of worth. They have the capacity to engage in close relationships, but these friendships require constant approval from others.

◆ DEPENDENT PERSONALITY DISORDER

A person with dependent personality disorder has a very poor sense of self and demonstrates a low level of self-confidence. He or she cannot make independent decisions or function as a responsible adult. The dependent person consistently defers or represses his or her own needs in order to gain the acceptance and approval of others. Interactions with others are marked by passivity. He or she finds it difficult, if not impossible, to travel alone and be self-reliant, which leads to social limitations.

◆ OBSESSIVE–COMPULSIVE PERSONALITY DISORDER

The person with this disorder demonstrates a limited or constricted range of emotions. Warmth, spontaneity, and a feeling of emotional "connectedness" with others seem lacking in his or her personality. He or she ceaselessly strives for perfection and is stubborn. Decision making is difficult for obsessive–compulsive people, who overly attend to trivial details and are unable to carry through the decision-making process to form a conclusion. Compulsive people are frequently overinvolved with their work to the exclusion of normal pleasure and satisfaction in the workplace. They commonly spend excessive time at work and lose time with family and in normal recreational activities.

◆ PERSONALITY DISORDER NOT OTHERWISE SPECIFIED

This category is for disorders that do not meet criteria for any of the specific personality disorders listed previously. An example includes mixed personality disorder, in which features of more than one specific disorder are present but do not meet the full criteria for any one disorder. This category also includes disorders not covered by the above classifications, such as depressive personality disorder and passive-aggressive personality disorder.

◆ TREATMENT OF THE PERSONALITY DISORDERS

People with personality disorders are rarely hospitalized. Their personality traits may cause difficulty in their relationships with others in the family, at work, or in social settings. If outpatient psychiatric care is sought, the most appropriate treatment mode is individual or group psychotherapy, depending on the severity of the disorder. There are no specific recommendations for nursing care, because these clients usually are not treated in inpatient settings.

CHAPTER 27 SUMMARY

- Coping and defense mechanisms allow a person to channel excess anxiety and balance needs. Adaptive mechanisms allow a person to develop a healthy personality.

- If a person builds too many defenses, he or she may not be able to reduce tension and anxiety. Pathologically exaggerated or disorganized defenses can lead to a personality disorder. The kind of disorder a person develops when coping mechanisms fail depends largely on the basic personality structure developed during childhood.

- Personality disorders and their characteristics are:
  — Paranoid—suspiciousness, with a tendency to blame others
  — Schizoid—emotional coldness, tendency to withdraw
  — Schizotypal—vague or abstract speech, preoccupation with own thoughts
  — Antisocial—unable to form any significant attachments or tolerate frustration
  — Borderline—instability, inappropriate mood shifts, self-harmful activities

— Histrionic—exhibitionism, provocative sexual behavior

— Narcissistic—egocentric, requires constant attention, grandiose

— Avoidant—fear of rejection and avoidance of conflict, humiliation, or shame

— Dependent—consistently represses own needs to gain others' approval

■ Obsessive–compulsive disorder is characterized by a constricted range of emotions with a ceaseless striving for perfection and overattention to trivial details. This person is often unable to make decisions or form a conclusion.

■ Treatment of personality disorders is rarely conducted on an inpatient basis. The most appropriate treatment mode is individual or group psychotherapy.

CHAPTER 27 QUESTIONS

1. Which of the following could cause a person to develop a personality disorder?
   a. A build-up of defenses
   b. An inability to reduce tension and anxiety
   c. Pathologically exaggerated or disorganized defenses
   d. All of the above

2. A person who exhibits emotional coldness, sensitivity, inability to socialize, and a tendency to withdraw from reality may manifest
   a. histrionic personality disorder.
   b. schizoid personality disorder.
   c. borderline personality disorder.
   d. none of the above.

3. Egocentricity is a characteristic of which personality disorder?
   a. Narcissistic
   b. Histrionic
   c. Antisocial
   d. Schizotypal

4. The provocative or seductive sexual behavior seen in people with histrionic personality disorder
   a. shows that they enjoy sexual activity.
   b. occurs because they seek independence and "free love."
   c. may mask feelings of sexual inadequacy.
   d. is a positive response to frustrations of reality.

BIBLIOGRAPHY

Barry, P.D. (1996). *Psychosocial nursing: Care of physically ill patients and their families* (3rd ed.). Philadelphia: Lippincott-Raven.

Diagnostic and statistical manual of mental disorders (4th ed.). (1994). Washington, DC: American Psychiatric Press.

Eisendrath, S.J. (1994). Psychiatric problems. In F.S. Bongard & D.Y. Sue (Eds.). *Current critical care diagnosis and treatment.* Norwalk, CT: Appleton & Lange.

Kaplan, H.I., & Sadock, B.J. (1995). *Comprehensive textbook of psychiatry/VI* (6th ed.). Baltimore: Williams & Wilkins.

Kaplan, H.I., & Sadock, B.J. (1994). *Synopsis of psychiatry: Behavioral sciences, clinical psychiatry* (7th ed.). Baltimore: Williams & Wilkins.

Lego, S. (1996). *Psychiatric nursing: A comprehensive reference* (2nd ed.). Philadelphia: Lippincott-Raven.

McFarland, G.K., Wasli, E.L., & Gerety, E.K. (1996). *Nursing diagnoses and process in psychiatric mental health nursing* (3rd ed.). Philadelphia: Lippincott-Raven.

Nehls, N. (1994). Brief hospital treatment plans for persons with borderline personality disorder: Perspectives of inpatient psychiatric nurses and community mental health center clinicians. *Archives of Psychiatric Nursing, 8*(5), 303–311.

Nettina, S.M. (1996). *The Lippincott manual of nursing practice* (6th ed.). Philadelphia: Lippincott-Raven.

Wilson, H.S., & Kneisl, C.R. (1996). *Psychiatric nursing* (5th ed.). Redwood City, CA: Addison-Wesley.

DEVELOPING CRITICAL THINKING SKILLS THROUGH CLASS DISCUSSION

UNIT SIX Case Study
Categories of Mental Disorder

Rhonda is a 45-year-old housewife who has a long-standing depressive order. She is married to a controlling and unsupportive partner. Over the past 20 years she has been admitted to the psychiatric unit on three occasions when she experienced suicidal despair. Her most recent admission occurred following the marriage of her last child, who had been living at home. Her symptoms include severe depression, suicidal ideation and plan, and poor response to a new antidepressant medication.

DISCUSSION QUESTIONS

1. What would it be like to sit with Rhonda on the day of her admission? How would you begin to talk with her? What would you say?

2. Name five nursing diagnoses that you might expect to see in Rhonda's chart. Using Maslow's Hierarchy of Human Needs in Chapter 9, can you prioritize the importance of the diagnoses and explain the reasons for your choice?

3. What normal activities of daily living most likely would be affected by depression? How would you begin to assess whether they are being carried out by Rhonda?

4. Would it be appropriate if Rhonda's clinical treatment plan included family or couple therapy while she is hospitalized? Why?

5. Can you describe the personal and family developmental issues that may be additional contributing factors to Rhonda's depression?

6. Can you name one nursing diagnosis that pertains to one of these developmental factors? Can you think of a nursing intervention that would be included in addressing this diagnosis?

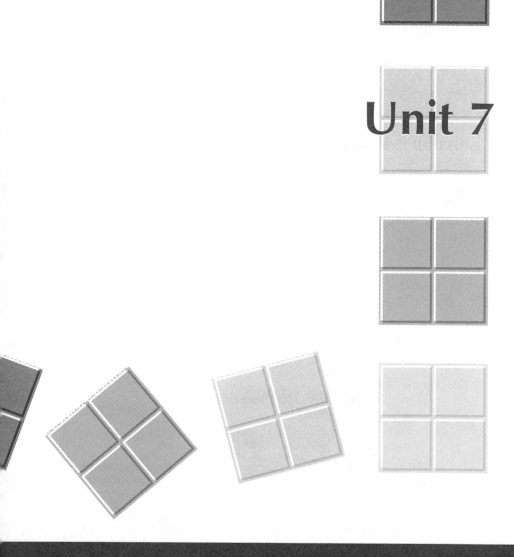

Unit 7

INTERVENTION
AND TREATMENT
OF MENTAL DISORDERS

28

Crisis Intervention

Behavioral Objectives

After reading this chapter the student will be able to:

■ Describe the ways in which events can lead to crisis.

■ List the sequence of developments after a critical event that can lead to crisis.

■ Explain the symptoms of maladaptation exhibited by a person after crisis.

■ List the main developmental stages and describe two major developmental issues under each.

■ Describe the five types of situational events that are most likely to cause crisis.

A crisis of some type usually causes the onset of mental illness. There may be a specific event that triggers a deteriorating capacity for mental functioning—for instance, a new situation with which the person has no previous experience. Accordingly, there are no specific automatic behaviors or coping responses available to respond to or relieve the person of the anxiety associated with such an event.

There may be a number of stressful life experiences, compounded by a new situation, which are often "the straw that breaks the camel's back." The person's coping abilities are already taxed and do not respond as well as they did to earlier difficulties. Finally, the crisis may be one that appears to have no known cause or identifiable **triggering** or **precipitating event.** In such cases, subtle changes in the client's perception of events often cause distorted or disoriented awarenesses that are stressful in and of themselves. These distorted awarenesses most often occur in schizophrenia, manic–depressive illness, psychotic depression, and delirium or dementia due to a general medical condition or substance abuse.

◆ SEQUENCE OF DEVELOPMENTS FOLLOWING A CRITICAL EVENT

A number of factors determine whether an event has crisis potential:

1. The perception of the event by the person, which is strongly influenced by his or her:
   a. Value system (what is important to the person)
   b. Normal personality style
   c. Normal ego strength
   d. Response to issues of trust, self-esteem, control, loss, guilt, intimacy
   e. Coping skills during normal stresses of living
   f. Level of stress in the past year
   g. Availability of support from family, friends, caregivers
2. The degree of threat, as perceived by the person, to his or her:
   a. Personal safety
   b. Life goals
   c. Normal role functioning
   d. Family stability
3. The person's coping style: effective coping versus ineffective coping

When a person is functioning well mentally, his or her ego is able to tolerate the stress of a difficult new event by developing an ever-expanding set of responses to decrease his or her anxiety. Eventually, the new relief behaviors or conscious coping strategies decrease his or her anxiety, and crisis is avoided. He or she has adapted to the new event or life change. When effective coping does not occur, a maladaptive response develops. At times maladaptation becomes chronic. Crisis does not occur, but there is a change in the quality of the individual's life and the life of his or her family. The quality-of-life changes are due to diminished capacity to function both psychologically and socially in the way that the person did before the triggering event occurred.

Another possible outcome is that a maladaptive response results in a decreasing ability to deal with anxiety and the emotional, intellectual, and physiologic stresses accompanying it. While this is occurring, the person feels increasingly out of control. His or her awareness of environmental stimuli is decreased. The two possible outcomes of this progressive deterioration are immobility or panic. In either case, the person's capacity to help himself or herself is temporarily lost. Crisis results.

A crisis occurs over a limited period of time. It can last anywhere from a few days to a few weeks. It either decreases, because the client's coping strength gradually returns and he or she has an available support system, or it causes the person's mental functioning to deteriorate to the point at which hospitalization is necessary to protect the client or others.

◆ CATEGORIES OF CRISIS

Two main categories of circumstances can challenge a person's ability to cope and adapt. The potential outcomes are developmental crises and life change crises (also known as situational crises).

DEVELOPMENTAL CRISES

The normal stages of development, as described by Erik Erikson, include many issues that must be worked through and resolved to allow normal progression into the next stage. On occasion, individuals are unable to make the transition, and one or more of these issues are unresolved. When a large number of the issues proves too taxing to resolve, crisis can occur. Box 28–1 outlines the developmental stages and the outcomes that may occur if the issues are not resolved.

Although aging from one decade to the next can stress the psyche, it is usually less disruptive than the significant development stages described earlier, and the person adjusts to a changed self-image. At times, however, self-esteem temporarily decreases until the person accommodates to the change.

BOX 28–1 DEVELOPMENTAL STAGES

INFANCY AND EARLY CHILDHOOD (BIRTH TO 3 YEARS)

Major issues (progressive from birth): trust, dependency, awareness of separateness from mother, development of autonomy

When issues are not resolved: distrust, poor self-confidence, fusion of self with caregiver, poor self-control

CHILDHOOD (3–11 YEARS)

Major issues: identification with significant elders; development of initiative, security, and acceptance within family and eventually within peer group; mastery of age-appropriate skills and intellectual challenges

When issues are not resolved: guilt, lack of direction and purpose, self-undermining behavior, feelings of inadequacy

ADOLESCENCE (12–20 YEARS)

Major issues: reawakening of oedipal conflicts (see Chapter 11, The Structure and Development of Personality), idealization of significant others, resolution of loss of childhood, development of sexual identity, acceptance by peer group, psychological separation from family as adolescent develops his or her own perceptions of the world (physical separation usually occurs a few years later)

When issues are not resolved: inability to separate from family and assume independence, sexual confusion, self-consciousness, inability to form relationship with person of opposite sex, poor object relations

EARLY ADULTHOOD (20–30 YEARS)

Major issues: ability to develop intimacy and commitment within a relationship, commitment to employment, exploration, and clarification of societal norms as they pertain to self

When issues are not resolved: superficiality in relationships with others, poor goal setting, drifting in and out of relationships and employment, lack of responsibility to self and others

MIDDLE ADULTHOOD (30–50 YEARS)

Major issues: maintenance of life goals, creativity, and spontaneity; ability to maintain meaningful relationships; appropriate channeling of emotions

When issues are not resolved: inability to work or to feel pleasure, poor motivation, egocentrism in relationships and in goal setting

LATE ADULTHOOD (50 YEARS AND OLDER)

Major issues: ability to resolve losses of aging and to integrate ongoing losses, maintenance of hope, acceptance of uncertain future

When issues are not resolved: continual wishing to relive past experiences, inability to take pleasure in the present, loss of hope, depression

SITUATIONAL CRISES

Life change events that can cause crisis include death, divorce, major illness, marriage, childbirth, loss of a job, and retirement. Many times, a life change event occurs at the same time a person is adapting to a new developmental stage. When this happens, the person is at greater risk for inadequate coping. The life change events and their accompanying effects are described in the following sections.

Death

Death of a loved one or one's own anticipated death is the most severe social stressor that most people encounter in their lives. The losses associated with a death are many. A relationship with a significant other person contains connections to innumerable ongoing experiences and memories, as well as irreplaceable loss of support and caring that the other person provided. In some cases, the relationship with the other person was permeated with conflict. In either a loving or conflicting relationship, the loss results in the eruption of strong feelings of grief, anger, guilt, and fear.

Before a person dies, there is often a period of months or years of physical decline that allows the person and those who know him or her gradually to work through (at least partially) the anticipated death. When this occurs, the coping process commonly follows a pattern similar to that described by Elisabeth Kubler-Ross, including stages of denial, anger, bargaining, depression, and acceptance. The dying person and the various family members frequently progress through these stages at different times. One or more family members may deny the illness, express anger, and become depressed, thereby increasing the stress on the family system.

Sudden, unexpected death has even greater crisis potential because family members have had no time to develop their coping ability. Such a death suddenly disrupts their entire world without warning. Even a few days of critical illness allow a family time to adjust, at least minimally, to the imminent death. When sudden death of a loved one occurs, the bereavement process in one or more family members often lasts beyond the normal 1-year period.

Divorce

Divorce was second in the list of most disruptive events reported by people in the Holmes and Rahe research study on life change stressors. Divorce, similar to death, results in multiple changes within the family. However, the dynamic of choice is involved for one or both members of the couple. This element increases the potential for anger, guilt, and loss in both partners. The children, regardless of their ages, can be profoundly affected as well. Increased levels of anxiety and decreased self-esteem and role-functioning ability frequently occur.

Major Illness

Major illness, mental or physical, presents a moderate-to-severe challenge for individuals and their family members. Usually, they have had no experience with illness in the past, and their ability to cope and adapt is severely challenged. The ongoing effects of psychiatric illnesses, such as schizophrenia and major depressive illness, and chronic physical illnesses, such as cancer and heart disease, pose threats to self-image, body image, self-esteem, loss of control, issues of dependence and trust, separation from family, and changes in role functioning. Just as the ill person is under increased psychological stress, so are his or her family members, because they must adapt to losses associated with the changed health status and role functioning of their loved one. Communication patterns in the family are often permanently altered as a means of coping with the many changes in the family created by the illness.

Marriage

Although marriage is usually a happy event for a person and his or her family, it often creates a number of stresses for the couple as well as for their families. These include the couple's anticipated role changes and a heightened sense of responsibility. Family members may or may not agree with their loved one's choice of spouse. Often, as the time of marriage approaches, there is a greater awareness of differences in values pertaining to family, tradition, religion, and so on, leading to increased potential for interpersonal and psychological conflict.

Marriage also creates many losses. It may involve the first time a young person has lived apart from his or her family. The anticipated separation is usually accompanied by feelings of sadness and fear in the person about to be married and in his or her parents and siblings. If a man has been excessively emotionally close to his family, he will be unable to reach independent decisions or to reach an agreement with his new wife, if her views differ from those of his family. The issue of emotional separation from one's own family is significant in the development of a healthy marital relationship.

Childbirth

The implications of raising children have become increasingly important to young people during the past two decades. The decision about whether to have children is an important one in the developing relationship between two young people who are contemplating marriage. The values and beliefs about pregnancy, childbirth, and child-rearing have strong potential for conflict and are best addressed during the courtship period.

The arrival of a child causes a major shift in the interpersonal dynamics between a husband and wife. Many couples find that the arrival of the first child is a crisis event. Regardless of their psychological preparation, it involves changes in their lives and normal roles that were not anticipated. In most instances, the crisis is short-lived. Within 4 to 6 weeks, adaptation begins to occur.

◆ TREATMENT SITES FOR CRISIS INTERVENTION

THE FAMILY AND SOCIAL NETWORK

Crisis intervention can occur anywhere. Ideally, whatever the precipitating event, the individual in crisis will have a supportive environment that can provide support and problem solving during the crisis period. Social network crisis intervention with the individual can provide needed support. When the individual has adequate inner strength and reserves and social support, a crisis can be averted in most circumstances.

THE HOME VISITING NURSE CRISIS INTERVENTION TEAM

Visiting nurse and home care organizations in many communities have developed emergency crisis intervention teams that intervene early with individuals and families in crisis. The purpose of early intervention is to decrease the risk of hospitalization by introducing medication, coping support, problem solving, and consultation about community resources to the unique crisis situation. Chapter 3, The Home Care Setting: Client and Family Issues, describes more dimensions of home care crisis intervention.

COMMUNITY CRISIS INTERVENTION IN OUTPATIENT CLINIC SETTINGS

Community outpatient centers have been created to meet the needs of individuals of all social groups, including the homeless. The purpose of community mental health centers is to provide crisis support in the center by intervening before the crisis requires inpatient hospitalization.

COMMUNITY CRISIS INTERVENTION IN THE EMERGENCY ROOM

Admission to the emergency room is an option when the crisis has quickly escalated and immediate stabilization is necessary. Emergency room mental health crisis staff attempt to gather information about possible family or social network supports that can be available to the individual during the stabilization period. When the crisis requires hospitalization, the emergency staff will triage the individual to an appropriate inpatient facility.

PARTIAL HOSPITALIZATION

When crisis is occurring, another option to consider is partial hospitalization. This choice can be useful if the individual requires structure and problem solving as a means of reducing the crisis symptoms. Partial hospitalization is also a helpful choice when the family or social network of the individual is not able to provide 24-hour availability to the person in crisis. Partial day or evening programs can provide the added comfort and safety of being in a supportive environment while the primary support person may be at school or work.

INPATIENT CRISIS STABILIZATION

When all other options have been considered and the security and acute crisis stabilization resources of the hospital setting are necessary, the hospital is chosen as the treatment setting.

◆ USE OF NURSING PROCESS WITH CLIENTS IN CRISIS

When a client is admitted in crisis, begin the nursing process immediately. You can provide support while you are admitting the client. Such availability of support from other people is a key factor in the resolution of crisis. The more you understand the frame of reference of a client, the less isolated he or she feels. Major exceptions to this approach are with the client who is suspicious or paranoid.

ASSESSMENT

In caring for a client who is not coping, remember that each human being perceives the world in a different way from every other person. The unique set of circumstances that each person encounters in his or her development from infancy to adulthood creates different personality dynamics. As a result, the way that one person copes with a given situation can be quite different from another.

For example, if you were a passenger in a race car in the Indianapolis 500, traveling at 120 miles per hour around a curve, you might expect that the perceptions of the driver and passenger regarding the experience are quite different. The passenger may feel a high level of anxiety; the driver, on the other hand, thrives on the experience. It is the frame of reference of each that determines the overall response. Accordingly, the more you understand about what a particular event means to a person, the more complete will be the data on which you base your care plan.

PLANNING

Most likely a client in crisis with whom you are working will have been hospitalized by the time you are planning his or her care. One of the most important elements in the client's ability to resolve the crisis will be the sense of support he or she feels in the treatment setting. One of the ways you can ensure this is to develop a team plan with members of the various disciplines who will be caring for the client. This is also known as systems planning. The caregiving team is usually made up of a psychiatrist, psychologist, family therapist, nurse, occupational therapist, drama therapist, and members of whatever other disciplines your institution uses in the care of clients.

Without such teamwork, each of these caregivers might otherwise work toward opposite directions. The person who suffers is the client. He or she will not feel you are helping if all members of your treatment plan are not working toward similar goals. For this reason, it is important to attend a team conference and understand the treatment plan of the psychiatrist or psychologist in charge of caring for the client. You can ask questions at this conference to clarify your understanding of the client and can also share any information you may have obtained from the client.

In the development of the care plan, be attentive to the client's most active concerns. A short-range care plan can be developed with specific dates to attend to these concerns. A client who is in crisis feels overwhelmed and finds it difficult to think of the mid- or long-term future. During the planning stage, the short-term and intermediate plan should be reviewed in the team conference with the other caregivers so that all understand the nursing goals.

As the specific goals of the short-term care plan are developed, share them with the client and discuss his or her reaction to each. He or she will feel less alone and more secure. Share the plan with the client, even if depression makes him or her unresponsive; at the very least, he or she will be listening. If the client is psychotic or violent, wait until medication has increased his or her ability to participate in a discussion about a care plan before you share it.

Never assume that a mentally ill person is helpless; it is counter-therapeutic. The more you promote a client's feeling of helplessness and dependency, the longer you are prolonging his or her illness. Accordingly, if the client is able to participate, even in the most minimal way, in the planning of care, his or her sense of control and personal strength will increase.

IMPLEMENTATION

During this step of the nursing process, you begin to undertake what you developed in the nursing care plan. As you implement your plan, watch and listen carefully to the client. His or her verbal and nonverbal responses can give you an indication about whether or not the nursing approach is therapeutic.

EVALUATION

During the last step of the nursing process, use the intermediate goals to review the client's response to nursing intervention. Usually, however, new information is obtained, the client's condition improves or worsens, new medication is begun, or some other factor intervenes that requires you to use new data to modify or change the original plan. In essence, you must reinstitute the nursing process of assessing, planning, implementing, and evaluating in order to develop a plan that adjusts to the client's changed condition.

CHAPTER 28 SUMMARY

- A crisis that causes the onset of mental illness may be an event with which the person has no experience and thus has developed no coping responses. It may also be a series of stressful life experiences. In some cases, a crisis may have no identifiable trigger or precipitating event.

- When a person is functioning well mentally, he or she can tolerate the stress of a new event and develop responses to decrease anxiety. When a person does not cope effectively, a maladaptive response occurs.

- Maladaptive response results in change to the person's quality of life and capacity to function. It may also result in a person's decreasing ability to deal with anxiety, which may lead to immobility or panic.

- Crisis results when the person temporarily loses the capacity to help himself or herself.

- Certain life change events can cause crisis. These situational events are death, divorce, major illness, marriage, and childbirth.

- Nursing care for a client in crisis includes assessing what events mean to the person, particularly regarding a client's frame of reference about the events that led to the crisis. Nursing care also includes creating a care plan that offers the client consistent support and monitoring the client's responses to the care.

CHAPTER 28 QUESTIONS

1. Which of the following is *not* true about crisis?
   a. It usually causes the onset of mental illness.
   b. It always has an identifiable trigger or precipitating event.
   c. It can occur when a person's coping capacities are already taxed to the limit.
   d. None of the above

2. The factor that determines whether an event has crisis potential is the person's
   a. perception of the event.
   b. perceived degree of threat to safety, life goals, family stability, or role functioning.
   c. coping style.
   d. all of the above.

3. The most severe situational crisis that people encounter is
   a. joblessness.
   b. death of a loved one or one's own anticipated death.
   c. marriage.
   d. development.

4. Which of the following best describes the reason for a developmental crisis?
   a. When a person does not reach normal adult height and becomes self-conscious
   b. When a person is immature and can't find a job
   c. When numerous developmental issues prove too taxing to resolve
   d. When a person has his or her 40th birthday

BIBLIOGRAPHY

Aguilera, D.C. (1994). *Crisis intervention: Theory and methodology* (7th ed.). St. Louis: Mosby Year Book.

Barry, P.D. (1996). *Psychosocial nursing: Care of physically ill patients and their families* (3rd ed.). Philadelphia: Lippincott-Raven.

Bartolovic, M. (1996). Psychosocial intervention in the emergency department. In P. Barry (Ed.). *Psychosocial nursing assessment and intervention* (3rd ed.). Philadelphia: Lippincott.

Groves, J.E., & Kurcharski, A. (1997). Brief psychotherapy. In N.H. Cassem (Ed.). *Massachusetts General Hospital handbook of general hospital psychiatry* (4th ed.). St. Louis: Mosby Year Book.

Hoff, L.A. (1995). *People in crisis: Understanding and helping* (4th ed.). San Francisco: Jossey-Bass.

Holdsworth, N., & Guy, W. (1994). Problems of service assessment *ab intra*: Research and evaluation relating to a new early intervention community psychiatric nursing service. *Journal of Advanced Nursing, 19*, 290–298.

Kaplan, H.I., & Sadock, B.J. (1995). *Comprehensive textbook of psychiatry/VI* (6th ed.). Baltimore: Williams & Wilkins.

Kubler-Ross, E. (1975). *Death: The final stage of growth*. Englewood Cliffs, NJ: Prentice-Hall.

Lego, S. (1996). *Psychiatric nursing: A comprehensive reference* (2nd ed.). Philadelphia: Lippincott-Raven.

McFarland, G.K., Wasli, E.L., & Gerety, E.K. (1996). *Nursing diagnoses and process in psychiatric mental health nursing* (3rd ed.). Philadelphia: Lippincott-Raven.

Nettina, S.M. (1996). *The Lippincott manual of nursing practice* (6th ed.). Philadelphia: Lippincott-Raven.

Reding, G.R., & Raphelson, M. (1995). Around-the-clock psychiatric crisis intervention: Another effective alternative to psychiatric hospitalization. *Community Mental Health Journal, 31*(2), 179–187.

Wilson, H.S., & Kneisl, C.R. (1996). *Psychiatric nursing* (5th ed.). Redwood City, CA: Addison-Wesley.

29

Milieu Therapy and Behavior Modification

Behavioral Objectives

After reading this chapter the student will be able to:

■ Explain how tranquilizing drugs have helped change the manner of treating mentally ill clients.

■ Identify the members of the hospital team who deal with emotionally ill clients.

■ Describe the type of atmosphere and attitudes that help establish a therapeutic milieu.

■ List the eight aims of staff members working with clients who are hospitalized for mental illness.

■ Explain why counseling family members is important in the treatment of mentally ill clients.

■ Describe the role of halfway houses in the rehabilitation of clients with emotional problems.

■ Describe the ways that a client's behavior may be modified or changed by the techniques of relaxation and desensitization, condition avoidance, and operant conditioning (token economy).

■ Explain the limitations of behavior modification as a therapeutic modality.

◆ History of Development of the Therapeutic Milieu Concept

Under the old concept of custodial care for the mentally ill, many clients regressed, relinquished their responsibilities, and were relegated to "back wards." Here, they were provided with minimal physical care, locked in, and essentially left alone. Most of their decisions were made for them. They were dehumanized, garbed in unattractive clothing, and placed on a rigid institutional routine. When they acted out their hostility, they were subdued with sedative drugs, harsh commands, and, at times, manhandling. If they did not respond to these methods they were put into restraints, such as strait jackets or hand and ankle cuffs. Even those living on the better wards had to submit to regimentation and locked doors and lost their personal belongings and freedom. The staff members who cared for these clients often had little, if any, training in psychology or psychotherapy. The attendants or guards were hired and placed on the wards without in-service training, and they learned to cope with the behavior of their clients to the best of their abilities.

The **milieutherapie** approach was introduced during the first two decades of the 1900s by Hermann Simon, a German psychiatrist. Although brief references in historical accounts acknowledge the importance of environment in the treatment of mental disorders, Simon's approach was the first use of the therapeutic milieu on a large scale. The major focus of this approach is that a client's social environment can be therapeutic for him or her. When all those around the client, staff members and other clients alike, are working to support his or her rehabilitation, their restoration to health can be more effectively ensured.

◆ Acceptance of the Therapeutic Milieu Concept

The therapeutic milieu concept was not widely adopted in this country until the 1960s. A number of dynamics operating before that time supported its gradual acceptance. The introduction of the major tranquilizers during the mid-1900s had the greatest impact on treatment of the mentally ill client, adding another dimension to psychiatric therapy. They lowered the anxiety level, thus producing sustained relief of the symptoms of many disturbed mentally ill clients. As these drugs became more widely used, the amount of disturbed behavior on the nursing units decreased. The clients became less disorganized and more compliant. Their destructiveness decreased greatly. Accordingly, it became possible to improve the physical surroundings and to gain clients' cooperation in efforts being made for them.

While the severity of the clients' symptoms yielded to these tranquilizing drugs, great strides were also being made in the psychiatric field. Training was begun at all levels to teach hospital personnel the theory of psychiatric care. A client's behavior was regarded as an indication of his or her needs. The different care disciplines began to pool their knowledge and efforts to assess the needs of the client. Thus, the psychiatric team was born. It came to include all levels of professionals and paraprofessionals who had actual client contact. Today, in many hospitals, these teams include psychiatrists; psychologists; physicians; nurses; social workers; therapists for drama, art, recreation, and other therapies; teachers; counselors; pastors; and technicians.

When a new client is admitted, he or she is usually apprehensive, upset, and disturbed. This is a strange new world he or she is entering. Every effort is made to convey that the client will be accepted as he or she is, without criticism, reprimand, or judgment. His or her legal rights are explained. The client is evaluated physically, mentally, and emotionally during the first few days after arrival in order to determine his or her needs. On the basis of these evaluations, the team outlines a treatment program. If the client is able to participate in this planning, he or she is involved and aware of what forms of treatment are being scheduled and why.

◆ THE TREATMENT MODEL

Clients are encouraged to set up their own council and to form their own rules and regulations. When it is possible for them to do this, they are also expected to enforce these rules. When a resident breaks one of these rules or shows grossly unacceptable conduct, the entire ward then exerts social pressure on this person. This has proved much more effective in reshaping behavior than when the staff has enforced the hospital rules.

Clients are encouraged to be answerable for their behavior as much as possible, but are not required to assume responsibility that they cannot handle. As they improve, more and more responsibilities are offered. Clients should be encouraged to help other clients as much as possible in order to experience responsibility and satisfaction in tasks that hold real meaning.

Clients who tend to withdraw and isolate themselves socially should be placed in a unit that has as one of its primary goals the interaction of its members. The staff should continually reach out toward these withdrawn people and allow them plenty of time to respond. A one-to-one relationship is advisable.

In the past, staff members were cautioned not to become involved in the clients' problems. Their role was that of observing, recording, and controlling the clients' activities. A wide gulf existed between the controlled patient and the controlling staff. Today, emphasis is placed on the necessity of becoming involved with the clients, of participating with them in order to positively influence the course of their illness. In this way, they can feel accepted and learn to trust and feel that their rights as an individual are respected, that their treatment needs are being explored, that all efforts are directed toward helping them, and that there is a genuine expectation that they will improve.

These changed attitudes, plus a realistic social setting on the units, add up to what is called a **therapeutic milieu**. *Milieu* is a French word meaning a trusted environment. When the environment acts constructively to help clients function comfortably, encourages improved behavior and self-confidence, and enables them to assume responsibility and to socialize effectively, we say that a therapeutic milieu has been established (see Chapter 4 for more on the therapeutic milieu).

One of the most important elements in the hospital environment is the nursing staff. Nurses are largely responsible for creating an environment that will be health-producing for their clients. Of great importance are the interactions that exist among the clients and between the clients and you. The clients must be the focus of interest and concern, so that you may help them to handle stressful situations better. Encourage them to become active participants in all aspects of unit living. Give them the opportunity to discuss fears, problems, observations, successes, and failures openly and frankly with the staff and fellow clients. Group therapy sessions and informal, small, spontaneous interchanges are the best methods.

Each member of a therapeutic staff trained to understand the dynamics of behavior should reinforce each client's strengths and help reduce his or her weaknesses. A client often needs assistance in reestablishing contact with reality. Encourage participation in unit activities. Work and play can be used therapeutically, helping to work off pent-up emotions. A client can be encouraged to satisfy creative needs by making beautiful and useful objects. The social interchange on the unit tends to pull a client back into reality.

Direct your efforts in the hospital toward the following:

Convince the client that he or she is a person of worth and dignity.

Convince the client that you and the staff have realistic expectations that he or she can and will improve.

Provide the client with a therapeutic milieu that will act as a realistic social setting for his or her therapy.

Meet the client's physical, intellectual, and emotional needs as much as possible.

Emphasize and provide meaningful tasks and experiences for the client.

Reduce the social distance between you and the client.

Reduce the client's anxiety and fear.

Bring the client slowly but steadily closer to reality and to the community.

While the client is undergoing therapy in the hospital, his or her family should also enter family therapy. They should explore their own problems and anxieties in relation to their family members and each other. Since the client became ill within the family, work, and social settings, these settings should be examined and obvious areas of stress identified. Above all, family, friends, employer, and fellow workers should try to achieve a deeper understanding of the client's feelings and the reasons for his or her behavior if they are going to be able to accept and assist him or her when he or she returns from the hospital. As the client improves, he or she should be allowed short visits home to help reestablish emotional ties there and to progress toward eventual complete recovery.

If most of the emotional stress appears to develop within the family setting, complete rehabilitation in a halfway house may be advisable when the client is well enough not to need around-the-clock care. The client can live there for a number of weeks until he or she is able to adjust better to the home setting. Some hospitals have special living units where clients may come and go daily to work. Some clients spend their evenings and nights at a halfway house and return daily to the hospital for therapy.

◆ BEHAVIOR MODIFICATION

Behavior modification uses systems theory (see Chapter 10, Influence of Family and Social Environment on the Individual) to bring about change in the client. What the client *does* is the focus, rather than how he or she feels or why the client is as he or she is.

The field of behavior modification or behavior therapy is strongly based on the psychology of the learning process. Reports of treatment of behavioral disorders by this method or related forms of this method can be found throughout history. It was during the 1960s that behavioral therapy began to be used actively in the treatment of various types of mental disorders.

Behavior therapy differs from the traditional psychoanalytic approach to mental illness by focusing on the behavior of the person, rather than on an underlying cause. It is an appropriate therapeutic approach for certain types of mental disorders. Table 29–1 lists the conditions that have had positive response rates to specific behavioral therapy approaches. The therapy approach appears next to the condition.

◆ TABLE 29-1. Behavior Therapy Approaches to Mental Disorders

Mental Disorder	Therapeutic Approach
Phobias or phobic disorders	Desensitization
Anxiety or chronic pain	Relaxation Biofeedback
Dependent or passive personality style	Assertiveness training
Alcoholism or smoking	Aversive conditioning Conditioned avoidance

The following terms describe the learning principles used in behavior modification or behavior therapy:

Operant conditioning—Conditioning or influencing behavior by rewarding a person for positive forms of behavior; also called **behavioral psychology** and **behavior modification**.

Positive reinforcement—When a person's behavior results in a positive response from others, he or she experiences a feeling of acceptance and internal pleasure; he or she is likely to repeat the same behavior.

Negative reinforcement—Rewarding a stoppage of an undesirable event or behavior.

Aversive stimulus—Any event that results in an unpleasant feeling.

Punishment—A type of reinforcement in which a negative behavior elicits a negative response from the environment. The outcome is a cessation or stopping of negative behavior.

Extinction—The complete inhibition of a conditioned reflex as a result of failure of the environment to reinforce it.

Behavioral modification involves modifying the environment of the client in such a way that desirable behaviors are rewarded and undesirable behaviors punished. An example of this is **operant conditioning** as seen in **token economy.** Here, each client on a small psychiatric inpatient unit or partial hospitalization unit has a **problem-oriented record,** on which problem behaviors are listed (such as pacing, excessive smoking, not socializing, talking to voices). A schedule is then drawn up to provide the client with tokens for desired behavior. For example, a client may be entitled to a token for every half hour in which he or she does not pace the floor, or for every 15-minute conversation he or she holds with another client. These tokens are used to purchase desired things. Perhaps the group is planning a picnic or a trip to an amusement park, and each client desiring to go will be charged 30 tokens. If a client does not have enough tokens, he or she is not permitted to go on the excursion. A token economy obviously takes a lot of staff and involves a lot of record keeping, but it does produce desired behaviors.

In a completely developed behavior modification program, the staff, too, may be rewarded for desired behavior (such as coming to work on time and getting the clients to cooperate). In this situation, there is usually a minimal base salary, and the staff can earn more if they produce more.

Another technique of behavior modification is termed **conditioned avoidance.** Here the habit pattern of the client is paired to an unpleasant stimulus so that the client learns to avoid both the stimulus and the habit. The classic example of this technique is the use of disulfiram (Antabuse) in the treatment of the alcoholic.

A classic use of behavior modification techniques is in the treatment of phobias by **relaxation** and **desensitization.** For example, if a client is afraid of flying, the therapist will compile a series of slides or photographs in hierarchical order from the most anxiety-provoking scenes to those that are completely neutral. Such a series may include: (1) a picture looking out of the window of an airplane on take-off (most anxiety-provoking), (2) a picture of the inside of the airplane, (3) the airport waiting room, (4) the airport ticket counter, (5) the airport parking lot, (6) the road to the airport, (7) the client's own car, (8) the client's driveway, and (9) the client's living room (least anxiety-provoking).

In an actual therapy situation there may be 20 or 30 items in the series. Then, the client is taught to relax by a method that is fairly similar to self-hypnosis. While the client is relaxed in the therapist's office, usually on a couch or in a lounge chair, the least anxiety-provoking scene is projected on a screen. The client learns to **pair** (associate) the feeling of relaxation and the picture he or she is viewing. Then the client works his or her way up the series of pictures until he or she comes to one that causes feelings of anxiety. The series is then stopped, the client returned to a state of relaxation, and the series continued (going back a few pictures to a non-upsetting one). After many tries, the client will learn to pair the feeling of relaxation with what was formerly the most anxiety-provoking scene.

Following this **desensitization** procedure, the client will usually be taken on a field trip to the airport by the therapist. If at any time the client feels anxious, he or she is encouraged to practice relaxation, and the steps are retraced to a non–anxiety-provoking stage. Finally, when the client is ready, he or she may be taken for an actual airplane ride. However, the pattern of relaxation that occurs during the symbolic representation of the feared event usually generalizes to the real-life situation itself, making a field trip unnecessary.

The behavior treated in this example was the fear of flying. Using this therapeutic approach, it is not necessary for the client to ever know *why* he or she became afraid of flying. It is only required that the fear be stopped.

Although these techniques appear to work on almost anyone, a client with a host of problem behaviors (eg, a chronic paranoid schizophrenic) presents too formidable a task for any behavior therapist. The approach works best with phobias, some sexual disturbances, and some obsessive–compulsive neuroses.

CHAPTER 29 SUMMARY

- Milieu therapy was introduced in the early 1900s. The major focus of this approach is that a client's social environment can be therapeutic for him or her.

- The introduction of major tranquilizers, which lessen anxiety and resulting disturbed behavior by clients, had a tremendous impact on the treatment of the mentally ill client.

- In milieu therapy, the environment acts to help the client function comfortably and encourages improved behavior and self-confidence. It also enables the client to assume responsibility and socialize effectively. This social interchange helps pull clients back into reality.

- In the milieu setting, clients are encouraged to set up and enforce their own rules and regulations. Having residents, rather than staff, do this is more effective in reshaping behavior. Clients are also encouraged to assume responsibility and to help other clients.

- The nursing staff is largely responsible for creating an environment that is health-producing for the client. Efforts can be directed to emphasizing the client's worth and dignity, meeting the client's needs as much as possible, providing meaningful tasks, and reducing the client's anxiety and fear.

- As the client improves, short visits home help reestablish emotional ties. In some cases, having a client complete rehabilitation in a halfway house may be preferable to discharging the client to an insufficiently supportive family setting.

- Behavior modification focuses on what the client does (behavior) rather than the underlying cause of the behavior. The learning principles used in behavior modification are operant conditioning, positive reinforcement, negative reinforcement, aversive stimulus, punishment, extinction, conditioned avoidance, and desensitization.

CHAPTER 29 QUESTIONS

1. The main premise of the milieu therapy approach is that
   a. the best environment for people with mental disorders is in hospitals.
   b. a client's social environment can be therapeutic for him or her.
   c. giving heavy doses of tranquilizers is the first step.
   d. none of the above.

2. With milieu therapy, clients are encouraged to
   a. be answerable for themselves.
   b. enforce rules about conduct and behavior for themselves and other clients.
   c. handle increasing responsibility and help other clients, as they are able.
   d. all of the above.

3. The social interchange of the milieu therapy setting tends to
   a. let clients feel free to do whatever they wish.
   b. encourage clients to become more dependent on staff.
   c. help clients avoid other clients with more severe mental disorders.
   d. pull clients back into reality.

4. The therapeutic approach of desensitization is used to deal with
   a. phobias.
   b. anxiety.
   c. alcoholism.
   d. chronic pain.

BIBLIOGRAPHY

Barry, P.D. (1996). *Psychosocial nursing: Care of physically ill patients and their families* (3rd ed.). Philadelphia: Lippincott-Raven.

Kaplan, H.I., & Sadock, B.J. (1995). *Comprehensive textbook of psychiatry/VI* (6th ed.). Baltimore: Williams & Wilkins.

Lego, S. (1996). *Psychiatric nursing: A comprehensive reference* (2nd ed.). Philadelphia: Lippincott-Raven.

McFarland, G.K., Wasli, E.L., & Gerety, E.K. (1996). *Nursing diagnoses and process in psychiatric mental health nursing* (3rd ed.). Philadelphia: Lippincott-Raven.

Nettina, S.M. (1996). *The Lippincott manual of nursing practice* (6th ed.). Philadelphia: Lippincott-Raven.

Sideleau, B. (1996). Activities of daily living. In J. Haber, P. Price-Hoskins, A. Leach McMahon, & B. Sideleau (Eds.). *Comprehensive psychiatric nursing* (5th ed.). St. Louis: Mosby Year Book.

Stuart, G.W., & Sundeen, S.J. (Eds.). (1994). *Principles and practice of psychiatric nursing* (5th ed.). St. Louis: Mosby Year Book.

Walker, M. (1994). Principles of therapeutic milieu: An overview. *Perspectives in Psychiatric Care, 30*(3), 5–8.

Wilson, H.S., & Kneisl, C.R. (1996). *Psychiatric nursing* (5th ed.). Redwood City, CA: Addison-Wesley.

30

Group Therapy

After reading this chapter the student will be able to:

■ List the three ways that group therapy can help clients with emotional problems.

■ Describe the differences between group therapy and psychotherapy and guidance therapy.

■ Describe the role of the leader in group therapy.

■ Explain why it can be helpful if the members of a therapy group share a degree of similarity in outlook and attitudes.

■ Indicate the method by which a qualified member of the health team would go about setting up a therapy group in the hospital.

There are many definitions and many concepts of **group therapy**. Group therapy is a treatment mode with the guiding principle that individuals function in groups using patterns they acquired in their original families. The purpose of group therapy is to contribute to a change in perception and reality of the group member. In fact, there are many concepts of just what constitutes a group, and just what therapy is. Actually, a well-functioning group may consist of as few as 4 people interacting together; the upper limit is 10 to 12.

◆ EARLY SOCIALIZATION IN GROUPS

We become members of many groups throughout our lives. At birth, we become members of the family group. Then come the play groups, groups in school and church, and the important teenage peer group; then the social groups, business groups, political groups, and parent groups. We remain in some of these groups temporarily, some permanently; some directly, and some indirectly; some voluntarily, and some involuntarily. But always, along life's way, we are involved in group activities.

 We are told that our behavior is formed, influenced, and controlled by the dynamic forces existing within groups. If the child's first group—his or her family—fails to provide positive, gratifying interpersonal learning experiences, his or her psychosocial development may well become impaired. For instance, the child who has never learned how to get approval from his or her mother and father tends in later life to develop insecure relationships with authority figures, such as teachers and employers. If he or she fails to relate well with peers in the latency period, and is unable to extract pleasure from association with them, he or she may have trouble in competition and with leadership skills, for it is during this period that leadership and the ability to compete are formed.

◆ THE PURPOSE OF GROUPS IN THE THERAPEUTIC SETTING

The concept of structured group interaction, the purpose of which is to promote well-defined therapeutic objectives, is based on the idea that people have a profound effect on one another, both constructive and destructive.

 One of the primary treatment modalities in the hospital setting, in addition to medication evaluation and administration, is group therapy. Most hospitalized individuals report that it was the most beneficial aspect of their treatment. Because of the crisis nature of the inpatient experience and the opportunity to meet and talk with others who are also in crisis, the therapeutic group becomes an important vehicle for self-understanding, self-acceptance, short-term planning, and general coping support.

The word **therapy** indicates therapeutic treatment of some sort. **Therapeutic** refers to any form of treatment or relationship in which the actions, techniques, and practices are purposefully planned and directed toward goals that offer a beneficial effect to the client.

The first clients treated in groups in the United States were tubercular clients. Later, others with various psychosomatic conditions were treated; then the neurotic, the socially maladjusted, and the psychotic. In the early stages of group psychotherapy, it was considered necessary for the therapist to be a psychiatrist. Later, the clinical psychologist was considered sufficiently trained to conduct such sessions. Eventually nurses assumed this role.

◆ THE PURPOSE OF GROUPS IN THE COMMUNITY SETTING

Regardless of the location of a therapeutic group, the purpose is always the same; to provide a safe and supported environment in which individuals can examine their current experiences and options. Many more therapeutic groups occur in the community than in the inpatient setting.

The goal of community groups is to support effective coping. A community group may be designed to meet the needs of individuals with specific types of issues, such as recovery from substance dependence, coping with the everyday challenges of chronic depression, or examining the effects of AIDS.

Within the community group setting, individuals have the opportunity to discuss issues that, if unaddressed, could undermine their decision making and adaptation. Another outcome of group therapy is that it provides additional support to the family or social network of the group member; the availability of group support to an ineffectively coping individual can assist in decreasing the demand on the coping ability of the remaining family members.

◆ THE NURSE'S ROLE IN GROUP THERAPY

Three types of groups most commonly have nurse leaders. One type is a **support group,** in which members explore feelings and thoughts related to a particular subject, such as women's issues or discharge from the hospital. The second is an **instructional group,** in which thoughts and feelings about particular needs related to discharge are discussed within the group. When appropriate, the group leader switches from a leadership role to a teaching role. In these first two groups, the major role of the leader is to promote participation from the group members and clarify and paraphrase their statements. This means the leader repeats the statements of others in his or her own words. Such groups have a structure that is preestablished.

Interpretation and explanation of the causes of clients' conflicts are not undertaken in this setting. A registered nurse functioning as a staff nurse who has had previous group coleadership and group participation experience is qualified to lead such a group. He or she should discuss the content and process of the group with a supervisor. Ideally, the supervisor should be a certified clinical nurse specialist, a nurse who holds a master's degree in psychiatric/mental health nursing. It is helpful to receive supervision from a person prepared to understand the nursing perspective of client care. Occasionally, people from other disciplines, although skilled as mental health clinicians, lack the ability to integrate the concurrent nursing needs of the client into the group therapy process.

The third type of group, usually called group therapy, has less formal structure than the first two. In it, the members' thoughts and feelings are subject to the analysis and interpretation of the leader. This type of group requires a leader with advanced knowledge of intrapsychic and group dynamics. Customarily, group psychotherapy is led only by people prepared at the master's or doctoral level in one of the mental health disciplines. The nurse-leader, when certified by the Psychiatric/Mental Health Nursing Division of the American Nurses Association, has met the following criteria:

1. Holds a master's degree in psychiatric/mental health nursing
2. Has 2 years postmaster's experience working in a psychiatric setting
3. Has spent 100 hours in supervision with a board-certified mental health clinician from one of the following disciplines:
   a. Nursing
   b. Social work
   c. Psychology
   d. Psychiatry
4. Has passed a board examination prepared by the American Nurses Association, Division of Psychiatric/Mental Health Nursing

◆ TYPES OF GROUP THERAPY

Group therapy is a method of treatment in which a number of clients with similar types of problems meet with the therapist in an organized, structured setting for the purpose of arriving at a better understanding of themselves and others, learning how to modify their behavior to a more socially acceptable form, and developing their ability to derive more satisfaction in their relationships with others.

Many varieties of therapy are included today under the general term of group therapy. Among those most commonly used are rehabilitation therapy, remotivation therapy, occupational therapy, physical therapy, play therapy (for children), work therapy, activity group therapy, psychodrama, art therapy, and the program of Alcoholics Anonymous, as well as therapy groups established for narcotic addicts, homosexuals, parents of cerebral palsy children, and parents of retarded children. There is no question that there can be some overlapping among these various therapies.

CODEPENDENCE

One of the most therapeutic mental health concepts that has developed in the past two decades is called codependence. In most psychiatric inpatient units there will be one or more ongoing therapeutic groups whose purpose is to increase awareness about codependence and how it can affect coping and healthy communication.

Codependency is a cluster of personality traits and patterns that are identified by the chemical dependency field. It is believed that a family that is coping with an alcoholic member develops codependence as a way to cope with the illness. It is also possible that codependent traits are present in the majority of families as a result of the need to avoid emotional distress or conflict.

The characteristics of codependence can create psychological pain in individuals and all of their relationships. Some of the patterns seen in codependence include:

- Having a strong, compelling desire to solve the problems of others
- Feeling the feelings of others
- Taking responsibility for the choices and actions of others
- Needing to deny one's own feelings
- Needing to please others
- Overcommitting one's time and energy
- Having low self-worth
- Feeling strong guilt and avoiding it by taking care of others
- Worrying frequently
- Feeling emotional turmoil

There are a number of groups in clinical settings, as well as self-help groups in the community, that utilize the codependency concept in their therapeutic approach. These groups include Alcoholics Anonymous; Al-Anon, the group for spouses and loved ones of alcoholics; Adult Children of Alcoholics; similar groups for other types of chemical addiction; and general groups on codependency.

◆ FORMATION OF THE GROUP

The leader should assume the responsibility for making all the arrangements for the group meeting. A treatment goal for the group should be established, as well as plans for its implementation. The nurse should then go to the treatment team and explain the plan for the group, asking for their cooperation in the project. The team members can help choose a balanced group of clients for these sessions, since they are usually quite familiar with the behavioral patterns of the clients under their care.

The next step is to involve the nurse specialist or staff psychiatrists (preferably the team psychiatrist whose clients are to be involved in the therapy) in the project, because supervision is essential to development of therapeutic leadership ability.

The leader should choose a room for the therapy that will accommodate the size of the group—one that is well lighted and ventilated and that is comfortably furnished. The chairs and couches should be arranged in a circle or semicircle.

When establishing a nurse-led group, the following suggestions can promote positive group process:

- The nurse-leader should interview potential group members to determine their appropriateness for the group.
- The group should consist of 8 to 12 people.
- The group can be homogeneous (people with similar problems, similar ages, and so on) or heterogeneous (people with a variety of backgrounds, mixed ages, and so on).
- The group meetings in an inpatient setting are usually scheduled from twice weekly to once daily, depending on the purpose of the group.
- The group should be relatively stable in order for the feeling of togetherness to develop. However, it can be "open-ended"; that is, when one or two members leave the group, another one or two can start with the group, so the majority of the group has not changed.
- The length of the therapy is variable. In some instances, it goes on year after year with a few entering and leaving it from time to time. In other instances, if the goal for which it was set up is reached, it may be disbanded.
- The meetings should last from 1 to 1½ hours.

LEADERSHIP STYLE

The way in which a leader conducts a group can have an important effect on the way the group reaches its objective. The process is what is happening in the group—what dynamics are occurring and why.

Some group therapists may establish themselves as the authority figure in the group. This might be advisable if the group consists chiefly of withdrawn schizophrenics, where the primary goal would be to get them to interact with other members of the group and where a great deal of direct intervention might be needed.

However, the method becoming more and more popular is the method by which the group leader, or therapist, sits quietly in the background, controlling the interaction by indirect guidance, sometimes so indirect that it seems as though the clients are running the whole show. The leader invites the clients to share their situations and explain their problems to the entire group. On occasion he or she must quietly redirect the focus to a better solution of the problem, often saying only a word or two.

Unlike psychoanalysis, counseling, or guidance therapy, this form of client interaction does not aim to solve a single, specific situational problem. Rather, its aim is to bring people with similar problems together to help them ventilate their feelings to each other, explore common emotional problems, face their traumatic memories together, and face up to their unacceptable feelings. The leader rarely directs the conversation or suggests remedies for problems but, rather, acts as a catalyst, helping the ebb and flow of strong emotion, group approval, or group criticism that results from the discussions. The leader encourages clients to express their feelings about people and situations, about themselves and their families, their fears and hopes, their hospitalization, and their illness.

THE GROUP PROCESS

At times a client will express deep hostility toward society, a family member, an employer, a fellow worker, and even another member of the group. The other clients can realize, through this anger, that other people can hate and plot revenge and desire to kill, even as they do. They can identify with this destructive form of hate. By assuring the angry client that they, too, entertain similar "bad" emotions, these other clients help restore his or her self-confidence and help channel the destructive impulses without harm to others.

Sometimes a group member receives hostility from fellow members. They may tell the person in no uncertain terms that his or her feeling, behavior, or thinking is wrong. This may result in a behavioral change or a changing concept in the person thus judged by his or her peers.

Slowly, a sense of belonging develops in the group. An increased sense of self-identity is noticeable in most of the participants. Eventually, the clients in the group start behaving like members of a strongly knit family. What threatens one, threatens all. When one member rejoices over a problem worked through there is a sense of elation in the entire group. This is truly a client-administered form of therapy—clients administer therapy to each other. This form of client-acting-on-client is therapy at its best, and it is a strong deterrent of unacceptable behavior and acting out.

Some people become very anxious as a result of the increased intimacy that such a group formation engenders. Some become overwhelmed and oppressed by shame when they yield to the invitation to disclose the disturbing facts in their past lives. Some cannot tolerate the criticism of their fellow members and may develop antagonism toward those who so criticize them.

On the whole, once a client joins such a therapy group, he or she usually perseveres in it, and very often, members of the group, working out their problems together, become deep friends and carry on these friendships after they leave the hospital.

CHAPTER 30 SUMMARY

- The concept of structured group action to promote therapeutic objectives is based on the idea that people have a profound effect on one another, both positive and negative.

- Support groups, instructional groups, and group therapy are often led by nurses.

- In support groups, members explore feelings and thoughts related to a particular subject.

- In instructional groups, members discuss thoughts and feelings about particular needs related to discharge.

- Group therapy is a method of treatment in which clients with similar types of problems meet with a therapist in an organized, structured setting. Their purpose is to better understand themselves and others, learn to modify their behavior, and develop their ability to derive more satisfaction from their relationships with others.

- In group therapy, the members' thoughts and feelings are subject to the analysis and interpretation of the leader. Thus, the leader must have advanced knowledge of intrapsychic and group dynamics.

- When the leader is making arrangements to form a group, he or she should involve the entire treatment team in reviewing the goals for the group and implementation.

- The way the leader conducts the group has an important impact on how the group reaches its objective. Depending upon the needs of the group members, the leader may be more directive or less directive.

- During the group process, members slowly begin to develop a sense of belonging and begin to behave like members of a strongly knit family. The result is "clients-acting-on-clients," which is a strong deterrent to unacceptable behavior.

- Codependence is a set of personality traits and patterns. It is believed these behaviors are developed as a means to avoid emotional distress or conflict.

CHAPTER 30 QUESTIONS

1. The purpose of group therapy is for clients to
   a. solve a single, specific situational problem.
   b. be firmly directed by the leader.
   c. ventilate feelings and explore common emotional problems.
   d. avoid talking about their families.

2. A pattern seen in codependence is
   a. having low-self worth.
   b. feeling other people's feelings.
   c. needing to please others.
   d. all of the above.

3. The size limit for a well-functioning therapy group is
   a. 20 to 24.
   b. 10 to 12.
   c. less than 6.
   d. 15.

4. In support and instructional groups, the nurse leader's role is to
   a. promote participation from clients and paraphrase their statements.
   b. create a plan for each client and make sure he or she follows it.
   c. keep the group totally focused on behavior rather than on feelings.
   d. write down what everyone says, to discuss it with them later.

BIBLIOGRAPHY

Barry, P.D. (1996). *Psychosocial nursing: Care of physically ill patients and their families* (3rd ed.). Philadelphia: Lippincott-Raven.

Husseini, M.B. (1996). Designing a residential aftercare and outreach program. In S. Lego (Ed.). *Psychiatric nursing: A comprehensive reference*. Philadelphia: Lippincott-Raven.

Kaplan, H.I., & Sadock, B.J. (1995). *Comprehensive textbook of psychiatry/VI* (6th ed.). Baltimore: Williams & Wilkins.

Lego, S. (1996). *Psychiatric nursing: A comprehensive reference* (2nd ed.). Philadelphia: Lippincott-Raven.

Lego, S. (1996). Psychodynamic group psychotherapy. In S. Lego (Ed.). *Psychiatric nursing: A comprehensive reference*. Philadelphia: Lippincott-Raven.

Long, P., & Leach McMahon, A. (1996). Working with groups. In J. Haber, P. Price-Hoskins, A. Leach McMahon, & B. Sideleau (Eds.). *Comprehensive psychiatric nursing* (5th ed.). St. Louis: Mosby Year Book.

McFarland, G.K., Wasli, E.L., & Gerety, E.K. (1996). *Nursing diagnoses and process in psychiatric mental health nursing* (3rd ed.). Philadelphia: Lippincott-Raven.

Nettina, S.M. (1996). *The Lippincott manual of nursing practice* (6th ed.). Philadelphia: Lippincott-Raven.

Nickerson, P.R. (1995). Solution-focused group therapy. *Social Work, 40*(1), 132–133.

Sideleau, B. (1996). Activities of daily living. In J. Haber, P. Price-Hoskins, A. Leach McMahon, & B. Sideleau (Eds.). *Comprehensive psychiatric nursing* (5th ed.). St. Louis: Mosby Year Book.

Walker, M. (1994). Principles of therapeutic milieu: An overview. *Perspectives in Psychiatric Care, 30*(3), 5–8.

Wilson, H.S., & Kneisl, C.R. (1996). *Psychiatric nursing* (5th ed.). Redwood City, CA: Addison-Wesley.

31

Psychopharmacology and Electroshock Treatment of Mental Disorders

Behavioral Objectives

After reading this chapter the student will be able to:

■ List the seven groups of antipsychotics, indicate the effects of each, and name one prominent drug under each category.

■ Identify the six major types of antidepressants and the physical side effects that may result from the use of each type.

■ List the two chemical families that constitute the antianxiety medications and indicate why their use should be limited.

■ Explain why antiparkinsonian agents are frequently prescribed along with antipsychotics.

■ Name the kind of mental disorder for which lithium carbonate may be prescribed.

■ Define electroshock therapy and describe the conditions under which it is used.

The treatment of mental disorders is increasingly being called biologic psychiatry. The name identifies the importance of diagnosing and treating the underlying physiologic changes in the brain that contribute to mental disorders. The development of medications that restore brain chemistry to near-normal levels has markedly altered the treatment of mental illness. The availability of these medications has been the single most important contributing factor to the discharge of hundreds of thousands of chronically mentally ill individuals from long-term mental institutions.

The knowledge and clinical use of medications in psychiatry is called psychopharmacology; medications used in the treatment of mental disorders are most commonly called psychotropic drugs. Psychotropic medications are those that affect behavior, psychological or cognitive function, or the sensory experience.

◆ GENERAL CONSIDERATIONS ABOUT PSYCHOPHARMACOLOGY

The role of the nurse and mental health worker in the administration of all medications is central and indisputable. Usually, they are the ones who first perceive the need for medication in a particular client or the need to change the drugs he or she is receiving. They may be the first to recognize side effects or adverse reactions and to call them to the physician's attention. The nurse instructs the client in precautions to observe with certain medications. The psychiatrist, working together with the other members of the mental health team in the area of psychopharmacology, delivers a safer, more comprehensive service to the client as a result of the information received from the nurse about the client's response to medication.

IMPORTANCE OF CLIENT CONSENT

The drugs used to treat mental disorders have many side effects (these will be discussed later in the chapter). Physicians and nurses are required to discuss these with their clients and, in doing so, can learn about the client's past experiences with psychotropic medication. Clients have the right to refuse to take these medications. They also have the right to know about the side effects caused by these medications before agreeing to take them.

MAJOR DRUGS

There are seven groups of drugs that are used most frequently for clients with mental disorders. These groups and their general function are as follows:

Antipsychotics alleviate psychosis.

Antidepressants reduce depression.

Antianxiety agents lower anxiety levels.

Sedative–hypnotics also lower anxiety levels.

Antiparkinsonian agents decrease the extrapyramidal symptoms that develop as side effects of major antipsychotics.

Anticonvulsants lower the potential for convulsions.

Antimanic drugs (lithium) are used to treat acute manic episodes.

There are subtle differences in the action of various members of the antipsychotics: some are more "alerting," some more sedating; each has particular side effects; some are more likely than others to cause symptoms mimicking Parkinson's disease. However, in terms of drug choice, the client's individual reaction, particular situation, and preference almost always cast the deciding vote.

Most clients can remember difficulties with drugs. A man who has experienced disturbed sexual functioning on thioridazine (Mellaril) will ask for something else. The person who has a tendency toward pseudoparkinsonism as a medication side effect and has had great difficulty in this regard with haloperidol (Haldol) or fluphenazine (Prolixin) may fear the same reaction will occur with other drugs. If the client's last medication experience was as an inpatient, the doses he or she remembers may be out of line for outpatient care. Too much sedation could make traveling dangerous or might result in the client staying at home in bed.

Nonetheless, wherever possible, the client's wishes are honored, and comments about his or her drug experiences are always listened to. If there is a clear contraindication to the client's drug or dose choice, or if the nurse or physician believes that there is great importance in using a different drug, all of the facts are explained to the client and his or her full cooperation is sought. Further discussion of ethical considerations in administering psychiatric medications can be found in Chapter 5, Legal and Ethical Issues in Mental Health Nursing.

When a client is started on psychotropic drugs *for the first time,* more caution is required, and a careful history of drug sensitivities in both the client and the family must be obtained. A family history of success with a particular psychotropic drug in a blood relative with a similar disease is considered as presumptive evidence that the present client may do best with the medication. For example, it is known that amitriptyline (Elavil) is more sedating than imipramine (Tofranil), and usually is a better choice when depression is accompanied by considerable anxiety, agitation, or insomnia. However, if two sisters in a family developed agitated depressions within a few years of each other and the first did well on Tofranil and less well on Elavil, using Tofranil in

the second sister should be considered from the beginning. Both consti-
tutional factors and family suggestibility play a role in drug response.
Accordingly, information about family drug experience is sought and
valued.

◆ ANTIPSYCHOTICS

These therapeutically important drugs, also called neuroleptic agents,
are divided chemically into seven groups: phenothiazines, thioxanthenes, butyrophenones, diphenylbutylpiperidine, dihydroindolone,
dibenzoxazepine, and dibenzodiazepine. Of these, the phenothiazines
are the largest and most important group. The incidence of side effects
from the major tranquilizer group is very high. Table 31–1 lists the various drugs and their normal dosages. Table 31–2 provides a comprehensive list of these drugs and their common side effects.

PHENOTHIAZINES

The introduction of phenothiazines in 1955 resulted in major changes in
the treatment of mental illness. Most antipsychotics fall into this group.
The oldest and most widely used drug in this category is chlorpromazine (Thorazine). It also has the highest incidence of allergic reactions, affecting the liver, skin, and blood; however, these side effects can
occur with any drug in the group. Promazine (Sparine) has a cross-sen-
sitivity with chlorpromazine (allergy to one will occur with the other),
but switching to other phenothiazines will usually diminish the allergic
reaction. One of the most common side effects of these drugs is that the
person develops parkinsonian symptoms. More information about
these symptoms and their treatment appears later in this chapter.

The most serious liver complication is obstructive jaundice; this
condition is usually reversible if it is noticed in time and the offending
drug is withdrawn. The skin complications include hypersensitivity to
sunlight and various skin eruptions and edema. Nurses who handle
Thorazine concentrate, in particular, may develop a contact dermatitis,
in which case further direct exposure of the skin to the chemical must
be avoided. Blood dyscrasias are not strictly dose related and occur
most frequently in white, elderly, debilitated women; the most serious
form is agranulocytosis. Most of this reaction occurs very rapidly, usually in the 6th to 8th week of treatment. Symptoms are sore throat, fever,
chills, and weakness. Treatment of agranulocytosis should take place in
the hospital; if treatment is not promptly undertaken, risk of death is
considerable. Following recovery, clients should never again be given
any phenothiazine, tricyclic drug (see antidepressants), or diphenylmethane derivatives (see minor tranquilizers). Be keenly aware of this

◆ **TABLE 31–1. Drug Therapy for Psychosis (listed in order from the most to the least sedating)**

Drug	Daily Intensive-Treatment Dose (mg)	Daily Maintenance Dose (mg)	Available Dosage Size (mg)
Chlorpromazine			10, 25, 50, 100, 200 (tablets)
(Thorazine)	150–500	50–100	30, 75, 150, 200, 300* (spansules)
Triflupromazine (Vesprin)	50–150	25–50	10, 25, 50
Thioridazine (Mellaril)	200–300	20–60	10, 25, 50, 100, 150, 200
Mesoridazine (Serentil)	50–100	10–25	10, 25, 50, 100
Chlorprothixene (Taractan)	50–100	25–50	10, 25, 50, 100
Loxapine succinate (Loxitane)	25–50	10–50	10, 24, 50
Promazine (Sparine)	200–600	50–100	10, 25, 50, 100, 200
Carphenazine (Proketazine)	50–100	25–50	25, 100
Thiopropazate (Dartal)	20–30	5–15	5, 10
Fluphenazine (Permitil, Prolixin)	2–8	1–4	1, 2.5, 5
Perphenazine (Trilafon)	4–16	2–8	2, 4, 8, 16
Prochlorperazine (Compazine)	50–150	25–50	10, 15, 30, 75
Trifluoperazine (Stelazine)	10–20	1–10	1, 2, 5, 10
Haloperidol (Haldol)	2–5	1–2	0.5, 1, 2, 5
Thiothixene (Navane)	10–20	5–10	1, 2, 5, 10
Clozapine (Clozaril)	300–900	300–450	25, 100
Risperidone (Risperdal)	3–6	3–6	1, 2, 3 (tablets)

* Note: Most of these medications are available in tablet or spansule form; liquid concentrate (to prevent the client from holding the pill in his or her cheek); and IM injectable form.

TABLE 31–2. Side Effects and Dose Equivalents of Antipsychotic Medications

Generic Drug Name (Trade name)	Side Effects*	Dosage Range† per 24-Hour Period (mg)	Chlorpromazine Oral Dose Equivalent (mg)
Aliphatic dimethylamine subgroup			
Chlorpromazine hydrochloride (Thorazine)	1–9, 11, 12–15, 23	300–1200	50
Triflupromazine (Vesprin)	1–12	60–150	12.5 to 15
Piperidine subgroup			
Thioridazine hydrochloride (Mellaril)	1–3, 6–7, 12, 13, 17–19	30–800	50
Mesoridazine besylate (Serentil)	1–7, 13, 19, 21	100–400	25
Piperacetazine (Quide)	1, 6, 7, 10, 11, 19, 20, 23, 29	20–160	5
Piperazine subgroup			
Acetophenazine dimaleate (Tindal)	1, 6	40–80	10
Carphenazine dimaleate (Proketazine)	1, 6, 8, 9	75–400	12.5 to 15
Fluphenazine hydrochloride (Permitil, Prolixin)	1–9, 11, 12, 15, 18	1–20	1
Perphenazine (Trilafon)	1–9, 11, 12	6–64	4
Prochlorperazine dimaleate (Compazine)	1–7, 9, 11, 12, 15, 20	15–150	5–10
Trifluoperazine hydrochloride (Stelazine)	1, 2, 4–9, 11, 12, 15, 18	2–20	2
Tricyclic dibenzodiazepine subgroup			
Clozapine (Clozaril)	1–9, 14, 24–29	250–900	50

(continued)

◆ TABLE 31-2. *Continued*

Generic Drug Name (Trade name)	Side Effects*	Dosage Range† per 24-Hour Period (mg)	Chlorpromazine Oral Dose Equivalent (mg)
Thioxanthene subgroup			
Thiothixene hydrochloride (Navane)	1, 3, 5–7, 10, 12–14, 18, 23	6–60	2–4
Chlorprothixene (Taractan)	1–10, 14, 15, 18, 20, 21, 23	30–600	50
Butyrophenone subgroup			
Haloperidol (Haldol)	1, 6	2–30	150–2250
Diphenylbutylpiperidine subgroup			
Pimozide (Ovap)	1, 3–5, 7, 8, 12, 28, 29	1–2	75–150
Dihydroindolone subgroup			
Molindone (Moban)	Similar to chlorpromazine hydrochloride (Thorazine)	50–200	100–400
Benzisoxazole subgroup			
Risperidone (Risperdal)	1, 3–7, 17 23–26, 30–32	3–6	Not available

* Side effects listed here are not intended to be a complete account of all possible adverse reactions reported.
† Drug dosage varies with the client's response and the severity of the disease.

Key to Side Effects
1. Sedation or sleep
2. Ataxia
3. Dry mouth
4. Constipation
5. Dermatitis
6. Extrapyramidal symptoms
7. Orthostatic hypotension
8. Blood dyscrasia (usually agranulocytosis)
9. Jaundice
10. Convulsions
11. Antiemetic
12. Blurred vision
13. Hypothermia
14. Tachycardia
15. Nasal congestion
16. Menstrual irregularities
17. Nausea and vomiting
18. Edema
19. Impotence
20. Increased appetite
21. Bradycardia
22. Increased gastric secretions
23. Photosensitivity
24. Dizziness
25. Insomnia
26. Headache
27. Seizures
28. Amenorrhea
29. Electrocardiogram changes
30. Aggression
31. Upper respiratory inflammation
32. Dyspnea
33. Fever

Reprinted with permission from Hahn, A., Barkin, R., & Oestrich, S. (1982). *Pharmacology in nursing* (15th ed.). St. Louis: C. V. Mosby.

most dangerous of all adverse reactions to psychoactive drugs and act quickly if sore throat or any other symptoms of infection occur, especially in the population at risk (elderly, debilitated, etc.).

Of the other phenothiazines, the one of exceptional value in the outpatient setting is fluphenazine enanthate (Prolixin enanthate) or fluphenazine decanoate, 0.25 to 2 mL IM every 6 hours. Given IM every 10 days to 2 weeks in a dose of 0.25 to 2 mL (25 mg/mL), this drug can effectively handle most psychotic symptomatology. It is widely used in outpatients when there is some question about whether the client will reliably take oral medication. Prolixin enanthate has a higher-than-average incidence of extrapyramidal reactions. Usually the client is instructed to take an antiparkinsonian agent by mouth concurrently and is warned about the possibility of such reactions. If the reaction is severe, 50 mg of diphenhydramine (Benadryl) or 1 to 2 mg of benztropine mesylate (Cogentin) can be given IM.

The other phenothiazines differ somewhat in dose and severity of adverse reactions—drowsiness, hypotension (especially postural), extrapyramidal reactions, appetite and weight increase, depression, atropine-like effects (dry mouth, blurred vision, amenorrhea), and allergic reactions (see chlorpromazine).

THIOXANTHENES

This category includes chlorprothixene (Taractan) and thiothixene (Navane). Navane appears to cause less drowsiness and more extrapyramidal effects than Taractan and also, like Thorazine, may produce lenticular pigmentation. Other side effects are similar to the other major tranquilizers.

BUTYROPHENONES

Haloperidol (Haldol) is similar in effect and side reactions to the other major tranquilizers. It may, however, produce very severe extrapyramidal effects. It tends to cause less appetite increase and weight gain than the others.

DIBENZOXAZEPINES

Loxapine succinate (Loxitane) is chemically related to the tricyclic antidepressants and is used for treatment of the symptoms of schizophrenia. It comes in three strengths—10 mg, 25 mg, and 50 mg. The starting dose ranges from 20 to 50 mg per day, with a maximum dose of 250 mg per day suggested. Twenty milligrams of Loxitane is roughly equivalent to 200 mg of Thorazine. In its sedating qualities, it is similar to Stelazine.

TRICYCLIC DIBENZODIAZEPINES

A new type of medication has been introduced as an antipsychotic treatment for chronic psychotic mental disorders. The generic name of this drug is clozapine (Clozaril), and it belongs to a drug class called tricyclic dibenzodiazepines. It reduces the psychotic mental symptoms of schizophrenia with fewer side effects. The response of long-term chronic schizophrenics to clozapine has been very positive and more therapeutic than any other class of antipsychotic medications, including the phenothiazines.

The starting dose is half of a 25-mg tablet every day. The dose is increased slowly by 25 to 50 mg daily until either adverse effects or the normal therapeutic range of 300 to 450 mg per day is reached. There are individuals who take up to 900 mg per day with therapeutic effects and no adverse effects. Side effects can include hypotension, seizures, and agranulocytosis. A baseline and weekly white blood cell count is required while a client is on this medication.

DIPHENYLBUTYLPIPERIDINE

This category includes the generic medication pimozide (Orap) that is occasionally used to treat Tourette's disorder. The symptoms that respond to pimozide are facial, motor, and phonic tics. The normal daily dose is usually 1 to 5 mg. Side effects include extrapyramidal symptoms, as well as breast enlargement, blood dyscrasias, mood alterations, and tachycardia.

DIHYDROINDOLONE

This category is a new chemical class of antipsychotics. It includes molindone (Moban). The normal daily range of medication is 100 to 200 mg. The effects of this medication are very similar to both the therapeutic and adverse effects of the phenothiazines.

BENZISOXAZOLE

Risperidone (Risperdal) is a drug that is increasingly being used for elderly adults with psychotic disorders. The advantage of this medication when used with elderly populations is that it has a decreased incidence of neuroleptic syndrome (extrapyramidal tract symptoms) and agranulocytosis. The recommended dose for elderly adults is usually one half that used in the general population.

OTHER PHARMACOLOGY ADJUNCTS IN THE TREATMENT OF PSYCHOTIC DISORDERS

Anticonvulsant medications are used to treat the psychotic symptoms associated with a rare form of complex epileptic seizure that results in bizarre behavioral effects and confusion.

Antianxiety agents are used in conjunction with the antipsychotic drugs when the psychotic episode is accompanied by severe anxiety. Sedatives and hypnotics are also used in conjunction with antipsychotic medications when normal sleep patterns are disrupted by the psychotic mental state. Antimanic agents are those drugs used during the manic phase of bipolar disorder; the manic phase is often accompanied by a psychotic mental state.

◆ ANTIDEPRESSANTS

Five chemical groups of drugs have marked effect on depressive syndromes. They are the dibenzazepines (the tricyclics), tetracyclics, bicyclics, triazolopyridines, aminoketones, and monoamine oxidase inhibitors (MAOIs). The differences in these antidepressants and their effects can be seen in Table 31–3.

Antidepressant effects of these drugs are generally not noticed for 2 to 3 weeks, and the client must usually be encouraged to continue taking his or her medicine even though at first there is little improvement. Initially, the client's psychomotor retardation, often part of the depressive picture, may seem increased by the drowsiness that the medication causes.

Once his or her depressive symptomatology is relieved, the client tends to discontinue the medication prematurely. However, he or she should ordinarily continue on the antidepressant for 3 to 6 months, and then undergo gradual dosage reduction for up to a total of 1 to 1½ years.

TRICYCLICS AND TETRACYCLICS

The **tricyclic antidepressants** include amitriptyline (Elavil), clomipramine (Anafranil), desipramine (Norpramin), doxepin (Adapin, Sinequan), imipramine (Trofranil), nortriptyline (Averntyl, Pamelor), protriptyline (Vivactil), and trimipramine (Surmontil).

The side effects of the tricyclics closely resemble those of the phenothiazines to which they are related. They frequently have toxic effects on many of the body's physical systems, notably the cardiovascular system. The section on adverse effects covers these side effects in greater

◆ TABLE 31–3. Antidepressants

Generic Name	Trade Name	Usual Dosage per Day (mg)	Side Effects*
Tricyclics			
Amitriptylene	Elavil	50–100	1–17
Clomipramine	Anafranil	50–100	2–8, 10, 11, 14, 18–21
Desipramine	Norpromin	25–100	5–8, 11, 12, 14, 15, 18, 21–27
Doxepin	Sinequan, Adapin	75–100	1–9, 11–13, 16, 29
Imipramine	Tofranil	50–150	2–8, 10, 12, 14, 15, 16, 24, 27, 29
Nortriptyline	Pamelor	25–100	1–15, 22, 24, 26, 27
Protriptyline	Vivactil	15–30	1–9, 11–15, 17, 21
Trimipramine	Surmontil	50–100	1–12, 14, 15, 16, 25, 27, 29, 30
Tetracyclics			
Amoxapine	Asendin	150–400	1–9, 11–14, 18, 25, 29
Maprotiline	Ludiomil	100–200	1–16, 18, 25–27, 29
Bicyclics			
Fluoxetine hydrochloride	Prozac	20–40	1, 6, 8, 11–13, 18, 21, 22, 28, 31–39
Setraline	Zoloft	50–200	3, 6, 8, 11–13, 19, 21, 28, 34, 36, 37, 40–45
Triazolopridine			
Trazodone	Desyrel	50–300	1, 3, 6, 9–11, 13, 14, 18, 19, 21, 25, 36, 43, 46–49
Aminoketones			
Bupropion	Wellbutrin	100–300	2, 3, 6, 8, 11, 18, 21, 22, 28, 31

*Side effects

1. Sedation
2. Constipation
3. Dry mouth
4. Blurred vision
5. Urinary hesitancy
6. GI upset
7. Tachycardia
8. Weight gain
9. Fatigue
10. Blood dyscrasia
11. CNS stimulation
12. Rash
13. Headache
14. Hypotension
15. Hypertension
16. Photosensitivity
17. Changes in blood sugar
18. Seizures
19. Sexual dysfunction
20. Dyspepsia
21. Insomnia
22. Anxiety
23. Agitation
24. Allergic reactions
25. Extrapyramidal effects
26. Arrhythmias
27. Jaundice
28. Weight loss
29. Edema
30. Heat or cold intolerance
31. Restlessness
32. Nightmares
33. Impaired motor performance
34. Tremor
35. Diaphoresis
36. Diarrhea
37. Manic episodes
38. Weakness
39. Pruritus
40. Dermatologic problems
41. Decrease in serum uric acid
42. Abdominal pain
43. Dizziness
44. Confusion
45. Chest pain
46. Malaise
47. Fainting
48. Hallucinations
49. Delusions

detail. Note the tendency to aggravate or precipitate narrow angle glaucoma. Before starting tricyclics, ask the client whether he or she has this condition, has experienced eye pain, or has seen halos around lights. The client should be examined for the presence of infected conjunctivae (reddened eyes). The hypotensive effect (as with the phenothiazines) is the most serious side effect in the elderly, and older clients should be told not to stand up too quickly. Tricyclics also tend to produce withdrawal symptoms upon abrupt discontinuation of a dose over 150 mg per day for 6 to 8 weeks. Withdrawal consists of nausea, vomiting, abdominal cramps, diarrhea, chills, insomnia, and anxiety. Withdrawal begins 4 to 5 days after discontinuation and last 3 to 5 days; it is avoided by gradual withdrawal over 3 to 4 weeks.

Tricyclics cause two types of toxic mental effects. The first consists of a shift from the original depression to a state of manic-like excitement, and the second resembles an organic brain syndrome, especially in the elderly, ranging anywhere from a transient defect in recent memory to delirium.

The **tetracyclic antidepressants** include amoxapine (Asendin) and maprofiline (Ludiomil). They are a more recent chemical class of antidepressants than the tricyclics. Their therapeutic and adverse effects are similar to those of the tricyclics.

The following conditions are contraindications for the use of tricyclic or tetracyclic antidepressants: agitation or overstimulation, alcoholism, angina pectoris, asthma, benign prostatic hypertrophy, blood disorders, congestive heart failure, epilepsy, glaucoma (narrow angle), hyperthyroidism, impaired liver function, kidney disease, myocardial infarct (within 1 year), paroxysmal tachycardia, pregnancy, preoperative status, and pyloric stenosis.

BICYCLICS (SEROTONIN REUPTAKE INHIBITORS)

An important new class of antidepressant drugs, called serotonin reuptake inhibitors, has recently been introduced to the treatment of depression. These drugs alter the availability of serotonin, a neurochemical that is decreased in the brains of depressed people. The action of the new class of drugs is to increase the presence of serotonin in the brain structures involved in the regulation of emotion.

Because these antidepressant medications are chemically different from the tricyclic and tetracyclic antidepressants, their side effects are different. They also can be reviewed in Table 31–3.

TRIAZOLOPYRIDINE

This class of drug includes trazadone hydrochloride (Desyrel). This medication has high sedating properties; low cardiovascular toxicity, unlike the tricyclics and tetracyclics; and no anticholinergic properties. It can be a good drug of choice for use in the elderly.

AMINOKETONES

Another new antidepressant class includes bupropion (Wellburtrin). This medication has a stimulant effect, no anticholinergic effects, and low cardiovascular toxicity.

MONOAMINE OXIDASE INHIBITORS

The MAOIs can be useful in some clients not affected by the tricyclics. However, they cause potentially serious side effects. Accordingly, they are considered by some authorities to be unacceptable for general use in a community mental health setting. Be sure to caution the physician in cases where the client's reliability or ability to understand and follow directions is questionable.

The dangers of MAOIs are twofold. First, hypertensive crisis may occur in clients on MAOIs who eat foods that contain tyramine or dopa. Such foods include aged cheese, broad beans, yeast products, Chianti wine, pickled herring, chocolate, and chicken livers. The symptoms of such a crisis are sharp elevation in blood pressure, throbbing headache, nausea, vomiting, elevated temperature, sweating, and stiff neck. Chlorpromazine (50 to 100 mg IM) is often effective in aborting the episode.

The second danger of MAOIs is potentiation of other drugs. The list is long and contains many drugs in common use in medical problems, such as central nervous system (CNS) depressants, sympathomimetics, ganglion blocking and anticholinergic agents (used in peptic ulcer and other gastrointestinal conditions), antihistamines, opiates, diuretics, chloroquine, hypoglycemic drugs, corticosteroids, antirheumatic compounds, and the tricyclic antidepressants.

◆ ANTIANXIETY DRUGS

These drugs can be divided into three chemical families: benzodiazepines, which include chlordiazepoxide (Librium), diazepam (Valium), and oxazepam (Serax); diphenylmethane derivatives, such as hydroxyzine (Atarax, Vistaril); and propanediols, which include meprobamate (Miltown) and tybamate (Solacen, Tybatran). Buspirone hydrochloride (Buspar) is a nonbenzodiazepine used in the treatment of anxiety disorders.

The antianxiety agents have limited usefulness in the outpatient setting, unless the anxiety is incapacitating. Anxiety normally accom-

◆ **TABLE 31–4. Antianxiety Drugs**

Drug Class	Drug Name	Side Effects
Benzodiazepines	Alprazolam (Xanax) Chlordiazepoxide (Librium) Chlorazepate (Tranxene) Diazepam (Valium) Flurazepam (Dalmane) Lorazepam (Ativan) Oxazepam (Serax) Prazepam (Centrax) Quazepam (Doral) Temazepam (Restoril) Triazolam (Halcion)	Sedation, dependence, decreased memory, hypotension, nausea, blood dyscrasias, vertigo, drowsiness, paradoxical agitation, slurred speech
Diphenylmethane derivatives	Hydroxyzine (Atarax, Vistaril)	Dry mouth, drowsiness, tremor convulsions, allergic reactions
Propanediols	Meprobamate (Equanil, Miltown) Tybamate (Solacen, Tybatran)	Same as benzodiazepines
Other	Buspirone hydrochloride (BuSpar)	Sedation, headache, nausea, increased nervousness faintness

panies growth and change and is an important ingredient in providing the motivation for most psychotherapeutic work. Most clients can tolerate a moderate level of anxiety without medication. They find that it rapidly diminishes as their energies are directed toward therapy and growth. Further, these drugs are more similar than not to the barbiturates and other CNS depressants. They have a high potential for habituation and addiction and carry the same danger on withdrawal (convulsions and delirium tremens) as the other CNS depressants. See Table 31–4 for a more complete description of the side effects of this family of drugs.

◆ SEDATIVES AND HYPNOTICS

Chemically, these CNS depressants are divided into barbiturates and nonbarbiturates. These drugs have a very limited but important place in psychiatry. They have withdrawal effects (e.g., convulsions) when discontinued abruptly, especially at high dosages. Withdrawal from severe abuse situations should always be carried out in a hospital. When severe sleep disturbances are a problem and cannot be handled by the sedating phenothiazines, either paraldehyde or chloral hydrate are recommended, since these drugs carry the least potential for abuse of the sedative–hypnotics. A list of popular sedatives is given here for completeness, not as a recommendation for use.

- Barbiturates
  Amobarbital (Amytal)
  Butabarbital (Butisol)
  Pentobarbital (Nembutal)
  Phenobarbital (Eskapen, Eskabarb, Luminal)
  Secobarbital (Seconal)
- Nonbarbiturates
  Chloral hydrate (Felsules, Rectules, Noctec)
  Ethchlorvynol (Placidyl)
  Ethinamate (Valmid)
  Flurazepam (Dalmane)
  Glutethimide (Doriden)
  Methyprylon (Noludar)
  Quazepam (Doral)
  Paraldehyde
  Zolpiden (Ambien)

◆ ANTIPARKINSONIAN AGENTS

Benztropine (Cogentin), biperiden (Akineton), procyclidine (Kemadrin), and trihexyphenidyl (Artane) are used most frequently. If one does not work well enough after a trial, the client is switched to another. More and more physicians use these agents only after dystonic effects appear, whereas others prefer to start them simultaneously with the major tranquilizer. After accommodation to the tranquilizer (6 to 8 weeks), the antiparkinsonian dose can usually be lowered or a milder agent used (Cogentin is the most powerful). Some clients remain convinced, however, that the antiparkinsonian agent is the real tranquilizer and will not be without it. The atropine-like effect of these agents adds to the similar effect of the tranquilizers and causes blurred vision and dry mouth. If the vision is not improved with dosage reduction, nonprescription reading glasses are recommended (especially for clients who must read). Hard candy is recommended for the dry mouth.

◆ ANTICONVULSANTS

Occasionally, seizures occur as a symptom with certain types of mental disorders, particularly those with mania. When they occur or are anticipated, there are two drugs of choice most often used in the psychiatric setting. They include carbamazepine (Tegretol), ordered at 200 mg intervals twice a day until symptoms are controlled. The second medication is divalproex (Depakote). The usual daily dose is 750 mg.

◆ ANTIMANIC DRUGS

LITHIUM CARBONATE

This drug (Eskalith, Lithonate, Lithane) is the treatment of choice in acute manic episodes, which it can terminate within 10 days in 90% of clients. Lithium is an essential pharmacologic agent in the treatment of bipolar disorders. A bipolar disorder can include acute episodes of psychosis during the manic phase and severe depression during the depressed phase. Often, it is necessary to use antipsychotic and antidepressant medications in conjunction with lithium.

Lithium is also used with varying success in other forms of cyclic illness, whether or not there is a manic phase. Because the effective therapeutic dosage is fairly close to the toxic dosage, it is important to monitor the lithium blood level regularly. This is done with a laboratory test called a serum lithium level.

600 to 1800 mg of lithium carbonate per day in divided doses usually produces a serum lithium level of 0.5 to 1.0 mEq/L. This is within the therapeutic range and not significantly toxic. Because lithium is excreted at far different rates in various people, a serum determination must be made frequently at the beginning to be sure the 1.5-mEq/L limit is not exceeded. In the presence of febrile illness or in any situation that causes a loss of fluids (including administration of diuretics), the lithium level must be closely watched.

Common side effects are nausea, occasional vomiting and mild abdominal pain, fatigue, and thirst. These gradually subside and later recurrence may signal impending intoxication. Intoxication generally occurs when serum levels exceed 2 mEq/L, and it produces confusion, coarse tremor, muscle twitching, and difficult speech. More severe effects include ataxia, nystagmus, hyperreflexia, stupor, and coma. Fatalities are rare.

◆ ADVERSE EFFECTS OF PSYCHOTROPIC MEDICATIONS

The most severe side effect of the major tranquilizers and tricyclic antidepressants is that the extrapyramidal tract of the central nervous system can develop mild to severe reactions to the drugs. The exact cause of this action is unknown. It is thought to be related to the medication's blockade of the dopamine-mediated response.

The extrapyramidal effects that the antiparkinsonian agents are used to treat can be produced by all the major tranquilizers in large enough doses. These drug-induced effects can be divided into four classes:

1. Dystonic effects, which occur the first day of treatment, up to 1 week

2. Akathisia, which begins during the second week of treatment

3. Pseudoparkinsonism, which appears after 3 or 4 weeks of treatment

4. Tardive dyskinesia

Dystonia manifests as muscle spasms of the head, neck, lips, and tongue and appears as torticollis (severe neck muscle spasms), retrocollis, opisthotonus (arched position of body caused by neurologic disorder), oculogyric crisis (eyeballs are fixed in upward position), trismus (lock jaw), slurred speech, dysphagia (difficult swallowing), and laryngospasm (which can be life-threatening).

Akathisia, or motor restlessness, is seen as constant pacing and inability to sit down. It may often be impossible to tell except by trial and error whether the akathisia seen is the result of anxiety, which would require more phenothiazine, or is an extrapyramidal effect, which would require less.

Pseudoparkinsonism is characterized by a masked face (immobile) and shuffling gait with pill-rolling movements of hands, coarse tremor, drooling, and waxy skin. It is also seen as weakness, diminished drive, and muscular rigidity.

Tardive dyskinesia can occur with long-term treatment with some phenothiazines, especially in women, the elderly, and those with some brain damage. It is not relieved by antiparkinsonian drugs and is a permanent irreversible side effect. It is recognized by rhythmic facial and tongue movements. The problems with this side effect must be weighed against the problems of continuing psychosis in the population at risk.

Another major side effect is due to action of the major tranquilizers and tricyclic antidepressants on the autonomic nervous system. This results in anticholinergic, atropine-like effects such as dry mouth, constipation, and urinary retention. The autonomic effects also account for the hypotensive effects.

It is especially important to be aware of the more common adverse reactions or side effects of the psychotropic chemicals. Many of these have been discussed under the individual drug headings and in chart form for easy reference. Some drugs cause a sympathetic nervous system response (either fight or flight) and a group of symptoms related to this, such as tachycardia, high blood pressure, excitement, and hypomania. Others elicit a parasympathetic nervous system response (more vegetative) with a slowed pulse, hypotension, and drowsiness. Still others bring forth allergic responses and many cause primitive nervous system responses such as tremors and pseudoparkinsonism.

Drugs within a certain group (such as the tricyclics) also vary one from another in the severity of the adverse effects they cause. Finally, the individual client's response can cause a great difference in both a drug's therapeutic effectiveness and the type and degree of adverse effect seen.

When these adverse effects are bothersome to the client the problem is often dose-related, and it diminishes when the dose is reduced. It can usually be handled satisfactorily without discontinuing medication. However, these side effects are the most common reason that clients reduce or stop their medication. The nurse can question the client about these effects, reassure him or her, suggest measures to reduce the annoyance, and recognize and report the more serious and dangerous adverse reactions.

When there is a clear choice between having a nonpsychotic client with blurred vision and a dry mouth, or a psychotic client without these symptoms, almost everyone will opt for the former. Not every choice is clear; the nurse and psychiatrist must weigh the various choices until the best possible solution is found for the particular client at the particular time.

◆ NURSING RESPONSIBILITIES

What are your duties in administering and monitoring major and minor tranquilizers and mood-elevating drugs to clients? First, be well acquainted with their actions, dosages, forms, characteristics, and complications.[1] Use great care and caution in administering these drugs; observe the client closely, both for behavioral and physical reactions; and chart these observations. Record and report failure of the drug to produce the desired effect. Immediately report sensitivity or toxic reaction. Since the physician usually adjusts the dosage to the individual's physical and emotional requirements and since each person's tolerance or reaction to these drugs is specifically his or her own, you must judge whether the dosage is achieving the desired results. The physician must rely on these observations to decide whether the dosage should be maintained, decreased, or increased.

Realize that drugs, no matter how effective, are by no means the final answer to mental health problems, in spite of the excellent response of psychotic clients to modern therapy. Drugs cannot in themselves repair personality disorders, nor can they take the place of meeting soci-

---

[1] In addition, the nurse should be aware of the legal and ethical issues of psychotropic drug administration. See Chapter 5.

ologic needs. Their major contribution is symptom removal. This will enable the client to respond to other therapies more effectively.

◆ ELECTROSHOCK THERAPY

One of the alternatives to psychopharmacology when a client does not respond to treatment for depression is **electroshock therapy** (EST). (Electroshock therapy and electroconvulsive therapy, ECT, are the same treatment.) It is reserved for specific types of mental disorders that cannot be treated by medication—most effectively in treating moderate to severe depression. Because it carries some physical risks, it should be used only when one or both of the following conditions exist:

- The client cannot physically tolerate the many toxic physiologic side effects of the tricyclic or MAOI antidepressants. This client usually has heart disease, allergies, or other types of physical disorders that would be aggravated by antidepressant medications.

- The client has not responded favorably to treatment with antidepressant medication after a time period of several weeks and continues to be moderately to severely depressed.

ADMINISTRATION OF EST

A client receiving EST is placed on a stretcher and given a brief-acting general anesthetic. Next, he or she is given a muscle relaxant such as succinylcholine (Anectine) to counteract the grand mal muscular contractions that accompany electric shock. The client is also given a high concentration of oxygen by the anesthesiologist. Next, an electric current passes between two electrodes placed on the head and the client receives a shock that results in a mild to moderate convulsive movement. The client becomes confused within 5 to 15 minutes following the treatment. The confusion usually clears within a few hours; however, amnesia about the actual EST experience will remain indefinitely.

THEORIES ABOUT THE THERAPEUTIC EFFECTS OF EST

Researchers have discovered that there are specific brain neurotransmitters that underlie man's basic emotions of rage, fear, and so on. As research has revealed more about these neurochemical actions, scientists have theorized that EST causes a chemical reaction in the brain. This reaction results in a shift of the neurochemistry of depression. It is known, for example, that a chemical solution of any kind undergoes change when an electric shock passes through it. Psychobiologic research has indicated that norepinephrine and serotonin are implicated in depression. The effects of EST on these two neurotransmitters is, however, not fully understood.

NURSING CARE OF CLIENTS RECEIVING EST

EST is usually administered in a room adjacent to the psychiatric unit. During the procedure, a psychiatrist, an anesthesiologist, and a nurse are present. In order to ensure the client's safety, oxygen and suctioning apparatus, as well as emergency resuscitative drugs, are present. If needed, they are administered by the anesthesiologist. Nursing care involves obtaining the client's signature on the informed consent form and answering any questions the client may have. If it is the client's first EST treatment and if the client is unusually anxious or has not received an adequate explanation from the psychiatrist, you should ask the doctor to revisit the client before he or she is brought to the EST room. EST can be very frightening to clients, and because it is usually repeated 3 times a week for a total of 6 to 10 treatments, you should carefully prepare the client for the first treatment so he or she will not fear the remainder.

Bring the client to the EST room in loose-fitting clothing. Remove dentures and hairpins. While the electric shock is given to the client, hold his or her arms at his or her sides to prevent uncontrolled thrashing. Following the treatment, hold his or her head to the side to prevent aspiration of saliva. Closely monitor the client's vital signs and airway while he or she is waking from the treatment. Ensure his or her safety in bed, so confusion following EST will not cause harm.

Confusion and memory loss regarding recent events are the two most common changes in mental state that result from EST. Orientation returns more rapidly than recall of recent events. The severity of these two changes often depends on the client's age and the number of treatments he or she has received. Often, the client feels frightened by these changes in mental state. Quietly reassure him or her that these are the expected effects of the EST and that they will pass in time.

CHAPTER 31 SUMMARY

- The development of medications that restore brain chemistry to near-normal levels has markedly changed the treatment of mental illness.

- The role of the nurse in administering psychoactive medications is central, and nurses should be acquainted with the actions, dosages, forms, characteristics, and complications associated with them.

- Nurses should record and report failure of the drug to produce the desired effect, any sensitivity, or a toxic reaction. Physicians rely on the nurse's observations to decide whether dosage should be maintained, decreased, or increased.

- Clients have a right to know about the side effects caused by medications. Clients also have the right to refuse to take medications.

- The following classes of psychoactive medications are prescribed for specific types of mental disorders: phenothiazines (to alleviate psychosis), antidepressants, antianxiety drugs, antiparkinsonian agents, anticonvulsant medications, and lithium carbonate (for acute manic episodes).

- Tardive dyskinesia can occur with long-term use of some phenothiazines. This condition is characterized by rhythmic facial and tongue movements. It is a permanent, irreversible side effect that is not relieved by antiparkinsonian drugs.

- Electroshock therapy (EST) may be used to treat depressed clients who do not respond to medication. In the procedure, the client's head receives an electrical shock. He or she will be anesthetized and will not remember the treatment. Nursing care for clients receiving EST includes preparing the client for the treatment and closely monitoring the client's vital signs and airway after the treatment.

CHAPTER 31 QUESTIONS

1. Which of the following statements about clients and medications is not true?
   a. Client family history of response to psychotropic drugs should be considered.
   b. Clients are required to take all medications prescribed in an inpatient setting, regardless of side effects.
   c. Medication side effects are explained when the client is released from the hospital.
   d. Most clients do not notice or remember drug side effects.

2. Which is the most dangerous side effect resulting from phenothiazines?
   a. Drowsiness
   b. Agranulocytosis
   c. Amenorrhea
   d. Decreased appetite

3. Antianxiety drugs should be limited because
   a. anxiety often provides motivation for psychotherapeutic work.

b. most clients can tolerate a moderate level of anxiety without medication.
c. these drugs have a high potential for habituation and addiction.
d. all of the above.

4. Electroshock or electroconvulsive therapy is used when
a. a client becomes totally disruptive in the inpatient setting.
b. a client is diagnosed as schizophrenic.
c. a client cannot physically tolerate certain antidepressants.
d. none of the above.

BIBLIOGRAPHY

Barry, P.D. (1996). *Psychosocial nursing: Care of physically ill patients and their families* (3rd ed.). Philadelphia: Lippincott-Raven.

Cooper, J.R., Bloom, F.E., Roth, R.H., & Roth, R.Y. (1996). *The biochemical basis of neuropharmacology* (7th ed.). New York: Oxford University Press.

Facts and comparisons (49th ed.). (1995). Philadelphia: J.B. Lippincott.

Fink, M. (1994). Indications for the use of ECT. *Psychopharmacology Bulletin, 30*(3), 269–275.

Harris, B. (1996). Psychopharmacology. In J. Haber, P. Price-Hoskins, A. Leach McMahon, & B. Sideleau (Eds.). *Comprehensive psychiatric nursing* (5th ed.). St. Louis: Mosby Year Book.

Kaplan, H.I., & Sadock, B.J. (1995). *Comprehensive textbook of psychiatry/VI* (6th ed.). Baltimore: Williams & Wilkins.

Karch, A.M. (1997). *Lippincott's nursing drug guide*. Philadelphia: Lippincott-Raven.

Lego, S. (1996). *Psychiatric nursing: A comprehensive reference* (2nd ed.). Philadelphia: Lippincott-Raven.

Linden, M. (1994). Therapeutic standards in psychopharmacology and medical decision-making. *Pharmacopsychiatry, 27*(Suppl 1), 41–45.

McFarland, G.K., Wasli, E.L., & Gerety, E.K. (1996). *Nursing diagnoses and process in psychiatric mental health nursing* (3rd ed.). Philadelphia: Lippincott-Raven.

McKenney, L., & Salerno, E. (Eds.). (1997). *Mosby's pharmacology in nursing* (20th ed.). St. Louis: Mosby Year Book.

Nettina, S.M. (1996). *The Lippincott manual of nursing practice* (6th ed.). Philadelphia: Lippincott-Raven.

Physician's Desk Reference. (1996). Montvale, NJ: Medical Economics Company.

Stoudemire, A. (1995). Expanding psychopharmacologic treatment options for the depressed medical patient. *Psychosomatics, 36*(2), S19–S26.

UNIT SEVEN Case Study

Interventions and Treatment of Mental Disorders

Henry is a 59-year-old married man who has had a long-standing alcohol disorder. He was laid off from his construction job 3 years ago because of his poor attendance, fighting with co-workers, and poor attitude toward his supervisors. He has consistently refused to go into treatment. His wife, Susan, is a long-suffering person who makes excuses for him, buffers his difficult personality with their adult children, and works two jobs to meet family expenses. His children, while teenagers, encouraged their father to enter alcohol treatment. During their 20s, they actively encouraged their mother to leave the marriage, which she refused to do. One week ago Henry was driving while intoxicated; he struck and killed a pedestrian.

DISCUSSION QUESTIONS

1. As a result of the accident, this family is in crisis. The children are disgusted with their father. If you were a child in this family, how would you feel toward your father? Toward your mother?

2. Susan is in a state of exhaustion and shock. Using the list of crisis potential factors in the Sequence of Developments Following a Critical Event in Chapter 28, examine the current mental state, based on each of the factors, that Susan may be experiencing at this time.

3. If Susan continues to cope ineffectively with this crisis event, for what types of mental disorder described in Chapters 20 through 27 would she be at risk? Why?

4. When Susan recovered from the acute effects of this crisis, with what types of activities could she be encouraged to become involved?

5. What would be the advantages of Susan attending a self-help type of group?

6. If Susan were to become involved in Al-Anon or a codependents type of self-help group, how could her attitude toward her husband's alcohol disorder be altered?

7. What are the potential outcomes or results for Susan, Henry, and their marriage if her attitude toward his condition is changed?

ANSWERS TO MULTIPLE CHOICE QUESTIONS

Chapter 1
1. d
2. a
3. c
4. d
5. e

Chapter 2
1. c
2. d
3. a
4. c

Chapter 3
1. b
2. d
3. c
4. a

Chapter 4
1. c
2. a
3. b
4. d

Chapter 5
1. d
2. c
3. d
4. d

Chapter 6
1. c
2. b
3. c
4. d

Chapter 7
1. c
2. d
3. c
4. b

Chapter 8
1. d
2. b
3. a
4. c

Chapter 9
1. b
2. c
3. c
4. d

Chapter 10
1. b
2. d
3. a
4. a

Chapter 11
1. a
2. d
3. c
4. b

Chapter 12
1. b
2. d
3. c
4. a

Chapter 13
1. b
2. c
3. b
4. a

Chapter 14
1. d
2. b
3. d
4. c

Chapter 15
1. c
2. c
3. b
4. a

Chapter 16
1. c
2. b
3. d
4. b

Chapter 17
1. d
2. a
3. b
4. d

Chapter 18
1. a
2. d
3. d
4. c

Chapter 19
1. b
2. b
3. d
4. c

Chapter 20
1. c
2. d
3. a
4. b

Chapter 21
1. b
2. d
3. d
4. c

Chapter 22
1. d
2. c
3. b
4. d

Chapter 23
1. d
2. c
3. d
4. b

Chapter 24
1. c
2. d
3. a
4. d

Chapter 25
1. b
2. b
3. d
4. a

Chapter 26
1. c
2. d
3. c
4. b

Chapter 27
1. d
2. b
3. a
4. c

Chapter 28
1. b
2. d
3. b
4. c

Chapter 29
1. b
2. d
3. d
4. a

Chapter 30
1. c
2. d
3. b
4. a

Chapter 31
1. b
2. b
3. d
4. c

Glossary

acting out See *defense, mechanisms, immature.*

adaptation The process by which the ego uses unconscious coping strategies to adjust in a healthy manner to the stresses of life.

adjustment disorder A mental disorder in which a person is unable to resolve a crisis that occurred at least 3 months previously.

affect The mood or emotion an individual feels in repsonse to a given situation or thought. Affect may be described, according to its expression, as blunted, blocked, flat, inappropriate, or displaced.

aggression Excessive rage, anger, or hostility that is seemingly unrelated to a person's current situation.

agoraphobia A mental condition that manifests itself in excessive fear of open spaces.

akathisia Extreme restlessness.

akinesia The complete or partial loss of muscle movement.

altruism See *defense mechanisms, mature.*

ambivalence The coexistence of two opposing feelings toward another person, object, or idea. (For example, feelings of love and hate, pleasure and pain, or liking and disliking may exist simultaneously.)

amnesia Complete or partial inability to recall past experiences.

anorexia nervosa An eating disorder that occurs primarily in young females and in which there is a strong fear of becoming obese.

anticipation See *defense mechanisms, mature.*

anxiety Apprehension, tension, or uneasiness due to an unknown cause. Primarily of intrapsychic origin, unlike fear, which is the emotional response to a consciously recognized and usually external threat or danger. Anxiety and fear are accompanied by physiologic changes. Anxiety is pathologic when present to such an extent that it interferes with effectiveness in living, achievement of desired goals or satisfactions, or reasonable emotional comfort.

anxiety disorder A general category of mental disorder found in DSM-IV that is characterized by an excessively uneasy and tense mental state with no explainable cause. Includes the following major categories: panic disorders, specific and social phobias, obsessive-compulsive disorders, stress disorders, and posttraumatic stress disorders.

separation anxiety disorder of childhood A mental disorder that develops during early childhood or adolescence, characterized by developmentally inappropriate and excessive anxiety concerning separation from home or from major attachment figures. (See Index.)

aphasia Partial or complete loss of the power of expression or the ability to understand either written or spoken language. The cause may be functional, organic, or both.

apraxia The inability to carry out purposeful movement to achieve a goal.

assessment See *nursing process.*

attention-deficit/hyperactivity disorder A disorder diagnosed in childhood whose symptoms include fidgeting, distractbility, and difficulty sustaining attention.

autism A mental state in which a person seems unaware of external reality; primarily seen in schizophrenia or as a pervasive developmental disorder.

avoidance See *defense mechanisms, immature.*

awareness See *level of awareness.*

behavior The visible or observable signs of a person's psychological response to his or her internal and external environments.

behavior modification Changing a person's behavior by rewarding positive behavior and ignoring negative behavior. Also known as *behavioral psychology.*

biological psychiatry The use of biological means to treat mental disorders.

bipolar disorders A type of mood disorder characterized by strong, exaggerated, and cyclic mood swings.

blunted (or flat) affect Lack of a normal range of emotions.

boundary Within a family, the rules that keep the role of one family member separate from another.

bulimia An eating disorder seen primarily in adolescent or young adult females. It involves eating binges of high-calorie food.

catastrophic reaction Occurs when there is a sudden, unexpected stressor and the person's normal coping mechanisms fail.

catatonic A certain type of schizophrenia in which a person appears to be in a stupor. Rigid posture is also common. In addition, the person may be mute and unable to speak.

circumstantiality A speaking and thinking style in which the person frequently switches topics but eventually reaches a conclusion.

claustrophobia Fear of being in an enclosed space.

closed family A family in which rigidity allows for little change in family roles and patterns.

cognitive disorder A mental disorder characterized by a decrease in the intellectual aspect of mental functioning, including awareness, ability to focus, memory, orientation, and language. Dementia (including vascular dementia and dementia of the Alzheimer's type), delirium, and amnestic disorders are included in this category.

compensation See *defense mechanisms, neurotic.*

competency In law, the mental status of a person who is capable of sound decision making and management of his or her own life circumstances.

compulsion An act that a person finds himself or herself forced to do (generally against his or her wishes) in order to reduce anxiety. See also *obsession.*

conduct disorder A mental disorder of infancy, childhood, and adolescence in which a person violates the rights of others through aggression towards people and animals, destruction of property, deceitfulness or theft, and serious rule violations such as running away or truancy. Oppositional defiant disorder is also included in this category. (See Index.)

confidentiality The client's right not to have information revealed publicly without his or her consent.

consent A legal term for the agreement by a person to an act that will affect his or her body, or to disclose about himself or herself.

consent, informed In law, the agreement by a competent person who has been given the information necessary to weigh the advantages and disadvantages of what is being proposed.

consent, presumed In law, the type of agreement that occurs when an unconscious person is given life-saving treatment in a life-threatening situation.

consent, vicarious In law, the agreement given when a person is incapable of making decisions for himself or herself. Instead, parents, guardians, or conservators make the decision.

constricted personality A personality that is tightly controlled.

conversion An ego defense by which emotional conflicts are channeled into physical illness.

coping The way a person's psychological or intrapsychic system responds to external or internal awarenesses that are threatening.

covert Implies secrecy, or hidden reasons for conscious actions or behavior.

crisis An event or situation that triggers a deteriorating capacity for mental functioning. The result is that the person temporarily loses the capacity to help himself or herself.

crisis intervention therapy A type of brief psychiatric treatment in which individuals (and/or families) are assisted in their efforts to cope and to solve problems in crisis situations. The treatment approach is immediate, supportive, and direct.

cyclothymic Describes a person who has high and low mood swings that are not as pronounced as those experienced by a person with bipolar disorder.

decompensation The failure of the ego to use defense mechanisms.

defense mechanisms A mental maneuver performed by the ego to decrease the unpleasant feeling of anxiety. As the ego matures, it uses increasingly mature levels of defense mechanisms.

The levels, starting with the most basic, are: 1) narcissistic, 2) immature, 3) neurotic, and 4) mature.

1. *narcissistic defense mechanisms.* The most basic of the defense mechanisms used by the ego. They develop during the first year and are used during childhood. In addition, they are used by healthy individuals under moderate to severe stress and routinely by individuals with severe forms of certain types of personality disorders.

    a. *denial.* The first defense used in infancy, it remains the strongest defense we have to shut out painful awareness in the environment.

   b. *delusional projection.* The ego forms conclusions and beliefs that are not based on reality.

   c. *distortion.* The ego reshapes external reality to reduce anxiety and restore a feeling of emotional comfort.

2. *immature defense mechanisms.* Second level of defense mechanisms, developed during the toddler state.

   a. *acting out.* The result of conflict caused by anxiety that the person cannot tolerate. He or she impulsively acts out the conflict.

   b. *avoidance.* The ego causes a person to unconsciously stay away from any person, situation, or place that might cause unwanted sexual or aggressive feelings.

   c. *hypochondriasis.* The ego magnifies generally mild, vague physical symptoms into more severe symptoms of potentially serious illnesses.

   d. *projection.* A less pathologic form of delusional projection (defined above).

   e. *regression.* The ego is unable to tolerate severe intrapsychic or environmental stress, resulting in a behavioral retreat to an earlier stage of development.

3. *neurotic defense mechanisms.* The third level of defense mechanisms frequently used by all persons who are psychologically "healthy."

   a. *displacement.* The ego shifts unacceptable feelings about a person or thing to another object.

   b. *identification.* The ego causes a person to take on the thoughts, feelings, or particular circumstances of another person as if they were his or her own.

   c. *isolation.* The ego separates emotion from a thought. Also known as intellectualization or rationalization.

   d. *reaction formation.* A defense used by the ego when a thought, feeling, or impulse is unacceptable. Also called *compensation*.

   e. *represssion.* Considered one of the most important defense mechanisms, the ego causes anxiety associated with distressing internal awareness to be stored away in the unconscious.

4. *mature defense mechanisms.* The highest or fourth level of defense mechanisms used by the healthy, mature ego when it is under minimal stress.

   a. *altruism.* The ego channels the desire to satisfy one's own needs into meeting the needs of others.

   b. *anticipation.* The ego acknowledges, both intellectually and emotionally, an upcoming, anxiety-provoking situation.

   c. *humor.* A defense used by the ego when it cannot fully tolerate a difficult situation.

   d. *sublimation.* An ego defense in which unacceptable thoughts or feelings are channeled into more acceptable outlets.

   e. *suppression.* Differs from repression in that memories, thoughts, or feelings are quickly retrieved from the subconscious or preconscious rather than being deeply buried in the unconscious.

déjà vu A feeling that one has experienced a new situation on a previous occasion. (French for "already seen").

deinstitutionalization The act of transferring formerly institutionalized individuals from the hospital environment to the community environment.

delirium An acute organic brain syndrome that usually is reversible.

delusion A false belief or opinion that is unreasonable and causes distortion in judgment.

delusional projection See *defense mechanisms, narcissistic.*

dementia Chronic organic brain syndrome that usually is irreversible.

denial See *defense mechanisms, narcissistic.*

depersonalization A mental state in which a person experiences periods of unreality about who he or she is or about various aspects of his or her body.

depression A hopeless feeling of sadness, grief, or mourning associated with a loss. See also *depressive episode,* below.

depressive episode, major A mood disorder in which five of the following symptoms are present: depressed mood, diminished interest or pleasure in life, significant weight loss, insomnia or hypersomnia, psychomotor agitation or retardation, fatigue, feelings of worthlessness or excessive guilt, diminished ability to concentrate, and recurrent thoughts of death.

derealization A neutral state that can range from a mild sense of unreality to a frank loss of reality about one's environment.

disintegration The disruption of the normal influence of the ego on combining thoughts, feelings, memories, and perceptions into a realistic view of self and environment.

displacement See *defense mechanisms, neurotic.*

dissociative disorder A mental disorder in which a person experiences a sudden loss of self-identity and takes on the identity of another. It includes the following categories: dissociative amnesia, dissociative fugue, dissociative identity disorder, depersonalization disorder, and dissociative disorder not otherwise specified. (See Index.)

distortion See *defense mechanisms, narcissistic.*

double-bind A type of interaction, generally associated with schizophrenic families, in which one individual demands a response to a message containing mutually contradictory signals while the other is unable to respond or comment on the inconsistent and incongruous message. Best characterized by the "damned if you do, damned if you don't" situation.

dyad Refers to the relationship between two people; dyadic pair can be husband and wife, parent and child, sibling and sibling.

dynamic A constantly operating force within a system, such as a person's psyche, that results in some type of action or observable result.

dyskinesia Excessive movement of mouth accompanied by protruding tongue. Seen most often in tardive dyskinisia—a permanent negative side effect of phenothiazines.

dysphoria Unpleasant emotion that causes psychological distress or conflict.

dystonia Severely impaired muscle tone.

eating disorder A mental disorder that includes major disturbances in eating behavior. The category includes anorexia nervosa and bulimia. Eating and feeding disorders usually diagnosed in infancy or childhood include pica and rumination disorder. (See Index.)

echolalia The pathologic repetition or imitation of another's speech. Seen in some forms of schizophrenia.

echopraxia The pathologic repetition or imitation of another's movements. Seen in some forms of schizophrenia.

ego That part of the personality, according to Freudian theory, that mediates between the primitive, pleasure-seeking instinctual drives of the id and the self-critical, prohibitive, restraining forces of the superego. The compromises worked out on an unconscious level help to resolve intrapsychic conflict by keeping thoughts, interpretations, judgments, and behavior practical and efficient. The ego is directed by the reality principle, meaning it is in contact with the real world as well as the id and superego. The ego develops as the individual grows. See also *superego, id.*

egocentricity Describes a person's attitude and inner feeling that the world exists to meet his or her needs.

ego ideal A high standard within the ego that motivates the individual to continued growth and self-actualization.

ego-dystonic Describes thoughts, perceptions, or actions that are unacceptable and conflict producing within the ego.

ego-syntonic Describes thoughts, perceptions, or actions that are acceptable to the ego.

electroshock therapy (EST) A method of treatment in which an electric current is passed through the brain causing a grand-mal seizure. Useful in treating certain types of depression. Also known as electroconvulsive therapy (ECT).

empathy The ability to "feel with" another person while retaining one's own sense of objectivity.

encopresis A disorder in which feces are passed in socially inappropriate places.

eneuresis Involuntary voiding by a child beyond an age that is socially acceptable.

ethics The knowledge of the principles of good and evil.

euphoria An excessive and inappropriate feeling of well-being.

exaltation Intense elation accompanied by feelings of grandeur.

exhibitionism A sexual disorder in which a person (usually male) obtains sexual pleasure in displaying the genitals in a public setting.

explosive disorder An impluse-control disorder that results in episodes of severe violence, rage, or destruction as the result of a stressor that would not be responded to in a similar manner by normal persons.

extended family All family members other than mother, father, and siblings.

extinction The process of eliminating particular types of behavior due to a lack of response to that behavior by persons in the environment.

extrapyramidal reaction Refers to side effects of some major psychotropic drugs on the extrapyramidal system of the central nervous system. Characterized by a variety of physical signs and symptoms (similar to those seen in patients with Parkinson's disease) that include muscular rigidity, tremors, drooling, restlessness, shuffling gait, blurred vision, and other neurologic disturbances.

facies Facial expressions.

factitious disorder A mental disorder in which the person consciously pretends to have symptoms of a physical or mental disorder.

family of origin See *nuclear family.*

family rules Unwritten expectations about what types of roles or behavior will be acceptable or unacceptable to the family.

family therapy Psychotherapeutic treatment of more than one member of a family. The treatment may be supportive, directive, or interpretive.

fear Excessive fright of consciously recognized danger.

fetishism A sexual disorder in which a person derives abnormal sexual pleasure from an object or a body part.

functional Refers to mental disorders (disorders of functioning) in which no physical or organic cause in known.

general adaptation syndrome (GAS) Hans Selye's description of the physiologic response to stress.

gestalt psychology The study of mental process and behavior with emphasis on a total perceptual configuration and the interrelation of component parts. Generally refers to the "whole person" approach to assessment and treatment of psychiatric clients.

grandiosity An objective experience in which the person feels that he or she is very important and holds great power.

group therapy Application by one or more therapists of psychotherapeutic techniques to a group of individuals who may have similar problems and are in reasonably good contact with reality. The optimal size of a group is six to ten members. As a therapy procedure, it is popular because it is a versatile, economical, and, for certain individuals, successful modality.

habeas corpus Writ requiring an immediate court hearing to determine a person's sanity.

hallucination An imagined sensory perception that occurs without an external stimulus; can be auditory, visual, or tactile; usually occurs in psychotic disorders, but can occur in both chronic and acute organic brain disorders.

heterosexuality Sexual interest and behavior toward persons of the opposite sex.

holistic Approach geared to the whole person. See *gestalt psychology.*

homeostasis A term borrowed from physiology; the self-regulating intrapsychic processes that are optimal for comfort and survival.

homosexuality Sexual preference, attraction, and relationship between two people of the same sex.

homosexuality, ego-dystonic type A condition in which a person who is sexually aroused by persons of the same sex experiences psychological distress as the result of his or her sexual preference.

humor See *defense mechanisms, mature.*

hyperchondriasis A mental condition in which the angry feelings that a person cannot express toward another are transferred into physical symptoms.

hypochondriasis See *defense mechanisms, immature.*

id In Freudian theory, the id is identified as the storage place of psychic energy. It is guided by the pleasure principle, curbed by the ego, and is unconscious. (See *ego, superego.*)

identification See *defense mechanisms, neurotic.*
illusion A misinterpreted sensory impression, usually auditory or visual; or false interpretation of an actual stimulus.
impotence Condition in which there is sexual desire but the physiologic response is lacking or dimished.
impulse-control disorder A mental disorder in which a person is unable to control urges related primarily to his or her aggressive drive. The categories include pathologic gambling, kleptomania, pyromania, intermittent explosive disorder, trichotillomania, and impulse-control disorder not otherwise specified. (See Index.)
insight The ability of an individual to understand himself or herself and the basis for his or her attitudes and behavior.
insomnia A disturbance in a person's normal sleeping pattern.
instructional group A group in which persons learn and discuss new knowledge about a particular topic.
intellectualization Another name for isolation. See also *defense mechanisms.*
intimacy The capacity to trust another within a deep and committed relationship.
intrapsychic Refers to all that takes place within the mind (psyche).
isolation See *defense mechanisms, neurotic.*

judgment The ability of a person to behave in a socially appropriate manner.

kleptomania A condition in which a person spontaneously takes objects with no specific need for them.

la belle indifference A lack of concern in a situation that would cause worry in a normal individual.
lability Alternating periods of elation and depression; also known as mood swings.
latent Adjective used to describe feelings, drives, and emotions that influence behavior but remain repressed, outside of conscious thought.
lenticular pigmentation A condition in which the normally clear lens in the eye becomes colored.
learning disorder Disorders of childhood, in which achievement in comprehension, ability, or accuracy is substantially below that expected for the person's age, measured intelligence, and age-appropriate education. Categories include reading disorder, mathematics disorder, and disorder of written expression.
level of awareness A description of the client's wakefulness or consciousness.
liaison psychiatry A field that addresses the emotional stress of illness on the psyche.

major affective disorder A serious mental disorder marked by a severe disturbance in emotional state.
maladaptation An unhealthy outcome of an attempt by the ego to adapt to the stresses of life. The result is a decreased quality of life. See *adaptation.*

malingering A condition in which a person pretends to be physically ill.

manic episode A distinct period of abnormally and persistently elevated mood, characterized by extreme excitement, restlessness, talkativeness, inflated self-esteem, and decreased need for sleep. The manic phase of bipolar I disorder.

masochism A sexual disorder in which pleasure is obtained by having mental or physical pain inflicted by the sexual partner.

memory The ability of a person to recall past events, both recent and remote.

mental mechanism See *defense mechanisms.*

milieu The immediate environment of persons, objects, and general surroundings.

mood The internal feelings that a person experiences in response to a situation or thought.

motivation Describes the individual's will and determination to persevere and succeed.

mutism A condition in which a person is unable to communicate verbally.

narcissistic Describes an extreme form of self-love in adults. This form of self-love is normal, however, in toddlers and young children.

narcissistic defense mechanism The most basic level of defense mechanisms used by the ego. It is commonly used by normal children under 5 years of age, normal adults when under moderate to severe stress, and persons with certain types of personality disorders.

neologism A word that is invented or made up by condensing other words into a new one. Typical in schizophrenia.

neurotransmitter A biochemical substance (also known as catecholamine) that sends messages within the brain and from the central nervous system to the body.

norms The expectation that a society places on persons to behave in ways that it considers to be normal.

nosology The scientific classification of diseases.

nuclear family The immediate family into which a child is born.

nursing process The manner in which nursing care ideally occurs. It consists of the following four steps:

> *assessing.* First step in nursing process; gathering data to aid in developing a care plan for the client.

> *planning.* The second stage of the nursing process; the problem-solving process results in a nursing care plan.

> *implementing.* Putting the nursing care plan into practice.

> *evaluating.* The final step of the nursing process; observing and determining the outcome of nursing care.

nystagmus A condition in which there is constant movement of the eyeball.

obsession A persistent, recurring thought or urge occurring more or less against the person's wishes. Often leads to compulsive acts. See *compulsion.*

obsessive-compulsive personality disorder Person demonstrates constricted range of emotions, ceaselessly strives for perfection, overly attends to trivial details, and is unable to carry through the decision-making process to form a conclusion.

obsessive-compulsive disorder Repetitive, recurring thoughts accompanied by stereotyped act person feels compelled to perform to neutralize the thoughts.

oculogyric crisis A condition in which the eyeballs are fixed in an upward position.

open family A family in which members, especially parents, have developed as healthy, active members of society. Communications within the family are honest and not avoided.

operant conditioning Conditioning or influencing behavior by rewarding a person for positive forms of behavior.

opisthotonos An arched position of the body caused by severe neurologic disorder.

organic Refers to disorders in which a physical, chemical, or structural cause is discernible.

organic brain syndrome (OBS) Organic mental disorder. Mental status disorder caused by physiologic or anatomic changes in the brain.

overt Open, conscious and unhidden actions, behavior, and emotions.

panic disorders Cause symptoms of overwhelming anxiety that can include dizziness or feelings of faintness, difficult breathing, choking or smothering feelings, chest pain, palpitations, sweating, hot and cold flashes, tingling of the hands and feet, and trembling.

paranoid Used as an adjective to describe unwarranted suspiciousness and distrust of others. See also *schizophrenia* and *personality disorder*.

paraphilia Sexual perversion; any type of abnormal sex act that results in orgasm. It includes fetishism, transvestic fetishism, pedophilia, frotteurism, exhibitionism, voyeurism, sexual masochism, and sexual sadism. (See Index.)

parkinsonian movement A fine tremor accompanied by muscular rigidity.

pedophilia A sexual disorder in which a child is the sexual choice of an adult.

perception The way a person experiences his or her environment; includes his or her frame of reference about himself or herself.

personality The characteristic way in which a person behaves. It is the deeply ingrained pattern of behavior that each person evolves, both consciously and unconsciously, as his or her style of life or way of being.

personality disorder A mental disorder in which the ego overuses certain types of defense mechanisms that result in a variety of exaggerated personality or character traits. The category includes paranoid, schizoid, schizotypal, histrionic, narcissistic, antisocial, borderline, avoidant, dependent, and obsessive-compulsive personality disorders. (See Index.)

phenothiazines The major group of psychotropic drugs used in the treatment of mental illness, chiefly the psychoses. Their chemical action is on the central nervous system.

phobia An irrational, persistent, obsessive, intense fear of an object or situation that results in increased anxiety and tension and that interferes with the individual's normal functioning. May be specific (related to a particular object or situation) or social (fear of social or performance situations).

pleasure principle The concept that humans instinctually seek to avoid pain and discomfort and strive for gratification and pleasure.

positive reinforcement Occurs when a person's behavior results in a positive response from others.

posttraumatic stress disorder See *anxiety disorders.*

precipitating event The situation or event that causes a client to go into crisis.

preoccupation of thought A thought process in which a person connects all experiences to a central thought, usually one with strong emotional overtones.

projection See *defense mechanisms, immature.*

pseudoparkinsonism A condition that mimics the symptoms of Parkinson's disease.

psyche A term that refers to the mind. It is made up of the id, ego, and superego.

psychoanalysis A form of psychotherapy developed by Freud, based on his theories of personality development and disorder, generally requiring basic commitments from the client (analysand) to the therapist (analyst) regarding time, money, and procedure. The technique of psychoanalysis involves an examination of the thoughts of a client and the interpretation of his or her dreams, emotions, and behavior. Its focus is mainly on the way the ego handles the id tensions. In psychoanalysis, success is measured by the degree of insight the client is able to gain into the unconscious motivations of his or her behavior.

psychodrama A form of group psychotherapy in which clients dramatize their emotional problems. By assuming roles in order to act out their conflicts, they reveal repressed feelings that have been disturbing to them.

psychogenic Implies that the causative factors of a symptom or illness are due to mental rather than organic factors.

psychopathology Disease of the mind.

psychosexual disorder See *sexual disorder.*

psychosis A major mental disorder characterized by any of the following symptoms: loss of contact with reality, bizarre thinking and behavior, delusions, hallucinations, regression, disorientation. Intrapsychically, it results from the unconscious becoming conscious and taking over control of the individual. In psychosis, the ego is overwhelmed by the id and the superego.

psychosocial A term that describes the interrelationship between a person's psyche and his or her social system.

psychotherapy The treatment of mental disorders or a psychosomatic condition by psychological methods using a variety of approaches including psychoanalysis, group therapy, family therapy, psychodrama, hypnotism, simple counseling, suggestion.

psychotic Adjective describing a person experiencing psychosis.

pyromania A condition in which a person sets fires for no specific reason.

rationalization (Also known as isolation or intellectualization.) See *defense mechanisms, neurotic.*

reaction formation See *defense mechanisms, neurotic.*

reality The way things actually are.

reality-oriented therapy Refers to any therapeutic approach that focuses on helping the client to define his or her reality, to improve his or her ability to adjust, and to function productively and satisfactorily within his or her real situation.

regression See *defense mechanisms, immature.*

reinforcement An action that increases the likelihood of changing a person's behavior. It is used in behavior modification therapy.

repression See *defense mechanisms, neurotic.*

respite care Extended family or community resources that can be called on to provide care for the ill individual in the home, to support rest and recovery for the primary caregiver.

sadism A sexual disorder in which sexual pleasure is obtained by inflicting mental or physical pain on the sexual partner.

schizophrenia A severe mental disorder accompanied by psychosis. It includes hallucinations, delusions, and disturbed mood. The categories of schizophrenia all share the preceding symptoms. Each category, however, has a unique symptom that is described as follows:

1. *disorganized type.* Inappropriate, usually silly, emotion.
2. *catatonic type.* A mute, negative, immobile stupor.
3. *paranoid type.* Extreme, delusional suspiciousness.
4. *undifferentiated type.* Mixed untypical symptoms.
5. *residual type.* Chronic symptoms of schizophrenia described above but not severe enough to require hospitalization.

schizophrenogenic An adjective used to describe the object or situation that is believed to be causative in the development of schizophrenia.

sexual dysfunction A disorder in which sexual arousal is negatively affected by some physical or emotional cause.

sexuality Those aspects of the personality determined by a person's view of his or her sexual functioning, body image, and relatedness with other persons of the same or opposite sex.

socialization A developmental process during which the young child gains acceptance from his or her parents and other authority figures by conforming to their rules.

somatoform disorder A mental condition that results in physiologic symptoms through an unconscious process. It includes the following categories: somatization disorder, undifferentiated somatoform disorder, conversion disorder, pain disorder, hypochondriasis, and body dysmorphic disorder. (See Index.)

stereotypic movement disorder A mental disorder characterized by repetitive, seemingly driven, and nonfunctional motor behavior such as waving, rocking, or head banging.

stimulus An action or awareness that results in a response in a person.

stress The internal feeling of tension that is a response to a stressor.

stressor A threatening environmental event.

stuttering A condition marked by disruption of a normal flow of speech.

sublimation See *defense mechanisms, mature*.

substance-related disorder A mental disorder in which a person has a maladaptive pattern of substance (drug, alcohol, or both) use that leads to clinically significant impairment or distress. Substance-related disorders are further categorized into substance dependence and substance abuse. With *substance dependence*, the person is physiologically dependent on the drug, taking larger amounts over a longer period than was intended and spending a significant amount of time in activities necessary to obtain the substance. Withdrawal from the drug would result in a toxic physiologic action. Generally, it is a more severe form of drug use disorder than is substance abuse. With *substance abuse*, the person is unable to decrease use, experiences physical or mental complications because of the substance use, and experiences impairment of social functioning. Generally, a less severe form of substance-related disorder than substance dependence.

subsystem A concrete or abstract entity that belongs to a larger system and relates in specific ways with all parts of a larger system.

sundowning A decrease in orientation at night; caused by organic brain syndrome.

superego The third part of the Freudian personality theory; it guides and restrains, criticizes and punishes just as the parents did when the individual was a child. It is unconscious, and it is learned. Like the id, the superego also wants its own way. It is sometimes referred to as the conscience. See *ego, id*.

supersystem A large complex made up of many sytems, for example, a state department of mental health, made up of many hospitals and many different types of personnel.

support group A group in which persons with similar concerns explore thoughts and feelings related to these concerns.

suppression See *defense mechanisms, mature*.

sympathy The taking on of the feelings and circumstances of other people. The helper loses his or her own separate identity.

synergism The combined result of separate entities that together have a greater effect than the sum of their individual actions.

system An assemblage or combination of parts (subsystems) that form a complex or unified whole.

tangentiality A symptom of thought disorder in which the person switches topics frequently and fails to complete discussion of any of them.

tardive dyskinesia See *dyskinesia*.

therapeutic Any form of treatment or relationship in which the actions, techniques, and practices are purposefully planned and directed toward goals that offer a beneficial effect to the client.

thought disorder A mental status that is the result of a disturbance in normal thinking. It is usually seen in schizophrenia and is evidenced by behavior or spoken words that are confused and irrational.

tic disorders Characterized by sudden, rapid, recurrent, nonrhythmic stereotyped motor movement or vocalization. Includes Tourette's disorder.

torticollis Severe spasm of the neck muscles on the side of the neck.

transactional analysis A psychodynamic approach that attempts to understand the interplay between individuals in terms of the roles they have been assigned, have assumed, or play in their transactions with others.

unconscious The storage place of those mental processes of which the individual is unaware. The repressed feelings and their energy are stored in the unconscious, and they directly influence the individual's behavior.

value An affective disposition or deeply held belief about a person, object, or idea.

voyeurism A sexual disorder in which sexual pleasure is obtained by observing other people undress or engage in sexual activity.

waxy flexibility A pathologic condition in which the body maintains the position in which it is placed. Seen in some forms of schizophrenia.

word salad A jumbled mixture of words and phrases that have no meaning and are illogical in their sequence. Seen most often in schizophrenia. (For example, "Backter dyce tonked up snorfel blend.")

Barry Psychosocial Assessment

This comprehensive assessment tool uses Gordon's functional health patterns to facilitate the data-gathering process and promote the identification of corresponding nursing diagnoses.

The assessment categories include the following patterns:
• Health perception–health management
• Nutritional-metabolic
• Elimination
• Activity-exercise
• Sleep-rest
• Cognitive-perceptual
• Self-perception–self-concept
• Role-relationship
• Sexuality-reproductive
• Coping–stress tolerance
• Value-belief

These categories help the nurse focus on specific aspects of assessment and identify problem areas. Problem areas are identified through a focused assessment.

Assess all boxed questions subjectively, rather than asked of the client directly. Bold italic statements advise the nurse how to proceed.

Admitting Information

Name _____ Age _____ Date of admission _____

Marital status   S___   M___   W___   D___   How long? _____

Occupation _____ Years of education completed _____

Date of assessment _____ Admitting diagnosis _____

HEALTH PERCEPTION–HEALTH MANAGEMENT

Patient's Perception of Illness

What was the original problem that caused you to come to the hospital? _____

_____

On what date did you first become ill? _____

What caused this illness? _____

How do you feel about being in a hospital? _____

_____

How can the physician's and nurses help you most? _____

_____

How will this illness affect you when your are out of the hospital? _____

_____

Do you think it will cause any changes in your life? _____

How will it affect your family? _____

Barry Psychosocial Assessment (*continued*)

Potential for noncompliance?   Yes _____   No _____   Possible _____

Related to: _____ Anxiety
            _____ Negative side effects
                  of prescribed treatment

_____ Unsatisfactory relationship
      with care-giving environ-
      ment or care-givers

_____ Other

Explain:

Potential for injury?   Yes _____   No _____   Possible _____

Explain:

NUTRITIONAL-METABOLIC

How does your current appetite compare with your normal appetite?

Same _____   Increased _____   Decreased _____

How long has it been different? _____

How your weight fluctuated by more than 5 lb in the last several weeks?

Yes _____   No _____   How many pounds? _____

What is you normal fluid intake per day? ml* _____   Your current intake? ml _____

Nurse can substitute estimate of milliliters for client's reported fluid intake.

Aspects of client's illness or condition that could contribute to organic mental disorder?

No _____   Yes _____

Delirium type _____   Dementia type _____

Possible cause:

_____ Metabolic
_____ Electrolytes
_____ Other metabolic or endocrine
      condition
_____ Arterial disease
_____ Mechanical disease
_____ Electrical disorder

_____ Infectious disease
_____ Neoplastic disease
_____ Nutritional disease
_____ Degenerative (chronic) brain
      disease
_____ Drug toxicity

ELIMINATION

What is your current pattern of bowel movements?

Constipated _____ Diarrhea _____ Incontinent _____

How does this compare to normal?

Same _____ Different _____

Explain:

What is your current pattern of urination? _____

How does this compare to normal?

Same _____ Different _____

Explain:

Possibility that emotional distress may be contributing to any change?

High _____ Moderate _____ Low _____

ACTIVITY-EXERCISE

What is your normal energy level?

High _____ Moderate _____ Low _____

Has it changed in the past 6 months? Yes _____ No _____

To what do you attribute the cause?_____

_____

How would you describe your normal activity level?

High _____ Moderate _____ Low _____

How may it change following this hospitalization?_____

What types of activities do you normally pursue outside the home?_____

What recreational activities do you enjoy?_____

Do you anticipate your ability to manage your home will be changed following

your hospitalization?_____

Explain:

Barry Psychosocial Assessment (*continued*)

Current self-care deficits?
Feeding _____   Bathing _____   Dressing _____   Toileting _____
Anticipated deficits following hospitalization? _____
Current impairment in mobility? _____
Anticipated immobility following hospitalization? _____
Alterations in the following?
Airway clearance   How? _____
Breathing patterns   How? _____
Cardiac output   How? _____
Respiratory function   How? _____
Potential for altered tissue perfusion as manifested by altered
cognitive-perceptual patterns?

SLEEP-REST
Normal sleeping pattern
How many hours do you normally sleep per night?
From what hour to what hour? _____ to _____
Changes in normal sleeping pattern
Do you have difficulty falling asleep? _____
Do you awaken in the middle of night? _____
Do you awaken early in the morning? _____
Are you sleeping more or fewer hours than normal? _____   How many? _____

COGNITIVE-PERCEPTUAL
Are you feeling pain now? _____   How severe? _____   How often? _____
What relieves the pain? _____

What information does this client need to know to manage this illness or health state?

Ability to comprehend this information?

Good _____   Moderate _____   Poor _____

If poor, explain:

Mental Status Exam

Level of awareness and orientation _____

Appearance and behavior _____

Speech and communication _____

Affect (mood) _____

Thinking process _____

Related to: Inability to evaluate reality _____   Aging _____   Other _____

Explain:

If there is a distortion of the thought process, a focused assessment is indicated.

Perception _____

Abstract thinking _____

Social judgment _____

Memory _____

Impairment in short-term memory _____   Long-term _____

Is there evidence of unilateral neglect?   Yes _____   No _____   Does not apply _____

Self-perception

Does the client describe feelings of anxiety or uneasiness? _____

Is he able to identify a cause?   Yes _____   No _____

Cause? _____

If the client feels anxious but cannot identify a cause, assess for the major coping risks of physical illness below.

Barry Psychosocial Assessment (*continued*)

Is there anything you are frightened of during this hospitalization or illness?
Yes _____   No _____   What is it? _____
How will this illness affect your future plans? _____
Normally, do you believe that you control what happens to you (internal locus of control) or do you believe that other people or events control what happens (external locus of control)?

Internal locus of control _____
External locus of control _____

Will this illness affect the way you feel about yourself? _____
How? _____   About your body? _____

Psychosocial Risks of Illness
What are the major issues of this illness for this client? _____
For this family? _____
Use the following space to record client and family comments illustrating how they are coping with these issues.

Trust	Client _____
	Family _____
Self-esteem	Client _____
	Family _____
Body image	Client _____
	Family _____
Control	Client _____
	Family _____
Loss	Client _____
	Family _____
Guilt	Client _____
	Family _____
Intimacy	Client _____
	Family _____

Could one or more of these issues be contributing to feelings of anxiety, hopelessness, powerlessness, or disturbance in self-concept?
Yes _____   No _____   Possible _____
If so, explain which ones and proceed with a focused assessment.

ROLE-RELATIONSHIP

What is your occupation? _____

How many years have you been in this occupation? _____

Do you anticipate that this illness will have an effect on your ability to work?

Yes _____   No _____   How? _____

With whom do you live? _____   Are they supportive? _____

Who are the most important people in your life? _____

Do you ever feel socially isolated?   Yes _____   No _____

Explain:

Is there any indication in this history of social isolation or impaired social interaction?

Yes _____   No _____

Explain:

Ability to communicate

Within normal limits _____   Impaired _____

Describe:

FAMILY HISTORY

Who are the members of your immediate family? What are their ages and how are they related to you? Please include deceased members and when they died.

Name of family member _____

Relationship to you _____ Age _____ Date of death _____

Name of family member _____

Relationship to you _____ Age _____ Date of death _____

Name of family member _____

Relationship to you _____ Age _____ Date of death _____

Name of family member _____

Relationship to you _____ Age _____ Date of death _____

Name of family member _____

Relationship to you _____ Age _____ Date of death _____

What is your position in relation to your brothers and sisters? For example, are you the second oldest, the youngest . . .? _____

How often do you see your immediate family members? _____

What goes on in your family when something bad happens? _____

What do most of the members do? _____

Barry Psychosocial Assessment (*continued*)

Have any of your relationships within your immediate and extended family changed recently? _____

Which ones? _____

How have they changed? _____

Is there any change in the way you parent your children?

Yes _____   No _____

Is so, to what do you attribute the cause?

_____ New baby

_____ Death of family member

_____ Illness in other family member

_____ Change in residence (describe reason for change)

_____ Other (describe)

What is your normal role within your family? _____

What role do the significant other people in your family play? _____

Potential for disruption of these roles by this illness? High _____

Moderate _____   Low _____

Explain:

While the client is describing the family, is there any indication of uncontrolled anger or rage?

Yes _____   No _____

Related to a specific issue or person?

Explain:

Open (trusting) or closed (untrusting) communication style in family? (Can be initially determined by statements and emotional expression of client.) _____

Developmental stage of family

_____ Early married

_____ Married with no children

_____ Active childbearing

_____ Preschool or school-age children

_____ Adolescent children and children leaving home

_____ Middle-aged, children no longer at home

_____ Elderly, well-functioning

_____ Elderly, infirm

Is there any other aspect of your family or the way your family normally operates that you think should be added here? What is it?

If any item discussed in this section appears to be a current stressor for this client or family, it can be assessed using a focused approach with the other items under coping-stress tolerance pattern.

Interpersonal style

_____ Dependent   _____ Superior

_____ Controlled   _____ Uninvolved

_____ Dramatizing   _____ Mixed (usually two styles

_____ Suspicious   predominate)

_____ Self-sacrificing   _____ No predominant personality
                                            style

Write a brief sentence explaining your choice.

Response to you as the interviewer.   Guarded? _____   Open? _____
Is the client able to maintain good eye contact?

SEXUALITY-REPRODUCTIVE

Have you experienced any recent change in your sexual functioning?

Yes _____   No _____

How? _____

For how long?_____

Do you associate your change in sexual functioning with some event in your life?

_____

Do you think this illness could change your normal pattern of sexual functioning?

_____

How? _____

_____

Is this change in sexuality patterns related to:

_____ Ineffective coping

_____ Change or loss of body part

_____ Prenatal or postpartum changes

Changes in neurovegetative functioning related to depression

Explain:

Use focus assessment if necessary.

Barry Psychosocial Assessment (*continued*)

COPING–STRESS TOLERANCE
Level of Stress During Year Before Admission
How long have you been out of work with this illness? _____

Have you experienced any recent change in your job? _____

Have you been under any unusual job stress during the past year? _____

What was the cause?

_____ Retirement

_____ Fired

_____ Other. Explain:

_____ Same job, but new boss or working relationship

_____ Promotion or demotion

Do you expect the stress will be present when you return to work? _____

The preceding questions should be adapted for students to a school situation.

Have there been changes in your family during the last 2 years?

Which family members are involved? Include dates.

Death _____

Was this someyou you were close to? _____

Divorce _____

Child leaving home _____

Cause? _____

Other _____

Has there been any other unusual stress during the last year that is still affecting you?

Describe:

Any unusual stress in your family?

Describe:

Normal Coping Ability
When you go through a very difficult time, how do you handle it?

_____ Talk it out with someone

_____ Drink

_____ Ignore it

_____ Become anxious

_____ Withdraw from others

_____ Become depressed

_____ Get angry and yell

_____ Get angry and clam up

_____ Get angry and hit or throw something

_____ Other (explain)

How often do you experience feelings of depression? _____

In the past, what is the longest period of time this feeling has lasted? _____

Have you felt depressed during the past few weeks? Yes _____   No _____
To what do you attribute the cause? _____
If rape trauma is the cause of this admission do not explore the psychological reaction with the client until reading the report of the rape crisis counselor, who should have met with the client within an hour of arrival at the emergency department. Either follow the recommendations on the report for ongoing assessment or proceed with gentle questioning about current feelings.
What is the most serious trauma you have experienced? _____
What was the most difficult time you have experienced in your life? _____
How long did it take you to get over it? _____
What did you do to cope with it? _____
Potential for Self-Harm
This part of the assessment should be included if moderate to severe depression is present.
Have you ever thought of committing suicide? Yes _____   No _____
If yes, continue on.
What would you do to end your life? No plan _____   Plan _____
Describe:

What would prevent you from committing suicide? _____
Substances That May Be Used as Stress-Relievers
Smoking history
Do you smoke? _____   How long have you been smoking? _____
How many packs per day? _____
Alcohol use history
Do you drink? _____   How often? _____   How much? _____
Is there a history of alcoholism in your family? _____   Who? _____
Drug use
What prescribed medications are you currently using?
Name of medications _____
Dose or schedule _____ Prescribing physician _____
Are you currently using any other drugs? Yes _____   No _____
What are they? _____
How long have you been using them? _____
What is the usual amount? _____ How often? _____
Have you ever been treated for substance abuse? _____

VALUE-BELIEF
What is your religious affiliation? _____
Do you consider yourself active or inactive in practicing your religion?
Active _____   Inactive _____

Barry Psychosocial Assessment (*continued*)

Is your religious leader a supportive person?   Yes _____   No _____
Explain:

What does this illness mean to you? _____
Are you experiencing spiritual distress?   Yes _____   No _____
Explain:

What would you consider to be the primary cause of this spiritual distress (ac-
tual, possible, or potential)?
_____ Inability to practice spiritual rituals
_____ Conflict between religious, spiritual, or cultural beliefs and prescribed
       health regimen
_____ Crisis of illness, suffering, or death
_____ Other (explain)

Do you expect there will be any disparity in your care-givers' approach that could
present a problem to you? _____
Any problems in the areas of
_____ Spiritual rituals   _____ Communication
_____ Cause of illness   _____ Problem solving
_____ Perception of illness and sick   _____ Nutrition
       role   _____ Family response
_____ Health maintenance
Explain:

How has this illness affected your relationship with God or the supreme being of
your religion?
Explain:

The 11 functional health patterns were named by Marjorie Gordon (1987) in
Nursing diagnosis: Process and application, New York: McGraw-Hill.

From Barry, P.D. (1994). Psychosocial nursing: Care of physically ill patients and
their families (3rd ed.). Philadelphia: J.B. Lippincott.

B DSM-IV Classifications

DISORDERS USUALLY FIRST DIAGNOSED IN INFANCY, CHILDHOOD, AND ADOLESCENCE

MENTAL RETARDATION

317	Mild Mental Retardation
318.0	Moderate Mental Retardation
318.1	Severe Mental Retardation
318.2	Profound Mental Retardation
319	Mental Retardation, Severity Unspecified

LEARNING DISORDERS

315.00	Reading Disorder
315.1	Mathematics Disorder
315.2	Disorder of Written Expression
315.9	Learning Disorder NOS

MOTOR SKILLS DISORDER

315.4	Developmental Coordination Disorder

COMMUNICATION DISORDERS

315.31	Expressive Language Disorder
315.31	Mixed Receptive-Expressive Language Disorder
315.39	Phonological Disorder
307.0	Stuttering
307.9	Communication Disorder NOS

PERVASIVE DEVELOPMENTAL DISORDERS

299.00	Autistic Disorder
299.80	Rett's Disorder
299.10	Childhood Disintegrative Disorder
299.80	Asperger's Disorder
299.80	Pervasive Developmental Disorder NOS (including Atypical Autism)

ATTENTION-DEFICIT AND DISRUPTIVE BEHAVIOR DISORDERS

Attention-Deficit/Hyperactivity Disorder

314.01	Combined Type

314.9   Attention-Deficit/Hyperactivity Disorder NOS

314.00   Predominantly Inattentive Type
314.01   Predominantly Hyperactive-Impulsive Type
314.9   Attention-Deficit/Hyperactivity Disorder NOS
312.8   Conduct Disorder
313.81   Oppositional Defiant Disorder
312.9   Disruptive Behavior Disorder NOS

FEEDING AND EATING DISORDERS OF INFANCY OR EARLY CHILDHOOD
307.52   Pica
307.53   Rumination Disorder
307.59   Feeding Disorder of Infancy or Early Childhood

TIC DISORDERS
307.23   Tourette's Disorder
307.22   Chronic Motor or Vocal Tic Disorder
307.21   Transient Tic Disorder
307.20   Tic Disorder NOS

ELIMINATION DISORDERS
787.6   Encopresis with Constipation and Overflow Incontinence
307.7   Encopresis without Constipation and Overflow Incontinence
307.6   Enuresis (Not Due to a General Medical Condition)

OTHER DISORDERS OF INFANCY, CHILDHOOD, OR ADOLESCENCE
309.21   Separation Anxiety Disorder
313.23   Selective Mutism
313.89   Reactive Attachment Disorder of Infancy or Early Childhood
307.3   Stereotypic Movement Disorder
313.9   Disorder of Infancy, Childhood, or Adolescence NOS

DELIRIUM, DEMENTIA, AND AMNESTIC AND OTHER COGNITIVE DISORDERS
DELIRIUM
293.0   Delirium due to [indicate the General Medical Condition]
—   Substance-Induced Delirium (refer to specific substance for code)
—   Substance Withdrawal Delirium (refer to specific substance for code)
—   Delirium Due to Multiple Etiologies (use multiple codes based on specific etiologies)
780.09   Delirium NOS

DEMENTIA

Dementia of the Alzheimer's Type

With Early Onset: If Onset at Age 65 or Below
290.11   With Delirium
290.12   With Delusions
290.13   With Depressed Mood
290.10   Uncomplicated

With Late Onset: If Onset After Age 65
290.3   With Delirium
290.20   With Delusions
290.21   With Depressed Mood
290.0   Uncomplicated
—   With Behavioral Disturbance (can be applied to any of the above
          subtypes)

VASCULAR DEMENTIA
290.41   With Delirium
290.42   With Delusions
290.43   With Depressed Mood
290.40   Uncomplicated
—   With Behavioral Disturbance (can be applied to any of the above
          subtypes)

DEMENTIA DUE TO OTHER GENERAL MEDICAL CONDITIONS
294.9   Dementia Due to HIV Disease (Code 043.1 on Axis III)
294.1   Dementia Due to Head Trauma (Code 854.00 on Axis III)
294.1   Dementia Due to Parkinson's Disease (Code 332.0 on Axis III)
294.1   Dementia due to Huntington's Disease (Code 333.4 on Axis III)
290.10   Dementia Due to Pick's Disease (Code 331.1 on Axis III)
290.10   Dementia Due to Creutzfeldt-Jakob Disease (Code 046.1
          on Axis III)
294.1   Dementia Due to Other General Medical Condition
—   Substance-Induced Persisting Dementia (refer to specific
          substance for code)
—   Dementia Due to Multiple Etiologies (use multiple codes based
          on specific etiologies)
294.8   Dementia NOS

AMNESTIC DISORDERS
294.0   Amnestic Disorder Due to a General Medical Condition
—   Substance-Induced Persisting Amnestic Disorder (refer to specific
          substance for code)
294.8   Amnestic Disorder NOS

OTHER COGNITIVE DISORDERS
294.9   Cognitive Disorders NOS

MENTAL DISORDERS DUE TO A GENERAL MEDICAL CONDITION NOT ELSEWHERE CLASSIFIED

293.89	Catatonic Disorder Due to a General Medical Condition
310.1	Personality Change Due to a General Medical Condition
293.9	Mental Disorder NOS Due to a General Medical Condition

SUBSTANCE-RELATED DISORDERS
ALCOHOL-RELATED DISORDERS

Alcohol-Induced Disorders

303.90	Alcohol Dependence
305.00	Alcohol Abuse
303.00	Alcohol Intoxication
291.8	Alcohol Withdrawal
291.0	Alcohol Withdrawal Delirium
291.0	Alcohol Intoxication Delirium
291.2	Alcohol-Induced Persisting Dementia
291.1	Alcohol-Induced Amnestic Disorder

Alcohol-Induced Psychotic Disorder

291.5	With Delusions
291.3	With Hallucinations
291.8	Alcohol-Induced Mood Disorder
291.8	Alcohol-Induced Anxiety Disorder
291.8	Alcohol-Induced Sexual Dysfunction
291.8	Alcohol-Induced Sleep Disorder
291.9	Alcohol-Related Disorder NOS

AMPHETAMINE (OR AMPHETAMINE-LIKE)—RELATED DISORDERS

Amphetamine Use Disorders

304.40	Amphetamine Dependence
305.70	Amphetamine Abuse

Amphetamine-Induced Disorders

292.89	Amphetamine Intoxication
292.0	Amphetamine Withdrawal
292.81	Amphetamine Intoxication Delirium

Amphetamine-Induced Psychotic Disorder

292.11	With Delusions
292.12	With Hallucinations
292.84	Amphetamine-Induced Mood Disorder
292.89	Amphetamine-Induced Anxiety Disorder
292.89	Amphetamine-Induced Sexual Dysfunction
292.89	Amphetamine-Induced Sleep Disorder
292.9	Amphetamine-Related Disorder NOS

CAFFEINE-RELATED DISORDERS

305.90	Caffeine Intoxication
292.89	Caffeine-Induced Anxiety Disorder
292.89	Caffeine-Induced Sleep Disorder
292.9	Caffeine-Related Disorder NOS

CANNABIS-RELATED DISORDERS

Cannabis Use Disorders

304.30	Cannabis Dependence
305.20	Cannabis Abuse

Cannabis-Induced Disorders

292.89	Cannabis Intoxication
292.81	Cannabis Intoxication Delirium
	Cannabis-Induced Psychotic Disorder
292.11	With Delusions
292.12	With Hallacinations
292.89	Cannabis-Induced Anxiety Disorder
292.9	Cannabis-Related Disorder NOS

COCAINE-RELATED DISORDERS

Cocaine Use Disorders

304.20	Cocaine Dependence
305.60	Cocaine Abuse

Cocaine-Induced Disorders

292.89	Cocaine Intoxication
292.0	Cocaine Withdrawal
292.81	Cocaine Intoxication Delirium
	Cocaine Psychotic Disorder
292.11	With Delusions
292.12	With Hallucinations
292.84	Cocaine-Induced Mood Disorder
292.89	Cocaine-Induced Anxiety Disorder
292.89	Cocaine-Induced Sexual Dysfunction
292.89	Cocaine-Induced Sleep Disorder
292.9	Cocaine-Related Disorder NOS

HALLUCINOGEN-RELATED DISORDERS

Hallucinogen Use Disorders

304.50	Hallucinogen Dependence
305.30	Hallucinogen Abuse

Hallucinogen-Induced Disorders

292.89	Hallucinogen Intoxication
292.89	Hallucinogen Persisting Perception Disorder (Flashback)
292.81	Hallucinogen Intoxication Delirium
	Hallucinogen-Induced Psychotic Disorder
292.11	With Delusions
292.12	With Hallucinations

292.84	Hallucinogen-Induced Mood Disorder
292.89	Hallucinogen-Induced Anxiety Disorder
292.9	Hallucinogen-Related Disorder NOS

INHALANT-RELATED DISORDERS

Inhalant Use Disorders
304.60	Inhalant Dependence
305.90	Inhalant Abuse

Inhalant-Induced Disorders
292.89	Inhalant Intoxication
292.81	Inhalant Intoxication Delirium
292.82	Inhalant-Induced Persisting Dementia

Inhalant-Induced Psychotic Disorder
292.11	With Delusions
292.12	With Hallucinations
292.84	Inhalant-Induced Mood Disorder
292.89	Inhalant-Induced Anxiety Disorder
292.9	Inhalant-Related Disorder NOS

NICOTINE-RELATED DISORDER

Nicotine Use Disorders
305.10	Nicotine Dependence

Nicotine-Induced Disorder
292.0	Nicotine Withdrawal
292.9	Nicotine-Related Disorder NOS

OPIOID-RELATED DISORDERS

Opioid Use Disorders
304.00	Opioid Dependence
305.50	Opioid Abuse

Opioid-Induced Disorders
292.89	Opioid Intoxication
292.0	Opioid Withdrawal
292.81	Opioid Intoxication Delirium

Opioid-Induced Psychotic Disorder
292.11	With Delusions
292.12	With Hallucinations
292.84	Opioid-Induced Mood Disorder
292.89	Opioid-Induced Sexual Dysfunction
292.89	Opioid-Induced Sleep Disorder
292.9	Opioid-Related Disorder NOS

PHENCYCLIDINE (OR PHENCYCLIDINE-LIKE)-RELATED DISORDERS

Phencyclidine Use Disorders
304.90	Phencyclidine Dependence
305.90	Phencyclidine Abuse

Phencyclidine-Induced Disorders
292.89   Phencyclidine Intoxication
292.81   Phencyclidine Intoxication Delirium
          Phencyclidine-Induced Psychotic Disorder
292.11   With Delusions
292.12   With Hallucinations
292.84   Phencyclidine-Induced Mood Disorder
292.89   Phencyclidine-Induced Anxiety Disorder
292.9   Phencyclidine-Related Disorder NOS

SEDATIVE-, HYPNOTIC-, OR ANXIOLYTIC-RELATED DISORDERS

Sedative-, Hypnotic-, or Anxiolytic Use Disorders
304.10   Sedative-, Hypnotic-, or Anxiolytic Dependence
305.40   Sedative-, Hypnotic-, or Anxiolytic Abuse

Sedative-, Hypnotic-, or Anxiolytic-Induced Disorders
292.89   Sedative-, Hypnotic-, or Anxiolytic Intoxication
292.0   Sedative-, Hypnotic-, or Anxiolytic Withdrawal
292.81   Sedative-, Hypnotic-, or Anxiolytic Intoxication Delirium
292.81   Sedative-, Hypnotic-, or Anxiolytic Withdrawal Delirium
292.82   Sedative-, Hypnotic-, or Anxiolytic-Induced Persisting Dementia
292.83   Sedative-, Hypnotic-, or Anxiolytic-Induced Persisting Amnestic
          Disorder
          Sedative-, Hypnotic-, or Anxiolytic-Induced Psychotic Disorder
292.11   With Delusions
292.12   With Hallucinations
292.84   Sedative-, Hypnotic-, or Anxiolytic-Induced Mood Disorder
292.89   Sedative-, Hypnotic-, or Anxiolytic-Induced Anxiety Disorder
292.89   Sedative-, Hypnotic-, or Anxiolytic-Induced Sexual Dysfunction
292.89   Sedative-, Hypnotic-, or Anxiolytic-Induced Sleep Disorder
292.9   Sedative-, Hypnotic-, or Anxiolytic-Related Disorder NOS

POLYSUBSTANCE-RELATED DISORDER
304.80   Polysubstance Dependence

OTHER (OR UNKNOWN) SUBSTANCE USE DISORDERS
304.90   Other (or Unknown) Substance Dependence
305.90   Other (or Unknown) Substance Abuse

Other (or Unknown) Substance-Induced Disorders
292.89   Other (or Unknown) Substance Intoxication
292.0   Other (or Unknown) Substance Withdrawal
292.81   Other (or Unknown) Substance-Induced Delirium
292.82   Other (or Unknown) Substance-Induced Persisting Dementia
292.83   Other (or Unknown) Substance-Induced Persisting Amnestic
          Disorder
          Other (or Unknown) Substance-Induced Psychotic Disorder

292.11	With Delusions
292.12	With Hallucinations
292.84	Other (or Unknown) Substance-Induced Mood Disorder
292.89	Other (or Unknown) Substance-Induced Anxiety Disorder
292.89	Other (or Unknown) Substance-Induced Sexual Dysfunction
292.89	Other (or Unknown) Substance-Induced Sleep Disorder
292.9	Other (or Unknown) Substance-Related Disorder NOS

SCHIZOPHRENIA AND OTHER PSYCHOTIC DISORDERS
SCHIZOPHRENIA

295.30	Paranoid Type
295.10	Disorganized Type
295.20	Catatonic Type
295.90	Undifferentiated Type
295.60	Residual Type
295.40	Schizophreniform Disorder
295.70	Schizoaffective Disorder
297.1	Delusional Disorder
298.8	Brief Psychotic Disorder
297.3	Shared Psychotic Disorder (Folie à Deux)

Psychotic Disorder Due to a General Medical Condition

293.81	With Delusions
293.82	With Hallucinations
—	Substance-Induced Psychotic Disorder (refer to specific substance for codes)
298.9	Psychotic Disorder NOS

MOOD DISORDERS
MAJOR DEPRESSIVE DISORDERS

296.2x	Single Episode
296.3x	Recurrent
300.4	Dysthymic Disorder
311	Depressive Disorder NOS

BIPOLAR DISORDERS

Bipolar I Disorder

296.0x	Single Manic Episode
296.40	Most Recent Episode Hypomanic
296.4x	Most Recent Episode Manic
296.6x	Most Recent Episode Mixed
296.5x	Most Recent Episode Depressed
296.7	Most Recent Episode Unspecified

296.89	Bipolar II Disorder (Recurrent Major Depressive Episodes with Hypomanic Episodes)
301.13	Cyclothymic Disorder
296.80	Bipolar Disorder NOS
293.83	Mood Disorders Due to a General Medical Condition
—	Substance-Induced Mood Disorder (refer to specific substances for codes)
296.90	Mood Disorder NOS

ANXIETY DISORDERS

300.01	Panic Disorder Without Agoraphobia
300.21	Panic Disorder With Agoraphobia
300.22	Agoraphobia Without History of Panic Disorder
300.29	Specific Phobia
300.23	Social Phobia
300.3	Obsessive-Compulsive Disorder
309.81	Posttraumatic Stress Disorder
308.3	Acute Stress Disorder
300.02	Generalized Anxiety Disorder (Includes Overanxious Disorder of Childhood)
293.89	Anxiety Disorder Due to a General Medical Condition
—	Substance-Induced Anxiety Disorder (refer to specific substances for codes)
300.00	Anxiety Disorder NOS

SOMATOFORM DISORDERS

300.81	Somatization Disorder
300.81	Undifferentiated Somatoform Disorder
300.11	Conversion Disorder
300.7	Hypochondriasis
300.7	Body Dysmorphic Disorder
300.81	Somatoform Disorder NOS

PAIN DISORDER

| 307.80 | Associated with Psychological Factors |
| 307.89 | Associated with Both Psychological Factors and a General Medical Condition |

FACTITIOUS DISORDERS
FACTITIOUS DISORDER

| 300.16 | With Predominantly Psychological Signs and Symptoms |

300.19   With Predominantly Physical Signs and Symptoms
300.19   With Combined Psychological and Physical Signs and Symptoms
300.19   Factitious Disorder NOS

DISSOCIATIVE DISORDERS

300.12   Dissociative Amnesia
300.13   Dissociative Fugue
300.14   Dissociative Identity Disorder
300.6   Depersonalization Disorder
300.15   Dissociative Disorder NOS

SEXUAL AND GENDER IDENTITY DISORDERS
SEXUAL DYSFUNCTIONS

Sexual Desire Disorders

302.71   Hypoactive Sexual Desire Disorder
302.79   Sexual Aversion Disorder

Sexual Arousal Disorders

307.72   Female Sexual Arousal Disorder
302.72   Male Erectile Disorder

Orgasmic Disorders

302.73   Female Orgasmic Disorder
302.74   Male Orgasmic Disorder
302.75   Premature Ejaculation

Sexual Pain Disorders

302.76   Dyspareunia (not due to a general medical condition)
306.51   Vaginismus (not due to a general medical condition)

Sexual Dysfunctions Due to a General Medical Condition

625.8   Female Hypoactive Sexual Desire Disorder Due to a General
            Medical Condition
608.89   Male Hypoactive Sexual Desire Disorder Due to a General
            Medical Condition
607.84   Male Erectile Disorder Due to a General Medical Condition
625.0   Female Dyspareunia Due to a General Medical Condition
608.89   Male Dyspareunia Due to a General Medical Condition
625.8   Other Female Sexual Dysfunction Due to a General Medical
            Condition
608.89   Other Male Sexual Dysfunction Due to a General Medical
            Condition
—   Substance-Induced Sexual Dysfunction (refer to specific
            substances for codes)
302.70   Sexual Dysfunction NOS

Paraphilias
302.4	Exhibitionism
302.81	Fetishism
302.89	Frotteurism
302.2	Pedophilia
302.83	Sexual Masochism
302.84	Sexual Sadism
302.3	Transvestic Fetishism
302.82	Voyeurism
302.	Paraphilia NOS

GENDER IDENTITY DISORDERS
302.6	Gender Identity Disorder In Children
302.85	Gender Identity Disorder In Adolescents or Adults
302.6	Gender Identity Disorder NOS
302.9	Sexual Disorder NOS

EATING DISORDERS
307.1	Anorexia Nervosa
307.51	Bulimia Nervosa
307.50	Eating Disorder NOS

SLEEP DISORDERS
PRIMARY SLEEP DISORDERS

Dyssomnias
307.42	Primary Insomnia
307.44	Primary Hypersomnia
347	Narcolepsy
780.59	Breathing-Related Sleep Disorder
307.45	Circadian Rhythm Sleep Disorder
307.47	Dyssomnia NOS

Parasomnias
307.47	Nightmare Disorder
307.46	Sleep Terror Disorder
307.46	Sleepwalking Disorder
307.47	Parasomnia NOS

SLEEP DISORDERS RELATED TO ANOTHER MENTAL DISORDER
307.42	Insomnia Related to [Axis I or Axis II Disorder]
307.44	Hypersomnia Related to [Axis I or Axis II Disorder]

OTHER SLEEP DISORDERS

Sleep Disorders Due to a General Medical Condition
780.52	Insomnia Type

780.54	Hypersomnia Type
780.59	Parasomnia Type
780.59	Mixed Type
—	Substance-Induced Sleep Disorder (refer to specific substances for codes)

IMPULSE-CONTROL DISORDERS NOT ELSEWHERE CLASSIFIED

312.34	Intermittent Explosive Disorder
312.32	Kleptomania
312.33	Pyromania
312.31	Pathological Gambling
312.39	Trichotillomania
312.30	Impulse-Control Disorder NOS

ADJUSTMENT DISORDERS
ADJUSTMENT DISORDER

309.0	With Depressed Mood
309.24	With Anxiety
309.28	With Mixed Anxiety and Depressed Mood
309.3	With Disturbance of Conduct
309.4	With Mixed Disturbance of Emotions and Conduct
309.0	Unspecified

PERSONALITY DISORDERS
CLUSTER A PERSONALITY DISORDERS

301.0	Paranoid Personality Disorder
301.20	Schizoid Personality Disorder
301.22	Schizotypal Personality Disorder

CLUSTER B PERSONALITY DISORDERS

301.7	Antisocial Personality Disorder
301.83	Borderline Personality Disorder
301.50	Histrionic Personality Disorder
301.81	Narcissistic Personality Disorder

CLUSTER C PERSONALITY DISORDERS

301.82	Avoidant Personality Disorder
301.6	Dependent Personality Disorder
301.4	Obsessive-Compulsive Personality Disorder
301.9	Personality Disorder NOS

OTHER CONDITIONS THAT MAY BE A FOCUS OF CLINICAL ATTENTION

PSYCHOLOGICAL FACTORS AFFECTING MEDICAL CONDITION

316   [Specified Psychological Factor;] Affecting; [indicate the general medical condition]

Mental Disorder Affecting General Medical Condition

Psychological Symptoms Affecting General Medical Condition

Personality Traits or Coping Style Affecting General Medical Condition

Maladaptive Health Behaviors Affecting General Medical Condition

Stress-Related Physiological Response Affecting General Medical Condition

Other or Unspecified Psychological Factors Affecting General Medical Condition

MEDICATION-INDUCED MOVEMENT DISORDERS

332.1	Neuroleptic-Induced Parkinsonism
333.92	Neuroleptic Malignant Syndrome
333.7	Neuroleptic-Induced Acute Dystonia
333.99	Neuroleptic-Induced Acute Akathisia
333.82	Neuroleptic-Induced Tardive Dyskinesia
333.1	Medication-Induced Postural Tremor
333.90	Medication-Induced Movement Disorder NOS
995.2	Adverse Effects of Medication NOS

RELATIONAL PROBLEMS

V61.9	Relational Problem Related to a Mental Disorder or General Medical Condition
V61.20	Parent-Child Relational Problem
V61.1	Partner Relational Problem
V61.8	Sibling Relational Problem
V62.81	Relational Problem NOS

PROBLEMS RELATED TO ABUSE OR NEGLECT

V61.21	Physical Abuse of Child
V61.21	Sexual Abuse of Child
V61.21	Neglect of Child
V61.1	Physical Abuse of Adult
V61.1	Sexual Abuse of Adult

ADDITIONAL CONDITIONS THAT MAY BE A FOCUS OF CLINICAL ATTENTION

V15.81	Noncompliance with Treatment
V65.2	Malingering
V71.01	Adult Antisocial Behavior
V71.02	Child or Adolescent Antisocial Behavior
V62.89	Borderline Intellectual Functioning
780.9	Age-Related Cognitive Disorder
V62.82	Bereavement

V62.3	Academic Problem
V62.2	Occupational Problem
313.82	Identity Problem
V62.89	Religious or Spiritual Problem
V62.4	Acculturation Problem
V62.89	Phase of Life Problem

ADDITIONAL CODES

300.9	Unspecified Mental Disorder (nonpsychotic)
V71.09	No Diagnosis or Condition on Axis I
799.9	Diagnosis or Condition Deferred on Axis I
V71.09	No Diagnosis on Axis II
799.9	Diagnosis Deferred on Axis II

Diagnostic Criteria from DSM-IV, Washington, DC, American Psychiatric Association

Index

Page numbers followed by *f* indicate figures; *t* following a page number indicates tabular material.

Ego-syntonic, 327
Elavil. *See* Amitryptyline (Elavil)
Elderly persons, home mental health care
 for, 12
Electrical disorders, psychosis from, 261
Electroconvulsive therapy (ECT), 399–400
Electrolyte imbalances, mental status
 changes from, 260–261, 261*t*
Elimination disorders, 244
 DSM-IV codes for, 433
Emergency room
 crisis intervention in, 356
 mental health care in, for homeless per-
 sons, 17–18
Emotions
 commonly experienced, 138
 control of, 137–138
 definition of, 136
 physiologic responses to, 136–137
Empathy
 in infants, 99
 in therapeutic relationship, 65, 74
Encopresis, 244
Enuresis, 244
Environment
 concept of, 72
 and human development, 95
Epilepsy, 261
Erikson, E., theory of personality development, 124–128
Esteem, need for, 101
Ethical issues, 43–55
 code of nursing and, 44–46
 nursing profession and, 49–50
 practice standards and, 46–49
Ethics, definition of, 45
Etiologic risk factors, in nursing diagnosis, 196
Evaluation, in nursing process, 186
 with client in crisis, 358
 for client with schizophrenia, 294
Exchanging, nursing diagnoses involving,
 190–191, 195
Exophthalmic goiter, 260
Explanations, in therapeutic relationship,
 63
Explosive disorder, intermittent, 332
Expressive language disorder, 238
Expressive therapist, on treatment team,
 37
Extinction
 in behavioral therapy, 366
 in learning, 98
Extrapyramidal side effects, 396–397

F
Facial expression, in mental status exami-
 nation, 169
Factitious disorders, 332
 DSM-IV codes for, 441

Family
 boundaries in, 111
 of client with schizophrenia, 294
 of client with substance-related disorder, 281–282
 of cognitively impaired older adult,
 stress on, 222–223
 definition of, 23
 homeostasis in, 106–107, 112
 nuclear, 108–109
 rules in, 111
Family dynamics, mental illness and,
 110–112
Family of origin, sibling position in,
 110–111
Family systems, open *vs.* closed, 109
Family systems theory, 108–109
Fear, 139
Feeding disorders, 240–241
 DSM-IV codes for, 433
Feeling, nursing diagnoses involving,
 194–195
Feelings. *See also* Emotions
 expression of, in therapeutic relation-
 ship, 63–64
Fetishism, 329
Fight or flight response, 136
Flat affect, 172
Flight of ideas, 172
Fluoxetine (Prozac), 391*t*
Fluphenazine (Permitil, Prolixin)
 dosage of, 385*t*, 388
 side effects of, 386*t*
Foster care, 86*t*
Freud, S., theory of personality develop-
 ment, 116–117, 121–124
Fromm, E., theory of personality develop-
 ment, 121
Frotteurism, 329
Fugue, dissociative, 326
Funding, of community mental health
 care, 12

G
Gambling, pathologic, 332
Gender identity disorders, 330–331
 DSM-IV codes for, 443
General adaptation syndrome, 148–149
Genital stage, of psychosexual develop-
 ment, 124
Gestures, in mental status examination,
 169
Gilligan, C., 102
Goiter, exophthalmic, 260
Graves' disease, 260
Grieving, dysfunctional, nursing care plan
 for, 208
Group homes, 86*t*
Groups, early socialization in, 372

Thermoregulation, ineffective, clozapine and, 206–207
Thiamine, deficiency of, 265
Thinking, assessment of, in mental status examination, 172–173
Thiopropazate (Dartal), dosage of, 385t
Thioridazine (Mellaril)
    dosage of, 385t
    side effects of, 386t
Thiothixene (Navane)
    dosage of, 385t
    side effects of, 387t, 388
Thioxanthenes, side effects of, 387t
Thorazine. See Chlorpromazine (Thorazine)
Thought processes, altered, in manic client, nursing care plan for, 210
Tic disorders, 243–244
    DSM-IV codes for, 433
Tindal. See Acetophenazine (Tindal)
Tofranil. See Imipramine (Tofranil)
Token economy, 366–367
Tourette's syndrome, 243
Tranquilizers, and cognitive disorders, 259
Transitional housing, 86t
Transvestic fetishism, 329–330
Trauma, to head, and mental status changes, 263
Trazodone (Desyrel), 391t
Treatment. See Mental health care
Treatment team
    communication within, 38
    in home care, 27–28
        and collaboration with other health care providers, 28–29
    members of, 36–38
    therapeutic interventions by, 39–40
Triage, 17, 83
Triangulation, 29
Triazolopyridine, 391t, 392–393
Trichotillomania, 333
Tricyclic antidepressants, 390, 391t, 392
Tricyclic dibenzodiazepines, 389
Trifluoperazine (Stelazine)
    dosage of, 385t
    side effects of, 386t
Triflupromazine (Vesprin)
    dosage of, 385t
    side effects of, 386t

Trihexyphenidyl (Artane), 395
Trilafon. See Perphenazine (Trilafon)
Trimipramine (Surmontil), 391t
Trust, in therapeutic relationship, 64
Trust vs. mistrust, development of, 125–126

U
Unconscious mind, 117–118
Understanding, in therapeutic relationship, 64–65
Unit manager, on treatment team, 36

V
Vaginismus, 330
Values, development of, 95
Valuing, nursing diagnoses involving, 192, 195
Verbal communication, in therapeutic relationship, 75–76
Vesprin. See Triflupromazine (Vesprin)
Vicarious consent, 52
Violent client, nursing care plan for, 213
Vivactil. See Protriptyline (Vivactil)
Vocal tic disorder, 244
Vocational nurses, code of nursing for, 45–46
Voyeurism, 330

W
Wellbutrin. See Bupropion (Wellbutrin)
Withdrawal
    from alcohol, 274
    from heroin, 277
    from nicotine, 277–278
    from opioids, 258
    in schizophrenia, 288
    from sedative-hypnotics, 259
Women
    needs of, 102
    personality development in, 121
Word salad, 287
Worry, value of, 153

Z
Zoloft. See Sertraline (Zoloft)